Dr. Jerry Sutton's work is brilliant in encapsulating the who, what, where and most importantly the why of the commitment of the Southern Baptist Convention to be "salt" and "light" in the public square through the work of the ERLC. As one who works alongside Dr. Richard Land on national policy issues and as a Southern Baptist who supports the ERLC, I encourage you to understand the history and the present and future importance of this ministry of the SBC.

TONY PERKINS, PRESIDENT
FAMILY RESEARCH COUNCIL

This book skillfully places the story of the Southern Baptist Convention's Ethics & Religious Liberty Commission in the wider context of American Christianity, Baptist history, and the worldwide evangelical movement. There is conflict here but also consensus—not a perfect story of unbroken progress, but the triumph of conviction over accommodation and the emergence of a witness for which all followers of Jesus Christ can be grateful.

TIMOTHY GEORGE, FOUNDING DEAN OF BEESON DIVINITY SCHOOL OF
SAMFORD UNIVERSITY AND A SENIOR EDITOR OF *CHRISTIANITY TODAY*

Dr. Jerry Sutton's *A Matter of Conviction* is thorough, enlightening, encouraging, and convicting. Using the studied approach already associated with Sutton's previous writings, the reader is taken on a journey through the remarkable metamorphosis of a Southern Baptist Convention entity as it moves from mere social accommodation to become a powerful catalyst for societal change. Sutton's book is a textbook for change, and for the importance of properly stewarding the influence entrusted to each of us.

TOM ELLIFF, SENIOR VICE PRESIDENT FOR SPIRITUAL NURTURE AND
CHURCH RELATIONS, INTERNATIONAL MISSION BOARD,
SOUTHERN BAPTIST CONVENTION

Another priceless and accurate history of the Southern Baptist entity whose responsibility has been to relate to public policy and inform the churches about the great ethical and moral issues of our day. Dr. Jerry Sutton, a distinguished graduate of the Ph.D. program in Church History here at Southwestern, has demonstrated once again his ability to find the sources, understand them, and write a riveting historical account of the entity that is today called the Ethics & Religious Liberty Commission.

PAIGE PATTERSON, PRESIDENT
SOUTHWESTERN BAPTIST THEOLOGICAL SEMINARY
FORT WORTH, TEXAS

With great insight and based on painstaking research, Dr. Jerry Sutton has shown one of the results of the conservative resurgence in the Southern Baptist Convention. The book is informative, well written, and well documented. Every Southern Baptist and everyone interested in government in the United States should read this book.

PAUL PRESSLER, RETIRED, JUSTICE FOR THE 14TH COURT OF APPEALS
HOUSTON, TEXAS

A Matter of Conviction is well researched and encyclopedic in documentation. It is also an easy, interesting, and at times fascinating read! Dr. Jerry Sutton provides a fine survey and analysis of the SBC entity charged with guiding Southern Baptists in being "salt" and "light" to our culture.

DANIEL AKIN, PRESIDENT
SOUTHEASTERN BAPTIST THEOLOGICAL SEMINARY
WAKE FOREST, NORTH CAROLINA

The Ethics & Religious Liberty Commission is the "mouse that roared." With little funding and often going cross grain with cultural norms, the prophetic voices of Richard Land and his predecessors carried out their biblical mandate. Speaking "to" Southern Baptists and speaking "for" Southern Baptists without fear or favor is the hallmark of the ERLC. This book chronicles the incredible work of one of God's valuable ministries.

JIM RICHARDS, EXECUTIVE DIRECTOR, SOUTHERN BAPTISTS OF TEXAS
CONVENTION AND FIRST VICE-PRESIDENT, SOUTHERN BAPTIST CONVENTION
2007–2008

Dr. Jerry Sutton has done all of us a great favor in writing *A Matter of Conviction*. This book is a must-read for anyone interested in the critical moral and civic issues which we face as people of faith and as Americans. By tracing the history of the Ethics & Religious Liberty Commission, Dr. Sutton has given us a road map for impacting our culture now by studying our past.

JAY SEKULOW, JD, PHD
CHIEF COUNSEL, AMERICAN CENTER FOR LAW & JUSTICE

A Matter of Conviction powerfully tells the story of Southern Baptists' wide-ranging efforts to engage the culture throughout the past century. Here we read of the effective work of the Commission that has called Southern Baptists to be "salt" and "light" in the areas of religious liberty, race relations, marriage, family, life, and much more. Readers will find this informative and challenging historical survey to be both helpful and hopeful.

DAVID S. DOCKERY, PRESIDENT, UNION UNIVERSITY

A MATTER OF CONVICTION

A MATTER OF CONVICTION

A History of Southern Baptist Engagement with the Culture

JERRY SUTTON

Foreword by James T. Draper, Jr.

PUBLISHING GROUP

Nashville, Tennessee

Contents

Acknowledgments

In preparing this manuscript I have had a great deal of help. Some thanks are certainly in order.

I would like to thank my friend Richard Land for asking me to write this project, as well as the fact that he made himself available for interviews and feedback.

I would also like to express my gratitude to Harold Harper and Bobby Reed, who work at the Commission, for their encouragement, assistance, and patience. Thanks also goes to Pat Clark for running down numerous details.

I am appreciative for much of the work done by the late Jim Hefley who also loved the Ethics & Religious Liberty Commission.

Two research assistants who greatly enabled my work were Robert Matz from Southwestern Seminary and Hilary Sutton from Liberty University. Both went way above the call of duty to ensure that the subject matter was thoroughly researched.

I wish to express my appreciation to those who read the first draft and offered very helpful suggestions on improving the manuscript: Joe Atchison, James Draper, Hal Lane, Gary Ledbetter, Paige Patterson, Paul Pressler, Jim Richards, Kerry Bural, Barrett Duke, Dwayne Hastings, Harold Harper, and Bobby Reed.

I would also like to express my gratitude to Kathy Helmers, who assisted me and the Commission to make this project a reality.

I am very appreciative of the Two Rivers Baptist Church and especially our staff for their prayers, encouragement, and willingness to pick up some of my workload. Special thanks to Sam Mallory, Jerry Highfill, Weldon Doherty, and Scott Hutchings.

I am grateful for my Baptist history professors, who taught me to love research, to be exact in my choice of words, and through experience to be graciously tenacious in standing by my findings.

I am profoundly appreciative of my administrative assistant, Charlotte Kolbe, who spent long hours typing the manuscript, and her husband, Bob Kolbe, who assisted proofreading multiple drafts.

I am grateful to the Lord for my precious wife, Fern, who has been exceedingly patient and profoundly encouraging as I have labored through the process of putting the ideas of this book on paper and transforming it into a completed manuscript.

I wish to express my appreciation also to my daughter and son-in-law, Ashli and Matt Arbo, for their constant encouragement.

And lastly, I thank the Lord Jesus for His grace which has enabled me to walk in obedience to Him. May this volume bring Him glory and further His Kingdom.

Foreword

To be a Christian today is to be engaged in a historic struggle. There is ample evidence that our nation was founded upon Judeo-Christian values. Yet serious attempts are being made to remove nearly every vestige of Christian and biblical influence from America's history. Because this struggle is for the soul of our nation and the heart of our culture we need a champion to lead us in the fight to restore these values to their proper place in our nation. The Ethics & Religious Liberty Commission (ERLC) is such a champion. Calling us to moral purity, personal and public integrity, spiritual devotion, civic responsibility, and ethical convictions, the ERLC has challenged and inspired Southern Baptists to biblical faith and action.

The control and power of public institutions and public policy has fallen increasingly into the hands of influences today that run counter to biblical standards. These conditions require God's people to be vigilant. We must be sensitive to the critical issues of our time. The ERLC is an instrument God is using to create in us a biblical conscience.

This has been the entity's role for a century since the Southern Baptist Convention first took steps in 1907 to address formally moral attitudes with the establishment of the Committee on Civic Righteousness. Since that day there has been a continuous presence, now called the ERLC, which has called Southern Baptists and other Evangelicals to action.

We have been challenged to live out our faith in the culture. Christianity is not a way of doing certain things, but a certain way of doing everything! To that end the ERLC has called us to be "salt" and "light" in our insipid and darkened culture.

The hallmark issue has been the battle for religious liberty. Even before the birth of our nation, Baptists have been in the forefront calling for freedom for all to worship—or not worship—as they choose. This country was founded by those who were unwilling to compromise on this issue, leaving their homeland at great cost and risk in search of this "soul freedom."

The struggle over the years has been to protect that liberty and to properly interpret it. Religious liberty means freedom to worship without government interference or establishment. Known popularly as the "separation of church and state," our society now broadly calls for separation of God from government, thus endeavoring to create an agnostic society that denies any acknowledgement of the reality of God.

The ERLC has led the way in positioning Southern Baptists in the lead in confronting the culture with the biblical worldview. The agency has consistently provided resources imploring Southern Baptists to oppose the use of alcohol and drugs, gambling, and racial injustice, while promoting the biblical model of the family, sanctity of human life, care for the poor and disadvantaged, Christian citizenship, and a host of other issues. As early as 1929, the Southern Baptist Convention passed a resolution urging individuals not to support any candidate for president of the United States who supported the repeal of prohibition. It was clear that Southern Baptists were serious about influencing public policy and civic affairs.

In the 1960s, many of us experienced first-hand the leftward drift of the Christian Life Commission (now ERLC). When I wrote to the Executive-Secretary of the CLC, Foy Valentine, urging him to speak out against the tragedy of abortion, he refused to do so and replied that I should leave it alone because it was a Roman Catholic issue.

It soon became apparent that the CLC was losing touch both with its constituency and with biblical morality. To have been so strong and so right on so many issues and then to fail to stand for the right of the unborn to have life was a tragic revelation to Southern Baptists of the posture of this convention entity.

While nationally some were seeking to rewrite American history in an attempt to eradicate the evidence of Judeo-Christian influence, the election of Richard Land as president of the CLC served to stem the leftward drift within teh Convention's moral affairs entity. He began his service to Southern Baptists at the ministry with energy and enthusiasm. He quickly took steps to save the CLC from bankruptcy and to move it back to its historic purposes. Without any obscurity of expression or hesitation of conviction, his leadership has been one of God's greatest blessings to Southern Baptists.

Richard Land has consistently reminded us that what is right should be supported and what is wrong should be opposed. The standard by which right and wrong are determined is the Word of God! He speaks loudly for the dignity of all citizens and their freedom of worship. Richard Land calls for a national moral righteousness by challenging believers to be "salt" and "light" and thus to impact, challenge, and change the culture.

He reminds us that we are here to reflect God's presence and to make a difference in this world, that we are participants and not spectators in the cultural challenges of our day. Most of all, Richard Land challenges us to never quit, but to stay engaged, standing for moral and civic virtue and integrity. Richard Land and the Ethics & Religious Liberty Commission are giving a voice to the average citizen who believes in God and in the biblical principles and values that have made America the greatest nation in the world.

The history of the ethical consciousness of Southern Baptists certainly goes back beyond Richard Land. However, no one since the leadership of A. J. Barton (1910–1942) has more exemplified the spirit of biblical concern for social justice, biblical morality, Christian conduct, and involvement in the public arena than Richard Land.

His influence in our world, our nation, and our convention is enormous. He is recognized as a brilliant thinker and strategist, a consistent man of integrity, devotion, and compassion, and has been a counselor for many in the public sector over the years.

Jerry Sutton has done a magnificent and monumental work in these pages. He has set a fitting context for the entrance of Southern Baptists into the field of public morality and ethics. He has skillfully traced the development of our SBC in crucial areas of moral concern which began to emerge in the early years of our convention. He has pointed out the significant strengths of this ministry over the past 100 years, as well as chronicled its weaknesses and failures. He moves us forward with brilliance and renewed confidence as we follow the lead of the ERLC in applying our faith to all of life and culture.

The ERLC is a remarkable ministry of the SBC whose influence transcends our convention, partisan politics, and diverse theological positions. These pages will make you glad to be a Southern Baptist and amazed and grateful for the ERLC, which has done so much on limited resources to impact our world for Christ.

—James T. Draper Jr.

Introduction

The Southern Baptist Convention is the largest Protestant Christian denomination within inarguably the greatest nation on God's earth. As such, the Convention exercises great influence, if for no other reason than the sheer force of its millions of members. For an entire century, Southern Baptists have intentionally attempted to engage the American culture with a view to establishing righteousness as the prevailing virtue. The principal organization with the task assignment of leading that engagement and speaking for Southern Baptists in the areas of moral and religious liberty issues and public policy is the Ethics & Religious Liberty Commission. This volume is the story of that engagement.

This is a fascinating story and the one hundred year anniversary of Southern Baptists' engagement in moral and ethical matters and public policy issues deserves to be both celebrated and commemorated. Al Mohler said several years ago, "The burden of history falls upon all of us, but Christians bear a particular responsibility to make sense of the past and to evaluate events, issues and decisions from the framework of Christian moral teaching."[1] We have attempted to do that as we tell the story of the Ethics & Religious Liberty Commission.

On a recent trip to Starbucks, an encounter with a barrista at the store had me drinking out of a cup with "The Way I See It #182" printed on the side. This insightful observation stated,

In my career, I've found that "thinking outside the box" works better if I know what's "inside the box." In music (as in life) we need to understand our pertinent history . . . and moving on is so much easier once we know where we've been."

This was signed by Dave Grusin, an award-winning composer and jazz musician. In short, he says, to think outside the box is greatly assisted when you know what is inside the box. And, moving ahead is easier when you know where you've been. This is good advice for historians as well as musicians.

This volume is a meager attempt to describe what's inside our box and review where we have been. In order to set the stage for telling the Ethics & Religious Liberty Commission's story, it is only appropriate to set both the cultural and historical context.

Chapter 1, "Western Civilization, Culture Wars, and Christian Activism," presents an overview of the cultural context of the Commission's story. In short, it is an effort to answer the questions, "Why bother and what is at stake?"

Chapter 2 will identify, in broad strokes, the historic context of the role of biblical Christianity in creating and sustaining Western civilization. It will begin with the biblical foundation and proceed by touching upon the high points of history.

Chapter 3 will describe the Baptist influence in what historian and missiologist Kenneth Scott Latourette calls the Great Century or the nineteenth century. It will review Baptist influence and contributions before, during, and after the Civil War.

Chapter 4 will describe the beginnings of formal Southern Baptist engagement in cultural matters in 1907, tracing the development of the Committee on Civic Righteousness, the Committee on Temperance, and the Social Service Commission. Of particular interest will be the profound contribution made by Arthur J. Barton and the major Southern Baptist involvement in Prohibition.

Chapter 5 will chronicle the transition years of 1947–1960, when the Social Service Commission was led by Hugh A. Brimm and Acker C. Miller.

Chapter 6 addresses the early years of Foy Valentine's leadership (1960–1972), particularly his role in the civil rights debate in America.

Chapter 7 (1973–1988) begins with the landmark *Roe v. Wade* decision and reviews how Valentine's Commission positioned Southern Baptists vis-à-vis the important issue of the sanctity of human life. It will also cover the beginning years of the Conservative Resurgence and the transitional 19-month tenure of Larry Baker as head of the Commission.

Chapter 8 (1988–1997) tells the story of the beginning of Richard Land's years as executive director and later president of the Christian Life Commission. His leadership marked a major transition in philosophy and policy. During his early tenure the Commission was reassigned the responsibility for representing Southern Baptists in the arena of religious liberty and First Amendment concerns.

Chapter 9 (1997–2007) begins with the Southern Baptist reorganization, "Covenant for a New Century," which changed the Commission's name to "The Ethics & Religious Liberty Commission" and vastly expanded its reach and influence. Not unexpectedly, it will highlight the role of Richard Land as one of the top Christian influencers in U. S. domestic and foreign policy.

Chapter 10, the Epilogue, will review the historical, theological, philosophical, and practical framework and foundation of the Ethics & Religious Liberty Commission's work, touch on some of the critical issues addressed by the Commission, and conclude with a challenge for all who come under the influence of the Ethics & Religious Liberty Commission to work and pray for a greater tomorrow.

So, let's begin the story with an examination of the cultural context, which in many ways sets the stage and communicates the urgency of supporting the work of the Ethics & Religious Liberty Commission.

Notes

1. Al Mohler, "Hiroshima and the burden for history," *Baptist Press*, August 8, 2005.

CHAPTER

Western Civilization, Culture Wars and Christian Activism

Although the purpose of this volume is to tell the story of Southern Baptists and the Ethics & Religious Liberty Commission, the story would be incomplete without providing the context, and the context in broad strokes consists of the story of the developing of Western civilization and the role of the church in that development. When Francis A. Schaeffer wrote his monumental work, *How Should We Then Live?*, his subtitle was *The Rise and Decline of Western Thought and Culture.* In his study of Western culture, he noted that he was providing an "analysis of the key moments in history which have formed our present culture, and the thinking of the people who brought those moments." Throughout his text, Schaeffer points out the critical role played by the church in the development of Western civilization.[1]

Schaeffer and many others have addressed the critical issues they perceive as vital to the survival of Western civilization.

No one has done a better job of highlighting the critical nature of the days in which we live than Samuel P. Huntington. In his national best seller, *The Clash of Civilizations and the Remaking of World Order*, Huntington contends that Western civilization is in the "fight for its life." As he draws conclusions about the present time, he states,

> The overriding lesson of the history of civilizations, however, is that many things are probable but nothing is inevitable. Civilizations can and have reformed and renewed themselves. The central issue for the West is whether, quite apart from any external challenges, it is capable of stopping and reversing the internal processes of decay. Can the West renew itself or will sustained internal rot simply accelerate its end and/or subordination to other economically and demographically more dynamic civilizations?[2]

Huntington's assessment is that the West will collapse because of its moral decline, cultural suicide, and political disunity rather than by any external threat. He goes on to explain that the erosion of Christianity among Westerners is a principal cause of the threatening decline. Then as a major conclusion he states,

> A more immediate and dangerous challenge exists in the United States. Historically, American national identity has been defined culturally by the heritage of Western civilization and politically by the principles of the American creed on which Americans overwhelmingly agree: liberty, democracy, individualism, equality before the law, constitutionalism, private property. In the late twentieth century both components of American identity have come under concentrated and sustained onslaught from a small but influential number of intellects and publicists.

He points out that the trend toward multiculturalism is damaging and then concludes that "the futures of the United States and of the West depend upon Americans reaffirming their commitment to Western civilization." He maintains that the responsibility of Western leaders should be to "preserve, protect, and renew the unique qualities of Western civilization." And then he follows up that assessment by stating, "Because it is the most powerful Western country, that responsibility falls overwhelmingly on the United States of America."[3]

As a sequel to his *Clash of Civilizations*, Huntington wrote *Who Are We?*, in which he addressed issues raised about the challenges to America's national identity. Again, it is his contention that part of what makes Western civilization, and the United States in particular, unique is its heritage of Christianity.[4]

Christianity and the Formation of Western Civilization

Many writers of late have demonstrated the critical role of Christian thought in shaping Western civilization. Alvin J. Schmidt wrote *How Christianity Changed the World*. Rodney Stark wrote both *The Rise of Christianity* and *For the Glory of God*, and Thomas E. Woods wrote *How the Catholic Church Built Western Civilization*. Each of these volumes highlights the critical components of Western civilization and how Christian thought was formative in their development. Western civilization's philosophy of history, its common identity, its understanding of both politics and government, as well as its understanding of the law, all find roots in Christianity. Christianity provided the foundation for education, science, medicine, art, architecture, economics, and the work ethic, which has supported the superstructure of Western civilization. The place of charity, the value of the family, the importance of morality and peace find their philosophical roots in Western civilization in the Christian church.[5]

For a variety of reasons, Christianity provided a new and unique philosophy of history. In fact, unlike any other religion in history, Christianity rises and falls on the historicity of the events in Jesus' incarnation, death, burial, and resurrection. Christianity rejects Persian dualism, pantheism, and even the idea that history is exclusively cyclical. Some interpretations of history anticipate the emerging of an ideal society or human perfection. Christianity does not deny the idea of progress but does embrace an understanding that humanity is flawed and as a result of the reality of sin will always be less than perfect. For the Christian, history has to be understood as surrounded by eternity. History is understood as linear, moving from past events of creation, fall, and redemption through to a climax and culmination of judgment and eternity. In the midst of all of this, there is a tacit assumption that God is sovereign and that His creation was designed by intelligence and with purpose. This philosophical foundation has helped to shape Western civilization.[6]

A second component of Western civilization provided by the Christian heritage is the idea of a common identity. From the first century, as Christianity spread westward and particularly with the embracing of Christianity by Rome and what became the *Corpus Christianum* for the Holy Roman Empire, Christianity provided a common identity for Western Europe, the Americas, and Australia. Even with the fragmentation of Christianity into the East and West and then later with the Reformation, the Judeo-Christian heritage provided an identity that was not always embraced but was understood.[7]

When we come to the study of politics and government, we must acknowledge the debt to both the Greeks and the Romans and to intellects like Cicero, Socrates, Aristotle, and Plato. But as we watch the development of Western culture and Western civilization, numerous principles are embodied in Western culture and particularly nations that submit to the rule of law and find their foundational axioms in Christianity. Jesus Himself said that we are to render unto Caesar the things that are Caesar's and unto God the things that are God's. As the years transpired, men like Augustine, Aquinas, and John Locke, not to mention Ambrose and Hildebrand, and so many others, each contributed to a body of political thought that has shaped the modern world. Concepts such as no one is above the law, that there is a natural law which correlates into natural rights, personal freedom and rights of the individual, the idea of equality among individuals, and even the separating of the institutions of church and state are each found in germinal form in Scripture. Even concepts of the separation of powers and the checks and balances which we take for granted are found in Scripture.[8]

Much of the Western legal tradition can be traced directly to the unfolding of canon law in the Roman Catholic Church. In fact, Thomas Woods points out, "As the first systematic body of law in medieval Europe, canon law (that is, church law) became the model for the various secular legal systems that would now begin to emerge." Around AD 1140, a monk by the name of Gratian penned *A Concordance of Discordant Canons.* Considered a historic milestone, one legal scholar, Harold Berman, noted that "it was the first comprehensive and systematic legal treatise in the history of the West, and perhaps in the history of mankind—if by 'comprehensive' is meant the attempt to embrace virtually the entire law of a given polity, and if by 'systematic' is meant the express effort to present the law as a single body, in which all the parts are reviewed as interacting to form a whole."[9]

Laws relating to marriage, contracts, criminal activity, liability, and intent find their foundation in canon law. Again, the concept of natural rights of individuals based on a universal moral law is also found in canon law. Concepts of the rights of man and the philosophy of rights as well as the applicability of rights of those living in a foreign land were developed by the church and became the foundation of international law.[10]

Another pillar of Western civilization is its emphasis on education. Ancient Judaism was known for its education, and that same love for learning was quickly adapted by the early church. In fact, Jesus Himself said that the believers and disciples were to teach. So it is not surprising that throughout the entire story of the unfolding of the church there has been an emphasis on teaching and education. Thomas Woods points out that the entire "university system" was a product of the church and as such "it was the only institution in Europe that showed consistent interest in the preservation and cultivation of knowledge." In fact, by the time of the Reformation, eighty-one universities existed in the Western world. In the Reformation era, Martin Luther advocated establishing public schools, and both he and John Calvin argued for universal education. Luther, along with Phillip Melanchthon, advocated that schools should be tax supported and that education should be compulsory. In that same era, Johann Sturm, a Lutheran, became an advocate for graded education so that students would be more apt to learn. Almost all of the universities in the Americas were established first as institutions to train ministers and to further the cause of Christ. Alvin J. Schmidt points out that 92 percent of the 182 colleges and universities established in the United States prior to the Civil War were founded by Christian denominations.[11]

Even though conventional wisdom affirms that religion or faith and science are at polarities and that sometime during the Enlightenment period science finally won over the church, the truth is that Christianity and religion were the foundation of the development of science in the West. In his monumental work *For the Glory of God*, Rodney Stark states, "I argue not only that there is no inherent conflict between religion and science but that Christian theology was essential for the rise of science." He then proceeds to survey a litany of examples in which Christians convinced that God had created an orderly world sought inductively and empirically to discover the principles by which God had designed and was maintaining His world. Stark concludes his survey saying: "Despite its length, this chapter consists of only two major points. First, science arose only once in history—in medieval Europe. Second, science could only arise in the culture dominated by belief in a conscious, rational, all-powerful Creator. Thus, it could be said that the rise of science required an Eleventh Commandment: 'Know thou my handiwork.'" Both Schmidt and Woods argue for the same conclusion, demonstrating with repeated examples the influence of Christians who, convinced that God had ordained an orderly world, were seeking to understand the order by which God ran His universe.[12]

Anyone who travels to Italy and visits Florence, Milan, or the Vatican in Rome no doubt is impressed by the art and the architecture of the Christian church. Stunning cathedrals, breathtaking sculptures, and incredible works of art depicting numerous Christian themes can be found throughout the Western world. Some of the greatest music ever written—music by Bach, Handel, and Beethoven—was inspired by Christian themes. Magnificent murals and mosaics can be traced back to the early church. Beautiful stained glass depicting biblical characters and brilliantly copied manuscripts are part of the Christian heritage of Western civilization.[13]

Another contribution to the development of Western civilization was the Christian understanding of the dignity of work and its formative influence in the field of economics. Apart from Judaism and prior to the rise of Christianity, the Greco-Roman world considered labor to be demeaning; it was restricted only to slaves, and the consideration was that free citizens did not participate in labor. In contrast the Hebrew Scriptures taught that labor was honorable, that the worker deserved his or her wages, and that property rights were normative, hence Exodus 20:15, "Thou shalt not steal" (KJV). As the New Testament era unfolded, Paul likewise taught that labor was honorable. He also communicated that the laborer deserved his wages and those who were unwilling to work should not be permitted to eat. As time passed, the Christian church taught the dignity of work. In fact, an old Benedictine proverb says, "To work is to pray." As Woods demonstrates, the late scholastics developed much of the economic theory upon which modern civilization is based—the theory of money, the destructive effects of inflation, the expectations theory in economics, the subjective theory of value, the concept of the just price, and much more. In the Reformation era, Martin Luther saw that work was not only pleasing but also a calling, *vocatio*, to serve God. Likewise, John Calvin has been credited with contributing much to the Puritan work ethic and the rise of capitalism in Western civilization. In 1905, the German sociologist Max Weber articulated the phrase the Protestant Ethic or the Protestant Work Ethic and coupled it with the rise of capitalism. Those who have studied what Weber has written argue that it should have been the "Christian work ethic" because the foundation of all these things was laid early in the writings of the New Testament. When Christianity came to the New World, particularly in the establishments of Jamestown and the Plymouth Colony, both attempted early on to create a socialist commonwealth and both failed dismally; only when the concepts of private property and economic freedom were established did these colonies flourish. As time passed, it became clear that only in Western civilization where Christianity was embraced did a stable middle class develop. Schmidt summarizes the contribution of Christianity by stating:

> Thus, while Christianity does not advocate a given economic ideology, its support of human freedom and private property rights provides fertile ground for the existence of a free enterprise economic system as opposed to a planned or command economy such as socialism or communism, where human freedom is severely curtailed and private property proscribed. Nor is Christianity opposed to people being thrifty and productive, which can and often have resulted in many individuals becoming wealthy. . . . Christians have always been expected to use their acquired wealth to God's glory and to the welfare of their neighbor, as Luther and Calvin frequently emphasized.[14]

Still another contribution of Christianity to Western civilization was its emphasis on charity and caring for those in need. Along with the Old Testament emphasis on giving to the poor and providing gleanings from the harvest (i.e., Ruth), the early church promoted highly the importance of giving to the poor and of taking care of those who were less fortunate. Paul talked about taking relief offerings to certain churches. In Acts 6, we find the concern to take care of widows. James speaks of taking care of both widows and orphans. As history unfolds, the cultural distinction between giving by the Greeks and Romans and then the Christians is noteworthy. Greeks and Romans seem to have given for the purpose of notoriety and the benefit of the one giving whereas Christians would give with no expectation other than to help those in need. Repeatedly we find the church being a center of charitable activity. Tertullian wrote of having a common fund to take care of people in need. When Pachomius saw how the Christians took care of wounded and sick soldiers in Constantine's army, he was moved by the Christian compassion. Many of the Catholic orders gave primary attention to caring for people in need. As time passed, the Christian church set aside specific ministries for orphans, for the elderly, for attacking child labor laws, for providing mental asylums, providing care for the blind and also establishing health care institutions and hospitals. Charitable giving became a distinctive mark of Western civilization that can be traced uniquely to the influence of Christianity.[15]

Additional major contributions of Christianity to Western civilization were its emphasis on the home and morality. From the beginning, Christianity emphasized the sacredness of life. In fact, early on, it attacked the pagan practices of infanticide, along with abortions, and even suicide. Christianity was the force that finally brought to a conclusion the bloody sport of the gladiatorial games in Rome, not to mention much of the pagan practice of human sacrifice. Christianity finally halted the practice of dueling and also cultivated the theory of just war. Whether it was violence against the individual or nation against nation, Christianity worked to bring peace. In the arena of morality, Christianity worked from the outset to honor the sacredness of marriage. It dignified the responsibilities of husbands, wives, and children in the home. As a result, the Christian church became a great adversary to promiscuity, adultery, homosexuality, prostitution, and other forms of sexual improprieties. In Schmidt's assessment, he notes that "by opposing the Greco-Roman sexual decadence, whether it was adultery, fornication, homosexuality, child molestation, or bestiality, and by introducing God-pleasing sexual standards, Christianity greatly elevated the world's sexual morality." Schmidt then provides this assessment, "It was one of its major contributions to civilization, a contribution that too many Christians today no longer seem to appreciate, much less defend, as feverish efforts are underway to bring back the sexual debauchery of ancient paganism." Likewise, Woods notes:

> Faithful to the mission she has fulfilled for two millennia, however, the church still holds out a moral alternative to young people immersed in a culture that relentlessly teaches them to pursue immediate gratification. The church recalls the

great men of Christendom—like Charlemagne, St. Thomas Aquinas, St. Francis of Assisi, and St. Francis Xavier, to name a few—and holds them up as models for how true men live. It's message? Essentially this: You can aspire to be one of these men—a builder of civilization, a great genius, a servant of God and men, or a heroic missionary—or you can be a self-absorbed nobody fixated on gratifying your appetites. Our society does everything in its power to ensure that you wind up on the latter path. Be your own person. Rise above the herd, declare your independence from a culture that thinks so little of you, and proclaim that you intend to live not as a beast but as a man.[16]

It is easy to conclude by reviewing the previous examples that Christianity has provided both the foundation and the fabric of Western civilization, and yet today in an incredible way that entire fabric of civilization is being threatened.

The Assault on Western Civilization

In two of his most insightful works, *The Clash of Civilizations and the Remaking of World Order* and *Who Are We?*, Samuel Huntington clearly makes the case that civilizations are clashing. In the second of these two works, Huntington "turns his attention from international affairs to our domestic cultural rifts as he examines the impact other civilizations and their values are having on our own country." His principal argument is that if we are to survive as a nation we must determine the answer clearly to the question, who are we? The answer to that question will determine whether or not we as a nation will survive. We are locked in an ideological war for the survival both of Western civilization and America as we know it.[17]

One of the most astute observers of the war of ideas is Summit Ministries' president David A. Noebel. In his major work *Understanding the Times*, he argues that four principal worldviews are contending for dominion. These include secular humanism, Marxist/Leninist ideology, cosmic humanism (which is essentially the New Age movement), and then biblical Christianity. No doubt Huntington and many others would add a fifth ideology, Islam. According to James Dobson and Gary Bauer, "nothing short of a great civil war of values rages today throughout North America."[18]

Since the middle of the twentieth century, numerous volumes have been written detailing the assault on Western civilization and Western culture. Among the more prominent of these are *Ideas Have Consequences* by Richard M. Weaver (1948), *How Should We Then Live?* by Francis Schaeffer (1976), *Christian Countermoves in a Decadent Culture* by Carl F. H. Henry (1986), *The Devaluing of America* by William J. Bennett (1992), *The American Hour* by Os Guinness (1993), *When Nations Die* by Jim Nelson Black (1994), *America's Real War* by Daniel Lapin (1999), *Civilization and Its Enemies* by Lee Harris (2004), *The West's Last Chance* by Tony Blankley (2005), and *The Marketing of Evil* by David Kupelian (2005).

One of the best summary treatments of the assault on America's traditional values is found in Pat Buchanan's *The Death of the West*. He explains that America is being offered a new faith which "refuses to recognize any higher moral order or moral authority." Citing the *Humanist Manifesto* of 1973, he points out that the new gospel "has as its governing axioms: there is no God; there are no absolute values in the universe; the supernatural is superstition. All life begins here and ends here; its object is human happiness in this, the only world we shall ever know." He notes that there are two principal values. First, that "all lifestyles are equal" and second, that "thou shalt not be judgmental." In other words, there are no moral absolutes. At the same time we find an intentional revision of history in which Western history is essentially a catalog of crimes committed by nations that profess to be Christian. He further points out that "eradication of the idea of superior cultures and civilizations is thus a first order of business of the revolution."[19]

Buchanan goes on to identify four key leaders of the "revolution." He notes that the common denominator of all four is the conviction that "unless and until Christianity and Western culture, the immune system of capitalism, were uprooted from the soul of Western man,

Marxism [which he identifies as the driving force of this attempted philosophical *coup d'etat*] could not take root, and the revolution would be betrayed by the workers in whose name it was to be fought." The first leader was the Hungarian, George Lukacs, who said, "A worldwide overturning of values cannot take place without the annihilation of the old values and the creation of new ones by the revolutionaries." He was convinced that the nuclear family must be destroyed in order to succeed.[20]

A second leader of the revolution was Antonio Gramsci who was convinced that governments "grounded in Judeo-Christian beliefs and values could not be overthrown until their roots were cut." Gramsci further noted that the best assault on the West was to initiate a cultural revolution which would require "a long march through the institutions." His conviction was that if Christianity could be eradicated from the cultural identity, the West could be overthrown.[21]

In time the radicals who had originally been located at Frankfurt University in Germany fled to America and were embraced by Columbia University. One of the key leaders of this newly arrived institution was Herbert Marcuse. Buchanan points out that one of the weapons developed by the Frankfurt School for the cultural conflict was "critical theory," which was an "essentially destructive criticism of all of the main elements of Western culture, including Christianity, capitalism, authority, the family, patriarchy, hierarchy, morality, tradition, sexual restraint, loyalty, patriotism, nationalism, heredity, ethnocentrism, convention, and conservatism." The primary *modus operandi* was to embrace an "attack politics," which introduced a "cultural pessimism," the intention of which was to destroy Western culture and replace it with a Marxist ideology. One of his primary allegations was to argue that conservative Christian culture breeds fascism, and therefore it needs to be replaced by a "therapeutic state . . . where sin is redefined as sickness, crime becomes anti-social behavior, and the psychiatrist replaces the priest." A fourth contributor to this revolution was Theodor Adorno, who contended that the traditional patriarchal family was the natural habitat for the traditional culture and must be dismantled. Buchanan points out that "for cultural Marxists, no cause ranked higher than the abolition of the family, which they despised as a dictatorship and the incubator of sexism and social injustice."[22]

According to Buchanan, Lukacs, Gramsci, Adorno, and Marcuse, the Frankfurt School had "immense influence on America's cultural and intellectual history." Citing James Cooper, Buchanan notes:

> By the end of World War II, the liberal left had managed to capture not only the arts, theater, literature, music, and ballet, but also motion pictures, photography, education and the media.
>
> Through its control of the culture, the left dictates not only the answers, but the questions asked. In short, it controls the cosmological apparatus by which most Americans comprehend the meaning of events.
>
> This cosmology is based on two great axioms: the first is there are no absolute values in the universe, no standards of beauty and ugliness, good and evil. The second axiom is—in a godless universe—the left holds moral superiority as the final arbiter of man's activities.[23]

Next Buchanan begins to delve into the tactics used by the left. Citing Alexander Solzhenitsyn, Buchanan notes, "To destroy a people, you must sever their roots." He then asks the question, "How do you sever a people's roots?" and he answers his own question by saying, "You must destroy its memory." He then looks back to Ronald Reagan's farewell address to the American people in which he said, "If we forget what we did, we won't know who we are . . . . I am warning of the eradication . . . of the American memory, that could result, ultimately, in an erosion of the American spirit."[24]

The ultimate intention of the revolutionaries, according to Buchanan, is to capture the cultural institutions, de-Christianize America, and set up a purely secular culture. At that juncture, any direction is possible. Buchanan points out that the courts, in particular, have done everything possible to remove Christian ideas and symbols from the public arena. He argues that "Christians who still believe the Court only created a level playing field for all faiths are whistling past the graveyard. The Court just took their stadium into receivership and turned it over to their rivals. What Christians have lost, they will not get back without a struggle." The old moral order based on Judeo-Christian convictions has been assaulted and removed to the periphery. According to Buchanan, "the old moral consensus has collapsed, and the moral community built upon it no longer exists."[25]

The Culture Wars

In 1991, sociologist James Davison Hunter popularized the term "culture wars" in his book by the same name. He states that the culture wars revolve around the issues of what is ultimately good and finally intolerable in our communities. He notes that "personal disagreements that fire the culture war are deep and perhaps unreconcilable." He goes on to explain "that these differences are often intensified and aggravated by the way they are presented in public." He concludes by saying, "At stake is how we as Americans will order our lives together."[26]

As Hunter begins to develop his arguments and his reasoning, he states, "I define cultural conflict very simply as political and social hostility rooted in different systems of moral understanding." He then concludes, "The end to which these hostilities tend is the domination of one cultural and moral ethos over all others." His belief is that two polarities are at odds. The first is orthodoxy and the second is progressivism. These two, he argues, maintain a constant tension in our culture. He further notes that the public discourse where these battles are fought is largely engaged in by the elites of the culture, which he identifies as "traditional" and "organic." He then concludes: "They become polarized to the point of an all out contest over the nature and content of the public order. The end of the struggle, according to Gramsci's model [recall Columbia University's Frankfurt School], is either the restoration of the old hegemony or the establishment of a new hegemony in the realm of public culture." Hunter further observes, "In all of this, the language of confrontation, battle, even war, then, is not merely a literary device but an apt tool to describe the way in which the many issues contested in American public culture are being settled."[27]

As Hunter draws his conclusions and makes his final assessments, he determines:

> The culture war is rooted in an ongoing realignment of American public culture and has become institutionalized chiefly through special purpose organizations, denominations, political parties and branches of government. The fundamental disagreements that characterize the culture war we have seen become even further aggravated by virtue of the technology of public discourse, the means by which disagreements are voiced in public. In the end, however, the opposing moral visions become, as one would say in the tidy though ponderous jargon of social science, a reality suigeneris: a reality much larger than, and indeed autonomous from, the sum total of individuals, and organizations that give expression to the conflict. These competing moral visions, and the rhetoric that sustains them, become the defining forces of public life.[28]

Noting that, "it is considerably more difficult to alter the ethos of national public life for those operating in large measure from the periphery of social power than for those whose efforts are concentrated in the center," (i.e., Washington, D.C., and New York City), Hunter speculates that the progressivist vision has an advantage in the present and finally concludes optimistically that a resolution will be arrived at which will include "a principled pluralism and a principled toleration." As one can tell, Hunter is more optimistic than Buchanan.[29] Yet the question for us is, what role will Southern Baptists play in this ongoing struggle? And what difference can they make?

Engagement

In the pages ahead we will review a litany of issues in which the Southern Baptist Convention (America's largest Protestant denomination) and its Ethics & Religious Liberty Commission (formerly the

Christian Life Commission) have engaged in what is commonly called the culture wars. We will review issues of freedom and religious liberty; equality and race; the issues of life, family, and education; as well as issues related to national security and the problems of abuse and addiction in our culture. We will also review the distortions made by our critics and hopefully provide a reasoned response. These items will be examined in light of our common life together as Americans and as Southern Baptists.

When it comes to the issue of Christian activism in the public arena, Evangelicals often face a divide. One school of thought argues that Christians should not be involved in the public arena and that Christian activism is a waste of time. In contrast, others argue the absolute necessity of Christians being involved and fighting for the survival of a traditional culture based on Judeo-Christian values. The former school of thought is represented by leaders like John MacArthur who wrote *Why Government Can't Save You* and edited a volume entitled *Fool's Gold?*, which includes a chapter by Phil Johnson, "Let Your Light So Shine: Examining the American-Christian Approach to Politics," in which he argues that the thrust of Matthew 5:16, which is often cited by Evangelicals to encourage involvement in the political process, is misused. In contrast, men like Tom Minnery and James Dobson of Focus on the Family and Chuck Colson of Prison Fellowship argue that it is absolutely essential for Christians to be involved in the public arena. Historically, Southern Baptists have always aligned themselves with the latter group and been involved from one degree to another in the public discourse. The monumental task for Southern Baptists, therefore, is the issue of effective engagement.

In his *Fit Bodies, Fat Minds* (1994), Os Guinness, critiquing evangelicals' poor showing in the cultural exchange and the consequential lack of influence in the public policy arena, assigns this ineffectiveness to an inherent anti-intellectualism. Although he provides four reasons for our inability to compete on the intellectual level, for our purposes one stands out. Guinness suggests that "there has been no generally accepted, constructive formulation of an Evangelical public philosophy (which translates into effective public policy) for the last hundred years." Although his conclusions are open for debate, it is wise at least to consider his rationale.[30]

In essence, Guinness argues that two factors undergird Evangelicals' ineffectiveness in public life. First, he raises the specter of an education gap, pointing out that "those more educated now tend to be significantly less religious, those more religious tend to be significantly less educated." Citing the sociologist Peter Berger, he notes that "the United States is distinctive among modern nations for having a populace as religious as India's but an elite as secular as Sweden's." He concludes that "Evangelicals who have failed to think Christianly in this era of the so-called 'knowledge elite' and the 'information explosion' have taken themselves out of the running for natural influence in our culture."[31]

A second factor identified by Guinness is the "lack of an Evangelical public philosophy, or common vision for the common good." The tendency among Evangelicals, he suggests, is to be partisan and sectarian. He moves on to conclude that "without a public philosophy that defends the common good, outsiders tend to view evangelicals' public involvement as constitutionally legitimate but intrusive and unwelcome." In short, Evangelicals, among whom Southern Baptists would be perceived as a significant subset, have been considered either irrelevant or a nuisance to public policy discussions.[32]

Guinness moves on to point out what he considers four strategic errors Evangelicals have repeatedly committed which have led to the present state of affairs. First, he believes they have concentrated their power with respect to location in "the peripheries of modern society rather than the center." Second, "Evangelicals have relied on populist strengths and rhetoric rather than addressing the gatekeepers of modern society—those whose positions of office or responsibility enable them to stand at the doorways of public power and influence." Third, "Evangelicals have sought to change society through politics rather than changing the culture;" that is, they are no longer attempting to change society by bringing transformation to individuals. Finally, all too often, "Evangelicals have chosen to rely on a rhetoric of protest, pronouncement, and picketing rather than persuasion." In short, it appears that "the winning of hearts and minds" needs to be elevated to a greater priority.[33]

Southern Baptists may or may not agree with Guinness's assessment. Nonetheless, it is wise to consider his observations as we attempt to engage the culture and bring a Christian perspective into the public arena. We do well to consider his words of caution.

According to its printed material, "The Ethics & Religious Liberty Commission is the public policy arm of the Southern Baptist Convention. We are dedicated to addressing social, moral, and ethical concerns with particular attention to their impact on American families and their faith."[34]

According to the Vision Statement of the Ethics & Religious Liberty Commission, the ERLC looks forward to "an American Society that affirms and practices Judeo-Christian values rooted in biblical authority." Its Mission Statement is "to awaken, inform, energize, equip, and mobilize Christians to be the catalyst for the biblically based transformation of their families, churches, communities, and the nation." For Southern Baptists, being involved in the public arena and defending Christian values is a matter of conviction.[35]

The following pages will provide a narrative history of how Southern Baptists have been involved in the public arena. But before unfolding the story of Southern Baptists, it would be wise to provide the historical context of how Christians from biblical times forward have been involved in the public arena throughout the history of the Christian church.

Notes

1. Francis A. Schaeffer, *How Should We Then Live?* (Westchester, Ill., Crossway Books: 1976), 15.

2. Samuel P. Huntington, *The Clash of Civilizations and the Remaking of World Order* (New York: Touchstone, 1996), 303.

3. Ibid., 305, 307, 311.

4. Samuel P. Huntington, *Who Are We?* (New York: Simon and Schuster, 2004), 81–106, 340–54.

5. Alvin J. Schmidt, *How Christianity Changed the World* (Grand Rapids, Mich.: Zondervan, 2001, 2004); Rodney Stark, *The Rise of Christianity*

(Princeton and Oxford: Princeton University Press, 1996); Rodney Stark, *For the Glory of God* (Princeton and Oxford: Princeton University Press, 2003); Thomas E. Woods, *How the Catholic Church Built Western Civilization* (Washington, D.C.: Regnery, 2005).

6. Kenneth Scott Latourette, "The Christian Understanding of History," in C. T. McIntire, ed., *God, History and Historians* (New York: Oxford University Press, 1977), 46–47.

7. Kenneth Scott Latourette, *A History of the Expansion of Christianity* (7 vol.), (New York: Harper, 1937–1945).

8. Schmidt, *How Christianity Changed the World*, 248–71; Woods, *How the Catholic Church Built Western Civilization*, 187–202.

9. Woods, *How the Catholic Church Built Western Civilization*, 190–202.

10. Ibid.

11. Ibid., 47–66; Schmidt, *How Christianity Changed the World*, 170–93.

12. Stark, *For the Glory of God*, 123, 197; Schmidt, *How Christianity Changed the World*, 218–47; Woods, *How the Catholic Church Built Western Civilization*, 67–114; Schaeffer, *How Should We Then Live?*, 130–43.

13. Schmidt, *How Christianity Changed the World*, 292–313; Woods, *How the Catholic Church Built Western Civilization*, 114–32.

14. Schmidt, *How Christianity Changed the World*, 194–217; Woods, *How the Catholic Church Built Western Civilization*, 153–67.

15. Schmidt, *How Christianity Changed the World*, 125–69; Woods, *How the Catholic Church Built Civilization*, 169–86.

16. Schmidt, *How Christianity Changed the World*, 94; Woods, *How the Catholic Church Built Western Civilization*, 214–15.

17. Huntington, *Clash*, dust jacket.

18. David A. Noebel, *Understanding the Times*, (abridged ed.), (Colorado Springs, Colo.: Association of Christian Schools International and Summit Ministries, 1995), 1–10.

19. Patrick J. Buchanan, *The Death of the West* (New York: Thomas Dunne Books, 2002), 51, 55, 57–58.

20. Ibid., 73, 75.

21. Ibid., 76.

22. Ibid., 78, 80, 82.

23. Ibid., 91, 95. The most thorough critique of the Frankfurt School of Thought is Rolf Wiggershaus, *The Frankfurt School: Its History, Theories and Political Significance* (Cambridge, Mass.: MIT Press, 1995).

24. Buchanan, *The Death of the West*, 147.

25. Ibid., 184, 186–89.

26. James Davison Hunter, *Culture Wars* (New York: Basic Books, 1991), 31, 33–34.

27. Ibid., 42–43, 59, 61, 64.

28. Ibid., 290–91.

29. Ibid., 302, 325.

30. Os Guinness, *Fit Bodies, Fat Minds* (Grand Rapids, Mich.: Baker, 1994), 14.

31. Ibid., 15–16.

32. Ibid., 16–17.

33. Ibid., 17–18.

34. See www.erlc.com.

35. ERLC Vision and Values Statement, 2006.

CHAPTER

The Context of History

From the beginning of biblical days until the founding of the Southern Baptist Convention in 1845, an incredible amount of history had already transpired. After introducing this volume with a survey of the rise and development of Western civilization with its heavy formative Christian influence, and then reviewing the contemporary culture wars which are threatening to bring its disintegration, it is wise to stop and recall in broad brushstrokes the historic context that provides the backdrop for both church-state relations and the incitement for Christians to be involved in formulating and engaging in public-policy issues.

This chapter will begin by surveying briefly the biblical basis from which Christianity draws its ideas about church-state relations and public-policy convictions. Next it will provide an overview of how these ideas were expressed and embodied in history. The survey will move from the Patristic era through to the Medieval church to the Reformation and post-Reformation eras. At this juncture we will refocus on the Americas and review the colonial period and the birth of the nation. All of this is designed to provide a backdrop of our study on how the Southern Baptist Convention has engaged in church-state and public-policy concerns.

The Biblical Foundation

In our survey of the biblical material relevant to church-state issues and public-policy issues, primarily moral and social, two approaches are at our disposal. The first is to approach the subjects thematically, that is, what does Scripture say about life, family, or marriage? The second approach is to provide a chronological survey, Genesis onward. We will opt for the latter.

In the Pentateuch, the first five books of the Bible, numerous issues can be identified. Genesis begins by declaring the reality of God, "In the beginning God created the heavens and the earth." By this His authority as Creator and Sustainer is declared. In that same opening chapter, we find that God created man in His own image and directed him to exercise dominion over the created order. Next we find God placing limits on man's freedom, forbidding him to eat of the fruit of the tree of the knowledge of good and evil. Next God made a helper or a completer for Adam in the form of Eve. This clearly teaches that God is intentional in His design for the nuclear family. When Adam and Eve rebelled against God, the human race became cursed with sin. Evidence of this was seen when Cain killed Abel and climaxed when God said, "I am just going to destroy the entire human race," and yet showed mercy on Noah and his family as the surviving remnant. As the human race began to expand once again, we discover God's hand in establishing nation states particularly in His promise to Abraham, yet we still see God judging the iniquity of nations, but with great patience. Nevertheless, we do discover that he destroyed Sodom and Gomorrah because of their great wickedness. God is not neutral to the unrighteousness either of mankind or of nations. Genesis concludes with the story of Joseph—his tragedies and triumphs—and explains to us how God Himself orchestrated the events to place Joseph in a position of leadership in ancient Egypt. In explaining God's ways to his brothers who had betrayed him, Joseph simply stated, "What you meant for evil, God Himself meant for good."

In Exodus and Leviticus we find the story of God delivering and birthing a nation, Israel. Several salient points deserve to be mentioned. The first and most obvious is that Moses confronted Pharaoh for his refusal to free the slaves. Inherent here is the right of the dignity of all men to be free. In Exodus we find God giving the Law to the nation and establishing a new social order. In the follow-up of Leviticus, we find God giving specific laws concerning both religion and morality. God was clear that the reason He was displacing the nations and establishing Israel was because those nations practiced perversions that He abhorred.[1]

In the historical books, we discover God's direction in establishing a new nation. According to Joshua, behaviors exist that bless and curse nations according to God. In the book of Judges, we learn that God is infuriated over idolatry and immorality, and it is His intention to purify His people. In 1 Samuel we find the people petitioning Samuel, the prophet, saying, "We want a king and God"; and finally God acquiesced and allowed them to have a king so they could be like the other nations around them (see Deut. 17:14). After the Babylonian exile, we find Nehemiah, a faithful man and an effective leader, being led to return to Jerusalem, which by report was in ruins. We read here about the restoration of the city, how the gates that had been burned with fire and the walls that had been torn down were now restored. We find in Nehemiah an incredible example of strong leadership, and at the same time we find him addressing the issues of social injustice and oppression. He was the man who led Jerusalem once again to establish security and at the same time engage in necessary reforms. In the book of Esther we find several themes of importance. First, we discover a great example of how to live godly in ungodly circumstances; and second, we see the nature of divine providence as it leads Queen Esther to deliver her people.[2]

The books of poetry, consisting of the writings and collections of David and Solomon, provide insights into areas of praise, pain, purity, and wisdom. In Psalms we find at least five issues addressed that are germane to our subject. David relates that God is concerned about justice for the fatherless and the oppressed. He further notes that God Himself is a shield to all those who take refuge in Him. Later he makes the declaration, "Blessed is the nation whose God is the Lord" (Ps. 33:12 KJV). Moving to the issue of leadership, David notes that God Himself exalts leaders and deposes leaders. And finally, in an autobiographical section, David clearly articulates that life begins at conception. In Proverbs, Solomon reiterates two ideas that we have already read. First, he declares that "righteousness exalts a nation but sin is a reproach to any people" (Prov. 14:34 NKJV); and later he makes the observation that a king's heart is like a water channel in the hand of the Lord, which is to say that God Himself provides direction to those who are leaders.[3]

The books of prophecy continue to give insight into God's expectations and standards for humanity. The prophet Isaiah writes, "Woe to those who call evil good and good evil" (Isa. 5:20). He also provides a prophetic declaration that one was to come to the world about whom was said, "The government shall be upon His shoulders, that He will have dominion that will never end, and that He will mandate both justice and righteousness" (see Isa. 9:6). Jeremiah, whose ministry was to ancient Jerusalem and Judah during a period of great decline just prior to the Babylonian exile, makes the declaration that God Himself is the God of all flesh. By this Jeremiah was stating that God is not only the God of Israel but He is the living God who is Lord over the entire earth. The book of Daniel, which was written during the exile to Babylon, provides much insight into God's ways with mankind. The book states clearly that God's people being taken into captivity was God's judgment. In fact, the text states, "The Lord handed [them] . . . over" (Dan. 1–2 NIV). In the following chapter, however, we find the declaration that God Himself is establishing a kingdom that will never be destroyed. In the remainder of Daniel's prophetic book, we read about God's greatness, about how He rules, and about how He has the authority to rule over the entire earth. In short, Daniel was teaching that our Lord is the true God of history and that all people are ultimately accountable to Him.[4]

Moving to the New Testament, the Gospels provide for us additional insight into God's expectations and standards of the human race. In Matthew 5:13–16, we find Jesus teaching in the Sermon on the Mount how believers should be "salt" and "light" in a decaying culture. In that same sermon, Jesus provided what is commonly called the Golden Rule, which states, "Whatever you want others to do for you, do also the same for them—this is the law and the Prophets" (Matt. 7:12). Later, the Gospel of Matthew records for us an encounter Jesus had with someone who was attempting to entrap Him in His own words. In response to the question, Jesus simply retorted, "Render therefore unto Caesar the things which are Caesar's; and unto God the things that are God's" (Matt. 22:21 KJV). On the heels of that declaration, Jesus was asked, "What is the greatest commandment?" (see Matt. 22:36) to which He responded that it is the responsibility of mankind to love God and then one's neighbor as one's self. Toward the conclusion of the book of Matthew, Jesus was asked about what would happen in the future, and in one insight He provided the story of the sheep and goat judgment. This judgment, according to Jesus, would involve all mankind and would be based on our willingness to assist and minister to those in need. The final verses of Matthew's Gospel include the words of Christ commonly called the Great Commission. The overriding mandate is to "make disciples of all nations" (Matt. 28:19) which, among other things, implies that the Gospel of Jesus Christ is for the entire world and not simply for a small group of Jewish disciples. Additionally, Luke's Gospel records for us that Jesus will usher in a "kingdom [which] will have no end" (1:33). One statement from John's Gospel worth mentioning is when Jesus was addressing His disciples the night before He went to the cross. At that time Jesus said, "By this shall all men know you are My disciples because you have love one for another" (see John 13:35). Historically, one validating mark of the authenticity of the Christian faith has been not only the fulfillment of prophecy but also the lifestyles of those who profess to follow Jesus Christ. When Christians love one another and then express that love through service and ministry, those outside the Christian faith are drawn to it because of the contrasting life and lifestyle of the believer.[5]

The book of Acts is the New Testament's historical book, which records for us the expansion of Christianity in the early church. Several of its insights are germane to our subject. Early on, the Jewish Sanhedrin forbade the disciples to preach the gospel of Jesus Christ. In short, it was the state and the state church, if you please, attempting to muzzle the church. In the second event, similar to the first, Peter makes the declaration, "We must obey God rather than men" (Acts 5:29). As the Gospel expands to the Mediterranean basin, we find Paul and his associates on their second missionary journey preaching the gospel in Philippi. As a result, Paul and Silas were arrested and thrown into prison. When the word came down that they were to be released from prison, Paul, a Roman citizen, exercised his right as a Roman. Paul demanded that the magistrates themselves come and escort them out of the jail and out of the city. In short, Paul took advantage of his Roman citizenship when it was advantageous to further his work of spreading the gospel of Jesus Christ. In the next chapter Paul and his party move on to the city of Athens. In Paul's address to the citizens of that city, Paul engaged them on an intellectual level in which he used his knowledge of the culture to build a relational bridge in order to share the gospel of Jesus Christ. In his message Paul both assumed and was an advocate of the universal jurisdiction of the Christian faith. Toward the end of Acts, Paul had been arrested in Jerusalem, sent to Caesarea Philippi where he was interviewed successively by Festus, Felix, and Agrippa, and when faced with the dilemma of being returned to Jerusalem, stated that he had not sinned against the state and, therefore, appealed to Caesar. As a result, again, of Paul's taking full advantage of his Roman citizenship, he was transported to Rome where he would eventually give a defense of his life and his faith before Caesar.[6]

The New Testament Epistles are for the most part occasional letters sent by different apostles to various congregations or areas. They address issues that were raised concerning the normative belief and behavior of the early church. Most of the Epistles were penned by the apostle Paul. In his letter to the Romans, particularly 13:1–7, Paul delineates the Christian's responsibility to the government. In this passage, Paul writes:

> Everyone must submit to the governing authorities, for there is no authority except from God, and those that exist are instituted by God. So then, the one who resists the authority is opposing God's command, and those who oppose it will bring judgment on themselves. For rulers are not a terror to good conduct, but to bad. Do you want to be unafraid of the authority? Do good and you will have its approval. For government is God's servant to you for good. But if you do wrong, be afraid, because it does not carry the sword for no reason. For government is God's servant, an avenger that brings wrath on the one who does wrong. Therefore, you must submit, not only because of wrath, but also because of your conscience. And for this reason you pay taxes, since the authorities are God's public servants, continually attending to these tasks. Pay your obligations to everyone: taxes to those you owe taxes, tolls to those you owe tolls, respect to those you owe respect, and honor to those you owe honor. (Rom. 13:1–7)

In Paul's letters to Timothy he provides two insights about Christian's responsibility and liability. In 1 Timothy 2 he makes the plea, "I urge that petitions, prayers, intercessions, and thanksgivings be made for everyone, for kings and all those who are in authority, so that we may lead a tranquil and quiet life in all godliness and dignity." Yet, in his follow-up letter to Timothy, he notes that everyone who desires to live godly in Christ Jesus can expect to be persecuted.[7]

Paul was not the only writer of the Epistles. Two others who contributed to our study are James and Jude. James, known as the practical Epistle, provides much instruction on how Christians are to live in the world. For example, James declares that it should be the responsibility and intention of believers to care for widows and orphans in their distress. He also instructs believers to pay honest wages to those who work for them. In James we find a practical principle on how Christians should relate to the world: "For the one who knows to do good and does it not, to him it is sin" (see James 4:17). And finally, the book of Jude says to the Christians being instructed, "Contend earnestly for the faith which was once for all delivered to the saints" (1:3). Here is a strong reminder that God Himself will judge every human being. Each of us should live in such a way that we are prepared to give an account of our lives to Almighty God.[8]

We assume the biblical material to be normative in both belief and behavior. It provides guidelines for believers in how to relate both to the state and to the world in which we live. Scripture is both inerrant and sufficient for all matters of faith and practice. It provides the standard by which all ideas and practices should be evaluated.

From the Birth of the Church to the Reformation

The birth of the church until the Reformation spans some fifteen hundred years. Countless volumes have been written recounting in detail the growth and expansion of the church. For our purposes, it is necessary only to hit the highlights of the people and movements which greatly influenced the church with respect to church-state issues and public-policy-type issues. Because of the need for brevity, we will address only five epochs. First, we will consider the persecution and reform in the early church. Then, in turn, we will review the influence of Constantine, Augustine, Charlemagne, and Thomas Aquinas.

The expansion of the early church was marked by both pagan opposition and reforms that were fostered by the Christian worldview. In the first three hundred years of its existence, Nero, Domitian, Decius, Valerian, and Diocletian persecuted the church for a variety of reasons. The principal reason for opposition was because of the exclusive nature of Christianity. In the words of Bruce Shelley, "One simply could not reject the gods without arousing scorn as a social misfit." Christians condemned the gladiatorial combats as immoral, provided a revolutionary perspective toward human life, denounced abortion and infanticide, and set a high standard with respect to morality. On the other hand, some criticized Christianity because of misunderstandings. Worship services which were often held in secret were thought to be covers for sexual orgies and cannibalism. Obviously, this was a misunderstanding of the Lord's Supper and Jesus' command to love one another. Still others criticized the early Christians because they were "atheists." That is, they would not worship any gods other than Jehovah God and the Lord Jesus Christ. The greatest challenge, however, had to do with Rome's policy with respect to what was considered acceptable and unacceptable religions. Rome, because of its need for unity, instilled and enforced the policy of emperor worship where all residents within the Roman Empire were commanded once a year to declare allegiance to Caesar with the burning of incense and the declaration of "Caesar is Lord." Christians in the early church, however, refused to make this declaration of allegiance and stated rather "Jesus is Lord." As a result, Christians found themselves and their movement characterized as an illicit religion and, therefore, persecuted by the Roman Empire. Nevertheless, it seems that the more Christians were persecuted, the more they expanded.[9]

One of the major turning points in the history of the expansion of Christianity was when Constantine embraced Christianity in 313 with the Edict of Milan. Shelley concludes that this was the beginning of the age of the Christian Empire. He observes, "Courageous martyrs were a thing of the past." He then went on to express his conviction that "the Christianization of the empire and the imperial interference in the affairs of the church begins." The Roman Empire embraced Christianity as the normative religion. But with that embracing came a series of new challenges. First, the emperor ruled the Christian bishops as he did his civil servants. We also find a stream of the unconverted becoming part of the visible church. Shelley notes that by 380, "rewards for Christians had given way to penalties for non-Christians." Nonetheless as time passes we find tensions between the state and the church, with each attempting to control the other.[10]

One of the greatest events in the history of Christianity was the conversion of Augustine in 387. When Alaric, the Visigoth, conquered Rome in 410, the question asked was, "Why?" Augustine felt compelled to address the issue. His classic treatise, *The City of God*, provides his theological view of history and particularly explains why the great city, Rome might fall. One writer describes *The City of God* this way. It was:

> a monumental work written in response to the fall of Rome to the Visigoths. Some people blamed the Christians, arguing that Rome fell because its people had neglected the native gods. So Augustine responded by defending and explaining God's plan and working in history. Since Cain and Abel, he said, there had been two cities in the world: the city of God (the faithful) and the city of man (pagan society). Though they intertwined, God will see that the city of God, the church, will endure through eternity.
>
> Though Augustine wrote at the end of the ancient world, his thoughts would dominate scholars of the Middle Ages and last into the Reformation.[11]

Augustine helped to delineate the great idea of embracing a Christian worldview. He saw God at work in the world and proceeded to exhort Christians to be involved in bringing about the city of God. At the same time he minimized what some would call the tragic unfolding events in history and thought that even these were still under the control of Almighty God.

Christmas of 800 brought what some scholars have called the "culmination of Christendom." On this date Charlemagne was crowned Emperor of the Holy Roman Empire by Pope Leo III (795–816). Shelley, commenting on this development, notes:

> Modern times were marked by the idea of autonomous, sovereign states without religious affiliation and by the concept of the church as a voluntary association apart from the rest of organized society. But neither of these ideas existed in the Middle Ages.
>
> Drawing upon Augustine's vision of the "city of God," Charles the Great engrafted the Christian concept of a universal, catholic church on the stock of the traditional Roman view

of empire and gave to the medieval world Christendom, a uni-
fied society mingling religious (or eternal) concerns with the
earthly (or temporal) affairs. . . .

In medieval theory church and state were but two aspects
of Christendom; the one representing Christian society organized to secure spiritual blessings, the other the same society
united to safeguard justice in human welfare. Theoretically
church and state were in harmonious interplay, each aiming to
secure the good of mankind.

In fact, however, the pope and emperor were contestants.
The ever-present question was, should the church rule the state
or the state control the church?[12]

Over the next several hundred years, the church continued to gain
strength of influence. One of its strongest leaders was Hildebrand,
known as Pope Gregory VII (1073–1085). During the time that he
served as Pope, he used three devices to impose his will on the state.
First, he used "excommunication," then the "interdict," and finally
the "ban." The test of wills came when Pope Gregory VII challenged
Henry IV, the German Emperor, over the appointment of bishops. The
emperor declared the papal office vacant, and the Pope used the tools
in his arsenal. The situation reached its climax at Canossa, "where the
emperor stood outside the castle in the snow, barefooted, for three days,
begging the privilege of asking the Pope's forgiveness." The struggle
continued to 1215 at the Fourth Laterine Counsel, which marks the
height of Roman Catholic dominion. Here Innocent declared, "To
Peter was given . . . not only the universal church, but the whole earth
that he might rule it." And the argument was made that there should
be a "subordination of all civil authority under the pope."[13]

The greatest theologian of the Middle Ages was Thomas Aquinas,
whose massive *Summa Theologica* was a grand attempt to demonstrate that Aristotelian philosophy is compatible with Christianity.
Besides arguing for the supremacy of the pope, he also declared that
the church had the right to "punish heretics with death." Historian
Philip Schaff explains, "As the head of the mystical body of Christ,

the Pope is supreme over the civil estate, even as the spiritual nature is superior to man's physical nature." He continues, "Christian kings owe him subjection, as they owe subjection to Christ Himself for the pope is Peter's successor and the vicar of Christ." Schaff goes on to explain, "In his declaration about heresy and its treatment, Thomas Aquinas materially assisted in making the persecution of heretics unto death the settled policy of the church and the state." And then Schaff notes, "At any rate he cleared away all objections as far as it was possible to clear them away."[14] From the perspective of politics, Aquinas articulates a doctrine of natural law that expresses itself in human law. The doctrine and philosophy of natural law would emerge later in the time of the Reformation as well as the time of the birth of the United States of America.[15]

Each of these ideas and personalities would help set the stage for what would transpire during the period of the Reformation. Moreover, these would help shape the context of world history in the development of Western civilization.

The Reformation Era

In 1054, the Roman Catholic Church and the Orthodox Church divided. It is called the Great Schism. Not until 1517 would the Western church, the Roman Catholic Church, divide again. The Protestants separated from the Roman Church in the era identified as the Protestant Reformation. In fact, 1517 is the climax of twenty-five years that changed the world. It began with Columbus's voyage to the Americas in 1492, which initiated the age of exploration and the worldwide expanse of Christian influence. This same period climaxed with Martin Luther nailing his 95 Theses to the church house door of Wittenberg on October 31, 1517.

The Reformation took two forms: (1) the Magisterial Reform, in which the territorial churches broke away from Roman Catholicism and became state churches; and (2) the Radical Reformation, which consisted of Anabaptists and those who embraced the Free Church Movement. All of this occured in the context of the Holy Roman

Empire when the state and church were locked in a symbiotic, love-hate relationship. The state protected the church, and the church supported the state. The state used the church and the church manipulated the state. With the 1517 Reformation the monolithic control by the Roman Catholic Church came to a conclusion. The two brightest lights in the Reformation firmament were no doubt Martin Luther and John Calvin. Because Luther, Calvin, Zwingli, and even the Reformation in England took essentially the same form—that is, churches within Germany, Switzerland, and England became part of the state church—we consider Luther the prototype of the magisterial reformer.

Consider first the political, intellectual, and religious factors leading to the Reformation. The political factors are a combination of the rise of strong monarchies, which could support or oppose the papacy, as well as a universal discontent, particularly in Germany because of thirteen successive years of crop failure beginning in 1490. In fact, peasant revolts were all too common. The intellectual factors are also noteworthy. We find a widespread use of pamphlets and books. The attitude of the common man because of what he had read had been changing toward the Papacy, and a recollection of the recent Papal Schisms served to undermine papal authority. The rise of the printing press also contributed to the growing ferment of resentment and made communication possible. Religious factors include the history of dissenting movements, which had set precedents, as well as the recent abuses by the Catholic Church—for example, their sale of indulgences. Into this cultural melee stepped Martin Luther, who built his reform movement around the authority of Scripture and German patriotism. In fact, many see him as representative of the German peasants who had been grieved by the papal tyranny for over half of the present millennium.[16]

We will consider Luther's assessment of the relationship of church and state as well as his understanding of Christian social and moral policy. We will not address all of the nuances of the Protestant Reformation with respect to Luther. At the same time, we will assume that the same mind-set that Luther carried with his reformation in

Germany was also manifest in Calvin in Geneva, as well as the reformation in England.

Luther's Reformation actually began as he struggled personally to experience God's salvation. He struggled greatly with bondage to sin and an overwhelming fear of being lost. The harder he worked for his salvation the more lost he felt. Multiple forms of self-discipline and even a trip to Rome did nothing to satisfy his hunger. He found relief, however, as he began to study the Word of God, and the reality of salvation by grace through faith made a profound impact on him. In his "Tower Experience," Martin Luther finally found the peace he had been seeking. Against this backdrop of a sincere seeking of God, Luther reacted almost violently to the Roman Catholic Church's latest attempt to raise money by selling indulgences. For a fee, they taught, *your* deceased loved ones could be removed from purgatory and be taken right into heaven. As a matter of fact, *you* could take almost two million years off *your* loved ones' time in purgatory. The Dominican monk who was pedaling the indulgences was a man named Tetzel, and he used the slogan, "As soon as the coin in the coffer rings, a soul from purgatory springs." Luther passionately reacted against this issue of a works salvation and a salvation for sale as he nailed his 95 Theses on the church house door on October 31, 1517. His theses were really a proposal for debate of the whole legitimacy of the indulgence system and the theology and philosophy which undergirded such a system.[17]

In August 1518, Luther appealed to Frederick the Elector for his assistance since he was increasingly being attacked by the Roman Catholic machine. In 1520, Luther wrote three treatises: *The Address to the German Nobility, The Babylonian Captivity of the Church,* and *The Freedom of the Christian Man.* In the first pamphlet Luther pleaded with the magistrates to intervene in the affairs of the Catholic Church to stop its abuses, to remove the bishops and abbots of their wealth and their worldly influence. He advocated that they establish a state church or a national German church. In the second pamphlet he criticized from Scripture the whole sacramental system, concluding that only two sacraments were valid, baptism and the Lord's Supper. In Shelley's words, "Luther brushed aside the traditional view of the church as a sacred hierarchy headed by the pope and returned to the early Christian view of a community of Christian believers in which all believers are priests called to offer spiritual sacrifices to God." Luther's third pamphlet argued that good works do not result in salvation but are the result of salvation.[18]

As the result of these three treatises, Luther was declared a heretic and summoned to defend his teachings or recant them at the Imperial Diet of Worms in 1521. When asked to recant, Luther responded: "Since then your Majesty and your lordships desire a simple reply, I will answer without horns and without teeth. Unless I am convinced by Scripture and plain reason—I do not accept the authority of popes and councils, for they have contradicted each other—my conscience is captive to the Word of God. I cannot and I will not recant anything, for to go against conscience is neither right nor safe. God help me. Amen." And Roland Bainton, in *Here I Stand,* notes that the words, "Here I stand, I cannot do otherwise," were inserted in the earliest printed versions of his statement.[19]

This reformation age, however, was also rife with other reformers who were much more radical than Luther. For example, Thomas Muntzer, a radical millennarian, greatly influenced numerous peasants, provoked them to a revolt, and led countless thousands into a merciless death. Historian Robert Baker noted the Peasants' Revolt in 1925 resulted in Luther losing "his faith in the common man and thereafter looked to the nobility as the hope of the reform movement." Although Luther originally had been supportive of the peasants' complaints and even sympathetic, he was fearful that the violence that ensued would create chaos and destroy the established authority. As a result, Luther wrote a strident pamphlet, *Against the Thievish and Murderous Hordes of Peasants,* in which he called on the princes to "knock down, strangle, and stab . . . and think nothing so venomous, pernicious, or Satanic as an insurgent." It is estimated that in 1525 more than 100,000 peasants were killed in the uprising. Some have suggested that Luther lost the support of many of the surviving peasants because of his staunch refusal to support their movement.[20]

Jesse Lyman Hurlbut summarizes the Magisterial Reform with these words:

The tactical working of the Reformation was that a national church was established as distinct from one universal. The aim of the papacy and the priesthood had been to subordinate the state to the church, to make the pope supreme over all nations. Wherever Protestantism triumphed a national church arose, self-governed, and independent of Rome. These national churches assume different forms, Episcopal in England, Presbyterian in Scotland and in Switzerland, somewhat mixed in northern lands. The exception was the Anabaptist movement which emphasized a free church.[21]

Hurlbut introduces us to the second side of the Protestant Reformation, the side that is identified as the Radical Reformation. The common denominator of all the Anabaptists and radical reformers was that they advocated a "free church." Here the church would be separate from the state, the state would not manipulate the church, and the church would not manipulate the state. One of the finest treatments of the birth and expansion of the Radical Reformation is William R. Estep's *The Anabaptist Story*. He traces the birth of Anabaptism from 1525 and lays out its development in the Reformation era. With respect to the relationship between church and state, Estep observes:

> If the sixteenth century looked askance at the Anabaptist concept of the church, it is completely unprepared for the Anabaptist view of the state. The radical position . . . was undoubtedly beyond the comprehension of most of their contemporaries. Thought patterns of the day were enmeshed in, and determined by, the traditional medieval framework of the Holy Roman Empire. Neither civil nor religious leaders could ordinarily conceive of a stable society that did not unite church and state (*Corpus Christianum*). And yet, the Anabaptists' view of the state was to prove their most far-reaching contribution to the modern world. It is important to see that this view was derived from their view of the church and a corresponding

understanding of the Christian religion. Their position was based on Christian involvement—not religious indifference.

For the Anabaptists, the most damaging element in the fall of the church (the point at which it was connected to the state during the time of Constantine) was its alliance with the state. When church and state were joined, the church ceased to be the church. Anabaptists, and their attempt at a restitution of the apostolic church, did not deny the right of the state to exist. They did deny it any jurisdiction in religious affairs. Therefore, their attitude toward the state was not wholly negative. It was their customary reliance upon biblical authority which saved them from this.[22]

Many of the Anabaptist groups advocated a form of pacifism; however, not all Anabaptist theologians and leaders embraced that posture. Balthasar Hubmaier wrote in 1527 a brief "On the Sword" in which he explains, "Hence, it is evident that if men are pious, good and orderly, they will bear the sword for the protection of the innocent, according to the will of God, and for a terror to evildoers, according as God has appointed and ordained." Hubmaier goes on to explain, "To him (the magistrate) according to the divine order the sword is entrusted, not that we may fight, war, strive and tyrannize with it, but to defend the wise, protect the widow, maintain the pious, and to tolerate all who are distressed or persecuted by force." And then he concludes, "This is the duty of the magistrate, as God Himself many times in the Scripture declares it, which may not take place without blood and killing, wherefore God has hung the sword at His side, and not a fox's tail."[23]

Looking back at the Reformation era, we can identify six distinct conclusions. First, a linkage still exists between church and state in the magisterial reformers. With that we see a caution against rebelling against the state by most of the reformers. With the Anabaptists, however, we find a distinct quest to separate the church and state as institutions. Moreover, there is an insistence that the church has a responsibility to promote biblical values. Among all of the reformers, we find an insistence on leaders having the courage of their convictions to obey God rather than men, and finally, all of these leaders are products of their age and find it difficult to escape many of their preconceptions.

The Post-Reformation Era

Three groups emerged during the post-Reformation Era: the Puritans, the Separatists, and the Baptists. Each of these groups came out of the English Reformation and had a bearing on Christianity that eventually surfaced in the Americas. The Puritans were those within the Church of England who desired to purify it from Catholic influence. According to Shelley, Puritanism went through three phases. First, under Queen Elizabeth (1558–1603), they attempt to purify the Church of England, similar to what Calvin had done in Geneva. Next, under James I and Charles I (1603–1642) Puritanism resisted the monarchy and the pressures to conform to a high-church style of Christianity, which really reflected Catholicism without the pope. In the third phase, during England's Civil War and the rule of Oliver Cromwell (1642–1660), the Puritans shaped the national Church of England. Eventually, their movement collapsed because of internal dissension. Puritanism has been called England's second Reformation. Leland Ryken does a fine job explaining the Puritan attitude toward social action. Ultimately, Puritanism made a distinct contribution to the birth of the Americas.[24]

Some would never be satisfied with efforts to purify the existing church. As a result, some of those began to separate themselves from the established Church of England, just as those on the continent had separated themselves from Roman Catholicism. The Anabaptists separated themselves from the state church. A. C. Underwood writes, "Towards the end of Elizabeth's reign small groups appeared among the Puritans who had come to feel how hopeless it was to stay within the state church, working and hoping for better days." Baker identifies some of the leaders of early separatism. For example, in 1580 an outspoken Puritan minister, Robert Browne, embraced the Separatist ideals and yet eventually returned to the established church. Due to the persecution, however, he did spend some time as a religious refugee in the Netherlands. Another Separatist group went to Amsterdam. This group from Gainsborough, England, was led by Thomas Helwys and John Murton and later John Smyth. And still another congregation went to Leyden in 1607 and was led by William Bradford, William Brewster, and John Robinson, who are better known as the Pilgrims who emigrated to New England in 1620.[25]

Underwood highlights the special role played by John Smyth, who eventually became the pastor of the first English Baptists. He notes, "In his own life he epitomized all its main stages. He began as a son of the Church of England and took her orders, and progressively became a Puritan, Separatist, and then a Baptist Separatist."[26] When Leon McBeth introduces *Differences of the Churches of the Separation* (1608) written by John Smyth, he makes this observation:

> John Smyth constantly faced the necessity of defending
> his separation from the Church of England. In several writ-
> ings, he justified the withdrawal positively by showing that the
> separated churches restored New Testament patterns in wor-
> ship, doctrine, and ministry. On the negative side, he argued
> that the Church of England was a false system from which all
> true Christians had to separate or risk spiritual contamination.
> He thus took the position of strict separatism as compared,
> for example, with the mild semiseparatism of Henry Jacob
> who wanted to separate only from the corruptions within the
> Church of England.[27]

John Smyth became the leader of the early Baptist movement. Concluding that infant baptism was both unscriptural and illogical, he convinced about forty members of his congregation to be baptized or, as some would say, be rebaptized. Eventually this group, led by Thomas Helwys after Smyth's death by tuberculosis, became the first Baptist church in England. In his monograph, *A Short Declaration of the Mystery of Iniquity*, Helwys, who sent an autographed copy to King James, said, "The King is a mortal man and not God, therefore hath not power over the immortal soul of his subjects to make laws and ordinances for them and to set spiritual Lords over them." Eventually, Helwys was arrested for his rebellion and thrown into New Gate Prison. At that point John Murton became the pastor and the leader of the first English Baptist church which was identified as part of the General Baptist movement because they believed in a general atonement. They stood in contrast to the Particular Baptists, who followed the Calvinist idea of a limited atonement. This latter group, the Particular Baptists, can ordinarily be dated from 1638 under the leadership of John Spilsbury.[28]

Increasingly, Christians gathered themselves into congregations which moved progressively away from the strict notion of the state church. However, as these groups migrated to the Americas, many of them desired to reestablish their own state church.

The Colonial Experience in America

When the question is asked, "Why did people come to America?" the simple answer is that some came for God and others came for gold. Notwithstanding the occasional explorer who stopped in and did not stay, the official beginning of the Americas, at least the part that eventually became the United States of America, was with the sailing and the landing of the Mayflower and the settlement of the Plymouth Colony. Although they originally intended to sail to Virginia, because a storm blew them off course they eventually landed in Plymouth, Massachusetts. One Pilgrim described the land as "a hideous and desolate wilderness." In order to form a sound government, forty-one of the men signed what has come to be known as the *Mayflower Compact*. The document reads:

> Having undertaken, for the glory of God and advancement
> of the Christian faith in honor of our king and country, a voy-
> age to plant the first colony in the northern parts of Virginia,
> do these present solemnly and mutually in the presence of
> God and one of another, covenant and combine ourselves
> together into a civil body politic, for our better ordering and

preservation, and furtherance of the ends aforesaid; and by virtue hereof to enact, constitute and frame such just and equal laws, ordinances, acts, constitutions and offices, from time to time, as shall be thought most meet and convenient for the general good of the colony, unto which we promise all due submission and obedience.[29]

The Plymouth Colony had the benefit of strong leadership. Men like William Bradford, William Brewster, Edward Winslow, John Carver, and Myles Standish helped to form this small colony, which by its "Compact" had been established "for the glory of God and advancement of the Christian faith" with the ultimate goal being "the general good of the Colony." Again, notice how there is a mutual submission and mutual obedience.[30]

Ten years after the Pilgrims landed at Plymouth and signed the *Mayflower Compact*, another larger group journeyed from Europe to America, this time to settle the Massachusetts Bay area. They were led by the great Puritan layman, John Winthrop. Wrestling over whether or not to come to the Americas, Winthrop wrote in his journal, "When God intends a man to a work he sets a bias on his heart so as though he be tumbled this way and that yet his bias still draws him to that side, and there he rests at last." And Winthrop's bias was leading him to the New World. In April 1630, four ships led by the *Arbella* sailed for America. According to Francis Higginson, the purpose of this journey was "to practice the positive part of church reformation." In the words of Winthrop S. Hudson, "America was for them, as it was to become for others, a land of opportunity, a land where a 'wide door' of 'liberty' had been set open before them." He goes on to say, "The more important was the freedom they possessed to undertake a radical reconstruction of church life to conform to what they regarded as the plain prescriptions of God's 'most Holy Word.'" In other words, they wanted to restore the church to all of its original glory. Writing of those days, Increase Mather asserted, "There never was a generation that did so perfectly shake off the dust of Babylon . . . as the first generation of Christians that came to this land for the Gospel's sake."[31]

Baptists trace their roots in America back to Roger Williams, who landed in New England in 1631. Banished from Salem in 1635, he eventually became the founder of Providence, Rhode Island. In the words of Perry Miller, "He became a Baptist in 1639, but in a few months renounced even that creed, and for the rest of his life called himself a 'seeker,' who was always searching for the pure truth but did not expect to find it in this world." Williams became a champion of religious freedom. In July of 1644, he wrote a tract, *The Bloody Tenet of Persecution for Cause of Conscience.* Concerning the tract, Smith, Handy, and Loetscher explain: "However crude its style, it was competently argued, based on analysis of crucial passages of Scripture, examination of relevant facts of history, and appeal to fundamental doctrines of theology. It was a bold book, concerned with ultimate principles and not intermediate steps. Its appeal for full religious liberty was in advance of its time, but it brought the future nearer." They go on to explain, "For he viewed the alliance of the church with civil powers nothing short of a major disaster. He firmly believed that any coercion in religion cut squarely across the doctrines of predestination and justification by faith." Besides being an advocate for religious liberty, Williams also insisted on the importance of treating the American Indians with respect in buying and not taking land.[32]

One man who found himself out of step with colonial New England was Obadiah Holmes, who actually left England to escape religious persecution but then found it in America. He was an active Baptist from Rhode Island. When he ventured down to Boston in 1651, he was brutally whipped for his denial of infant baptism. According to McBeth, "His courage on that occasion, as told in the vivid detail by John Clark in *Ill News from New England* (1652) and by Isaac Backus in *A History of New England with Particular Reference to the Baptists* (1777) helped make this, perhaps, the most familiar case of Baptist persecution in America." Describing this horrid experience, Holmes wrote:

> And as the man began to lay the strokes upon my back,
> I said to the people, though my Flesh should fail, and my Spirit

should fail, yet God would not fail; so it pleased the Lord to
come in, and sort of fill my heart and tongue as a vessel full,
and with an audible voice I broke forth, praying unto the Lord
not to lay this Sin to their charge, and praying the people, That
now I found He did not fail me, and therefore now I should
trust Him forever who failed me not; for in truth, as the strokes
fell upon me, I had such a spiritual manifestation of God's
presence, as the like thereto I never had, nor felt, nor can with
fleshly tongue express, and the outward pain was so removed
from me, that indeed I am not able to declare it to you, it was
so easy to me, that I could well bear it, . . . when he had loosed
me from the Post, having joyfulness in my heart, and cheerful-
ness in my countenance, as the Spectators observed, I told the
Magistrates, you have struck me as with Roses.[33]

By the time of the impending Revolutionary War, Baptists had
become a major religious community in the Americas. Benefiting
greatly from the First Great Awakening, Whitefield said concerning
his converts, "All of my chicks have become ducks," referring to the
fact that instead of staying or remaining Anglican or Methodists, they
were becoming Baptists. As the Revolutionary War approached, there
were many strong Baptist leaders in America such as Isaac Backus and
John Leland.

The Birth of the Nation

Prior to the birth of the United States on July 4, 1776, Great
Britain passed a progressive series of laws that irritated and infuriated the colonists. The Royal Proclamation Act of 1763 divided the
New World into four provinces. An imaginary line was drawn down
the crest of the Alleghenies and all land west of it was for the Indians. In 1764, the *Sugar Act* was passed, which taxed molasses and
other types of sugar. That same year, the *Currency Act* was passed,
which outlawed the printing of paper money and insisted that
the colonies use gold. The following year, 1765, introduced the

Stamp Act, where all newspapers and legal and commercial documents were required to have a royal stamp. That same year the *Cordoning Act* required the colonial governments to furnish barracks and provisions for the royal troops. The *Townshend Acts* levied import duties on a variety of objects, and all of this finally climaxed with the 1773 Boston Massacre, in which three colonists died and two others were mortally wounded. This event became a major focal point of anti-British propaganda. By 1773, as a conciliatory gesture, the British government removed many of the taxes, but one tax that did remain was the tax on tea and the monopoly of the sale of tea by the East India Company. As a reaction to what appeared to be blatant heavy-handedness, on December 16, 1773, a group of Bostonians poorly disguised as Indians dumped the cargo of the tea chests from three ships into the Boston Harbor; hence, it was called the Boston Tea Party. As a result, the *Intolerable Acts* were passed, which only created more misery in the colonies.[34]

As a result of the increasing tyranny of Great Britain, a congress representing twelve of the thirteen colonies (Georgia failed to send representatives) met in Philadelphia in September 1774. This First Continental Congress, led by men like Thomas Jefferson and John Adams, attempted a conciliation with Great Britain. This was rejected by the House of Lords, and as a result, Massachusetts, particularly, was declared to be in rebellion. As a consequence of mounting hostilities, on April 19, 1775, the Revolutionary War began with the "shot heard around the world." The Battle of Bunker Hill, more appropriately identified as the Battle of Breed's Hill, saw an amphibious attack of twenty-five hundred British soldiers, one thousand of which perished in the battle.[35]

When the Second Continental Congress met and offered its "olive branch petition" to King George III and it was spurned once again, representatives from all thirteen colonies unanimously supported the move to resist the British government. With patriots like Thomas Jefferson, George Washington, and Benjamin Franklin, as well as Thomas Paine, the patriots quickly penned what we now identify as the Declaration of Independence. Although we celebrate its adoption on July 4, 1776, the day that it was signed was actually August 2. It should be noted that neither Washington nor Paine signed the Declaration of Independence because of other obligations that precluded their participation.[36]

The Declaration of Independence is the foundational document justifying the separating of the thirteen colonies from Great Britain and is not only a monumental historic and political document, it is also a religious document. In fact, the Declaration of Independence makes four clear, distinct references to Almighty God. The first paragraph refers to the "laws of nature and of nature's God." The next paragraph states that "all men are created equal, that they are endowed by their Creator with certain unalienable rights, that among these are life, liberty and the pursuit of happiness." The concluding paragraph of the Declaration of Independence declares that they were "appealing to the supreme judge of the world for the rectitude of our intentions." And the final statement of the Declaration reads, "And for the support of this declaration, with a firm reliance on the protection of Divine Providence, we mutually pledge to each other our lives, our fortunes, and our sacred honor."[37]

The delegates of the thirteen colonies unanimously agreed that the colonies united together under the leadership, guidance, and jurisdiction of Almighty God would form a new nation. This document is the foundation of every other document in the history of American jurisprudence. It is the document that legitimizes the Constitution, the Bill of Rights, and our form of government. To pretend that these statements are not present or to minimize their significance does not negate the reality that they are the founding principles upon which this nation is based, and to attempt to remove or explain away the substance of these four references to God is disingenuous at best or maliciously wicked at worst. In short, this is who we are, like it or not.

After the Articles of Confederation proved to be too fragile to support the superstructure of a new nation, the delegates eventually adopted our present Constitution in their meeting at Philadelphia in May 1787. Fifty-five delegates convened there and elected George Washington the President of the Convention. The Constitution itself was adopted by the ninth state, New Hampshire, in June 21, 1788, and was finally put into effect on March 4, 1789. George Washington was unanimously elected as the first President of the United States with John Adams elected the Vice President. President Washington was inaugurated in New York City on April 30, 1789.[38]

One reason that the Constitution was passed was because of an agreement that a Bill of Rights would be forthcoming. These first ten amendments to the Constitution were adopted in 1791; and for our purposes, the most important of the amendments is the first, which in many ways reflected the Virginia Declaration of Rights, which had been adopted in 1776.[39]

The First Amendment states, "Congress shall make no law respecting an establishment of religion, or prohibiting the free exercise thereof; or abridging the freedom of speech, or of the press; or the right of the people peaceably to assemble, and to petition the government for a redress of grievances." Three clauses provide a major bearing on the issue of religious liberty: the establishment clause, the free exercise clause, and the freedom of speech. The original intention of those who penned the First Amendment was to ensure that the nation would not provide a state church, as was prevalent in much of Europe, and consequently, one institution would not be permitted to manipulate the other; that is, the church would not manipulate the state, and the state would not manipulate the church. Again, the issue was separating institutions. Based on extensive documentation, there was never an intention to separate the acknowledgment and the accommodation of God in the government. Rather, as will be addressed later in this volume, the normative principle was that the state would accommodate the church and the church would be supportive of the state.[40]

The postrevolutionary era saw the disengaging of the established churches in the United States. The next chapter will address that disengagement, trace the rise of the Southern Baptist Convention, and detail its initial engagement in religious liberty issues as well as review its attempted engagement in the great moral issues of the day.

Notes

1. Genesis 1:1, 26–28; 2:17–18; 2:24; 12:2–3; 15:16; 19:1–29; 41:41; Exodus 5:1–14:31; 20:1–26; 21:1–23:33, 34:1–35; Leviticus 18:24.

2. Joshua 1:1 ff.; Judges 2:11–13; 1 Samuel; Nehemiah; Esther.

3. Psalms 10:17–18; 18:30; 33:12; 75:6–7; 139:13–16; Proverbs 14:34; 21:1.

4. Isaiah 5:20–21; 9:6–7; Jeremiah 32:26; Daniel 1:2; 2:44; 4:34–35; 5:21–22; 7:14.

5. Matthew 5:13–16; 7:12; 22:21, 37–40; 25:31–36; 28:18–20; Luke 1:31–33; 21:25–28; John 13:34–35.

6. Acts 4:19–20; 5:29; 16:37–39; 17:26; 25:8–12.

7. Romans 13:1–7; 1 Timothy 2:1–2; 2 Timothy 3:12.

8. James 1:27; 4:17; 5:1–6; Jude 14–15.

9. Robert A. Baker, *A Summary of Christian History* (Nashville: Broadman Press, 1959), 15–22; Bruce L. Shelley, *Church History in Plain Language* (updated 2nd ed.) (Dallas: Word Publishing, 1982, 1995), 37–45; see Herbert B. Workman, *Persecution in the Early Church* (Oxford: Oxford University Press, 1980).

10. Shelley, *Church History in Plain Language*, 91–98; see Henry Bettenson, *Documents of the Christian Church* (Oxford: Oxford University Press, 1978), 7–22.

11. Shelley, *Church History in Plain Language*, 124–31; Kenneth Curtis, et al., *The 100 Most Important Events in Christian History* (Grand Rapids, Mich.: Fleming H. Revell, 1991), 42–43; see St. Augustine, *City of God* (New York: Image Books, reprinted 1958), and A. M. Atkins and R. J. Dodaro, eds., *Augustine: Political Writings* (Cambridge: Cambridge University Press, 2001).

12. Mark Noll, *Turning Points: Decisive Moments in the History of Christianity* (Grank Rapids, Mich.: Family Christian Press, 1997, 2000), 107–27; Shelley, *Church History in Plain Language*, 174, 177.

13. Baker, *A Summary of Christian History*, 126–29; Philip Schaff, *History of the Christian Church* (Grand Rapids, Mich.: Eerdmanns, 1907, 1995), 5:775; Shelley, *Church History in Plain Language*, 183.

14. Schaff, *History of the Christian Church*, 5:673–75.

15. Harvey Mansfield, *A Student's Guide to Political Philosophy* (Wilmington, Del.: ISI Books, 2001), 26–29; see St. Thomas Aquinas, *Treatise on Law* (Washington, D.C.: Regenery, 1956, 2001); see J. Budziszewski, *Written on the Heart* (Downers Grove, Ill.: InterVarsity Press, 1997), 51–94.

16. Baker, *A Summary of Christian History*, 186–93.

17. Roland Bainton, *Here I Stand* (Nashville: Abingdon, 1950), 68–83.

18. Shelley, *Church History in Plain Language*, 241–42.

19. Bainton, *Here I Stand*, 185–86.

20. Baker, *A Summary of Christian History*, 203; Shelley, *Church History in Plain Language*, 243.

21. Jesse Lyman Hurlbut, *The Story of the Christian Church* (Grand Rapids, Mich.: Zondervan, 1918, 1974), 128.

22. William R. Estep, *The Anabaptist Story* (Grand Rapids, Mich.: Eerdmans, 1975), 194; see for reference Irvin Buckwalter Horst, *The Radical Brethren* (The Hague: Nieuwkoop—B. DeGraaf, 1972) and William R. Estep Jr., ed., *Anabaptist Beginnings* (The Hague: Nieuwkoop—B. DeGraaf, 1976).

23. Estep, *The Anabaptist Story*, 108–25.

24. Leland Ryken, *Worldly Saints* (Grand Rapids, Mich.: Zondervan, 1986), 173–86; Shelley, *Church History in Plain Language*, 291–300.

25. A. C. Underwood, *A History of the English Baptists* (London: The Baptist Union of Great Britain and Ireland, 1947, 1970), 32; Baker, *A Summary of Christian History*, 237–38.

26. Underwood, *A History of the English Baptists*, 33.

27. H. Leon McBeth, *A Sourcebook for Baptist Heritage* (Nashville: Broadman Press, 1990), 14.

28. Baker, *A Summary of Christian History*, 238–40; Curtis, et al., *The 100 Most Important Events in Christian History*, 113–14.

29. Shelton Smith, Robert Handy and Lefferts Loetscher, *American Christianity* (New York: Charles Scribner's Sons, 1960), 1:96; Nathaniel Philbrick, *Mayflower* (New York: Viking, 2006), 41; Sydney Ahlstrom, *A Religious History of the American People* (New Haven and London: Yale University Press, 1972), 136–37.

30. Philbrick, *Mayflower*, 40–43.

31. Winthrop S. Hudson, *Religion in America*, 2nd ed. (New York: Charles Scribner's Sons, 1965, 1973), 17–18; Smith, Handy and Loetscher, *American Christianity*, 97–98; Edmund S. Morgan, *The Puritan Dilemma* (Boston: Little, Brown and Co., 1958), 38.

32. Smith, Handy and Loetscher, *American Christianity*, 151–52; see Edwin S. Gaustad, *Roger Williams* (Oxford and New York: Oxford University Press, 2005).

33. McBeth, *A Sourcebook for Baptist Heritage*, 93, 95.

34. Alan Axelrod, *American History*, 4th ed. (Indianapolis: Alpha Books, 2006), 69–73.

35. Ibid., 74–82.

36. Ibid., 79–82.

37. The Declaration of Independence of the United States of America, July 4, 1776.

38. Axelrod, *American History*, 98–103.

39. Virginia Declaration of Rights, 1776 in Robert A. Baker *A Baptist Source Book* (Nashville: Broadman Press, 1966), 33–34.

40. The Bill of Rights of the United States of America, 1789.

CHAPTER

Baptist Influence and the
Great Century

For Baptists in America, the Great Century, the nineteenth century, brought both incredible growth and incredible challenges. Winthrop Hudson notes that by 1800 the Baptists were the largest denomination in the United States. In this fledgling nation Baptists experienced blessings, victories, hardship, and vast opportunity.[1]

This chapter first looks at "the Early Years" (up to 1845), including the disengagement of the state church and the role Baptists played in assisting this, along with their emphasis on religious liberty. Also in the Early Years, we will review the establishment of the General Missionary Convention in 1814 and the early Baptist emphasis on unity. We will also review the growing tensions over the presence of slavery in the United States.

The next section, "the Middle Years" (1845–1877), will detail the beginning of the Southern Baptist Convention, the Civil War years with all of their hardship, and finally the period of Reconstruction from 1865 until 1877. With the birth of the Southern Baptist Convention, we have records of both deliberations as well as resolutions passed by the convention in session, which will help us see some of the issues Southern Baptists were dealing with in these Middle Years.

The last section of this chapter, "the Later Years" (1877–1907), looks at the end of the Great Century. As will readily be seen, Southern Baptists were dealing with a variety of moral issues as well as issues relating to church-state relationships. For the sake of understanding the nineteenth century, it will be necessary to backtrack to the 1700s as well as moving forward into the early years of the twentieth century.

The Early Years (Up to 1845)

The first principal issue for Baptists in the nineteenth century was legitimacy. This issue was resolved officially with the passage of the Bill of Rights and specifically the First Amendment, which guaranteed that the new United States would neither embrace a state church nor interfere in the free exercise of religion. Baptists, historically, were identified with the dissenters. From the earliest days in Europe, they were part of the Free Church Movement, which perceived any church-state connection with great suspicion, and for good cause.

The established churches in the colonies included the Church of England, or Anglican Church, in five southern colonies and New York, and the Congregational Church in New England. Colonies with no established churches were Rhode Island, New Jersey, Delaware, and Pennsylvania.[2]

The colonies that embraced an established church practiced a litany of measures used to keep the established church in power and the dissenters in their place. These theocracies taxed citizens for the purpose of paying established ministers' salaries, buying land for the church, building church buildings, and in general taxed the population for the ongoing support of their establishment. At the same time dissenters were treated in a variety of ways, from persecution and oppression to simple harassment.[3]

Two movements which assisted in overcoming the established churches were the First and Second Great Awakenings and the influence of the Enlightenment. The awakenings caused major growth among the dissenters, so much so that they could influence public opinion. The Enlightenment caused some in the political arena to question the role of religion with the correlative concept that persecution was hardly worthwhile.[4]

In New England, the Cambridge Platform (1648) had solidified the established church with corresponding laws. Even though there were steps possible to obtain exemptions, the dissenters did not want to be tolerated; they wanted religious liberty and equality. Isaac Backus and the Grievance Committee worked hard to overcome the oppression and finally decided on the twofold strategy of appealing directly to London for assistance and resisting the established church by refusing to pay church taxes and desisting from applying for exemptions. In fact, the same "no taxation without representation" argument used to fuel the Revolution also drove Baptists in their resistance and resolve. McBeth summarizes this situation by saying:

> The growing spirit of revolt against England in the 1770s helped Baptists in a number of ways. First, American leaders wanted to head off any plan of Baptists to send agents to London to argue against the colonial governments. Second, patriot complaints against English oppression were precisely the same as those of Baptists against state-church oppression, as many came to realize. Third, Baptists had become so numerous that their support was essential if war came. The colonial legislatures, faced with these factors plus Backus' flaunting of their certificates, had little choice but to make concessions to the Baptists.[5]

The issue of religious liberty in most of the Middle Colonies was vastly different from New England due to the history of religious toleration. Between the example of the Quakers and the practical pluralism due to the diversity of religious opinion, the Middle Colonies provided welcome relief. McBeth identifies two benefits for Baptists in this region. First, "This area provided a model, a living laboratory of society as Baptists claimed it could be organized." Second, the region "provided a haven where Baptists could flee when persecution became too severe elsewhere." He noted that much of the Baptist evangelism of the South was launched from this area.[6]

Religious liberty in the South was another matter altogether. Virginia was notorious for its persecution of Baptists. Yet, because of the support of leaders like Thomas Jefferson, James Madison, and Patrick Henry, Virginia was the leader in embracing religious liberty by the time of the Revolution. And men like John Leland and the Baptist General Committee of Virginia lobbied for relief in the form of the state guarantee of religious liberty as well as the national guarantee through the 1791 Bill of Rights.

John Leland, the principal leader of the Baptist lobby for religious liberty, wrote many tracts and articles advocating his position. The most potent was *The Rights of Conscience Inalienable* (1791). According to McBeth:

> This hard-hitting defense of full religious liberty represented the mature culmination of Leland's thought. The longer title is descriptive: *The rights of conscience inalienable, and therefore, religious opinions not cognizable by law; or, the high-flying chuchman, stripped of his legal robe, appears a yaho.* In this treatise, Leland argued three basic points: (1) That the rights of conscience are inalienable, not subject to either government permission or restrictions; (2) That establishment of religion by law always damages religion; and (3) That the real motives for establishment are not to benefit religion but to buttress the power of civil rulers and augment the purses of ambitious clergy.
>
> Leland said the rights of conscience are inalienable, for "Every man must give an account of himself to God, and therefore every man ought to be at liberty to serve God in a way that he can best reconcile to his conscience."

Leland concluded by saying: "Government has no more
to do with the religious opinions of men, than it has with the
principles of mathematics. Let every man speak freely without
fear, maintain the principles that he believes, worship according
to his own faith, either one God, or three Gods, no God, or 20
Gods; and let government protect him in doing so."[7]

Even after the Revolutionary War, Baptists were not free to worship as they desired. And even though Virginia passed legislation guaranteeing religious liberty (1785), much remained to be done. When the
new Constitution was drafted, many Baptists were concerned about
"whether the new Federal Constitution, which had now lately made its
appearance in public, made sufficient provision for the secure enjoy-
ment of religious liberty." Most Baptists thought not. Leland wrote a
list of ten objections to the new Constitution, most of which centered
in the lack of a Bill of Rights. Finally, in 1791, Baptists received their
request when the Congress passed and the states ratified the Bill of
Rights.[8]

Yet, strictly speaking, this provided the opportunity, but not
the guarantee, of complete religious liberty in the United States. The
monumental task had now begun of disengaging the remaining state
churches. What should be noted is that although the Bill of Rights
guaranteed that the United States would not embrace an established
church, individual states would argue that theirs would remain
untouched because of the federal and state separation of powers.
Nonetheless, efforts were underway, in many places led by the Baptists, to disengage the established churches.

What began after the Revolution took until 1833 to complete. The
Anglican establishment fell first. Here in order is the sequence of disengaging the state churches: North Carolina (1776), New York (1777),
Georgia (1777) established "free exercise" and in 1789 removed a
religious test to hold office, South Carolina (1778 and 1790), Virginia
(1786), and Maryland (began in 1785 and completed in 1810).[9]

The Congregationalist disengagement took longer than the
disestablishment of the Anglicans primarily because Revolutionary

sympathy viewed the latter as sympathetic to the British cause while the Congregationalists were viewed as stridently patriotic to the colonies. Nonetheless, Connecticut disengaged in 1818, New Hampshire in 1819, and finally Massachusetts acquiesced in 1833–1834. Vermont, the nation's fourteenth state, disengaged its Congregational alliance in 1807.[10]

Religious liberty and the disengagement of the state church go hand in hand. The former would not be a reality until the latter was in force. More than any other lobby, Baptists in America were directly responsible for them both.

A second critical development in the Early Years of the nineteenth century was the newfound emphasis on unity for the sake of world missions. Due to a set of circumstances which could only have been orchestrated providentially, Baptists in America came together in a surprising show of unity and purpose.

To understand the significance of this unexpected show of force, consider the growth and expansion of Baptists up to 1814 when the General Missionary Convention of the Baptist Denomination in the United States for Foreign Missions was organized on May 18, 1814, at the First Baptist Church in Philadelphia, Pennsylvania. In 1700, Baptists in America numbered twenty-four churches with 839 members. In the 1740s, the first Great Awakening significantly expanded their presence. By 1790, Baptists numbered 979 churches with 67,490 members. McBeth writes:

> By 1800, they were a different people with a different spirit. Their outward transformation to become the largest denomination in America seems less significant than their inward transformation into a confident, aggressive, evangelistic people. The scattered churches had become a denomination. They had discovered purpose and evangelism, missions, and education and had organized to pursue those objectives.
>
> Without doubt, the event which did most to transform the Baptists was the First Great Awakening. Their greatest achievement was their struggle for religious liberty.

By 1814, Baptists had 1,282 churches with 110,514 members, and they were by far the strongest religious denomination in the United States.[11]

Most students of history are aware that William Carey, who published *An Enquiry into the Obligations of Christians to Use Means for the Conversion of the Heathens* in 1792, became the father of the modern missions movement when he sailed to India in 1793. He and John Thomas were commissioned as missionaries to Bengal in India. In 1800, Carey moved to Serampore and began his fruitful association with William Ward and Joshua and Hannah Marshman. His work was done under the auspices of the newly formed Baptist Missionary Society (1792). Francis Wayland wrote of this missionary pioneer, "Like most of the master minds of the ages, Carey was educated in the school of adversity." And for those in America, the entire world of mission enterprise held a vast sea of potential which beckoned their engagement.[12]

Interestingly enough, the first foreign mission endeavor in the United States was not from the Baptists but from the Congregationalists. Part of its impetus came from the new religious fervor overflowing from the Second Great Awakening in the East. Coming out of the legendary Haystack Prayer Meeting (1806), a group of young people covenanted together to surrender their lives for foreign missions. This commitment eventually took fruition in the establishment of the American Board of Commissioners for Foreign Missions (1810). Two of the missionaries setting sail for India under this banner were Adonirum Judson and Luther Rice. Due to an extensive time of focused study in the New Testament, Adonirum Judson came to the conviction that baptism was for adult believers by immersion and not for infants by sprinkling. Rice came to the same conclusion shortly after arriving in India. As a result of studying Scripture primarily because they would have to give a defense of their Congregational infant-baptism beliefs to the Baptists upon their arrival, both came to the conclusion separately and on separate ships, that the Baptists were right. As a result, Adonirum and Ann Hasseltine Judson and Luther Rice were baptized by immersion in India in 1812.[13]

The Judsons and Rice immediately sent letters of resignation to the American Board and wrote to Baptists in America petitioning them to form their own foreign mission society of which they would be available to serve as the first of their missionaries. Until that time Carey wrote concerning the Judsons and Rice: "I consider their baptism as a glorious triumph of truth over prejudice, and bless the Lord for it. . . . I hope our Baptist friends in America will take these two brethren under their protection, and consider them as their missionaries. We shall not desert them, nor their companions, should they be in want."[14]

Rice wrote an organizational proposal for Baptists to form their own Foreign Mission Board. As Baptists prepared to gather for discussion and decisions, the *Massachusetts Baptist Missionary Magazine* (December 1813) included an article stating, "The expense of such a Convention would be trifling compared with the magnitude of the object: Our success, under God, in providing funds for the foreign mission, depends on union among ourselves." Through the efforts of Luther Rice, who returned to the United States, a Convention of thirty-three delegates met on May 18, 1814, to form The General Missionary Convention of the Baptist Denomination in the United States. Because they would meet every three years, the Convention was often called the Triennial Convention. Richard Furman of South Carolina was elected its first president. Although he declined to serve as president, he was nonetheless pressed into service and delivered its first address communicating to all interested parties the nature and intentions of this newly formed organization.[15]

Several years later the General Missionary Convention embraced additional responsibilities of home missions and publications. Nevertheless, after ten years, both of these were dropped from the task assignment of the Convention and were absorbed by other societies formed specifically for those purposes. The American Baptist Publication Society was formed in 1824 and the American Baptist Home Mission Society was established in 1832. During this period Baptists also began to form state conventions. The first one was established in South Carolina in 1821.[16]

We reviewed the foreign missions effort among Baptists to point out the short-lived nature of the unity among Baptists in the United States. For, even though the call to foreign and domestic missions had a hold on the Baptist imagination, the ugly reality of slavery brought increasing tension among Baptists, north and south. According to Baker, slavery in America can be viewed in three successive stages:

> Before 1830 slavery was viewed primarily as an economic system; from 1830 to 1840, an era of moral reform in America, slavery was seen as a moral issue; and after 1840, the political aspects of slavery came to the fore and ultimately led to the Civil War. However, from the first, many opposed slavery on principle, and some Baptists were among them.

> Before 1800 slavery had not become a sectional issue. One might find anti-slavery viewpoints in both North and South; indeed, the evidence confirms more anti-slave societies in the South before 1800. The immense profit in importing slaves accrued more to the North than the South. That importation was outlawed in 1807. The invention of the cotton gin in 1792 made slave labor more profitable in the South, whereas north-ern industry profited less from slave labor. Thus, around the turn of the century, the slave system lost its profitability in the North just as it gained new profitability in the South. These related realities must be assessed in any evaluation of evolving attitudes towards slavery in the two regions.[17]

According to Baker, the unity of the Baptists was actually threat-ened by two forces. One was the widespread belief that the Home Mission Society neglected to give the South enough attention and missionaries. Yet the greater conflict was generated over the growing polarization created by the presence of slavery.[18]

The slavery-abolition controversy found its roots in Great Britain. It should be noted that Virginia's colonists attempted to resist the importation of slaves when it was introduced by the British Crown in 1619 but to no avail. Two centuries later British Baptists, who were instrumental in the final dissolution of slavery in the British Empire, lobbied for Baptists in America to do the same. In the exchange of letters, Baptists in America attempted to explain the difficulties in disengaging the practice of slavery since it was an individual state issue and not something that could be legislated from the top down as in the Bill of Rights and religious freedom. Moreover, to dispense with slavery would take time, energy, and sacrifice.[19]

In time the antislavery forces in the North solidified into an intense abolitionist posture, and a militant mind-set prevailed. From the pen of Baron Stow, a member of the American Baptist Board, we find him declaring, "It would not be difficult to show that the influence of the American Church, is, at present, the main pillar of American slavery. . . . But, my dear brother, God is on our side and the cause will prevail." On May 11, 1839, the American Baptist Anti-Slavery Convention was established, arguing that they simply could no longer cooperate with those who had not condemned slavery. Letters of explanation were sent to Baptists in the North and South. The letter to Baptists in the South stated:

> Finally,—if you should, (which Heaven avert!) remain deaf
> to the voice of warning and entreaty,—if you still cling to the
> power-maintained privilege of living on unpaid toil, and of
> claiming as property the image of God, which Jesus bought
> with His precious blood,—we solemnly declare, as we fear
> the Lord, that we cannot and we dare not recognize you as
> consistent brethren in Christ; we cannot join in partial, self
> ish prayers, that the groans of the slave may be unheard; we
> cannot hear preaching that makes God the Author and the
> Approver of human misery and vassalage; and we cannot, at
> the Lord's Table, cordially take that as a brother's hand, which
> plies the scourge on women's naked flesh,—which thrusts
> a gag into the mouth of a man,—which rivets fetters on the
> innocent,—and which shuts up the Bible from human eyes.
> We deplore your condition; we pray for your deliverance; and
> God forbid that we should ever sin against Him by ceasing so
> to pray.

By May 1843, the American Baptist Free Mission Society was established, declaring, "We hereby separate ourselves now and forever from all connection with religious societies that are supported in common with slaveholders."[20]

The immediate posture among the established societies was to attempt to maintain a pretense of neutrality. Richard Fuller, a southerner wrote:

> Therefore, first: That to introduce the subject of slavery or anti-slavery into this body, is in direct contravention of the whole letter and purpose of the said Constitution, and is, moreover, a most unnecessary agitation of topics with which this Society has no concern, over which it has no control, and as to which its operations should not be fettered, nor its deliberations disturbed,
>
> Two: That the Home Mission Society being only an agency to disperse the funds confided to it, according to the wishes of the contributors, therefore, our co-operation in this body does not imply any sympathy either with slavery or anti-slavery, as to which societies and individuals are left as free and uncommitted as if there were no such co-operation.

By 1844, Baptists in the North were recommending the separation of Baptists north and south instead of permitting the rancor and turmoil to continue. The quest for neutrality in the General Missionary Convention (foreign missions) was no more effective than that among the Home Mission Society.[21]

In 1841 a group of leaders north and south did meet with the hopeful attempt to establish some kind of compromise. According to Baker, it simply delayed the inevitable parting of the ways.[22]

The final prelude to the parting of Baptists north and south came in two distinct actions. First, in 1844, Georgia Baptists offered James Reeves as a prospective missionary to the American Baptist Home Mission Society. Because Reeves was a slaveholder, this was indeed a test case. Reeves was rejected as a missionary candidate. As a follow-up to the Reeves' rejection, the Alabama Baptists requested the foreign mission body to provide a categorical declaration that slaveholders would be acceptable to serve as foreign missionaries, to be treated as all other members of the Society. On December 17, 1844, Baron Stow replied on behalf of the Board stating: "If, however, anyone should offer himself as a missionary, having slaves, and should insist on retaining them as his property, we could not appoint him. One thing is certain; we can never be a party to any arrangement which would imply approbation of slavery."[23]

As a result of the growing animosity and differences of perception and perspective, Baptists in Virginia issued a call for a consultative convention to be held in Augusta, Georgia, in the spring of 1845, noting that "it is important that those brethren who are aggrieved by the recent decision of the Board in Boston, should hold a Convention, to confer on the best means of promoting the Foreign Missions cause, and other interests of the Baptist denomination in the South"[24]

On May 10, 1845, Baptist history in America would be changed forever.

The Middle Years (1845–1877)

The Middle Years of the Great Century can be divided conveniently into prewar, Civil War, and Reconstruction phases. These years were rife with hopes, dreams, tragedy, and hardship, all of which can be traced to the terrible reality of and the sad economic dependence on slavery.

Conventional wisdom maintains that Southern Baptists left their northern counterparts due to their own stubborn insistence of the legitimacy of slavery. In fact, the militant abolitionists among northern Baptists forced the hand of Baptists in the South, thereby declaring to them, "There is no place for you in this house." One wonders what course history might have taken had cooler heads prevailed in the religious, political, and economic arenas. Had those north and south realized the terrible price that would be extracted in order to excise the cancer of slavery from the nation, it seems that a way of disengagement surely could have been developed and implemented. We will never know.

In response to the Southwide invitation, 293 delegates, 237 from three states, convened in Augusta, Georgia, on May 10–12, 1845, and formed the Southern Baptist Convention. What was formed was not identical to the organization from which these founders departed. In fact, these men crafted a new entity unlike those which preceded it.[25]

The new form, the brainchild of the first president, William Bullein Johnson, was established upon a Convention basis, which in turn would establish and coordinate the various boards and agencies. They would be distinct from and potentially stronger than those that adhered to a society approach for accomplishing their missions. In the words of Johnson, "The whole Denomination will be united in one body for the purpose of well-doing."[26]

Just prior to the organizational meeting, Francis Wayland, one of northern Baptists' most prominent leaders, wrote:

> You will separate of course. I could not ask otherwise. Your rights have been infringed. I will take the liberty of offering one or two suggestions. We have shown how Christians ought not to act, it remains for you to show us how they ought to act. Put away all violence, act with dignity and firmness and the world will approve your course.[27]

When the new Convention organized, it provided both a Preamble and a Constitution to articulate its reason for existence. Its purpose (design) is summarized in Article 2, which states, "It shall be the design of this Convention to promote Foreign and Domestic Missions, and other important objects connected with the Redeemer's kingdom, and to combine for this purpose, such portions of the Baptist denomination in the United States, as may desire a general organization for Christian benevolence, which shall fully respect the independence and equal rights of the Churches."[28]

In keeping with the custom of the day, the newly elected president, W. B. Johnson, delivered an inaugural address which attempted to explain the necessity and purpose of the newly formed organization. Johnson declared, "A painful division has taken place in the missionary operations of the American Baptists." He noted:

> Let not the extent of this disunion be exaggerated. At the present time it involves only the Foreign and Domestic Missions of the denomination. Northern and Southern Baptists are still brethren. They differ in no article of the faith. They are guided by the same principles of gospel order. Fanatical attempts have indeed been made, in some quarters, to exclude us of the South from christian fellowship. We do not retort these attempts; and believe their extent to be comparatively limited. Our christian fellowship is not, as we feel, a matter to be obtruded on any one. We abide by that of our God, his dear Son, and all his baptized followers. The few ultra Northern brethren to whom we allude, must take what course they please. Their conduct has not influenced us in this movement. We do not regard the rupture as extending to foundation principles, nor can we think that the great body of our Northern brethren will so regard it. Disunion has proceeded, however, deplorably far. The first part of our duty is to show that its entire origin is with others. This is its history.

Several times, Johnson argued the root cause of the division was that those in the North had "forbidden us to speak unto the Gentiles." This created an untenable situation that demanded relief. He went on to state, "Our objects, then, are the extension of the Messiah's kingdom, and the glory of our God."[29]

In the charter, Act of Incorporation, we read, "Said corporation being created for the purpose of eliciting, combining and directing the energies of the Baptist denomination of christians, for the propagation of the gospel, any law, usage or custom to the contrary notwithstanding." Driving the creation of this new convention was the over-riding desire to advance the gospel.[30]

Summarizing the small beginning of the Southern Baptist Convention, McBeth notes, "At its formative meeting, the infant SBC appointed boards for foreign and home missions." Yet, "delegates also discussed publication and educational work but caution prevailed and entrance into these areas were delayed."[31]

Resolutions voted on at the Southern Baptist Convention in session often provide a snapshot of prevailing sentiments and concerns. From the beginning, Southern Baptists preserved their thoughts. Resolutions capture for posterity the priorities and the understandings of the day.

At the first meeting of the Convention, Southern Baptists' three resolutions reflected their purposes. The first resolution of the Convention stated, "That the board of Domestic Missions be instructed to take all prudent measures, for the religious instruction of our colored population." Likewise was an appeal of support for the work among the "Aborigines of America," the American Indians. And finally, the Convention authorized its Foreign Mission Board, its first and most important agency, to work as necessary to settle any claims with the Baptist Triennial Convention. Notice that its subsidiary was to relate to the main body of work for the Northern Baptists.[32]

In 1846, resolutions were offered requesting prayer for world evangelism and endorsing Southern Baptist participation in the "Monthly Concert of Prayer for the revival of genuine religion, and the success of the Gospel throughout the earth." Resolutions also endorsed expansion of mission work into the new settlements and new states, rejoiced over successful work among the Indian population, and encouraged educational efforts. The Concert of Prayer request was repeated again in 1849, as well as another plea to take the gospel to the "colored" population.[33]

Several years after the conclusion of the Mexican-American War (1848), we read of a resolution advocating the evangelization of Mexico's large cities, the West Indies, and South America.[34]

Following the period of Matthew Perry's venture taking his squadron of ships into Tokyo Bay and opening up Japan (1853) with its follow-up treaty of 1854, Baptists twice requested the U.S. Government to push for the acceptance of religious liberty abroad (1853 and 1855). Again in 1859, we find another resolution pleading with Congress to provide assistance to secure for its citizens religious liberty overseas.[35]

On the heels of the Kansas-Nebraska Act (1854), which advocated that its citizens should vote and decide on the presence or absence of slavery, the 1855 Southern Baptist Convention, "resolved, That the Board of Domestic Missions be instructed to occupy Kansas, as a field of missions as soon as practicable." One wonders if this was politically motivated.[36]

Meanwhile, tensions over slavery continued to intensify. The year 1851 saw the Fugitive Slave Law enacted. In 1852, Harriet Beecher Stowe released her *Uncle Tom's Cabin*. With the Kansas-Nebraska Act in 1854 and the Dred Scott Decision in 1857, which in effect made slavery legal everywhere, tension continued to escalate. In 1859, John Brown's attack on Harper's Ferry added fuel to the oncoming fire. America, it seemed, had reached a point of no return.[37]

Summarizing the dynamics which led into the Civil War, Greg Ward writes:

> Purely as an economic system, slavery was not in decline in 1860. Plantation agriculture had never been more profitable. The South produced three-quarters of the world's cotton, provided sixty percent of the U.S. exports, and led every one of the top 116 counties in terms of per capita wealth. Southern confidence was perhaps best expressed in James Hammons' *King Cotton* speech to the Senate in 1858, when he credited the South with rescuing the Union from the Depression of 1857: "The difference between us is, that our slaves are hired for life and well compensated . . . yours are hired by the day, not cared for, and scantily compensated."

Ward further notes that

> The two sides squared up to fight the Civil War were clearly demarcated by slavery. Slaves constituted on average forty-six percent of the population in the seven Deep South states that originally formed the Confederacy—South Carolina, Mississippi, Florida, Alabama, Georgia, Louisiana and Texas— and 28.5 percent of the four upper South states that joined once war began—Virginia, Arkansas, North Carolina and Tennessee. Overall, more than a third of the southern population were

slaves; the corresponding figure for the North was just one percent.[38]

By nearly everyone's assessment the Civil War was a tragedy and a travesty. The war, which began on April 12, 1861, concluded on April 9, 1865, in the Appomattox Courthouse when General Lee surrendered to General Grant.

South Carolina was the first state to secede from the Union on December 20, 1860. More southern states followed. The primary resolution offered at the May 1861 Southern Baptist Convention requested, "That a Committee be appointed to consider the propriety of changing the term 'United States' into 'Confederate States.'" It further requested that same committee to "recommend such vital changes in the Constitution and Minutes as may be necessary, growing out of the recent formation of the Southern Confederacy."[39]

As the war unfolded, Lincoln made his famous Emancipation Proclamation on January 1, 1863. The following November he gave his classic Gettysburg Address. In 1865, the Thirteenth Amendment outlawed slavery.[40]

During the course of the war, the Southern Baptist Convention, meeting again in Augusta, Georgia, offered this "Resolution on Peace" which provides a glimpse into the horror of the war:

> Resolved, 1st. That the events of the past two years have only confirmed the conviction expressed by this Convention at its last session, that the war which has been forced upon us is, on our part, just and necessary, and have only strengthened our opposition to a reunion with the United States on any terms whatsoever; and while deploring the dreadful evils of the war, and earnestly desiring peace, we have no thought of ever yielding, but still render a hearty support to the Confederate Government in all constitutional measures to secure our independence.
>
> Resolved, 2nd. That we gratefully acknowledge the hand of God in the preservation of our government against the power and rage of our enemies, and in the signal victories with which He has crowned our arms; and encouraged by the experience

of the past, and by the present condition of affairs, and humbly relying on the divine blessing, we confidently anticipate ultimate success.

Resolved, 3rd. That while we justify ourselves in this conflict with our enemies, we acknowledge that our sins have deserved the terrible calamities that God has sent upon us, and view them as a solemn and imperative call to penitence, humiliation and a hardy turning to God.

Resolved, 4th. That the religious destitution of our armies is a cause of deep solicitude, and calls for renewed, vigorous and liberal efforts that it may be supplied.

Resolved, 5th. That the privations of those reduced to poverty by the war, and especially the wants of the families of our soldiers, demand our sympathies, our kind attentions, and our generous contributions.

Resolved, 6th. That the serious interruption of education, and the growing neglect of domestic discipline which the war has caused, are evils of the greatest magnitude, and we earnestly urge upon our brethren and fellow citizens to keep their children steadily at school, and to give diligent attention to their moral and religious training.

Resolved, 7th. That we just heard with unutterable grief of the death of that noble Christian warrior, Lt. General T. J. Jackson; that we thank God for the good he has achieved, and the glorious example he has left us, and pray that we may all learn to trust, as he trusted, in the Lord alone.

Another resolution called for "vigorous efforts to secure the service of Chaplains, and to send forth Missionaries and Colporteurs into this field."[41]

The war years were difficult for Southern Baptists. Funds for their foreign mission endeavor were scarce. Home mission activity almost disappeared. Baptists from the North made inroads into what Southern Baptists considered their territory. Baker summarizes the war years and their impact on Southern Baptists this way:

Every phase of the work was either destroyed or impaired. More than 150 missionaries had been engaged before outbreak of hostilities, but their work was suspended. Army missions became the principal work. Southern Baptists were particularly displeased with the action of the American Baptist Home Mission Society in securing authorization to take possession of Baptist meetinghouses in the South.[42]

Yet hope for future reconciliation remained. From Abraham Lincoln's perspective, "Both parties deprecated war; but one of them would make war rather than let the nation survive; and the other would accept war rather than let it perish." He lamented, "And the war came." He concluded his Second Inaugural Address (March 4, 1865) by stating, "With malice toward none; with charity for all; with firmness in the right, as God gives us to see the right, let us strive on to finish the work we are in; to bind up the nation's wounds; to care for him who shall have borne the battle, and for his widow, and his orphan—to do all which may achieve and cherish a just, and a lasting peace, among ourselves, and with all nations."[43]

Only a few days after the conclusion of the war, sadly, Abraham Lincoln was struck down by an assassin's bullet. In the words of William J. Bennett, "Reconciliation was lost in the aftermath."[44]

As stated earlier, the war extracted a terrible toll on the nation. Ward summarizes the war's impact on America:

> The final Union victory is often attributed to sheer weight of numbers, and the economic might that went with it. In total, the war pitted the Union of 23 northern states, holding over 22 million people, against the Confederacy of 11 southern states, with 9 million people. As for potential combatants, the North initially drew on 3.5 million white males aged between 18 and 45—and later recruited blacks as well—whereas the South had more like one million. In the end, around 2.1 million men fought for the Union and 900,000 for the Confederacy. 620,000 soldiers died during the conflict, around one-third of

them in battle and the rest from disease; 360,000 of those were from the North, but the 258,000 who came from the South represented four percent of its total population and one-quarter of its white men of military age.[45]

John M. Blum concludes that the war settled three questions. First, the Union was indivisible and indissoluble. Second, the institution of slavery was swept away. And third, the North would dominate politics in the aftermath.[46]

The latter part of these Middle Years is commonly called the period of Reconstruction. It lasted from the war's conclusion until 1877 when Rutherford B. Hayes agreed to terminate Reconstruction for southern support in the electoral college and his win of the presidency by one single vote.

The aftermath of the Civil War brought the Fourteenth Amendment (1866), which forbade states from depriving anybody of life, liberty, or property without due process. The Fifteenth Amendment was passed in 1869 and guaranteed the right to vote regardless of race, color, or previous condition of servitude. At the same time, the South saw the birth of the Ku Klux Klan (1866) as well as legislation outlawing it in 1870.[47]

Bennett notes that at the conclusion of the war, the United States had the largest army in the world and the second largest navy. The plan for Reconstruction after Lincoln's death was harsher than it might have been had he lived. In 1867, the South was divided into five military districts. All military decisions were filtered through General Grant because Congress distrusted President Andrew Johnson. Also in this legislation, the Tenure of Office Act required the President to obtain the Senate's consent to dismiss or appoint officeholders. In essence, the radical reconstructionists in the Congress were ruling the nation with an iron fist.[48]

Meanwhile, Indian uprisings were growing more common in the West. In 1866, eighty U.S. soldiers were killed in Wyoming by Crazy Horse and his warriors. In 1876, 266 soldiers of the Seventh Cavalry, including George Armstrong Custer, were killed at Little Big Horn in the Dakota Territory. By the end of the decade, President Grant would decisively defeat the Native American resistance.[49]

In this same era the Transcontinental Railroad was completed, opening up America's interior. Yet the overwhelming assessment of the post Civil War Reconstruction era was that the South was an "economic basket case." And the newly emancipated "freedmen" had an incredibly difficult time. Poverty was rampant in the South.[50]

In the Reconstruction era, Southern Baptists struggled but gradually dug out of the war-wrought depression. It should be noted that Southern Baptists had 650,000 members in 1860 just prior to the war. By 1875, in the concluding years of Reconstruction, they had grown to more than 1,260,000 members.[51]

The resolutions during the Reconstruction era are revealing. First, numerous resolutions urged Southern Baptists to give to missions causes (1866, 1868, 1869, 1871, 1875, and 1877). Even though the South had been economically devastated, Baptists were asked to give and give sacrificially. The only resolution in 1867 was, "Resolved, That this Convention recommend to the churches to observe Saturday, before the fourth Sunday in June, as a day of fasting, humiliation and prayer, on account of the distressed condition of the country."[52]

Second, immediately after the war, the Southern Baptist Convention affirmed a resolution on "Religious Liberty," which states:

> We solemnly resolve, in the face of the world, and in the fear of God—1. That we believe civil government to be of divine appointment, and that magistrates should be prayed for, and obeyed, in all things, not contrary to the rights of conscience and the revealed will of Christ. 2. That Christ is the Supreme Ruler, of the Church—that it is His prerogative to put men into the Gospel ministry, and that they are amenable only to Him for the discharge of its functions—that all interference with these functions on the part of conscience; and that when the claims of civil rulers come in conflict with those of Christ, it is our duty to "obey God rather than men" and endure the

consequences. 3. That we express our sincere sympathy and high regard for those ministers, who, in following the dictates of their consciences, and maintaining the authority of their supreme lawgiver, have cheerfully submitted to fines, imprisonments, and other "pains and penalties," and that we will earnestly pray that rulers may be so considerate and just, and that Christian ministers may be so discreet and upright, that the cause of Christ may not be hindered, and the name of God blasphemed. 4. That in adopting these resolutions, the Convention expressly disavow any disposition to interfere with political affairs, and have regard solely to the question of religious liberty.[53]

With respect to missions, Southern Baptists were urged to evangelize and minister to the "colored population" (1868, 1869), the Jews (1873, 1875), the Indians (1877), and the "destitute parts of our country." During this era of great difficulty, Southern Baptists stayed true to their mission of taking the gospel to a lost world.[54]

Instead of rejoining the Baptists of the North, Southern Baptists opted to continue as a separate entity. McBeth suggests that part of the reason for this was because they were now confronting different issues. Baptists in the North were addressing issues of European immigration, the rise of organized labor, the industrialization of the economy, compromising theology, and the rise of the Social Gospel. In contrast Baptists in the South were attempting to address issues concerning the four million newly freed black slaves, political turmoil, and economic devastation.[55]

As Southern Baptists emerged out of the Reconstruction era and these Middle Years (1845–1877) of the Great Century, they were still concerned about religious liberty and sharing the gospel with a lost world and yet were humbled and even humiliated by the tragedy of slavery and the awful price that it extracted. As we turn our attention to the Later Years, notice how Southern Baptists began to expand their concerns to additional moral and social issues that affected society.

The Later Years (1877–1907)

The Later Years span a period of three decades beginning with the conclusion of Reconstruction up to the period where Southern Baptists began intentionally to engage the culture through a concerted effort in 1907. Over this period Southern Baptists continued to grow and expand. In 1875, right before the conclusion of the Reconstruction era, Southern Baptists had 1,260,000 members. By 1905, they had 1,900,000 members, a 50 percent increase in thirty years.[56]

Post-Reconstruction America was a period filled with challenges. It reflected in a real sense the continuing unfolding of the nation's "Manifest Destiny," a term coined by John O'Sullivan in the *New York Morning News* at the beginning of the Middle Years. He wrote that it is "our manifest destiny to overspread and to possess the whole of the continent which Providence has given us for the development of the great experiment of liberty and federated self-government."[57]

Blum writes that "by constitutional amendment and by detailed statutes, the United States was presumably committed to the principle of equal civil and political rights and to use the federal power to guarantee them." He goes on to explain, "Yet after Reconstruction the country quickly broke this commitment and virtually forgot about it for two generations." Blum further explains that, "In a long series of decisions the (Supreme) Court underwrote white supremacy, states rights, and *laissez faire* and virtually nullified the Fourteenth and Fifteenth Amendments insofar as they applied to the rights of freedmen."[58]

Yet, even while Jim Crow laws were being enacted, the United States was still embracing the world and standing as a bastion of freedom and hope. Here, reality met idealism. Yet, with the 1886 unveiling of the French gift, the Statue of Liberty, poet Emma Lazarus's words hold a significant place in our national experience. She wrote, concerning the meaning of the statue to America and the world, "Give me your tired, your poor, your huddled masses yearning to breathe free, the wretched refuse of your teaming shore. Send these, the homeless, tempest tossed to me, I lift my lamp beside the golden door!"[59]

As this latter period unfolded, some states, like Mississippi (1890), rewrote their constitutions, including literacy tests as prerequisites for voting. In the West three hundred Sioux Indians were killed at Wounded Knee on December 29, 1890. A few years later (1892) lynchings in the South reached 161 murdered in a single year. Approaching the turn of the century, America went to war with Spain and won. In his unexpected presidency, Theodore Roosevelt introduced surprisingly progressive policies and in a saber-rattling exercise dispensed the Great White Fleet, consisting of sixteen battleships (1907), to a two-year, around-the-world tour. Even so, in 1907 Ellis Island saw more than a million immigrants pass through its turnstiles.[60]

During this tumultuous time, Southern Baptists were busy. Notwithstanding the doctrinal controversies of Crawford Toy (1879) and William Whitsitt (1899) experienced during this era, Southern Baptists were a diligent people who sacrificially worked at both missions and evangelism. Yet this was not the only priority even though it was the principal one. They continued to address both church and state issues as well as what they perceived to be the great moral issues of their day. In fact, by reviewing the resolutions approved at the Southern Baptist Convention as it met in session, ten major themes, or convictions, emerged.[61]

First, we find a priority placed on race relations. In a period where prejudice was high and segregation was the norm of the day, Southern Baptists, although paternalistic initially, worked at improving the lot of black Americans. In 1878, 1884 and 1886, resolutions were offered highlighting the priority of evangelizing the "colored people" as well as providing resources to educate their leader. In 1884, another resolution was offered with respect to working with America's Native American population. And twice, in 1906 and 1907, strong resolutions were offered condemning the practice of lynching. Although some consider these latter resolutions as coming late, at least Southern Baptists went on record decrying their practice as a monstrous evil.[62]

A second emphasis offered in resolutions (1882, 1891 and 1892) was the desire to maintain the Sabbath or Lord's Day practices. In effect, these resolutions affirmed that people need a day of rest and recreation. The latter two resolutions are occasional in the sense that they responded to major exhibitions being opened on Sunday and thereby, by implication, competing with the church.[63]

A third focus of the resolutions, not surprisingly, consists of repeated pleas for Southern Baptists to give sacrificially (1885, 1904, 1906). The purpose was not only an encouragement to be good stewards of resources entrusted by God but to give in order to impact their world and make a difference in people's lives.[64]

Fourth, beginning in 1886, Southern Baptists engaged in the Temperance Movement with the same ferocity seen in the Abolitionist Movement a quarter century earlier. In this thirty-year period, no fewer than ten resolutions were offered attacking the liquor industry. Indicative of the sentiment of Southern Baptists is the first resolution, which states,

> Whereas, the manufacture and sale of intoxicating liquors as a beverage, in the opinion of this Convention, are opposed to the best interests of society and government, and the progress of our holy religion, and believing that all honorable means should be employed for their suppression, therefore be it
>
> Resolved, that we, as members of the Southern Baptist Convention, do most solemnly protest against its manufacture and sale, and pledge our influence in the exercise of our rights as citizens of this free country, socially, morally, religiously and in all other proper ways, to work for its speedy overthrow, and to this end we invoke the aid and blessing of Almighty God.

It should be noted that although Southern Baptists went on record opposing the liquor industry, not until 1907 did they begin to organize. This would mark the beginning of their own cooperative engagement in public policy issues.[65]

A fifth issue, mentioned only once in this period but driven by the possibility of Louisiana doing away with state-sponsored gambling, was offered in 1890. In it Southern Baptists explained, "Believing that gambling in all its forms is demoralizing to our people, and that the Louisiana Lottery is an evil of great magnitude, and having learned that the charter of the iniquitous concern will soon expire unless renewed; therefore, Resolved, that we extend our hearty sympathy to the good people of Louisiana in their struggle to rid themselves of this great curse by preventing its renewal, and that we bid them Godspeed and pledge the moral sanction of this Convention." Based on the sentiment of this resolution, it is safe to say, had more occasions arisen to promote gambling, more resistance would have been offered.[66]

A sixth emphasis found in the resolutions is the affirmation of religious liberty. Having secured it for themselves, Southern Baptists urged Congress to advocate it in foreign policy engagements. They specifically mentioned Cuba (1898) in the aftermath of the Spanish American War, Russia (1899), the Congo (1904 and 1906), Great Britain (1906), France (1906), and Russia again (1906).[67]

A seventh issue raised in resolutions was a forerunner to the pro-family posture developed later in the Southern Baptist Convention. In 1904, a resolution was offered "On Divorce." Noting the growing ease of obtaining a divorce in the nation, they concluded, "It is the sense of this body that the Legislatures of the States represented in this Convention be requested to discourage this great and growing evil by more stringent laws regulating the same." Baptists were antidivorce because they were pro-family. They did note, "That it is the sense of this body that Baptist ministers should refuse to solemnize the rites of matrimony in cases where one or both parties concerned have been divorced on other than Scriptural grounds, as laid down in Matthew 19:9."[68]

An eighth emphasis among Southern Baptists was the intentional relief provided for the poor and needy. Particularly, in 1885, they went on record advocating that the work of Christianity is not only worldwide in its scope but also must be concerned with both the physical and the spiritual needs of people. The resolution states:

> Resolved, First, that in the evangelization of our own country, and the consecration to Christ of the spiritual power of its 50 millions of people, and in the subordination of the forces inherent in its vast material and industrial resources to the work of the Lord, is to be found the prime factor in the world's conversion.

Resolved, Second, that this result can be attained only
by broadening the sphere of Christian activity as to include
proper attention to all the wants of man, both for this life and
that which is to come; by the disciple, like his divine master,
embracing every opportunity to do good to the bodies as well
as to the souls of men.

Resolved, Third, that the accomplishment of so grand a
work requires only that measure of energy and that expenditure
of means demanded by our obligation to our Savior and by the
spirit of our holy religion.

In 1906, the year of the Great San Francisco Earthquake,
Southern Baptists rallied to disaster relief. The fruit of this early effort
would eventually grow into an ongoing ministry, which is a worldwide
hallmark of Baptist identity.[69]

A ninth issue raised among Southern Baptists (1907) was a resolution on peace. In the wake of the Spanish American War and the
commissioning of Roosevelt's Great White Fleet, they affirmed, "Peace
hath her victories no less renowned than war; and we desire and will
pray for the day to hasten when all nations will settle their difficulties
by arbitration rather than resort to armies."[70]

A final emphasis, perhaps ancillary to this presentation, is that
found in 1885, 1903, and 1904, where Southern Baptists articulated
their strong conviction that their scope of activity was not regional
but national and that the entire nation was their local sphere of influence. In fact, the 1903 resolution, "On Convention Name," advocated
changing their name to "The Baptist Convention of the United States,
so that the same may better harmonize with the true nature and
opportunities of this body."[71]

In his insightful work *The Quality of Mercy* (1996), Keith Harper
reviews in detail the relation of Southern Baptists and social Christianity between 1890 and 1920. For those who maintain that Southern
Baptists were being influenced by the social gospel, he points out that
the South maintained a type of Social Christianity which attempted to
transform and restructure society and not simply provide spiritual aid

to individuals. As a result of the Populist Movement, Southern Baptists did advocate the overarching posture that "better societies are built on better people." This, Harper maintains, was the backbone of the Southern Baptist social view. This humanitarian ethic, he points out, provided the impetus for piety to demonstrate itself in a definite plan of social action. Yet Southern Baptists with a social conscience remain bound to the prevailing notion that personal salvation is the prevailing theme of authentic religion.[72]

As we turn our attention in the next chapter to Southern Baptists' initial attempts at social and moral engagement, keep in mind that for them it is all a matter of conviction.

Notes

1. Winthrop S. Hudson, *Religion in America*, 2nd ed. (New York: Charles Scribner's Sons, 1965), 118.

2. Robert A. Baker, *A Baptist Source Book* (Nashville: Broadman Press, 1966), 33–34; Leon McBeth, *The Baptist Heritage* (Nashville: Broadman Press, 1987), 206–227; Robert C. Walton, *Chronological and Background Charts of Church History* (Grand Rapids, Mich.: Academic Books, 1986), 53. One very thorough treatise on the development of religious liberty is William R. Estep, *Revolution Within the Revolution* (Grand Rapids, Mich.: Eerdmann, 1990).

3. McBeth, *The Baptist Heritage*, 206–27.

4. Ibid., 254.

5. Ibid., 264.

6. Ibid., 267.

7. Ibid., 274–75.

8. Ibid., 280–81.

9. Walton, *Chronological and Background Charts of Church History*, 53.

10. William G. McLoughlin, *New England Dissent, 1630–1883*, 2 vols. (Cambridge, Mass.: Harvard University Press, 1971), 789–1274.

11. McBeth, *The Baptist Heritage*, 251; Baker, *A Baptist Source Book*, 51.

12. Timothy George, *The Life and Mission of William Carey* (Birmingham, Ala.: New Hope Publishers, 1999); Mary Drewery, *William Carey* (Grand Rapids, Mich.: Zondervan, 1979); George, *The Life and Mission of William Carey*, 94.

13. Sydney Ahlstrom, *A Religious History of the American People* (New Haven and London: Yale University Press, 1972), 423–24; Baker, *A Baptist Source Book*, 53.

14. Baker, *A Baptist Source Book*, 53–61.

15. Ibid., 61–65.

16. Ibid., 66–75.

17. McBeth, *The Baptist Heritage*, 383.

18. Baker, *A Baptist Source Book*, 84–85. According to McBeth, *The Baptist Heritage*, 381, Baker demonstrated that in the decade, 1832–1841, the states of the Deep South contributed $28,149 to the Home Mission Society and had only $13,646 expended by the Society in their states.

19. Baker, *A Baptist Source Book*, 87–89.

20. Ibid., 91, 94–95.

21. Ibid., 95, 97–98.

22. Ibid., 100.

23. Ibid., 104–106, 109.

24. Ibid., 112–13.

25. McBeth, *The Baptist Heritage*, 388. Richard Land provides this salient observation: "While the refusal to appoint a slaveholder as a missionary to the Native Americans was the precipitating event, other issues had been simmering and contributed to the division. Perhaps chief among them was a basic disagreement about how the denomination should be organized. Southerners, largely as a result of the influence of the Separate Baptists of the Great Awakening, wanted a stronger board structure with accountability of the boards directly to the convention, whereas Northerners wanted to retain a societal structure with semi-independent societies, such as the Home Mission Society, the Foreign Mission Society, and the Publications Society. Evidence of the importance of this structural issue is that Southerners within a year gathered together and formed the Southern Baptist Convention with a strong board-type structure. Northerners did not form a convention until 1907 when the Northern Baptist Convention was formed. They just maintained their loose societal structure." Interview with Richard Land, May 7–8, 2007.

26. Baker, *A Baptist Source Book*, 114.

27. Ibid., 116.

28. Ibid., 117.

29. Ibid., 118–22; Ergun Caner and Emir Caner, eds., *The Sacred Desk* (Nashville: Broadman & Holman Publishers, 2004), 5–10.

30. Baker, *A Baptist Source Book*, 122.

31. McBeth, *The Baptist Heritage*, 412.

32. Southern Baptist Convention, Resolutions, 1845.

33. Ibid., 1846, 1849.

34. Ibid., 1851.

35. Ibid., 1853.

36. Ibid., 1855.

37. John M. Blum, Bruce Catton, Edmund S. Morgan, Arthur M. Schlesinger, Jr., Kenneth M. Stampp, and C. Vann Woodard, *The National Experience*, 2nd ed. (New York: Harcourt, Brace and World, 1963, 1968), 320–49.

38. Greg Ward, *The Timeline History of the USA* (New York: Barnes and Noble, 2003, 2005), 136–37.

39. Southern Baptist Convention, Resolutions, 1861.

40. Ward, *The Timeline History of the USA*, 162–73.

41. Southern Baptist Convention, Resolutions, 1863.

42. Baker, *A Baptist Source Book*, 125–26.

43. Abraham Lincoln, "Second Inaugural Address" in *Lincoln: Selected Speeches and Writings* (New York: Vintage Books, 1992), 449–500.

44. William J. Bennett, *America: The Last Best Hope*, vol. 1 (Nashville: Nelson Current, 2006), 369.

45. Ward, *The Timeline History of the USA*, 137.

46. Blum, *The National Experience*, 2nd ed., 373.

47. Ibid., 379, 383–85, 397, 454.

48. Bennett, *America: The Last Best Hope*, 392.

49. Blum, *The National Experience*, 2nd ed., 416–18.

50. Bennett, *America: The Last Best Hope*, 418.

51. Historical Statistics of the United States (1976), series H 805.

52. Southern Baptist Convention, Resolutions, 1866, 1868, 1869, 1871, 1875, 1877.

53. Ibid., 1866.

54. Ibid., 1868, 1869, 1873, 1875, 1877.

55. McBeth, *The Baptist Heritage*, 392.

56. Historical Statistics.

57. Ward, *The Timeline History of the USA*, 129; Bennett, *America: The Last Best Hope*, 262.

58. Blum, *The National Experience*, 397.

59. Bennett, *America: The Last Best Hope*, 449.

60. Blum, *The National Experience*, 397–98, 400, 418, 525–34; Ward, *The Timeline History of the USA*, 215.

61. Baker, *A Baptist Source Book*, 168–74.

62. Southern Baptist Convention, Resolutions, 1878, 1884, 1886, 1906, 1907.

63. Ibid., 1882, 1891, 1892.

64. Ibid., 1885, 1904, 1906.

65. Ibid., 1886, 1887, 1890, 1891, 1896, 1898, 1904, 1905 (2), 1907.

66. Ibid., 1890.

67. Ibid., 1898, 1899, 1904, 1906.

68. Ibid., 1904.

69. Ibid., 1885, 1906.

70. Ibid., 1907.

71. Ibid., 1885, 1903, 1904.

72. Keith Harper, *The Quality of Mercy* (Tuscaloosa, Ala.: University of Alabama Press, 1996), 16.

CHAPTER

Southern Baptist Beginnings in Public Engagement (1907–1946)

To this point in history, Baptists have been instrumental in helping to establish religious liberty as the normative political philosophy and policy in the United States. This includes lobbying for and promoting the writing and ratification of the First Amendment, which included the nonestablishment clause, the free exercise clause, the freedom of speech and press clauses, and the freedom of the people peaceably to assemble. Likewise, they supported article 6 in the Constitution, which stated that "no religious test shall ever be required as a qualification to any office or public trust under the United States."[1]

With respect to church life in the United States of America, the First Amendment meant, as its implications unfolded, the disestablishment of the state churches. For the churches in America, this meant no guarantees and no restrictions and well suited the theological and philosophical presuppositions and opportunities of Baptists in America.

Up to this point in history, Southern Baptists were diligently working to influence their culture. A primary instrument with respect to social and moral issues is the passing of resolutions which express the sentiment of the Southern Baptist Convention meeting in session. The year 1907, however, brought a new dimension. Here the Convention took initial steps collectively to mobilize its people to influence public policy issues and, in fact, lobby for public policy positions that it viewed as biblical values. For Southern Baptists, biblical values are identical to one's public philosophy and mandate intense persuasion to be implemented into public policy in the political arena.

Yet the growth of Southern Baptists' engagement in public policy issues was tested over the years as theological moderates and conservatives vied for positions of power and influence. The unfolding story of the twentieth century would see three distinct phases. The initial phase (1907–1946) was marked by a dominant conservatism, although some issues seemed to push the proverbial envelope. The second phase (1947–1987) moved Southern Baptists toward a more leftward posture, and 1988 until the present saw the return of Southern Baptists to their conservative roots. This chapter will address the earliest period of Southern Baptists' public engagement.[2]

Beginnings of Engagement to Prohibition (1907–1919)

Little did Edwin William Stephens realize, when he recommended and appointed the "Committee on Civic Righteousness" at the 1907 meeting of the Southern Baptist Convention in Richmond, Virginia, that it would be the forerunner of Southern Baptists' collective engagement in attempting to influence the culture and public policy issues in our nation. He requested the committee devise plans for a mass meeting to be held at the following year's Convention. By resolution he instructed the committee "to consider and counsel together as to what may best be done by Christian men and ministers, especially Baptists, for creating a more wholesome public opinion; for making the criminal laws more certain, more prompt, and more effective; so as to take away the reproach resting on civilization and religion by the prevalence of crimes and lynchings; and so as to make the law respected and effective in all parts of our common country." The approval of this resolution was followed by another, which states that, "The greatest enemy of the cause of Christ which we as a Convention in part represent is the legalized liquor traffic."[3]

By the following year, as Southern Baptists met in Hot Springs, Arkansas, the resolve of the messengers was to do everything necessary to defeat the liquor industry and promote civic righteousness. The principal resolution, which this Convention adopted, established the Committee on Temperance with these words:

> WHEREAS, One of the very greatest obstacles in the way of the advancement of God's kingdom in the world, both at home and abroad, is the legalized liquor traffic, ruining homes, blighting characters, blasting lives, damning souls, and neutralizing to a large extent the work of pastors and missionaries on home and foreign fields.

> WHEREAS, It is a fight between the churches on one side and the liquor traffic on the other side, the churches standing for good and for God in the world, and the liquor traffic standing for evil in the world.

> RESOLVED, 1. That we, the Southern Baptist Convention, representing a constituency of over 2,000,000 members, hereby declare our determined and uncompromising opposition to the liquor traffic in all of its forms;

> 2. That we respectfully but very earnestly request the proper officers of our national government not to issue privilege taxes for the sale of liquor where its sale is prohibited by the laws of the State:

> 3. That we urge our Senators and Representatives in Congress to pass some measure to prevent the shipment of liquor into dry territory;

4. That we will preach temperance, practice temperance, pray for temperance, and vote for temperance;

5. That we urge people everywhere not to vote for anyone for any office who is known to be in sympathy with the liquor traffic;

6. That we express our joy and our deep gratitude to God because of the fact that since the last meeting of this Convention the prohibition territory in the bounds of the Convention has very largely increased, and we declare our purpose as Southern Baptists, joining hands with our brethren of other denominations and with every one who loves the churches and the homes and the schools, not to cease our efforts until every vestige of this accursed liquor traffic has been entirely banished from our land;

7. That this Convention appoint a standing committee of fifteen brethren, to be known as a Committee on Temperance, whose duty it shall be to promote in every way possible the cause of temperance, until there shall not be a licensed saloon in our land, and until the whole liquor traffic shall be banished not only from our land, but from all lands;

8. That a copy of these resolutions be furnished to the presiding officers and chairmen of the proper committees in each branch of Congress, to the Governor of each State of the South, and that the press be requested to publish them.[4]

As a standing committee, the Committee on Temperance was the forerunner of the Social Service Commission, which would become the Christian Life Commission, and eventually take the form of the present Ethics & Religious Liberty Commission.

Along with the temperance initiative, Southern Baptists also addressed other issues that were of grave concern. In 1907, Southern Baptists passed resolutions advocating world peace, pleading for law and order, which had as its end "to take away the reproach resting on civilization and religion by the prevalence of crime and lynchings," and against the liquor traffic. The next year the resolution establishing the

Temperance Committee dominated the scene. In 1909, a Resolution on International Justice requested the U.S. Government to take steps to protect missionaries overseas. It also approved a "Resolution on Cooperation with Other Baptists," but it actually contained a statement partnering with the Southern Negro Anti-Saloon Federation to oppose alcohol and advocate improved race relations. It also passed a "Resolution on Public Health" providing a hearty endorsement to the newly formed Department of Public Health. The following year we find a strong "Resolution on Child Labor" pleading that this abuse be abolished.[5]

At this point Arthur James Barton steps onto the scene of Baptist history as Chairman of the Committee on Temperance and eventually the Social Services Commission. He served Southern Baptists without pay until his death in 1942. Needless to say, he became a tireless advocate of Prohibition and a constant champion of morality in the United States. Barton, a Southern Baptist, worked in concert with the Anti-Saloon League, the most powerful temperance organization in the country. Speaking at the 1912 Southern Baptist Convention, Barton declared, "The bad citizenship of good men is not theory, but fact; not a dream, but a nightmare from which the Gospel must awaken us. . . . Let the clear, high note sound out from every pulpit and assemblying, leading the people of God in a higher and better social service than we have ever hitherto rendered, and marshalling the hosts of God for a victory sure and certain."[6]

By the next year Southern Baptists established the Social Service Commission.

For many years Barton brought detailed reports to the Southern Baptist Convention. He filled them with facts and statistics particularly reflecting his advocacy of Prohibition, but he also reported lobbying work done in Washington, D.C. and proposed actions and resolutions that could further the work of Southern Baptists in the arena of public policy. Although he often pleaded for financial support, the Convention would wait many years before providing necessary funding. Had it not been for the Baptist Sunday School Board's willingness to pick up Barton's expenses, much work might well have gone undone.

In 1913, Southern Baptists' involvement in the public policy arena took a major step forward as it established the Social Service Commission. "The Resolution on Christian Social Concerns" states,

> WHEREAS, The conflict this body, together with the Christian world, have waged upon the whiskey traffic, so specifically and successfully has broadened in its scope to include other such serious wrongs as the white slave traffic, and child labor, as promoted by Mr. John Rockefeller; therefore,
>
> RESOLVED, That without lessening our zeal in the matter of temperance, we broaden the scope of our endeavors by the appointment to deal with other such wrongs which curse society today, and call loudly for our help.
>
> RESOLVED, FURTHER, That there be appointed a standing committee upon Social Service, which committee shall report from year to year upon such other matters as should come before this body for discussion and action, to be called the Social Service Commission; and it be composed of seven members.[7]

Other resolutions during this time emphasized the desire for peace and the plea that disputes among nations be resolved without recourse to war. We also find another plea for law and order. Southern Baptists advocated supporting the development of the Baptist World Alliance while criticizing the Edinburg Missionary Conference because it did not recognize Baptist work in the "papal field." This provides a foreshadowing of Southern Baptists' decline when invited to join the World Council of Churches in years to come.[8]

Also during this time Southern Baptists reiterated their strong belief in the "complete separation of church and state." This resolution was really no surprise to anyone. As a common and often repeated theme, religious liberty and the separation of church and state are Baptist hallmarks. A strong reinforcement to this already important ideal is E. Y. Mullins's book *The Axioms of Religion*, and especially chapter 9, which addresses his "Religio-Civic Axiom: A Free Church in a Free State."[9]

Another resolution of significance occured in 1913 when Southern Baptists approved cooperation with the National Convention of Colored Baptists. The intention was to assist them to establish their own "Theological Seminary," with the prospect that "we will give practical financial assistance in such ways and by such means as may be determined upon hereafter." Integrating even theological education would have to wait for the next generation.[10]

Southern Baptists and their leaders early in the twentieth century were concerned about the unjust and unfair treatment of the black community. When William J. Northern, who served as Southern Baptist Convention president (1899, 1900, 1901), spoke at the Evangelical Ministers' Association of Atlanta in 1911, his topic was "Christianity and the Negro Problem in Georgia." This former governor of Georgia had previously led the state to make lynchings a felony. In this address he made a passionate plea for Christians to do everything necessary to affirm, educate, and protect the black citizens of Georgia. Identifying the acceptance of lynchings as a "criminal condition," he declared, "To you I make my final appeal for the preservation of our Christian civilization." He asserted, "In these criminal times it is my candid judgment the responsibility rests with the Christian element of our people."[11]

When the Social Service Commission met in its first year, William Louis Poteat was named the chairman. The reason Poteat received the office was because Barton was still chair of the Temperance Committee, and it was judged improper for him to chair both. The following year Barton stepped into the chairmanship of the Social Service Committee, maintaining that post until his death in 1942. Most observers believe that Barton was the perpetually preferred chair because Poteat, who served as president of Wake Forest College, a Baptist institution, favored evolution as the preferred explanation of how God brought life into existence. Because he did not embrace the Bible's literalism with respect to creation, Southern Baptists chose to look elsewhere for leadership.[12]

Barton, who was elected president of the National Conference on Temperance, worked diligently to oppose the liquor industry. As the

First World War approached, a greater and greater outcry surfaced, pleading for Prohibition in the United States. In the 1914 Convention, Southern Baptists went on record supporting Prohibition. Barton noted the SBC was the first general religious body to do so. In the report of the Social Service Commission brought by Poteat, a litany of moral and social issues were raised, not simply Prohibition.[13]

Even though the Southern Baptist Convention met only days following the sinking of the *Lusitania* (May 7, 1915), in which 128 American citizens died, the Convention remained focused on the approaching battle over alcohol. We must note that Barton was a principal architect of the congressional resolution for the proposed Eighteenth Amendment to the Constitution. Barton's chief activity in 1916 and 1917 was focused on securing the necessary votes in the various states to pass the Eighteenth Amendment.[14]

On April 6, 1917, the United States entered the First World War. In just a year and half, over 117,000 men were killed before November 11, 1918, when an armistice was signed. The war officially concluded with the Treaty of Versailles in 1919. More devastating in terms of human life than the war, however, was the world-wide flu epidemic between September 1918 and June 1919, in which more than 675,000 Americans died.[15]

With respect to the efforts for Prohibition and the Eighteenth Amendment, Nebraska became the thirty-sixth state to ratify, and with that vote Prohibition officially became the law of the land, going into effect on January 16, 1920.

Before moving into the Prohibition era, resolutions on religious liberty promoted repeatedly by the Social Service Commission were proposed and passed at each Southern Baptist Convention from 1913 until 1920, with the exception of 1918. Of particular interest is the 1919 "Resolution on Religious Liberty," where Southern Baptists affirmed:

> WHEREAS, During many centuries, in various countries
> of the globe, the driven, wandering Jews have suffered terrible
> persecutions and massacres, sometimes at the hands of profess-
> edly Christian nations; and

WHEREAS, All right-thinking men, and especially Christians, should let their voice be heard for the justice, humanity, mercy, forgiveness, and love of true Christianity, as taught by the Lord Jesus Christ; therefore, be it

RESOLVED, That we, the Southern Baptist Convention, do hereby respectfully petition Woodrow Wilson, President of the United States, and other officials of our Government, as soon as deemed advisable, to intercede with the governments of Europe for an International Conference to consider the conditions of the Jews, and to adopt such measures as may be deemed wise for their relief.[16]

Although Barton's work was still not funded by the Southern Baptist Convention, 1919 saw him working with J. B. Gambrell to recommend the $75 Million Campaign. Gambrell, in his presidential address, challenged the Convention with these words:

We stand today with many doors open before us and the inevitable "many adversaries." Let us gird up our loins and go forward. Baptists have always flourished by meeting issues bravely. It is my deep conviction that this Convention ought to adopt a program for work commensurate with the reasonable demands on us and summon ourselves and our people to a new demonstration of the value of orthodoxy in free action.[17]

The appointed committee of twenty-nine leaders met immediately, adopting the goal of $75 million which would be subscribed to immediately and paid out over a five-year period. Although Barton lobbied diligently for the campaign, still the Social Service Commission did not receive anything from the allotment.

The Prohibition Era (1920–1933)

When the 1920 Southern Baptist Convention met, Campaign Director Lee Scarborough announced that more than $92 million had been pledged with more than $12 million already collected. Still no money was allocated for the Social Service Commission. Barton, still jubilant over the victory for prohibition, declared, "This is the Victory Convention" for prohibition.[18]

At the 1920 Convention, three resolutions were passed concerning the Southern Baptist opposition to alcohol, and two more related to drugs, particularly opium production in India. Of particular importance was the resolution promoted by the Social Service Commission, which states:

> WHEREAS, Prohibition is now a part of the Constitution of the United States and is no longer a political question, but a question of respect for and the enforcement of law, a question of the authority of the whole people expressed in law, and

> WHEREAS, The brewers and their paid attorneys are making every possible effort to circumvent and nullify the law by making beer and wine the entering wedge for the return of the saloon; and

> WHEREAS, The said brewers and their paid attorneys claim that there is a reaction in the public mind against prohibition; therefore be it

> RESOLVED, By the Southern Baptist Convention in annual session assembled in Washington, D.C., May 12–17, 1920, with 8,000 messengers enrolled representing a constituency of 3,000,000 white Baptists, that we hereby respectfully and earnestly petition each of the two great political parties of the United States to put a plank in their respective platforms to be adopted at their approaching National Conventions declaring strongly for the maintenance and enforcement of the Eighteenth Amendment to the Constitution and of the law enacted for its enforcement.

> Second, that we also petition said parties not to nominate any man for the Presidency who is not known to be committed to this policy of law and order.

> Third, That the Committee on Temperance and Social Service be and the same is hereby authorized and instructed to

communicate a copy of these resolutions to the Chairman of the Executive Committee of each of the two great parties.[19]

Even though Southern Baptists pushed hard for Prohibition's enforcement, many other issues were pressing as well. While Southern Baptists were advocating for a more fair treatment of their black neighbors, as a whole they were not yet ready to embrace integration and honest equality. In his 1920 address to Southern Baptists, Barton addressed issues related to what he called the "Negro race." Maintaining the posture of institutionalized segregation, Barton affirmed that there would be "no change in the matter of individual social relations. . . . If any member of either race desires or cherishes hope [for social integration] he is doomed to disappointment." Barton then proceeded to call for "better housing conditions, . . . better economic and industrial opportunity," and "even more evenhanded justice in the courts" for the black community. He concluded by saying, "We white Baptists of the South . . . must . . . give to the Negro race the helping hand of a brother in all these matters." Because of the prevailing cultural standards of the time, this was apparently as far as Barton dared go.[20]

At this Convention Lee Scarborough offered a formal resolution to discontinue the Committee on Temperance and permit the Social Service Commission to absorb its responsibilities. Yet, the Convention declined to underwrite the work of the Commission.[21]

The Nineteenth Amendment, giving women the right to vote, passed on August 18, 1920, when Tennessee became the critical thirty-sixth state to ratify the amendment. Although it became the law of the land on August 26, 1920, surprisingly, Southern Baptists, as a corporate body, remained silent, neither encouraging nor discouraging its ratification.

During the decade leading up to the beginning of the Great Depression (1929), Southern Baptists' work with respect to the great moral issues of their day maintained a torrid pace. The nation continued to progress with great optimism yet much remained to be done.

In 1921 a terrible race riot exploded in Tulsa, Oklahoma, with eighty-nine deaths. Several years later President Harding died suddenly.

On the heels of his death, reports surfaced of his adultery and corruption. The Teapot Dome Scandal eventually sent Secretary of the Interior Albert Fall to jail for leasing oil reserves in Wyoming to his friends. During this time, concern over immigration climaxed, and as a result, Congress curtailed the number of immigrants allowed into the country. Meanwhile, crime (especially bootlegging illegal alcohol) continued to escalate. In 1925, Dayton, Tennessee, hosted the notorious Scopes Trial in which the law prohibiting the teaching of evolution was challenged but upheld. Biblical creationism was under an ongoing attack. In 1927, Charles Lindbergh made his historic flight from New York to Paris, the same year that introduced talking movies. The following year Herbert Hoover was elected president of the United States, and the Kellogg-Briand Pact, which supposedly outlawed war, was embraced. The year 1929, known for the Chicago-gangland Valentine's Day Massacre, saw the automobile replace cotton as the United States' top export. And October 29, Black Tuesday, marked the stock market crash and recorded what economist John K. Galbraith calls, "the most devastating day in the history of markets."[22]

During this decade of upheaval, we find Southern Baptists going through some interesting transitions. First, Southern Baptists approved the 1925 Baptist Faith and Message. Much of the impetus for finally embracing their own confession was the reaction both to the Fundamentalist-Modernist Controversy among northern Baptists and the threat to biblical Christianity being posed by the growing evolution-science alliance. A second notable development was the climax of the $75 Million Campaign and the birth of the Cooperative Program. Proposed in 1924, it was adopted and implemented the following year.[23]

While these mark advances for Southern Baptists, scandal also threatened the credibility of their agencies. In 1927, G. N. Sanders, treasurer for the Foreign Mission Board, was exposed as having embezzled more than $103,000. The following year, Clinton S. Carnes, treasurer of the Home Mission Board, reportedly stole almost a million dollars from the board. Both of these thefts created tremendous strain on the two boards, not to mention the overall fiscal credibility of the Southern Baptist Convention. It is little wonder that the Social

Service Commission remained unfunded by the Southern Baptist Convention during this period.[24]

The Social Service Commission, nonetheless, remained steadfast in its endeavors and continued to address issues supporting Prohibition, pleading for racial understanding, cautioning against the corrupting potential of the movies, lamenting the persecution of Christians, especially the Armenian Genocide by the Young Turks, advocating world peace and affirming the Kellogg-Briand Pact.

One interesting entry, probably motivated by W. L Poteat, who had become a labor activist while he remained on the Social Service Commission board, is contained in Barton's 1921 report to the Convention, in which he states, "The struggle between Capital and Labor has often been unequal, with the odds against Labor. . . . We record our deepest interest in the welfare of the laboring masses. . . . Let us preach the gospel of peace and brotherhood and service; and let both Capital and Labor avoid all extremes and each seek the other's good."[25]

At each Southern Baptist Convention, we find periodic resolutions which address in very pointed fashion some of the great issues of the day. In the aftermath of World War I, this resolution was offered "On World Peace":

> Whereas, The matter of the reconstruction of the world upon a permanent peace basis, is the supreme question of the present,
>
> And whereas, The adjustment of the perplexing world-problem which is filling all nations with unrest, can only be made by the use of those spiritual forces that have been especially committed to the churches,
>
> And whereas, The ethical principles of the Gospel of our Lord are the changeless truths both for personal and national life of the whole world,
>
> And whereas, there is a wide-spread expression that it would be wise and timely to call a conference of representatives of the leading nations to discuss in a friendly way, the question of disarmament,

Resolve, First; That, as a Convention of Christians, we
are glad to join other bodies in an endorsement of this seemingly, practical movement toward disarmament with the hope
and prayer that our torn and bleeding world may be restored
to peace under the guidance and benediction of the Prince of
Peace,

Resolved, Second; That, a copy of this Resolution be sent
to the President of the United States and to the Secretary of
State.[26]

In 1929, in what appears to be a simple support of Prohibition,
we find a resolution with considerable political teeth, which is actually
more in keeping with the traditional Baptist position of engagement in
the public arena of moral concerns:

4. Resolved, That we give our continued hearty support,
both moral and financial, to the Anti-Saloon League and the
Woman's Christian Temperance Union as the two great nationwide organizations through which our people have cooperated
effectively for the overthrow of the legalized liquor traffic and
through which we may continue to cooperate effectively for the
perpetuation of prohibition, for the creation and maintenance
of a proper sentiment for law enforcement and for the education
of the masses concerning the evils and destructiveness of strong
drink.

5. Resolved, That we express the hope that the Anti-Saloon
League will strengthen its organization and work within the
bounds of the Convention by replacing in any state any super-
intendent who may be superannuated, or for any other reason
may be incapable of aggressive organization, work and leadership, with a wise, capable and vigorous leader.

6. Resolved, That we commend especially the work of the
new department of education which the Anti-Saloon League has
established as furnishing a good and efficient agency and means
for the general dissemination of the truth about the evil and

destructive character of alcoholic beverages and the facts about prohibition.

7. Resolved, That we reaffirm our former action heretofore repeatedly taken that as citizens we will not support for President any candidate committed to the repeal of National Prohibition and that in every proper and legitimate way we will seek to accomplish the defeat of any such candidate, no matter of what political party he may be nominated.[27]

Notice that resolve "7." states, "We (Southern Baptists) will not support for President any candidate committed to the repeal of National Prohibition and that in every proper and legitimate way we will seek to accomplish the defeat of any such candidate, no matter of what political party he may be nominated." In short, Southern Baptists declared to the nation their decision not to support, or work to defeat, candidates who do not hold to our values. There was no law restricting churches from endorsing or opposing candidates until the middle of the twentieth century. For those who have studied the past, the present-day status quo is nothing short of government intrusion into the church's free exercise of religion and freedom of speech.[28]

At the same 1929 Southern Baptist Convention, Barton, commenting on both the pro-liquor press and the pro-liquor politicians, noted that their methods were to use vindictive criticism and slanderous charges to stop Prohibition forces. Because of this heated opposition, Barton believed it necessary to explain some of the Social Service Commission's fundamental principles related to Baptist polity with respect to the great national moral issues and government. At this point he launched into a long essay that expressed his own understanding of the critical importance played by the Social Service Commission. Here is what he said. Notice that Barton began by laying a foundation of Baptist polity and from there developed his argument of engagement in public policy issues:

—Membership and participation in every Baptist body is voluntary.

—No Baptist body can bind, nor seeks to bind the conscience of any individual, either in politics or in religion.

—The kingdom of God is promoted primarily by preaching
the gospel, and bringing people to know Christ.

—The kingdom of God has to do with the whole life of the
individual and with the whole social order.

—Baptists in all bodies and positions are within their rights
when they become the antagonists of evil and the promoters
of good [in society], whether in the realm of private morals or
public morals.

—Baptist bodies are in no sense . . . concerned with partisan politics, . . . but only with the great matters of vital civic
righteousness and public morality.[29]

Barton then embarked into a long discourse on the relation of
government and religion:

—The Baptist position has always been and always will be
the complete separation of church and state.

—The union of church and state has usually been sought
by ambitious ecclesiastical bodies and dignitaries who despise
voluntariness as the basis of all true religion.

—This union has expressed itself mainly in . . . levies on all
citizens for the support of the established religion and invok-
ing of the sword of the state by ecclesiastical authorities for the
imposition of religious faith upon all and the punishment of dissenters and heretics.

—Separation of church and state is the priceless heritage of
our American civilization, purchased largely by the preaching
and suffering of the Baptists.

—The fact that church and state are separated does not
mean that they are in no way related or that they do not act
and react each on the other. . . . Each has its duties and functions. . . . Each influences and affects the character and work of
the other. As concerning religion, the sole function of the state
is to guarantee to all the right to worship as . . . consciences

may direct and to guarantee them quiet and peace in the free
observance of all their religious beliefs and forms so long as
such beliefs and forms shall not interfere with the rights of others or with the public peace and morals.

—The church, as the symbol of organized religion, is concerned with beliefs, with faith and with the making of character
and influencing and determining conduct and actions which
are the expression of character. The church contributes more
to the making of right character than all other agencies combined. . . . Hence, it is the largest factor in producing the right
kind of material for building a worthy and permanent state.

—Government is ordained of God, and public officials are
the ministers of God, not for the promotion of religion, but for
the promotion of their peace, happiness and welfare.

—Since God is the author and human welfare the end of
government, . . . the government has no moral right to ally itself
with evil and to barter the health and happiness, the peace and
prosperity of its citizens.

—When the government does ally itself with evil, every citizen not only has the right but is duty bound to "cry aloud and
spare not."[30]

As usual, after Barton defined his public philosophy of social and
moral engagement, he reported on the most pressing events of the
previous year.

By the Southern Baptist Convention, which met in New Orleans
in 1930, America had changed; the public mood transitioned from
optimism to near despair in many quarters. On October 29, 1929, the
stock market suffered its worst crash in history. It is not surprising that
the request for funding for the Social Service Commission, although
needed and legitimate, again fell on deaf ears.

No doubt the lack of funding had a double sting for Barton, who
not only was refused funding but also had taken notice that in recent
years the Methodists opened a half-million dollar headquarters in
Washington, D.C., "devoted exclusively to the work of temperance and

social service." Barton noted that "other denominations are increasing their equipment and effort in this field" and then concluded, "We who pride ourselves on our evangelical views of the gospel . . . ought not to lag behind others in any department of Christian activity."[31]

By the time the Convention met in New Orleans (1930), Baptists all over the country, like everyone else, were feeling the sting of the onslaught of the Great Depression. In response to these economically trying times, the Social Service Commission recommended the following resolution, which Southern Baptists adopted:

> Concerning Industrial Relations:
>
> 1. That we recognize the right of labor to organize and engage in collective bargaining.
>
> 2. That we recognize the right of laborers who may not wish to join a labor organization to employment.
>
> 3. That we believe in a fair living wage for all who toil in factory and mine.
>
> 4. That we favor a day of not more than nine hours and a week of not more than forty-nine and one-half hours.
>
> 5. That we are opposed to the employment in factory or mine of children under fifteen years of age and we are opposed to all night work for women and minors.
>
> 6. That we favor good sanitary housing conditions for all factory and mine workers, such as will properly protect both the health and morals of their families.
>
> 7. That the teachings and spirit of the Gospel ought to control in all industrial relations and that they offer the only happy and peaceful solution of all our industrial problems.

Nonetheless, at this point, not much could be done to offset the sting of the growing depressed economic climate.[32]

The following year, the Executive Committee reported to the 1931 Convention on Barton's most recent request for funding. The committee said it "deeply appreciate[d]" the work of the Social Service Commission and "especially that of its Chairman, Dr. A. J. Barton." They recognized "the fact that the Commission could render a larger service if more funds were at its disposal." However, in view of the ongoing depression, the Committee did not deem it wise to authorize a headquarters for the agency. They encouraged the Sunday School Board to continue helping with expenses for meetings "as it had in previous years."[33]

Although Barton had done everything in his power to rally the troops, by 1932 the permanency of Prohibition was becoming more and more called into question. And although Southern Baptists passed in one form or another some resolution on alcohol each year of the Prohibition era, forces that would benefit from alcohol's legalization continued to promote their cause.

In 1932, Franklin D. Roosevelt was elected president of the United States in a landslide . Under his leadership, prohibition was repealed with the passage of the Twenty-first Amendment to the Constitution of the United States. Yet these final years saw the Social Service Commission addressing more issues than simply the evils of alcohol and the liquor industry. In fact, from 1931 to 1933, the Southern Baptist Convention at the Social Service Commission's behest, passed resolutions on religious liberty, divorce, the international court of justice, tobacco, gambling, and lynchings.

Barton gave a valiant effort in his attempt to maintain prohibition. In his 1933 Social Service Commission address to the Convention, he noted how Hoover, a Prohibition candidate, had been elected four years earlier, and lamented the prospect of days to come, conceding that "the long continued and terrible depression . . . created a demand for a change of administration, regardless of every other issue."[34]

With a Democratic Congress and a Democratic President, the repeal of the Eighteenth Amendment by passing and ratifying the Twenty-first Amendment would soon be law. Barton noted that a majority in Congress had been elected as "dry" and then turned once in office. Concerning their reversal, he declared that it "will go down in history as the greatest betrayal of a public trust and the greatest blow to the economic and moral welfare of the people." The Twenty-first Amendment was ratified on December 5, 1933, and alcohol again flowed throughout the land.[35]

One interesting development happened at the 1933 Convention. After the Social Service Commission report made by Barton omitted a request for funds that would provide an office and operating capital, Edwin McNeil Poteat, nephew of W. L. Poteat, moved to amend the report of the Social Service Commission by adding the following motion: "Believing that the time has come for a more comprehensive and direct dealing with the great social issues in the South, we move that a committee be appointed to consider the advisability of creating an agency of Social Research in connection with the Social Service Commission to study these pressing social problems, and to furnish as far as possible guidance for the definitive work of the Convention in the field." Surprisingly, the motion carried and a study committee was appointed, with the younger Poteat named as the chairman by SBC President, M. E. Dodd. Barton, surprised and suspicious of the motion, declined to serve.[36]

The Post-Prohibition Era (1934–1946)

The year 1934 ushered in the post-Prohibition era along with the multiple plans of Roosevelt's New Deal legislation. At the 1934 Convention, Barton, along with others, approved the younger Poteat's proposals. Although the appointed committee recommended hiring "A Secretary (Director) of Social Research" who would head the "Bureau of Social Research" and, "not be under the control of any agency of the Convention" that might "interfere with objective" reports of "studies," Barton opposed it. No doubt he viewed Poteat's recommendation with suspicion, perhaps even an end run around long-established precedent and direction, not to mention the fact that many viewed Poteat as potential trouble. By 1936, the recommendation to establish a "Bureau of Social Research" was dead in the water.[37]

In the years leading up to the Second World War, President Roosevelt was elected two more times to serve as America's president. During that time the New Deal saw multiple programs launched in an attempt to bolster America's people and their economy. The Social Security Act was passed during this time, and it created no small stir among Baptist ministers.

In the world of A. J. Barton, moral and social issues continued to keep him extremely busy. In his 1935 report to the Southern Baptist Convention, he again reminded the messengers that all the work done by the Social Service Commission, "has been done without compensation." He expressed his gratitude to the Sunday School Board for its kind assistance in covering expenses. His report covered the usual concerns with a new wrinkle. He drew attention to the gathering war clouds over Europe. He explained that the "repudiation of the Versailles Treaty by Germany and the setting up of a great military establishment by the Reich made the situation acute in all Europe."[38]

By 1936, along with the normal litany of moral issues, Barton declared, "We see no just ground for the enormous military and naval establishment now being built up and maintained at the expense of approximately one billion dollars a year." Barton was clearly an opponent of what he perceived as an unnecessary arms race. One wonders if he would have embraced that policy if he could have foreseen the events as they unfolded in the next few years.[39]

In 1936, the Southern Baptist Convention changed the name of the Committee on Chaplains, established during the First World War, to the Committee on Public Relations. It enlarged its work, "to confer, to negotiate, to demand just rights that are threatened or to have other inescapable dealings with the American or other [in the United States] Governments." By 1939, this committee worked in cooperation with the Northern Baptist Convention and eventually embraced nine different Baptist bodies. The principal task was to represent Baptist interests with respect to religious liberty issues.[40]

By 1936, the New Deal legislation was threatening some Baptist distinctives concerning religious liberty and the separation of church and state. In a 1936 Resolution on Freedom of Religion, Southern Baptists adopted the position, "That we hereby reaffirm our devotion to the fundamental New Testament doctrine and fundamental principle of the American Government, the separation of church and state; religion must be kept free from all entangling alliances with government and government must not assume patronage, sponsorship or control over religion in any form." This resolution concludes by stating that "we would enter our earnest protest against the violation of this principle by any Baptist church or Baptist institution or by others, and especially against the appropriation of public funds to sectarian institutions of whatever name or order."[41]

At this same Convention, Southern Baptists received and approved a "Resolution on Communism," which states, "Resolved, that this Convention warns its constituency, fellow Christians and all patriotic citizens to be discriminatingly alert and watchful with reference to the insidious encroachments of Atheistic Communism in every form."[42]

In 1937 and 1938, America became increasingly isolationist in its foreign policy. In many ways Southern Baptists were supportive of this direction and expressed their sentiments in the 1937 resolution:

> WHEREAS, We recognize the wide gulf existing between
> the varied practices of our modern society and the principles of
> Christianity;
>
> AND WHEREAS, We feel a deep sense of shame that
> many of these sins and problems exist because of our indifference to them;
>
> AND WHEREAS, We believe that a firm stand expressing
> our conviction and willingness to act will do much to eradicate
> some of these evils; therefore, be it
>
> RESOLVED,
>
> A. International Relationships;
>
> 1. We recognize that a warless world is the Christian ideal
> and that we Christians should throw all our weight and power
> into the balance for peace.
>
> 2. That we petition the President of the United States to
> consider the advisability of calling a conference of world powers
> to consider the possibility of disarmament, believing that this
> would do much to relieve strained international relationships
> which are endangering world peace at the present time.[43]

W. L. Poteat, who served on the Social Service Commission with Barton since its inception, died in March just prior to the 1938 Southern Baptist Convention. Although Barton and Poteat simply agreed to disagree on the theory of origins, they were two old warhorses who had braved many a battle on the social and moral front. At the 1938 Convention, Barton memorialized his old friend, calling him "a conspicuous figure" and a man "keenly interested in social righteousness," of whom the Convention felt sorrow "in the death of one of its valuable and valued members."[44]

Barton's report to the 1938 Convention was the longest in SBC history. Again, it covered numerous social and moral issues. Religious liberty, management-labor relations, race relations and the sinfulness of lynchings, the evils of a national lottery, alcohol, and child labor were all addressed. One issue not addressed was the need for more money. By this time Barton seemed to have given up on ever having a funded Social Service Commission, at least in his life-time. The following year's report and resolutions were similar. One interesting resolution, On Christian Education, resolves, "that the Baptists throughout the South be urged to acquaint themselves with the abundant opportunities afforded in our Baptist schools and colleges and to assist in turning Baptist students to them that the future for Christian education and Christian democracy, even Christian civilization itself, may be guarded with jealous care." Also included was a "Resolution on America and China's Invasion," which denounced any role that America played "in this war of conquest." It notes, "We understand and sympathize with the normal needs of Japan, but these cannot justify the imperialism of the militaristic regime by which the human rights of another people are ruthlessly disregarded."[45]

In September 1939, war broke out in Europe when Germany invaded Poland, and Great Britain and France responded by declaring war on the aggressor. On September 5, Roosevelt issued an official proclamation to the world declaring the neutrality of the United States. This was modified by November so that the United States could at least assist the Allies with materials.[46]

In 1940, Barton, who held virtually a conscientious objector position on war, noted that "we hate war with an intensity which cannot be expressed in words." He went on to say, however, "But we do not believe that the Christian Spirit forbids purely defensive war." Yet most of his address still focused on the moral issues of the day.[47]

The Southern Baptist Convention met in Birmingham, Alabama, in 1941. By this time almost everyone could see that America was being drawn into the war against the Axis powers. Since the Convention had last met, the U.S. government had registered more than sixteen million men for a "peacetime draft." In December 1940, Roosevelt, after his third election, called for the U.S. to become an "arsenal of democracy." Congress supported the prospective war effort by appropriating seven billion dollars in Lend-Lease aid to the Allies. By May 1941, Roosevelt declared an unlimited state of national emergency.[48]

At the 1941 Southern Baptist Convention, a "Resolution on Peace" dwarfed all other presentations and proposals by staking a claim for the war, which at that point seemed almost inevitable. In this resolution common themes were again sounded, yet without the naïve hope that America might somehow avoid the conflict. It was now abundantly clear that the world and its war was increasingly being perceived in terms of a titanic struggle between good and evil, with the outcome uncertain, but U.S. involvement now almost inevitable. Because of the importance of this resolution, it is replicated here in its entirety, along with two related resolutions adopted at that Convention:

> WHEREAS, Southern Baptists constitute one of the largest democratic and evangelical bodies of Christians in the United States; and whereas they have over 25,000 churches with more than 5,000,000 bona fide members; and whereas some 10,000 members and "messengers" (or delegates) from these churches are meeting in Annual Convention in Birmingham, Ala., May 14–18, 1941, they feel it incumbent upon them and altogether appropriate for them to declare publicly certain of their clear convictions at this time of world crisis, in order that our burdened President, Franklin D. Roosevelt, and our National Government may be appraised of the sentiments and convictions of the great majority of this body of patriotic and liberty-loving citizens. While they thus record and publish their sentiments and convictions by majority vote in Convention assembled, they

fully recognize and respect the inalienable right of conscientious objectors to hold and to voice contrary sentiments and conviction if they deem it wise to do so.

Therefore, Be it Resolved, by the Convention:

1. That we declare our abhorrence of war and all its insanity and brutality. We are a peace-loving people and we know of no issues, national or international, which could not be settled in fairness and equity by the orderly processes of civilized society if only the leaders of the nations were willing to practice the principles of justice, truth, and righteousness. We sincerely believe that the rank and file of our denomination, even as the rank and file of our nation and the other nations as well, much prefer that all international disputes and conflicting interests be composed by the processes of peace rather than by the arbitrament of war. But unfortunately men of evil mind and ungodly heart sometimes gain control within a nation, or nations, and with cruel and deadly intent thrust war upon the world in order to gratify their lust for glory and power and fancied gains for themselves and their associates. Such men at the present time have criminally conspired to impose their anti-social, anti-Christian, and anti-human wills upon much of the world. With fiendish force and diabolical scheming they have overrun Europe and threaten to gain the mastery over Asia and Africa. Human rights, freedoms, and liberties have promptly gone into eclipse wherever the power of these ruthless men have been established. They hold nothing as sacred, and they regard with scorn many of the treasured achievements of mankind. They deny the physical, intellectual, moral, social, economic, and spiritual rights and liberties of all who in any way oppose them. In other words, their principles and their practices are the absolute antithesis of everything we have been taught to believe is in line with the will of God, the mind of Christ and the kingdom of God on earth. If these men are allowed to attain their announced worldwide aims and goals, then many of the values which we esteem as more precious than life itself will be

lost, and the world will be immeasurably impoverished socially, politically, culturally, and spiritually. We know not what course others may pursue but as for us we hold it were better to be dead than to live in a world dominated by the ideals of these modern dictators.

2. We declare our belief that some things are worth dying for; and if they are worth dying for they are worth living for; and if they are worth living for they are worth defending even unto the death. Among these are liberty under law, that sacred shrine called home, wives and children, the honor of one's country, and last but not least freedom of worship. "Is life so dear or peace so sweet as to be purchased at the price of chains and slavery" forged by some cruel and godless tyrant? "Forbid it Almighty God!" Thus was it prayed in other days when a tyrant sought to enslave our colonial Fathers. We believe that Almighty God made answer to that prayer through the deeds of those fathers from Lexington to Yorktown. Our Baptist Fathers opposed that tyrant and we, their spiritual descendants, are ready to oppose any other tyrant who impiously aspires to deprive us of any of our God-given and inalienable rights. Shall we have a vision of eternal values less clear than had those early American Fathers? Shall we in our strength forfeit those price-less values which they purchased with their blood and in their weakness? May Almighty God forbid that also!

3. Baptists are a democratic people—none more so. Therefore, it is nothing but natural that our deepest sympa-thies should go out to those democracies of the world which have been crushed for the time being or now are sorely beset by ruthless powers which are committed to the overthrow of all democracies. We are convinced that England's heroic resistance to the Axis powers is one of the great sagas of the human Spirit. We, like the great majority of people in the United States, are in thorough sympathy with the efforts being made by our nation to reinforce England in many ways as she fights not only for her own life, but also, and incidentally,

fights a terrible battle for the other democratic nations of the world. It will be most gratifying to us if these efforts of the United States to reinforce England can be multiplied and be made increasingly effective. We trust our Government to work out the wisest and most effective means to aid England, our national ally, in this titanic struggle.

We desire to register with our Government our clear conviction that the United States and her citizens should promptly cease supplying Japan with materials which enable her to continue her war of conquest against China.

We also urge our Government to quicken rather than slacken all measures needed to strengthen the defenses of the Western Hemisphere against all kinds of aggression from any and all powers which seek to undermine and to overthrow our peaceful and democratic ways of life.

4. We pledge ourselves as Christian patriots to pray earnestly unto our God and Saviour that a righteous peace may soon be granted unto all the warring nations: that our own nation may be spared the horrors of war, if that be the divine will, and that our nation may be used as a mighty instrument of peace and truth and righteousness and brotherhood; that Almighty God will, in the power of his might, take charge of the nations and overrule their folly and sin to the praise of his great and holy name.

RESOLUTION III

WHEREAS, The nations of the world are at this moment engaged in one of the most tragic wars of human history, a war that is ruthless in its attack upon human life and upon all human values, both material and spiritual, and

WHEREAS, The role of our own nation in this international conflict becomes daily of increasing significance to all, and

WHEREAS, Not in all history has there been a greater need for divine vision and guidance on the part of these nations as each in his own way looks forward to the day when this war shall cease.

WHEREAS, The Word of God and the testimony of believers to the Living Christ point the way to divine wisdom and guidance, adequate to the needs of this grave hour, therefore,

Be it RESOLVED, That the Southern Baptist Convention, assembled in its ninety-sixth year in Birmingham, Alabama, do on this day, May 15, 1941, reaffirm its faith in the power of prayer and in the leadership of the Holy Spirit.

Be it RESOLVED, That with one accord we turn to Almighty God, through Christ his Son, in humble petition for the forgiveness of whatever measure of corporate guilt may be ours with regard to the present international conflict, and, that our nation, through repentance and faith in the Lord Jesus Christ may be so yielded to the Divine Plan, that we may be effectively used in helping to bring to the nations of the world a just and righteous peace.

Be it further RESOLVED, That we invite the membership of our churches and all Christian believers throughout the world, to pray daily at a given hour, both in public and in private places, to the end that such a "just and righteous peace" may be speedily achieved. And,

Be it further RESOLVED, That as Christians we recognize that there may be honest differences of opinion about the issue in the present conflict, but we are deeply resolved that any difference shall not cause any breach in our fellowship.

Be if further RESOLVED, That the officers of this Convention constitute a committee which shall seek to carry out the spirit of this resolution, to lend itself to the advancement of such Christian ideals as should lead to the establishment and maintenance of a just and righteous peace; shall call our people everywhere in unceasing intercession, and that this committee be instructed to put this resolution into effect at once.

RESOLUTION VI

WHEREAS, The Southern Baptist Convention in session at Birmingham, May 16, 1941, affirmed its loyalty to the United States Government, and its devotion to the ideals of its founding fathers, and

WHEREAS, The aforesaid resolution [offered by Powhatan W. James] may be misinterpreted by some as a committal to the principle of militarism, Therefore, be it resolved that the aforesaid resolution, in no way commits the Southern Baptist Convention to an approval of war, as a recognized principle in settling international differences.[49]

At the 1941 Convention, Barton was already suffering pain from the illness that subsequently took his life. In what would be his final appearance at the Southern Baptist Convention, he explained his methodology in drafting the annual Social Service Commission report for review by his fellow commissioners for presentation to the Convention. After "gathering and filing source material," he would spend "three months in organizing and classifying the material for the report and in the preparation of the report itself." In the 1941 report, Barton confided it had "been prepared under rather severe handicaps." And in his first-ever mention of health problems, he related the presence of "a prolonged attack of influenza which had disabled" him for six weeks. The 1941 report, thirteen pages long, addressed the normal ongoing concerns accompanied by six proposed resolutions, all of which were adopted: race relations, crime, freedom of religion, accidents, liquor, and usurpation of power by legislators in a way that ignored the rights of voters.[50]

On December 7, 1941, the inevitable finally occured. The Japanese Empire, without provocation, attacked Pearl Harbor, headquarters of the U.S. Pacific Fleet. On November 27, the U.S. government had issued secret "war warnings," which read, "Japanese future action unpredictable but hostile action possible at any moment. If hostilities cannot . . . be avoided the United States desires that Japan commit the first overt act." Within four hours of the attack, the U.S. lost eighteen warships and eighty-seven planes. In the attack, 1,178 military personnel were wounded and 2,403 were killed. In the words of President Roosevelt, it was "a day that will live in infamy." With the nation in shock and outrage, the United States declared war on Japan on December 8, 1941. The other Axis powers, Italy and Germany, in turn declared war on the United States.[51]

As the United States began its massive engagement in World War II, Southern Baptists lost a champion for the cause of righteousness. On July 19, 1942, A. J. Barton died in Nashville, Tennessee. Except for the initial year, 1913–1914, when W. L. Poteat chaired the Social Service Commission, Barton served as the unquestioned leader of the Commission. His tenure parallels the history of the agency. Barton must be recognized and celebrated as the founder and program builder of the little appreciated, especially in terms of financial support, Southern Baptist social concerns agency.[52]

Reflecting on Barton's influence, J. M. Dawson, who served as the executive director of the Baptist Joint Committee on Public Affairs from 1936 to 1953, said, "Few men in our ranks understood as well as he, the historic tradition, policies and principles of the Baptists, or were as loyal as he to them." Dawson went on to describe Barton: "Mighty as a preacher, heroic in achievement, spotless in character, tireless in his consecrated activities, fraternal and genial in his fellowships, boundless in his influence for righteousness, he has gone to unsurpassed, abundant reward, in our Father's house."[53]

When it became obvious that Barton would not be available to speak at the 1942 Southern Baptist Convention, the Commission elected J. B. Weatherspoon to succeed Barton as chairman. Barton had followed up by asking Weatherspoon to write the 1942 report to the Convention. By all appearances the transition in leadership was seamless, and Southern Baptists, under the leadership of the Social Service Commission, continued to address the critical moral and social issues of the day.[54]

When the leadership of the Commission changed, the operational headquarters of the Commission also changed. For Barton, Nashville and the Sunday School Board had been the most recent location. With Weatherspoon's ascension to leadership, the Southern Baptist

Theological Seminary in Louisville, Kentucky, where Weatherspoon had taught since 1929, became the new headquarters.

Weatherspoon, forever the diplomat, fell somewhere between Barton and Poteat in his theological convictions. He most certainly was not one who embraced biblical inerrancy. Yet neither was he on friendly terms with the northern liberal establishment, as had been the Poteats.

As a professor of homiletics at the Southern Baptist Theological Seminary, Weatherspoon was a tireless crusader for social justice. In an era when segregation went virtually unchallenged in the South, he often made other Baptist educators uneasy by writing to inquire if they offered opportunities for the education of black ministers. T. B. Maston, longtime professor of Christian ethics at South Western Baptist Theological Seminary, later credited Weatherspoon with serving as a conscience for the Convention in attitudes regarding race.[55]

Weatherspoon had not promoted himself as Barton's replacement. In fact, the 1942 report to the Southern Baptist Convention by the Social Service Commission was little more than four rambling pages, did not even include Weatherspoon's name, and was presented by the Tennessee commissioner, John W. McCall.[56]

Along with the familiar issues and a preoccupation with the war effort, several resolutions are worthy of mention. One resolution expressed a firm opposition and a critical resistance to the U.S. intentions of forming diplomatic relations with the Vatican. In a memorial addressing the war and sent to the president of the United States, the secretary of war, and the secretary of the navy, the Convention, in session, requested the nation's leaders take advantage of Southern Baptists' academic community in efforts to formalize a postwar public policy that would ensure a just and lasting peace. The religious community (the Southern Baptist Convention) saw absolutely no conflict in its offer with the common perception, which insisted on the absolutist perspective of separating church and state:

> WHEREAS, Southern Baptists as loyal citizens of the
> United States are cooperating and participating in all branches

of the present war, including the Army, the Navy, and the Air Corps, and

WHEREAS, The prosecution of the war for the maintenance, perpetuation and extension of our four freedoms, well known and enjoyed by American citizens in our constitutional democracy, may not accomplish the purposes for which it is fought unless a just and righteous peace follows the termination of the war, and

WHEREAS, It will be too late to make plans for a lasting peace if constructive and comprehensive plans are delayed until the conclusion of the war, and

WHEREAS, Our Baptist colleges and universities have on their faculties a number of renowned scholars in the fields of knowledge utterly necessary for making a worthy peace, and

WHEREAS, Three American statesmen who are in the highest ranking positions as chairmen of committees in the United States Senate, the treaty determining body of our Federal Government, Senator Tom Connally of Texas, Senator Walter F. George of Georgia, and Senator Josiah W. Bailey of North Carolina, being chairmen respectively of the Foreign Relations Committee, the Finance Committee, and the Commerce Committee, are graduates of our Baptist universities, Senator Connally of Baylor University, Senator George of Mercer University, and Senator Bailey of Wake Forest College,

Therefore be it RESOLVED, That the convention request the Education Commission to procure, assemble and transmit to our own three Christian statesmen a body of facts and principles involved in a Christian peace with the earnest hope that these facts and principles may be used in planning the new world order which may be in accordance with the sovereign will of God so that the paths of all mankind may ultimately be paths of peace.[57]

When the Executive Committee of the Southern Baptist Convention met on February 24, 1943, the decision was made to cancel the May Convention in response to the government's request. Since Southern Baptists would not meet that year, the decision was also made to have the Southern Baptist Convention president, Pat Neff, former governor of Texas and then president of Baylor University, address all Southern Baptists via radio. The address, "Christian Patriotism in a Chaotic World," hit numerous hot-button issues that crossed war concerns with the moral imperatives embraced by Southern Baptists. Although the entire address is well worth reading, the high point of Neff's message came when he observed:

> After the allied armies have made of German soil a victorious battlefield, after the war lords of Japan no longer lift their arrogant heads above the broken bulwarks of civilization, and after the totalitarian generals have been made to surrender their bloody swords on the open battlefield and not behind armistice doors, it will then be America's responsibility through her Christian patriots to take the lead in the formation of this federation of the nations. We should not dodge our responsibility and default as we did at the close of the other war. We won the last war but lost forever the peace. We refused to join the League of Nations. We scorned the world court. The clock of destiny struck, and we were so busy with radios, automobiles, refrigerators, bathtubs, gadgets, coupons, and partisan politics, we heard it not. Let us not default the second time.

No doubt Neff envisioned Christians taking a major role in crafting the postwar world as he reflected regrettably on the aftermath of the first Great War. Again, we find this as a common theme among Southern Baptists in the midst of the Second World War.[58]

As the Executive Committee prepared its 1943 proposed Convention operating budget, for the first time ever, a thousand dollars was designated to assist the Social Service Commission. Barton, not yet dead a year, would have rejoiced. Although not yet given a percentage allocation, at least the door had finally been cracked. Even though the distribution of funds waited for the following year, it was still a huge step in the right direction. At last, after many years of requests and pleading, the work of the Social Service Commission was finally transitioning to a funded effort.

The year the Convention did not meet, J. B. Weatherspoon's name appeared at the head of the Social Service Commission report for the first time. He paid tribute to his predecessor as "a distinguished member and untiring servant of our denomination." He expounded that although Barton did much in the denomination's life, his "chief interest was in the work of the Social Service Commission. . . . Year in and year out he keenly watched the currents, tides and eddies, and social morality in the nation, . . . putting his finger with remarkable accuracy on the spots of greatest danger and need, and urging with unabating insistence that Southern Baptists bestir themselves to the responsibilities of Christian citizenship." He concluded that the death of Barton "creates a crisis in the history" of the Commission. "Hitherto," Weatherspoon wrote, "We have depended almost wholly upon the Chairman; now of necessity there must be a division of responsibility and a wider collaboration."[59]

In his 1944 address Weatherspoon communicated a renewed blueprint for tackling social concerns. He addressed issues of race, peace, and alcohol. At this Convention, several long memorials were made about A. J. Barton and his influence for civic righteousness.[60]

Chairman Weatherspoon's report was prefaced by a wordy statement on "the Purpose and Work of the Social Service Commission." Its purpose, he noted, was to arouse "Christians to relate themselves in a Christian way to our common social life." He explained that the Commission's assignment was to keep before Southern Baptists three basic convictions. First, to "believe that the baseline of all social judgments and proposals is Christian moral teachings." Second, to "recognize that the social function of this Convention is not to promote social action as a substitute for evangelism and education, but rather to combine and coordinate . . . the three elements: evangelism, education, and action." Third, "the difficulty or the proximity of a problem should constitute a special challenge to Christians to give it their best."

He explained, "Organized Christianity should be in the vanguard of leadership in grappling with social wrongs that harass the people to whom it preaches." He concluded strongly that "pioneering for social justice must not be left to secular or political interests."[61]

Also in 1944, Weatherspoon presented a modus operandi of what he visualized as the agency's operating philosophy. First, collect and report information. Second, explain Christian responsibilities toward social problems. Third, recommend position statements for Convention adoption. The bottom line of "all social service recommendations and actions," he maintained, "should be the biblical teachings of Christian morality."[62]

Whereas Barton had been the crusader, Weatherspoon was more the planner, setting in motion the methodology that would be embraced for decades. In spite of the preoccupation with the war, the Social Service Commission continued to address other issues as they cropped up, even during wartime. The 1944 resolutions included concerns over Social Security, especially since it was perceived as a tax on the churches, a resolution on religious freedom in the Americas giving special attention to undue Roman Catholic influence in Latin America, and a new resolution on race relations. The same Convention also produced a resolution affirming the work of chaplains and encouraging the churches to assist the returning veterans into mainstream American life. As in past years, it is no surprise to find another resolution on alcohol.[63]

Because of the war, the 1945 Southern Baptist Convention, like the 1943 gathering, was postponed and the centennial celebration has delayed to the following year. Even so, 1945 was a dramatic year for America as well as Southern Baptists. On April 12, 1945, President Franklin D. Roosevelt passed away, and Harry S. Truman catapulted into the presidency. On May 7, Germany surrendered unconditionally to the Allies. Following a successful test in New Mexico on July 26, atomic bombs were dropped on Hiroshima (August 6), and Nagasaki (August 9), claiming in excess of 100,000 citizens. On August 14, Japan unconditionally surrendered, and the war was officially over. Instead of the long hoped—for peace, however, the haunting spectre of communism continued to hang over the world like a dark cloud.[64]

In the aftermath of the war, Weatherspoon turned his attention to what he considered his greatest issue of postwar America, the issue of race relations. At the 1946 Southern Baptist Convention meeting in Miami Beach, the following "Resolution on Race" is adopted along with the recommendation from the Social Service Commission:

WHEREAS, This unity is now endangered by the efforts of groups that are endeavoring to breed hate and confusion in our midst, and

WHEREAS, The faith we profess and the teachings of the Lord and Master we love and serve, expressly forbid hatred one of the other, therefore be it

RESOLVED, That the Southern Baptist Convention assembled at Miami, Fla., hereby repudiates, and urges the members of the churches of the Convention to refrain from association with, all groups that exist for the purpose of fomenting strife and division within the nation on the basis of differences of race, religion and culture.

SOCIAL SERVICE COMMISSION RECOMMENDATION
CONCERNING BAPTISTS AND RACE RELATIONS

We recommend, in the light of the relation of Southern Baptists to the racial problems of our land, and in the light of our brotherly relationship with three and a half million Negro Baptists in the South,

That the Convention appoint a committee of nine, composed of one member each from the Home Mission Board, the Commission on the American Baptists Theological Seminary, the Committee on Negro Theological Education, the Public Relations Committee and the Social Service Commission, and four additional members, to review the service now being rendered by Southern Baptists to the Negro race, to study the whole race situation, especially in its moral and religious aspects and meaning, to consider the responsibility of Baptists in the problems of adjustment of interracial relations, and make recommendations of procedure to the Convention, looking toward a larger fulfillment of our responsibility in the total situation and particularly with reference to helpful cooperation with our fellow Baptists in the Negro race.[65]

This special committee, Weatherspoon hoped, would deal with an assortment of race issues including equality in education, the removal of discriminatory restrictions, equality in employment opportunities, equality of the races in the military, equal justice, housing improvements and equality, and cooperative ways to train black clergymen.[66]

As 1946 passed, so did the Social Service Commission's role as a voluntary entity depending on the good graces of its denominational patrons. Had it not been for the Sunday School Board's generosity and the willingness of Barton and Weatherspoon to labor diligently with no recompense, Southern Baptists might not have exercised the influence they did. All in all, however, the first forty years of cooperative engagement produced abundant fruit. With 1947, a new chapter in Southern Baptists' engagement in social and moral concerns as well as religious liberty issues began. Yet, Southern Baptists came to the end of an era. Along with the passing of Poteat and Barton, George W. Truett died on July 7, 1944, and soon after Lee Scarborough died on April 10, 1945.

Looking back on these forty years, we might well ask, what motivated the Poteats, Barton, and Weatherspoon? In a phrase, for each of them, it was a matter of conviction.

Notes

1. The First Amendment to the Constitution of the United States of America (1791); the Constitution of the United States of America, Article 6, paragraph 3 (1788).

2. The earliest period of Southern Baptists' collective involvement in attempting to influence public policy (1907–1946) could easily be divided by U.S. presidents and their terms, Southern Baptists and their presidents, or even the major historical events, such as the world wars. Because Prohibition was such a

stackpole for Southern Baptists and their engagement in the public policy arena, our approach will be the activity of Southern Baptists before, during, and after Prohibition up to the time when they transitioned from a voluntary to a paid approach to leadership in the public policy arena.

3. Emir Caner and Ergun Caner, *The Sacred Trust* (Nashville: Broadman & Holman Publishers, 2003), 33–36; SBC Resolution on Law and Order (1907) and an Untitled Resolution (1907).

4. SBC Resolutions, 1908.

5. SBC Resolutions, 1907, 1908, 1909, 1910.

6. 1912 *SBC Annual*, 77. Barton graduated from Southwestern Baptist University (Now Union University) in Jackson, Tennessee. Although he was a constant in the Committee on Temperance and the then Social Service Commission, he would never serve any denominational or church employment longer than five years.

7. SBC Resolution on Christian Social Concern, 1913.

8. SBC Resolutions, 1911, 1912, 1913.

9. "E. Y. Mullins on Religious Liberty" in McBeth, *A Sourcebook for Baptist Heritage*, (Nashville: Broadman Press, 1990), 463–67.

10. SBC Resolution on Cooperating with Other Baptists, 1913.

11. Ergun Caner and Emir Caner, eds., *The Sacred Desk* (Nashville: Broadman & Holman Publishers, 2004), 39–46.

12. William Louis Poteat, *Can a Man Be a Christian Today?* (Chapel Hill: The University of North Carolina Press, 1925), 34.

13. 1914 *SBC Annual*, 33, 35, 37.

14. Greg Ward, *The Timeline History of the USA* (New York: Barnes and Noble, 2003, 2005), 225.

15. Ibid., 227–29.

16. SBC Resolution on Religious Liberty, 1919.

17. James Burton Gambrell, "Baptists and Religious Liberty—We Shall Lead" (1919 SBC Presidential Address) in Caner and Caner, *Sacred Desk*, 87.

18. 1920 *SBC Annual*, 94.

19. 1920 SBC Resolution.

20. 1920 *SBC Annual*, 97.

21. Ibid., 127.

22. Ward, *The Timeline History of the USA*, 230–38.

23. 1924 *SBC Annual*, 68–69.

24. Jesse Fletcher, *The Southern Baptist Convention* (Nashville: Broadman & Holman Publisher, 1994), 147–49.

25. 1921 *SBC Annual*, 84.

26. 1921 Resolution on Peace.

27. 1929 Social Service Commission Recommendation.

28. Resolutions in 1908, 1920, 1923, 1930, 1932, and 1933 each advocate that Christians and churches be involved in supporting or endorsing political candidates based on their willingness or refusal to embrace biblical values.

29. 1929 *SBC Annual*, 87–90.

30. Ibid.

31. 1930 SBC "Social Service Commission Recommendation Concerning the Work of the Commission on Social Service;" 1924 *SBC Annual*, 118.

32. 1930 SBC "Social Services Committee [sic] Recommendation Concerning Industrial Relations."

33. 1931 *SBC Annual*, 24–25; An interesting change was made at the 1931 SBC in which a new ruling was put into play that only churches could send messengers or representatives to the SBC.

34. 1933 *SBC Annual*, 108–109.

35. Ibid., 115.

36. Ibid., 118.

37. 1934 *SBC Annual*, 84; 1935 *SBC Annual*, 57–59; 1936 *SBC Annual*, 38.

38. 1935 *SBC Annual*, 61, 67.

39. 1936 *SBC Annual*, 35.

40. McBeth, *A Sourcebook for Baptist Heritage*, 661.

41. 1936 SBC Resolution on Religious Freedom.

42. 1936 SBC Resolution on Communism.

43. 1937 SBC Resolution on Race. Although the label is "On Race," the subject matter is broader and includes issues of war and peace as well as the Christian responsibility.

44. 1938 *SBC Annual*, 100.

45. 1938 *SBC Annual*, 100–15; 1939 Resolution on Christian Education; 1939 Resolution on America and China's Invasion.

46. Ward, *The Timeline History of the USA*, 249.

47. 1940 *SBC Annual*, 87.

48. Ward, 251–52.

49. 1941 SBC Resolution on Peace.

50. 1941 *SBC Annual*, 98–99, 123–126.

51. Ward, *The Timeline History of the USA*, 250–53.

52. "Arthur James Barton," *The Encyclopedia of Southern Baptists* 4 vols. (Nashville: Broadman Press, 1958), 1:146.

53. David C. Woolley, "A. J. Barton, Crusader for Righteousness," *Baptist History and Heritage*, July 1969, 123.

54. "Jesse Burton Weatherspoon," *The Encyclopedia of Southern Baptists*, 3:2044.

55. Letter from T. B. Maston to J. B. Weatherspoon, February 1946.

56. 1942 *SBC Annual*, 91.

57. 1942 SBC Resolution on Suggested Establishment of Diplomatic Relations with the Vatican; 1942, *SBC A Memorial.*
58. 1943 *SBC Annual,* 21; Caner and Caner, *The Sacred Desk,* 147–53.
59. 1943 *SBC Annual,* 103.
60. 1944 *SBC Annual,* 69.
61. Ibid., 29–30.
62. Ibid., 129–31.
63. 1944 SBC Resolutions.
64. Ward, *The Timeline History of the USA,* 262–64.
65. 1946 SBC Resolution on Race.
66. 1945 *SBC Annual,* 97–98.

CHAPTER

Transition of the Early Years
(1947–1960)

The year 1947 began a new chapter in Southern Baptists' involvement in moral, social, and religious issues. No longer were they just working together under the auspices of the Convention, but now after forty years they were finally financing those endeavors with Cooperative Program dollars. At last Southern Baptists provided financial support making it possible for the Social Service Commission to hire a full-time secretary-treasurer and provide for modest operating expenses. All of this was done while J. B. Weatherspoon was chairman of the Commission, an elected and honorary position.

When 1947 opened, Truman was president. Even though he professed to be a Southern Baptist and had a reputation for being a faithful and moral man, Truman had a penchant for using foul language. This did not set well with his Baptist kin and so made them reluctant to invite the first Southern Baptist president of the United States to address the Convention. During 1947, Truman instituted the Marshall Plan for Europe and the Truman Doctrine, which promised assistance to any anticommunist government that found itself under assault. The Republican Congress also passed the Taft-Hartley Act over Truman's veto.[1]

Prior to the time when Hugh Brimm would become the first secretary-treasurer, Weatherspoon guided the Social Service Commission with a deliberate direction. At the 1946 Miami Southern Baptist Convention, Weatherspoon persuaded the Convention to appoint a Special Committee on Race Relations. This would sound a clarion call that Southern Baptists, or at least their leaders, had every intention of promoting aggressively what they perceived to be the Christian viewpoint on racial matters.[2]

Weatherspoon also had other items in his bag of agendas. Besides arranging the first Social Service Commission conference on social concerns, to be held at Ridgecrest in August 1946, he worked with the Sunday School Board to publish a series of handbooks, which addressed a litany of subjects related to social issues. He also requested the Executive Committee of the Convention to restudy the proper role and function of the Commission so that support commensurate with that assessment might be allocated. Obviously, he was seeking more than the first token eighteen-hundred-dollar appropriation.[3]

At the 1947 Convention meeting in St. Louis, the Executive Committee took steps to narrow the responsibilities and increase the appropriation for their moral concerns agency. The most important recommendation made by the Executive Committee was to reassign issues related to "church and state" to the denominational Public Relations Committee that, as mentioned earlier, had evolved out of the Committee on Chaplains.

The recommendation entailed channeling ten thousand dollars to the Public Relations Committee in 1948 with the understanding that the Northern Baptist Convention would, as a partnership venture, designate an additional seven thousand dollars. In 1950, the Public

Relations Committee became part of the newly named Baptist Joint Committee on Public Affairs, representing, at its apex, nine different Baptist bodies as they attempted to work together addressing church and state matters.

With church-state matters reassigned, the Social Service Commission would be left to "promote morality in social relations" which included, "problems of marriage and the family, crime and juvenile delinquency, industrial relations, race relations, the alcohol problem, and other matters of social morality which press upon our people for a solution." The Executive Committee further recommended that the social concerns agency have "a continuous program" planned by its own executive committee "to be assisted by qualified personnel." For this next chapter, the Commission would be allocated ten thousand dollars for 1948 from the Convention's operating budget. What Barton and Poteat had failed to accomplish, Weatherspoon did in just seven years.[4]

At the 1947 Convention, Weatherspoon delivered his customary report on social and moral concerns. He also presented the report of the Special Committee on Race Relations, accompanied by a list of recommendations intended to assist the Convention to fulfill its responsibility for the promotion of interracial good will. Weatherspoon also urged the Public Relations Committee to keep Southern Baptists informed on "legislation and other governmental actions touching race relations" and "citizenship rights of minority groups."[5]

The Brimm Years (1947–1952)

At the August 1947 meeting of the Social Service Commission, Hugh Alexander Brimm was hired as the first secretary-treasurer (the standard title given agency heads at the time). Soon thereafter Brimm opened the first office on the Southern Seminary campus in a corner of Weatherspoon's office. Brimm, a former doctoral student under Weatherspoon, had written his 1944 doctoral dissertation on "The Social Consciousness of Southern Baptists." Most believe that Brimm was Weatherspoon's handpicked choice to head the agency on a day-to-day basis.

Brimm was diligent in his duties and well understood the power of networking to accomplish his intentions. In January 1948, Brimm communicated that he had established an Executive Committee for the Commission, which included T. B. Maston of Texas. Communicating with Maston and other commissioners on January 16, 1948, he wrote, "I would suggest that if you know of any matter which we ought to put on the agenda for discussion that you communicate with one of the members of the executive committee or with this office." On February 19, 1948, Maston received from Brimm a rough draft copy of the upcoming "Fortieth Annual Report of the Social Service Committee," in which Brimm solicited feedback and recommendations. No longer would the Report be considered a one-man show.[6]

An interesting tidbit of history in the opening remarks of the Report is that the formation of the Social Service Commission had come in the 1913 Convention in St. Louis in response to a memorial from the Baptist World Alliance. The request was "that such a Commission be established to study the further duty of the church to society and suggest ways whereby Jesus Christ may become a fact in the social life of the world."[7]

On February 24, 1948, T. B. Maston sent a three-page, single-spaced critique of the Report's rough draft in which he not only challenged generalizations but also provided wise counsel with respect to its approval. For example, Maston wrote, "Might it not be wise to be a little more cautious on the statement of such a generalization. I wonder if it is wisest for the Committee to question motives . . . , should the source of the statistics that are given be provided? . . . I would like to raise a question about the correctness of . . ." He concluded graciously by conceding, "You will understand again that these are merely made as suggestions and because I felt sure you wanted us to look at the report carefully."[8]

In a letter to Brimm leading up to the 1948 Convention in Memphis, Maston wrote, "I do hope you folks will formulate some recommendation concerning the so-called Civil Rights scrap." He later confided: "I hope also that a good strong recommendation can be made concerning the best approach to our churches to the crisis that we have in Western civilization and the world. Instead of falling in line with all the material preparation that is being made for war, our churches should call on the people to repent of their sins and come back to God. A deepening conviction of mine is that that will do more to our world than all the preparation we can make to defend our nation and to preserve 'the peace of the world.'"[9]

When the Convention met in Memphis in 1948, Weatherspoon gave the Commission report, and Brimm presented the recommendations. With respect to race, the Convention voted to reaffirm its 1947 St. Louis statement. Other issues raised by the Commission and approved by the Convention addressed concerns about movies, alcohol, tax laws affecting the churches, labor and management, marriage and family issues, and separation of church and state.

Maston, besides serving as a commissioner on the Social Service Commission, was also counsel to J. M. Dawson, the first executive director of the Baptist Joint Committee on Public Affairs. Dawson served several churches as pastor before going to First Baptist Church of Waco, Texas (1915–1946). *The Encyclopedia of Southern Baptists* describes Dawson this way:

> A passionate civil libertarian, he saw religious liberty as
> integral to the American Bill of Rights and genuine religious
> faith. A member of the Baptist World Alliance Commission on
> Religious Liberty, the Department of Religious Liberty of the
> National Council of Churches, and the American Civil Liber-
> ties Union, he helped found Protestants and Other Americans
> United for Separation of Church and State, and upon its organi-
> zation, served as temporary executive director, 1947–1948.[10]

In several ways Maston tied the Social Service Commission together with the Baptist Joint Committee and, in turn, the Protestants and Other Americans United for Separation of Church and State. Primarily, however, he was an unofficial advisor to Dawson. For example, he wrote to Dawson in March 1948 and counseled him thusly: "I wonder if it would not also be advisable for you to write an article for our state papers giving the background for the recent Supreme Court decision and its possible effects. I know that many of our people are considerably disturbed concerning it." Most likely, Maston was referring to the *McCollum v. Board of Education* decision handed down November 24, 1947, in which the "[Baptist] Joint Conference Committee on Public Relations set up by the Southern Baptist Convention and others, including the ACLU were permitted to file a supporting *amici curiae* brief supportive of McCollum." In this landmark case, the High Court "struck down a 'release time' program because tax-supported schools were 'used for the dissemination of religious doctrine' in classrooms." In essence the ruling concluded that the state was not permitted to use its tax-supported public school system (facilities and class time) to aid in providing religious instruction.[11]

Concerning Maston's plan to teach a course at Southwestern Baptist Theological Seminary on the "Separation of Church and State," Dawson wrote him stating, "I am convinced also that there is positive need for such a study from the single fact that, as I have tried to point out in my book, there has been a long period of neglect of this subject in which dangerous tendencies have grown up." Suffice it to say, Maston provided a link between the Social Service Commission and the Baptist Joint Committee.[12]

Before leaving the 1948 Southern Baptist Convention, it is wise to mention that a resolution was approved supportive of the "Protestants and Other Americans United for Separation of Church and State." The opening statements affirm:

> WHEREAS, There has recently been launched a movement composed of many groups known as "Protestants and Other Americans United for Separation of Church and State," which has proclaimed its purposes as follows: (1) to revive in the public mind a clear understanding of the Constitutional basis upon which religious liberty has been guaranteed, (2) to redress the specific violations which have recently come into force, and (3) to resist further encroachments upon this Constitutional principle;

The concluding declaration of this resolution states:

THEREFORE, BE IT RESOLVED, That (1) we commend
the purpose of "Protestants and Other Americans United for
Separation of Church and State" as declared in its "Manifesto,"
signed by John A. Mackay, President, Princeton Theological
Seminary, Edwin McNeill Poteat, President, Colgate-Rochester
Divinity School, G. Bromley Oxnam, Bishop of the Methodist
Church, New York Area, New York City, Louie D. Newton,
President, Southern Baptist Convention, and Charles Clayton Morrison, Former Editor "The Christian Century"; and
(2) That we commend the hopeful activities as conducted by
the trusted officials and widely representative members of the
National Advisory Council of "Protestants and Other Americans United for Separation of Church and State," believing that
only by united effort can we hope for the preservation of this
great American principle.[13]

What we discover at this point is worth reviewing. First, Southern
Baptists were tied philosophically to a strict separationist agenda with
respect to church and state. Unlike earlier times, it appears that there
was now no latitude permitted for any accommodation for faith in the
public square. Second, Southern Baptists could be seen identifying and
even informally establishing a connectionalism with the liberal spectrum of American Christianity. Third, the Social Service Commission,
minimally, was still involved in church-state matters. And fourth, by
association and passive concession, history was slowly being revised to
remove Christian influence from the public arena, with the consequential result of a burgeoning secularism filling the remaining void.

While the Southern Baptist Convention was underway in 1948,
the Middle East was heating up. With the British mandate over Pales-
tine expiring on May 14, Israel declared its independence on the same
day. Both the U.S. and Russia recognized the nation in short order. In
the fall, tensions mounted in Germany as Russia sealed its borders,
east and west. Truman responded with the Berlin airlift. The United
States entered the era of the Red Scare. Mao came to power in China.
Russia solidified its hold on the Eastern European block countries.

In the United States, Alger Hiss was accused of stealing secrets of nuclear technology. Needless to say, it was an uneasy time.[14]

In February 1949, Brimm continued to correspond with Maston. In a comment on family issues, Brimm suggested, "I have found that the use of the term 'planned parenthood' is a little less negative than the term 'birth control.'" He observed, "You know, I am sure, that the old Birth Control League of America changed its name to the Planned Parenthood Federation of America largely for this very reason."[15]

At the 1949 Southern Baptist Convention in Oklahoma City, surprisingly, the issue of communism was not mentioned in the Social Service Commission report. The explanation was that the Baptist Joint Committee should address those issues. The typical list of moral concerns was addressed but with less detail than previously. Instead of presenting a long discourse on problems, however, Weatherspoon and Brimm offered ideas for local conferences under the theme, "Religion in Life."

There was good reason for this. First, the SBC Executive Committee had requested that all agency reports be made more concise and brief. Second, the report information had already been disseminated through twice-monthly news releases to Convention publications, Baptist state papers, and to almost every district association. Materials for bulletins had also been sent to churches and a free monthly mail-out called *Light* had gone to thousands of pastors. Hence, there was no need to read long paragraphs from the report. In their report, however, they did draw attention to a new Annual Conference on Christian Living at Ridgecrest. In summary, they noted to the Convention, "Our staff is somewhat limited, but . . . we stand ready to do what we can to make . . . the vast ministry of our churches more vital, more dynamic, and more fruitful for the cause of Christ and His Kingdom."[16]

One interesting resolution, "On Displaced Persons," recommended the United States admit its fair share into our country of those who were unable or unwilling to return to their homes after a war. No mention was made of Israel or its legitimacy.[17]

After the 1949 Convention, Brimm wrote to Maston to discuss plans for the upcoming Commission meeting at Ridgecrest. He related that he believed the Commission needed both a Charter and a Constitution. Also, he wanted an expanded and more effective program for the Convention. He then asked Maston to "study carefully the Charter of Principles on Race Relations," explaining his intentions of making it "the core of our discussions on Next Steps on Race Relations when we meet at Ridgecrest." Brimm's assessment in counsel with others was that this document needed "more implementation."[18]

By the summer, Maston was preparing to teach his course on church and state. In corresponding with Dawson, he requested, "Will you be kind enough to give me the line up of the Protestant groups in the McCollum Case?" Needing additional information, he asked, "What groups entered the brief in the case and what has been the general reaction of other groups to the case?" In response Dawson sent Maston a copy of the brief along with an explanation of the process used by the Supreme Court to reach its decision. Again, in response to Dawson's information, Maston wrote:

> Thanks very much for the material you sent me. I am looking forward to teaching the course this Fall. Preparing for the course has opened my eyes again to see the threat of the Roman Catholic Church.[19]

In January 1950, Brimm wrote to Maston relating that he had been contacted by the chairman on boards requesting a list of upcoming vacancies on the Commission's board and soliciting suggestions of those who might fill those positions. Although issuing the disclaimer that ultimately it is a committee decision, it is interesting to note that new trustees came from the short list provided by the agency.[20]

In February 1950, Senator Joe McCarthy announced his list of 205 communist sympathizers in the State Department. In June the Korean War broke out when North Korea invaded the South on June 25.[21]

Meanwhile, the 1950 Southern Baptist Convention saw several changes. Noteworthy is the fact that Weatherspoon's name was not included above Brimm's on the published report. After reviewing briefly the history and purpose of the Commission, Brimm explained the "baseline" for the Commission's judgments in Christian moral teachings. He noted that social action serves to "coordinate in one harmonious whole the three elements—evangelism, education and action—of its task." He concluded that "pioneering for social justice must not be left to secular or political interests."[22]

Brimm's most noteworthy words to the 1950 Convention had to do with race relations. Quoting E. M. McNeil of North Carolina, he declared, "If segregation is not un-Christian, we must advocate it. If it is un-Christian, we must protest against it." No doubt, some segregationists viewed this "in your face" approach with alarm.[23]

At the 1950 Convention, the Committee on Public Relations became the Committee on Public Affairs. Sites for two new seminaries, Golden Gate and Southeastern, were announced. And a new seminary for black ministerial training was introduced as a joint venture by Southern Baptists and National Baptists. Southern Baptists were not yet ready to admit black students into their schools, but the time was growing closer. Needless to say, Brimm found himself criticized for his high priority emphasis on sound race relations.[24]

In his May 24, 1950, letter to his commissioners, Brimm related that the theme of this year's Ridgecrest Conference would be the "Alcohol Problem." This seems like a safe subject. Later in the year Brimm wrote Maston with reference to the 1951 conference which would be held jointly with the Committee on Public Affairs and address matters of mutual concern. A few days later Maston wrote to Brimm about the 1951 proposed conference, stating, "It seems to me that it has tremendous possibilities." He then confided, "It is certainly dealing with one of the major problems that we have in our nation."[25]

At the 1951 Convention meeting in San Francisco, Brimm was still being criticized. His presentation included a record-setting twenty-page report reviewing the social problems and recommendations from the previous fifteen years. Among the subjects included were alcohol, gambling, peace, militarism, war, labor relations, and race relations. Except for alcohol and gambling, these were sensitive subjects on which many Southern Baptists differed.

This particular year Brimm delved into detail on both labor relations and race relations. He also announced the subject of the joint conference at Ridgecrest. Incidentally, by virtue of his secretary-treasurer position on the Social Service Commission, Brimm served on the Public Affairs Committee. Brimm concluded his report by presenting six recommendations to the 1951 Convention. Each was readily accepted, including a Convention request that the federal government not "lead us into a military state" and a request that Southern Baptists support the United Nations. Wisely, Brimm backed away from further recommendations on race and labor relations. He had gone as far as possible with these subjects at that time.[26]

While no significant controversy rocked the Social Service Commission in 1951, other events made headlines across the country. President Truman removed popular General Douglas MacArthur from his command in Korea. Senator Estes Kefauver began an investigation of gambling and organized crime. Julius and Ethel Rosenberg were sentenced to death for spying for the Soviet Union. And CBS transmitted the first color television broadcast from New York.[27]

Two interesting developments, however, did occur in 1951 with respect to the Social Service Commission's work. First, the Commission's Executive Committee met to hammer out a working philosophy for their publication, *Light*. Of the four principles proposed with respect to their editorial policy, two stand out. First, the suggestion is made that, "it is primarily our task to set Christian goals. . . . [and] to keep a Christian objective in view, exercising care not to endorse completely one method as opposed to another." Second, "shall the bulletin be a means of advocating and agitating or shall it be one whose method is education and information? Concerning problems of the *status quo* we cannot afford to be uncritical 'stand-patters.' If this is our objective, we might better quit. In the face of contemporary social, economic, political and moral evils in today's world we must be out in front of but always connected with our people. We must maintain a creative tension between the 'actual' and the 'ideal,' a tension that moves toward the idea or Christian goal."[28] Brimm had every intention, it seems, of using it as a goad to move his agenda forward.

A second interesting development in 1951 is contained in a letter from Dawson to Maston, who related "that because of a handsome gift from the Baptist Sunday School Board this office is having printed 100,000 copies of a booklet to be entitled, 'The Battle for America: The Issue, An Ambassador to the Vatican'."[29]

Noteworthy in both of these instances is first, how the Social Service Commission embraced a policy of being intentional about its work. Second, we find a growing concern that historic principles of separation of church and state were apparently beginning to fracture, at least from the government's side of the wall.

The next year, 1952, was a year of change. For many Southern Baptists it began with a note of sadness. Former Convention president, commissioner of the Social Service Commission, governor of Texas, and president of Baylor University, Pat Neff, died in January. He was eulogized at the Convention as a "staunch prohibitionist, and an ardent Baptist, . . . always interested in the work of his church and denomination."[30]

The next month, Brimm received an interesting letter from the executive director of the Texas State Christian Life Commission, Acker C. Miller. Miller wrote, "It is my conviction along with yours that every state body within our Southern Baptist Convention should be organized to give the emphasis on the totality of the Christian life." He related, "I believe that we are developing a program that would be quite effective in reaching the individual member of any church large or small within our convention or anywhere else." Miller concluded, "I do not think that we can do in Texas or in any other state what ought to be done unless we become an integral part of a great convention-wide movement." Little did Miller realize that Brimm's responsibilities would be his the following year.[31]

In response to Brimm's rough draft of the 1952 Commission Report, Maston wrote back providing him with some wise feedback. Concerning one statement, Maston observed: "I have a little question about one of the statements that you made. Most of you fellows who are a little younger in this whole field tend to put a little too much barb in what you say sometimes. I think you know me well enough to know that I am very sympathetic with you in regard to it, but I think frequently it is self-defeating. . . . I believe that the better over-all strategy is to stay pretty close to the facts and to be just as objective and deliberate as possible and to reason with our people."

Concerning Brimm's use of ridicule, Maston noted, "I'm not sure but what that tends to needlessly antagonize some folks." Maston concluded with a word of encouragement:

> Let me say again that what suggestions I have made have not been in a critical spirit at all. I have always assumed that when you send the report to us that you would like for us to take time to think through it and make suggestions to you. I have a deep appreciation for what you are doing and also for the time and effort you put into the writing of this report.[32]

One issue that Maston raised was why Brimm makes no reference to church-state matters in his proposed report. Brimm responded, "I did not include a statement on Church and State inasmuch as I was afraid that Dr. Dawson might think we were taking some of his 'thunder.'" It is interesting to observe this meek attempt to maintain graciously the division of labor. In response to Brimm's inquiry about Maston's future plans (rumor had it that he was headed to Baylor), he wrote back, "I appreciate very much your interest and will also appreciate your prayers that I may do the thing that is best." Then in a moment of transparency, Maston related, "If I know my own heart, I want to spend the remainder of my days where I can count for the most for the cause." Well said.[33]

Brimm's seventeen-page report to the 1952 Convention meeting in Miami would be his final and most polemic address. First, he brought a scathing attack on militarism and war. He pleaded, "Do not tolerate any complacency about war." He continued, "Combat a mood of hysteria or blind hatred. . . . Reject fatalism about war. . . . We must avert the Hitlerism spirit in America." He urged Southern Baptists to "oppose primary reliance on military strategy to meet Communist aggression." He called for "positive aid programs" that would safeguard peace. He also argued against any form of universal military training. Yet, at a time when the growing Soviet threat loomed over the United States, too much talk of peaceful passivity was met with both resistance and reluctance.[34]

Brimm alienated many of his listeners when he sided strongly with labor against management. This came in the shadow of Truman's attempt to seize the steel mills when they had been paralyzed by strikes. Brimm received more of a sympathetic hearing when he addressed the issue of alcohol and drugs. Yet, he refused even to mention the use of tobacco. Then again, many Baptists in Kentucky, Virginia, and the Carolinas produced tobacco. Again, in his report, Brimm alluded to but did not out and out recommend that Southern Baptists integrate their schools.[35]

After his report and recommendations, the Convention accepted them without rancor. When the Convention was over, Brimm announced that he would be stepping down in order to accept a faculty post at the WMU Missionary Training School in Louisville, Kentucky. J. B. Weatherspoon, who had engineered Brimm's election as the Commission's first paid officer, would remain as chairman.

Brimm had served five difficult years. Some no doubt would be glad to see him depart. Yet his ideas would live on still under a Weatherspoon-guided Commission.

In a personal letter written to Maston, whom he called an understanding friend, and after the decision had been announced that he was moving to Louisville, Brimm wrote:

> These have been five rewarding years in the service of Southern Baptists as secretary of our Commission. There have been signs of progress here and there which more than compensates for the gloomy discouraging periods of anxiety when I wondered a thousand times if we had done the right thing or said the right word. Perhaps as much as any human asset was the realization that behind me were men like yourself—I knew I could count on you when the chips were down.[36]

The Miller Years (1953–1960)

In the August 1952 meeting of the Commission trustees at Ridgecrest, discussion was underway concerning a name change for the agency. Proponents noted that the term "social service" had come to be applied to organizations whose purpose was to raise funds and minister directly to social needs. The function of the agency as defined by the Convention, however, was to "help interpret the basic moral principles of our faith and to bring these principles to bear upon the conditions of life among us."

Evidently the need for a new name had actually been under discussion since 1949. In that time frame, the name "Christian Life Commission" had surfaced in the conversation between Acker C. Miller, then in Texas, and T. B. Maston, longtime professor at Southwestern Baptist Theological Seminary in Fort Worth. In discussions among the commissioners, agreement came to recommend the new name to the Convention in 1953. It was Maston's honor to recommend to the Convention the change in name, which easily garnered the two-thirds majority vote for approval.[37]

Upon Brimm's departure, Acker C. Miller, a former student of Maston's and presently director of the Texas Christian Life Commission, was drafted as the new executive secretary-treasurer of the Convention's moral concerns agency. A veteran pastor before becoming a denominational worker, Miller deeply admired the Poteat family. In fact, when Glenn Archer, executive director of Protestants and Other Americans United for Separation of Church and State, wrote Miller informing him that McNeill Poteat had died from a sudden heart attack, Miller replied, "It was McNeill Poteat's father who influenced the direction of my life and thought more than any other single individual."[38]

In a letter to Maston early in 1953, Miller confided his hope that the Texas Christian Life Commission would hire Arthur Rutledge as his successor but noted if he should decline the opportunity, "I hope Foy (Valentine) will be given an offer to come to it." He explained, "I am anxious about the pressure that will be put on the Executive Secretary to name some favorite son of somebody." He then confessed, "I do wish the brethren would tell those who resort to pressure to go jump in the lake," but conceded, "Maybe I would be the first to jump, but I sure don't like this pressure business anyhow."[39]

Miller wasted no time in trying to rally his commissioner troops. Although Maston was due to rotate off at the conclusion of the 1953 Convention, Miller attempted to bypass the bylaws and retain Maston. In a confidential letter to Maston, Miller wrote:

> The committee to nominate Boards and Commissions met here this week. Our mutual friend, Fred Swank, was on the committee. I had two talks with him about your six year tenure. I did not have to persuade him. He worked hard on the committee to get them to suspend the tenure rule in your case. I had tried to show him we were just starting over again in this work. You had had more than anyone else to do the new approach and that we just had to have you. But he was unable to get them to do it. I did not talk with him after the committee met, but my inside information is authentic. Fred asked me if in the event they would not suspend the rule, whom did I recommend. I named several. Tentatively they have agreed on Rutledge. So that's the story, My dear friend. I wish I could have done more about it. They left nearly all their work to be done at their meeting at the Convention in Houston. They will be under terrific pressure there. I don't know how they will come out. You understand no one is supposed to know these inside facts. I am not supposed to know them, but I do. We must be careful about discussing the matter.

In a follow up letter to Maston concerning a special meeting in Louisville on March 12, Miller pleaded: "I urge you to come. I do not contemplate with much pleasure the direction of this work without you on the Commission. I do not like that and did all I could to keep you on. But I am of the opinion that some of the dear brethren think only in terms of rules, laws, and controls. It is not a good sign."[40]

This correspondence is printed here to illustrate the inside working of an agency head trying to secure a supportive trustee.

At the 1953 Convention, Maston presented the agency's report. Miller then led the discussion. Weatherspoon, who continued as chairman, did not speak. Maston noted that the Commission would work through committees assigned to do research and writing on various topics. The committees would then "bring their findings and recommendations" to meetings of the full Commission for inclusion on the annual report. He affirmed that the Commission would cooperate fully with other Convention agencies, interface with state commissions, and provide assistance to Southern Baptists through conferences and literature.[41]

Neither Miller, nor Maston, nor Weatherspoon presented any recommendations on emotionally charged subjects to the 1953 Convention. They did, however, receive a record appropriation of $15,000 for the following year.

With the Korean War's conclusion, and with it the thirty-three thousand war dead, most Americans were finally breathing a sigh of relief. What captured the imagination of the messengers was the new membership campaign, "A Million More in Fifty-Four."

After the 1953 Convention and prior to the August meeting of the Commission and its corollary Christian Life Conference, Miller confided to Maston that he believed "It is necessary to make the conferences less cerebral." He wrote, "I think we should keep these discussions on a plane that will appeal to our intellects but at the same time to present them so they will move our hearts." He went on to explain, "I know that to some this kind of thing will be a letdown from what we have been having, but we can't reach Southern Baptists with an idea that is shut up to a minority group or that is raised so much above the common people that they cannot hear it, much less hear it gladly." Two weeks later Miller wrote, "You can see by this that our plans are beginning to work." He explained, "With a little time we hope to be in the middle of action among Southern Baptists and, at least, closer to their hearts."[42]

Only a week later, after receiving further feedback, Miller wrote, "There have been a few who have expressed the fear that we would surrender our freedom of expression [as a Commission] on moral issues." He confided, "While I have no one to talk with me about it, I am informed that some members of our Commission are afraid that we will go too far in cooperating with the denomination." Obviously, Miller is expressing his concern that the Commission not find itself out of touch with its constituency. Yet at the some time he was also concerned about not being muzzled.[43]

At the Commission meeting on August 20, 1953, at Ridgecrest, they adopted their first set of bylaws. The twenty-four commissioners were divided into eight committees and then approved a five-point program for the work of the Christian Life Commission:

(1) They would be "a source of information on moral issues and complex problems which face the Christian in his daily life."

(2) There would be a division of the Commission's 24 members into 8 committees "to make special studies and reports . . . on alcohol and drug addiction, obscene literature and amusements, gambling, the family and home, juvenile delinquency, progress in race relations, industrial relations, and Christian citizenship."

(3) They would sponsor state and regional workshops for leadership training "in cooperation with the State committees and Commissions in this field of work."

(4) They would also sponsor an annual Christian Life Conference, "devised in organization and subject matter" so it could be "replicated by a church or group of churches."

(5) It would prioritize the "creation of literature . . . to be used" in education "through the Christian Life Conferences and as supplemental material in group and class lessons."[44]

After the August meeting, Miller continued to depend on Maston as an advisor. Writing to Maston, he stated somewhat bluntly: "When you write me on these [Commission] matters please be as free and as frank and as direct as you would in appraising a paper or recitation of any of your students. None of us have time to spend in seeking to understand what the other might mean. I have many things to say to you but this letter will not contain them." In a letter two weeks later, Miller confessed to Maston, "A change of name was due more to your insistence than to anyone else."[45]

In the meantime Foy Valentine was hired to be the new executive director of the Texas Christian Life Commission, replacing Miller. In a confidential letter to Maston, Miller expressed his concern, stating, "I hope you will be able to keep Foy from striking back at some of the brethren who will continue to fret him." Evidently Valentine did not project the same gentleness as his mentor, Maston, or his predecessor, Miller.[46]

No doubt, 1953 proved to be the peaceful year that turned out to be the calm before the storm at the 1954 Convention in St. Louis. Nationally, the United States Government had announced a new policy of massive retaliation should the country be attacked with nuclear weapons. In hindsight this policy of mutually assured destruction (MAD) proved to be beneficial. On March 1, a hydrogen bomb was successfully detonated by the United States as a test at Bikini Atoll in the Marshall Islands. The next month, President Eisenhower put forth his "domino theory" in reference to the perception of communist intention and aggression. Yet nothing created turmoil in the nation like the Supreme Court's May 17 landmark decision on *Brown v. Board of Education of Topeka* in which racial segregation in schools was declared unconstitutional. The "separate but equal" philosophy in the 1896 *Plessy v. Ferguson* decision had been overturned by the Earl Warren court with a 9–0 decision.[47]

Miller had already planned to address the mistreatment of minorities, specifically the American Indian, in his 1954 report to the Southern Baptist Convention. Many fired-up segregation-minded messengers came to the Convention, meeting this year at an unusually late date of June 2–5, disagreeing with the Supreme Court's ruling. With the Court's decision, the stage was set for what might have been an ugly confrontation. The strongest debate came on Friday night when Convention President J. W. Storer presented Miller for the Commission's report. After reviewing a short list of typical issues, the proverbial water hit the wheel when Miller, without going through the

Committee on Resolutions, presented three recommendations from the Commission for Convention action. The first two, on opposing liquor advertising and juvenile delinquency, were acceptable to all. The Commission's recommendation to endorse the Supreme Court's new ruling aroused loud and prolonged debate.

Miller began by asking the Convention to recognize that the decision was "in harmony with the constitutional guarantee of equal freedom." He called for commendation of the Court's action and urged "all Christians to conduct themselves in . . . the spirit of Christ." He further pleaded for "Christian statesmen . . . to use their leadership in positive thought and planning . . . that this crisis . . . shall not be made an occasion for new and bitter prejudices, but a movement to a united nation." After considerable debate, which expressed both hopes and fears, as well as anger, the Convention approved the motion. One spokesman, not surprisingly, was Maston, who pleaded with the messengers "not to get on the wrong side of history" in this matter.[48]

Needless to say, Miller received much criticism in months to come from those not ready to change. Yet the deed was done and Southern Baptists, many grudgingly and fearfully, moved on.

By November other issues surfaced which created alarm in the minds of the social reformers like Maston. In a letter to Dawson who, like Miller, depended on Maston's ability to read the culture as well as the Bible, Maston articulated some major concerns, no doubt arising from his research and preparation for his own lectures on church and state matters:

> In recent weeks I wished very much for an opportunity to sit down and talk with you and others concerning some developments in our Southern Baptist life. I have had considerable misgivings about some things we have been doing and are doing. It seems to me that we are in danger of jeopardizing our historic position concerning the separation of church and state, and reducing considerably the effectiveness of our opposition to the position of the Roman Catholic Church concerning the state and the use of federal funds to support sectarian institutions. I have

in mind, particularly, two developments. First, the use of federal money to build dormitories on denominational school campuses. The other is the inclusion of denominational employees in the Social Security program. While I think it is true that neither one of these violates the constitutional provision for separation of church and state, I do think they tend to endanger to some degree the doctrine and possibly do violate the spirit of separation. There is always the danger that one will be willing to surrender a principle for some particular economic benefit that may come. I personally have not even liked the collecting of withholding tax by denominational institutions and agencies. . . .
I would certainly be glad to know your reaction to these things. It seems to me that our public affairs committee, or some group among us, needs to give some careful study to the whole matter of the relation of church and state and the possible effects of some of the things we are doing on our historic position.[49]

Again we see here a tight network of those involved with the Christian Life Commission and the Baptist Joint Committee. All too often we find an overlap of concerns between the two agencies. The separation of assignments at times seemed difficult to enforce, and in time the strain got worse as Southern Baptists perceived a growing distance between their convictions and their representatives.

In the aftermath of the 1954 Convention, Miller remained extra busy responding to calls and letters about race relations and militarism, the two hottest subjects for the Commission in 1955.

Early in 1955, Miller and the Commission's Administrative Committee agreed in principle to accept a grant of $15,000 from the controversial Fund for the Republic, to be used to address issues related to race relations. News of the grant's offer was not released to the press.[50] The fear was that it would be perceived as a bribe to buy influence by those who were proponents of integration. As a percentage of the Commission's budget, no doubt, it would make a sizable impact.

As mentioned earlier, Miller received hundreds of letters on controversial subjects, but more on race relations than anything else.

Miller also stayed under pressure by powerful members of the SBC Executive Committee, particularly Douglas Hudgins of Jackson, Mississippi's First Baptist Church, who chaired the finance committee. One of the staunchest segregationists in his state was U.S. Senator Ross Barnett, one of Hudgins' deacons. Writing to Brooks Hays, a Commission member and future Southern Baptist Convention president (1957–1959), Miller related: "As you know, our good friend, Douglas, is violently opposed to anything we do or say about the racial issue, and permits his deep and undying prejudice on that question to control him, and to keep our Commission on a very limited budget. However, last year they increased the number of the Finance Committee from seven to eleven men. We are hoping that these other men can be approached before December 14 and helped to see the need for the adequate financial support of our work." No doubt, Miller felt lodged between the proverbial rock and a hard place. It was mandatory that he walk a very tight, and at times confidential, line. Periodically he felt trapped by the race issue. To Garland Hendricks, Miller wrote, "The public is so obsessed with the idea of desegregation that it is difficult to get any other issue before the people."[51]

J. B. Weatherspoon, who stood behind Miller in almost every decision, marked his sixty-eighth birthday in 1955. He had served on the Commission since 1930 and was its chairman since 1943. More than any other, he was responsible for the opening of an office and hiring of a paid staff member for the agency. His last six years as chair had come under a special provision which allowed local members to continue when their experience was needed for the good of the agency. When the office was moved from Louisville to Nashville in 1953, the special provisions for Weatherspoon expired, and for the first time in a quarter century, his name did not appear on the roster of commissioners for the coming year.

After Miller reported on the list of Commission concerns to the 1955 Convention meeting in Miami, which incidentally did not include a plank that year on race relations, he recognized Weatherspoon to present the single recommendation on "peace." He spoke at a time when the world was experiencing a profound sense of anxiety due

to the prospect of nuclear war between the Western nations and the
Soviet Union. A summit conference between leaders of the two blocs
did little to ease concerns. Weatherspoon spoke passionately on the
subject of world peace. After heated debate, the motion carried.[52]

In light of Weatherspoon's long and devoted service to the Commission and Southern Baptists, at the Commission's July 1955 business session at Ridgecrest, a committee was appointed to formulate
an appropriate statement of appreciation for this faithful and capable
leader and for the contribution he made to Christian thought and life.
Weatherspoon would be praised significantly at the 1957 gathering of
the Convention.

In an almost unnoticed act of defiance, on December 5, 1955, a
black seamstress, Rosa Parks, traveled home by public transportation.
After a long day's work, she was arrested after she refused to give up
her seat on the bus to a white patron. When news of her arrest spread,
its backlash was embodied in the Montgomery bus boycott, which
would last for 381 days. The boycott, built on nonviolence and peaceful resistance, brought its spokesman, Martin Luther King Jr., into
national prominence. The boycott did not conclude until December
21, 1956, when the U.S. Supreme Court declared that segregation on
public transportation was unconstitutional. Concerning Parks, "Her
quiet, courageous act changed America and redirected the course of
history."[53]

In 1956, the year Fidel Castro rose to power in Cuba, the Christian Life Commission elected as its fourth chairman Brooks Hays.
An astute former Congressman from Arkansas, Hays supported the
Brown v. Board of Education of Topeka decision by the Supreme
Court yet was suspicious of Martin Luther King Jr. He also was
reluctant to provoke another (or reengage the previous) floor debate
over racial matters at the Southern Baptist Convention. Under the
leadership of Hays and Miller, the Commission backed away from
the confrontation with die-hard segregationists at the 1956 Convention in Kansas City.

In Miller's report, he touched briefly on the race issue but in a nonconfrontational manner. He communicated that the social attitudes and

actions of American citizens have a direct impact on "the reception of our witness on foreign fields." Here he made a nonjudgmental reference to race, saying, "We must face the present controversy on our relations with the Negro people. On this issue we are divided in opinion, but let us not be divided in fellowship." He explained, "No one person or group has the wisdom to lead us to a solution of the difficult situation that has developed." Most everybody would accept that. Some believed that the Commission's budgetary increase was granted because Miller downplayed the race issue in 1956.[54]

Writing to Maston in July 1956, Miller related the promised support from the Fund of the Republic had finally been received. He noted, "By this means we will be able to circulate our racial materials without charging for them except under certain circumstances." He concluded his letter stating:

> At our annual meeting at Ridgecrest, August 23-29, I am
> hoping we will map out a long-range program over a period of
> at least five years. I am anxious for us to work especially on
> the program we should promote relative to the racial problem,
> the alcohol problem, and the problems involved in industrial
> relations. We will need your help very much. This is our urgent
> invitation for you to attend our business meetings and assist us
> in every way you can. Please be free to write to me any sugges-
> tion you may have about any phase of our work.[55]

This was a great improvement over Miller's letter a year earlier when he related to Maston, "I do not find it easy to operate very far in advance on the funds that are available to us." And almost in resignation, he conceded, "I simply have to do the best I can with what I have."[56]

Consider here the incredible difference that a grant, a gift, a "love offering" can make in God's work. Consider also the fact that Miller was reaching out to Maston, understanding that even though he was not a commissioner he could still be a contributor. Titles do not a leader make. And consider, too, that sometimes accomplishing God's will simply takes time, patience, and wisdom.

Behind the scenes the Christian Life Commission was under the proverbial gun. Some on the Executive Committee would have been pleased if it simply disappeared.

In 1957, a special study committee reviewed the work of the Convention and Maston got wind of what he perceived to be some of their intentions. He wrote Barry Garrett, editor of the *Baptist Beacon* in Arizona:

> My understanding is that you are a member of the special
> study committee set up by the Southern Baptist Convention.
> I have heard rumors recently of a thing that has concerned me
> considerably. Just recently while in Arkansas, I was talking with
> a member of the Executive Committee of the Southern Baptist
> Convention, and he said that he was sure that if two or three
> members of that committee could have their way, the Christian
> Life Commission would be eliminated and the work would be
> turned over to the Sunday School Board. Of course I have heard
> rumors of that from time to time for the last few years, and
> I have known very definitely of the attitude of the men that he
> mentioned in his conversation with me. I am writing to you
> simply to find out how serious you think the matter is, and if
> any of us can do anything to head it off. I personally think it
> would be tragic if it is done, and would set back our work a
> good many years.[57]

Garrett responded to Maston three days later. He wrote:

> Thank you for your letter of April 22 in which you make
> inquiry concerning a possible proposal of the elimination of the
> Christian Life Commission from the Southern Baptist Conven-
> tion. I regret to say that it is true that there are some members
> of the survey committee who are bitterly opposed to the Chris-
> tian Life Commission and who would abolish it if they have
> their way. Thus far only one of these persons has made bold to
> suggest to our committee that the Christian Life Commission
> be abolished. Other than his suggestion there has been no dis-
> cussion of this question by our committee.[58]

After acknowledging that both he and Brooks Hays were on the study committee and that both were strong supporters of the Commission, he confessed: "Being an amateur in denominational politics and being very inexperienced in a fight of this kind, I am unable to say just exactly how serious this threat is to our Christian Life Commission. I would like to think that the threat is not as serious as the barking dogs would have us to believe, but secretly in my heart I am afraid that there might be a little bit of bite to these dogs as well as bark."[59]

Garrett concluded, advising, "It is my personal opinion that the Christian Life Commission and those of us who believe in what the Commission is doing need to improve our public relations as much as possible." He confessed, "We have been silent too long." And admitted, "We have made little effort to sell our cause to the constituency of the Southern Baptist Convention," and, "We have not made the function of the Christian Life Commission clear to our people." Garrett signed off saying, "I stand ready to participate in as strong a fight as necessary, not only to maintain it [the Commission], but to raise its importance in the Southern Baptist Convention."[60]

Just prior to the 1957 Convention in Chicago, Maston wrote to Miller and related that "I have been hearing some rumblings about this special study committee and its possible recommendations concerning the Christian Life Commission." He then stated, "I do hope that something can be done to keep some of the fellows from having their way regarding the commission." And then offered, "If there is anything that I can do to help, let me know."[61]

When the Convention met in Chicago in 1957, Miller reported that for the first time the distribution of over one million tracts in a single year had been accomplished. He also announced the formation of a research program to study a sampling of social attitudes among Southern Baptists. Miller went on to expound on the familiar themes of the Commission. He finally arrived at the race issue but again took a low-keyed approach, summarizing that at its root "the race problem is basically a moral and religious problem." Although he did not offer any resolutions or recommendations under the banner of the Christian

Life Commission, Miller did have a hand in writing the Resolution on Beverage Alcohol.[62]

Great relief surfaced among the supporters of the Christian Life Commission when its chairman, Brooks Hays, was elected president of the Convention, although it did mean that he would have to forego his lesser role. Adiel Moncrief of Missouri was elected the new chairman the following July. The Convention closed in 1957, as in 1956, without a floor debate on racial issues.

It was inevitable that information about the grant from the Fund for the Republic would eventually get out. Many criticized Miller and the Commission for taking funds from that "left wing" organization.

Writing to Maston after the Chicago Convention, Miller related two interesting bits of information. First, he admitted, "After extended discussion of the statement on the racial controversy we had prepared and submitted to them [the commissioners], the brethren decided it would be best not to present the statement during these sessions [of the Convention] at Chicago." He then commented, "It is significant to us that Mr. Hays was elected President." Miller explained:

> He stood at one end and the man from Jackson,
> Miss., [Hudgins], stood at the other. I think it is interesting
> that Mr. Hays has come to be known in the Convention by his
> service in this Commission, yet he was elected. The fact that
> he was a layman helped to carry his election, but I think that
> was not the only element of strength with this Convention. We
> have a chance to go forward now as never before. We must be
> aggressive but cautious.[63]

Maston replied to Miller a few days later, optimistically acknowledging, "The election of Brooks Hays was certainly encouraging in every way." He then conjectured, "From that it may be that we will get over the hump and will not feel that we will have to be on the defensive."[64]

The time of challenging the Commission's right to exist was over, but its critics were not yet finished. In an attempt to understand the whys of the move to disband the Commission, Garrett and Maston continued to correspond. Maston explained,

I think there are some historic reasons for the moral weakness of Southern Baptists. One was their aversion for a long period of time and even yet to a considerable degree, for the social gospel. You know of course that is due to the fact that they early identified the social gospel with liberal theology.[65]

Several days later Garrett responded to Maston, noting that "an effort was made in the Survey Committee of the Southern Baptist Convention to inaugurate a move to kill the Christian Life Commission." He then explained, "We had a right warm battle in the committee meeting but when the vote was taken only three votes were cast against the Commission." But then he added:

My interpretation of the discussion and of the vote, however, is that this will not settle the matter but that later efforts will be made to destroy the Christian Life Commission. This means that its friends and advocates must make "hay" while the sun shines, build the fences strong, and be ready for battle at any time and every time that the questions may arise.[66]

Ever an encourager, Maston wrote to Miller several weeks after his round of correspondence with Garrett and stated, "While there are some discouraging signs there are also many things to encourage us." He then pointed Miller to heaven saying, "The main thing is that we must have a strong abiding faith and a sovereign God whose will will be done."[67]

Responding to Maston, Miller noted, "The truth doesn't phase any man when he doesn't want the truth."[68]

In one of his last letters in 1957, Maston wrote to Emanuel Carlson, who replaced Dawson at the Baptist Joint Committee. Maston, ever gracious, wrote: "I want to express my appreciation for your sharing with me the discussions your committee recently had. It does seem to me that Baptists need to rethink and restate their position concerning separation of church and state, religious liberty, and related matters. There is quite evidently considerable differences of opinion among us concerning these important and distinctive tenets of our faith."[69]

Behind the scenes issues were constantly stirring and being stirred. Whether it was race, or the next somebody desirous of dismantling the Commission, or a strong disagreement on the nature of the First Amendment, or someone deciding it was time for regime change, it was always something. And the tension, suspicion, and accusations just would not die down. Perhaps some of it was justified.

Early in 1958, Reuben Alley, editor of Virginia Baptists' *Religious Herald*, printed an editorial entitled, "A Disturbing Transaction," critical of the Commission's reception of the grant from the Fund for the Republic. Alley opined that the Foundation was concerned with "creating public opinion and obtaining political action upon social problems." He also maintained that the Commission was becoming "the agent of an organization other than the Convention." He concluded, "The Fund of the Republic was probably well pleased to pay this sum for the influence of a Southern Baptist Convention agency."[70]

Responding to Alley's accusations, Miller wrote that the Fund "is not a racist organization, nor is it working to enforce integration." He explained, "Its approach to the racial field is strictly an educational approach in the areas of human freedom as guaranteed by our Constitution as those freedoms are threatened by social and economic discrimination." Miller finally confided, "The facts are that the Fund for the Republic has given us this financial assistance only on the basis of our own request." In other words, they did not approach us, but we approached them because they had grant money that we needed for our work.[71]

An old axiom is that your friends come and go, but you accumulate enemies. Such was the case for Miller. Not only was Alley on his case, but Hudgins of Mississippi was too. Herschel Hobbs was also numbered among Miller's critics. In a letter to J. D. Grey, Miller wrote, "I like Herschel Hobbs very much," but "he has always stood with Doug and Louis in fighting us and these three seem to have set out to weaken this agency by the choking process."[72]

This letter was a reflection back to the recent Houston Convention held May 20–23 where Brooks Hays was serving his second term as president. The Christian Life Commission report was printed in the Book of Reports so Miller did not feel it necessary to read to the Convention what was already in print.

Reviewing the printed report, messengers found the typical issues raised along with a request to hire an additional staffer. They also saw that a second $15,000 grant had been received, this time from the Ford Foundation, which was known for promoting social integration in the South.

Miller's call for racial reconciliation grabbed the greatest interest. Some had already read quotations in the press, notably an article by Associated Press religion writer George Cornell, declaring, "Officially the denomination is on record in support of integration." Cornell had apparently drawn this conclusion from reviewing the Commission's printed report, which was distributed to the press before the Convention began. And all this occurred before Miller ever said a word.[73]

In the discussion which followed Miller's address, several legitimate but touchy issues were raised. Could the Commission speak for the churches when the churches had not spoken? Was the pronouncement from the Commission binding on the churches? One messenger related concerns from his local Baptist Association in which the charge was made that the Christian Life Commission was active "in propagandizing churches and individuals with this racial integration matter."[74]

When debate was underway on the motion to delete the report's section 5, "A Call for Reconciliation," two who supported retaining it were Adiel Moncrief, the chairman of the Commission, and commissioner Avery Lee from Louisiana. Lee argued: "Brother Chairman, it seems strange to me that Baptists, of all people, should try to delete anything having to do with the term reconciliation. By the same logic of the gentleman from Georgia (who made the motion), we would likewise strike from this report all references to alcohol, gambling, narcotics, [and] salacious literature. . . . By the same reasoning we could see no report from any commission or agency that represents this Convention. I believe that this report in all propriety should be accepted by this Convention." Avery's logic prevailed and the Convention sustained the Commission's report as it originally appeared in print.[75]

It was not as though Miller was caught off guard regarding the growing resistance to his and the Commission's position on racial reconciliation. The previous March, Miller wrote to Maston saying, "I sometimes wonder how long the leadership of Southern Baptist[s] is going to permit these protest groups to dictate what they read and what they shall think." He concluded, "It makes me tremble to think of it."[76]

Again, writing to Maston concerning *The Bible and Race* manuscript's timid reception, Miller noted:

> There will evidently be a number of sentence revisions
> they will request. I have no idea what they will be—no one has
> sought to influence me in this statement that I hope you will
> not "hold the line" too tight. You are fishing in a turbulent sea.
> Give-give-give out as much as you can. Revise and keep your
> ideas—we need the message.[77]

Yet only a few weeks later, Miller wrote again to Maston saying, "I am writing to withdraw my appeal in my last note urging you to 'give'—'revise,' etc." He implored, "You will do all you can and then some." Miller then confided, "But I rebel when I think of how these denominational agencies become censors of our thought and convictions." He then related, "I still hope Broadman will print the book— but I can't put up with some of these things." He finished, saying, "The next issue of our Bulletin should be on Freedom—and maybe it will be."[78] Suffice it to say, Miller's disposition going into the 1958 Convention was one of both irritation and concern.

Later in the year, after Broadman agreed to publish *The Bible and Race*, Maston wrote to Miller about that manuscript and a second more detailed manuscript on the same subject matter. He confided:

> I have prepared both of these manuscripts with some mis-
> givings, but also with a deepening conviction that I should write
> them. I know full well that they will close some doors for me,

but I am far enough along in years that that does not concern me a great deal. I do not believe that I could live at peace with myself if I did not say something. I do trust that what I have said will help rather than hinder the general situation.[79]

Needless to say, this was a time of intense unrest due to the tensions over race.

Not far from the Christian Life Commission's concerns, however, was the matter of church and state relations. Again, prior to the 1958 Convention, Maston related his concerns to the Baptist Joint Committee head, Emanuel Carlson. He wrote:

> It seems to me that the contemporary period is so different socially, economically, and politically from the early days of our nation that we are going to have to rethink and to reinterpret the Baptist position regarding religious liberty and the separation of church and state. It is certainly quite clear that Baptists are not together in regard to that reinterpretation and to the application of our historic Baptist position or positions to the changing situation. The fact that we are not together may be a part of our strength. In other words, it may be an expression or an evidence of religious liberty which is so precious to us.

Maston went on to observe:

> In this area of religious liberty we may need to examine some trends within Baptist ranks. In some areas at least there is not as much freedom as there should be to express differing viewpoints. There is some tendency toward censorship which does not belong within Baptist ranks. My own personal fear is that we may develop a type of Baptist scholasticism.[80]

While for some men like Maston, Miller, and Carlson, issues like race and religious liberty were churning front burner concerns, for others, these did not hardly even register. In fact, when Robert Naylor released his *A Messenger's Memoirs*, which chronicles the sixty-one Conventions he had attended, he did not even make reference to these as significant concerns at the 1958 Convention meeting.[81]

In 1959, Miller wrote to Maston about the year's upcoming work. Concerning the August 1959 Ridgecrest conference on race relations, he noted, "I can't get away from the feeling that we must develop suggested methods and procedures for the communities on the issue of desegregation." He also commented that there was a perception "on the part of some that we [the Commission] are overlapping with the Baptist Joint Committee on Public Affairs."[82]

The 1959 Convention in Louisville, Kentucky, was peaceful. President Hays, in his address, noted, "In my official activities as your president, I have tried to keep in mind that there is a wide diversity of viewpoints with reference to race relations, but I have steadily insisted that this, the nation's number one problem, has an impact upon our missionary enterprise, and must be met with high statesmanship and Christian insight."[83]

The prolonged tension evidently was getting to Miller. Nearing seventy, he did not know how long he could withstand the pressure. He began intimating to friends that he was considering retirement.

In his last Commission report to the Convention in 1959, Miller tried not to provoke his opponents. He addressed issues like obscenity, supporting the United Nations, and alcohol. The closest he came to a tense moment was when he stated, "The time has come for the restoration of communication between white and colored peoples of the South." Yet he offered no recommendations for action, leaving all of that in the hands of the Resolutions Committee.[84]

In November 1959, Miller announced his intention to resign. Writing to Maston on December 2, Miller noted, "You have probably by this time heard of my intentions to retire as of January 31, 1960." He concluded, "We are looking forward to a few years of very pleasant and fruitful service in this place," as they retired to the First Baptist Church of Sedona, Arizona.[85]

Writing back to Miller on December 16, 1959, Maston expressed his concern, "I do hope and pray that the Commission will be very wise in selecting your successor," and then noted, "I'm praying to that end."[86]

At his retirement the Commissioners expressed "grateful recognition" to Miller "for his exceptional leadership during critical days. . . . He enlarged the scope and vision of the Commission's work."[87]

In these transition years before Valentine's tenure, several significant events unfolded. First, because the Social Service Commission finally received funding, the work became full-time and not part-time. Although the work was still intense, the issue of greatest concern shifted from alcohol to race, and, to a lesser degree, all the issues related to religious liberty. We also find a certain mind-set among those associated with the Commission, a willingness to embrace an elitist perspective, which tended at times to alienate them from their constituency. Yet the consistent plea among those associated with the Commission was that Christian beliefs must be demonstrated by Christian behavior. For each of the leaders during this period, their work was ever a matter of conviction.

Notes

1. Greg Ward, *The Timeline History of the USA* (New York: Barnes & Noble, 2003), 264–66.

2. Robert A. Baker, *The Southern Baptist Convention and Its People* (Nashville: Broadman Press, 1974), 441.

3. 1946 *SBC Annual*, 125–26.

4. 1947 *SBC Annual*, 34.

5. Ibid., 48.

6. Letter from Brimm to Maston, January 16, 1948; letter from Brimm to Maston, February 19, 1948.

7. Social Service Commission 40th Report, unpublished rough draft, 1.

8. Letter from Maston to Brimm, February 24, 1948.

9. Letter from Maston to Brimm, May 7, 1948.

10. "Joseph Martin Dawson," *The Encyclopedia of Southern Baptists* (Nashville: Broadman Press, 1958), 4:2181.

11. Letter from Maston to Dawson, March 15, 1948; See Peter Irons, *A People's History of the Supreme Court* (New York: Penguin Books, 1999), 410; Stanley N. Worton, *Leading Cases of the Constitution* (New York: Monarch Press, 1966), 165–69.

12. Letter from Dawson to Maston, November 18, 1948.

13. 1948 SBC Resolution on Protestants and Other Americans United for Separation of Church and State.

14. Ward, *The Timeline History of the USA*, 266–69.

15. Letter from Brimm to Maston, February 16, 1949.

16. 1949 *SBC Annual*, 336–39.

17. 1949 SBC Resolution on Displaced Persons.

18. Letter from Brimm to Maston, May 27, 1949.

19. Letter from Maston to Dawson, July 18, 1949; letter from Dawson to Maston, July 20, 1949; letter from Maston to Dawson, July 29, 1949.

20. Letter from Brimm to Maston, January 24, 1950.

21. Ward, *The Timeline History of the USA*, 270–71.

22. 1950 *SBC Annual*, 371–72.

23. Ibid., 378.

24. Ibid., 376; SBC Executive Committee Meeting Minutes, February 10, 1950.

25. Letter from Brimm to Maston, May 24, 1950; letter from Brimm to Maston, October 18, 1950; letter from Maston to Brimm, October 24, 1950.

26. 1951 *SBC Annual*, 52–53.

27. Ward, *The Timeline History of the USA*, 271–72.

28. Memo including the Report of the Meeting of the Executive Committee to Determine a Policy for *Light*, a Bulletin of the Social Service Committee, February 10, 1951, from Brimm.

29. Letter from Dawson to Maston, November 9, 1951.

30. 1952 *SBC Annual*, 57.

31. Letter from Miller to Brimm, February 15, 1952.

32. Letter from Maston to Brimm, February 22, 1952.

33. Letter from Brimm to Maston, April 3, 1952; Letter from Maston to Brimm, April 11, 1952.

34. 1952 *SBC Annual*, 408–14.

35. Ibid., 55–56.

36. Letter from Brimm to Maston, November 4, 1952.

37. 1953 *SBC Annual*, 53.

38. Letter from Miller to Glen Archer, December 21, 1955.

39. Letter from Miller to Maston, n.d. (but context and the response from Maston indicates early January 1953).

40. Letter from Miller to Maston, February 20, 1953; letter from Miller to Maston, February 27, 1953.

41. 1953 *SBC Annual*, 429–30.

42. Letter from Miller to Maston, May 26, 1953; letter from Miller to Maston, June 8, 1953.

43. Letter from Miller to Maston, June 15, 1953.

44. Minutes of the August 1953 Christian Life Commission Meeting at Ridgecrest, N. C.

45. Letter from Miller to Maston, September 18, 1953; letter from Miller to Maston, October 2, 1953.

46. Letter from Miller to Maston, December 30, 1953.

47. Ward, *The Timeline History of the USA*, 275.

48. 1954 *SBC Annual*, 407; Jimmy Allen delivered a fine lecture on Maston's life, entitled "Thomas Buford Maston—Baptist Apostle of Biblical Ethics," at the Divinity School of Wake Forest University published in *Christian Ethics Today*, 47, Vol. 9, No. 5, December 2003, p. 4. Allen, however, did miscite the year. It was 1954, not 1952.

49. Letter from Maston to Dawson, November 6, 1954.

50. Motion to accept the grant is in the A. C. Miller file at the SBC Historical Commission.

51. Letter from Miller to Brooks Hays, September 29, 1955; letter from Miller to Garland Hendricks, February 4, 1955.

52. 1955 *SBC Annual*, 335.

53. Ward, *The Timeline History of the USA*, 277; Rosa Parks with Gregory J. Reed, *Quiet Strength* (Grand Rapids: Zondervan Publishers, 1994), 11.

54. 1956 *SBC Annual*, 336.

55. Letter from Miller to Maston, July 5, 1956.

56. Letter from Miller to Maston, March 22, 1955.

57. Letter from Maston to Barry Garrett, April 22, 1957.

58. Letter from Garrett to Maston, April 25, 1957. Note that Garrett would leave Arizona to become the Assistant Director of the Baptist Joint Committee on Public Affairs.

59. Letter from Garrett to Maston, April 25, 1957.

60. Ibid.

61. Letter from Maston to Miller, May 16, 1957.

62. 1957 *SBC Annual*, 366–68.

63. Letter from Miller to Maston, June 5, 1957.

64. Letter from Maston to Miller, June 15, 1957.

65. Letter from Maston to Garrett, September 11, 1957.

66. Letter from Garrett to Maston, September 26, 1957.

67. Letter from Maston to Miller, October 14, 1957.

68. Letter from Miller to Maston, October 31, 1957.

69. Letter from Maston to Emanuel Carlson, December 12, 1957.

70. Reuben Alley, "A Disturbing Transaction," *Religion Herald*, January 1958.

71. Letter from Miller to Reuben Alley, January 20, 1958.

72. Letter from Miller to J. D. Grey, May 28, 1958.

73. 1958 *SBC Book of Reports*, 288.

74. From "Minutes of the Southern Baptist Convention," Houston, Texas, May 20–23, 1958.

75. Ibid.

76. Letter from Miller to Maston, March 20, 1958.

77. Letter from Miller to Maston, April 12, 1958.

78. Letter from Miller to Maston, May 2, 1958.

79. Letter from Maston to Miller, October 27, 1958.

80. Letter from Maston to Carlson, February 24, 1958.

81. Robert E. Naylor, *A Messenger's Memoirs* (Franklin, Tenn.: Providence, 1995), 103–107.

82. Letter from Miller to Maston, March 25, 1959.

83. 1959 *SBC Annual*, 85.

84. Ibid., 394.

85. Letter from Miller to Maston, December 2, 1959.

86. Letter from Maston to Miller, December 16, 1959.

87. 1960 *SBC Annual*, 274.

CHAPTER

The Middle Years: Part 1 (1960–1972)

With Foy Valentine's election as the next executive secretary of the Christian Life Commission, the entity's drift toward the left on the political, theological, and philosophical spectrums continued. Valentine, Miller's personal choice to be his replacement, was Maston's first doctoral student in ethics. His dissertation is entitled, "A Historical Study of Southern Baptists and Race Relations, 1917–1947." In it he writes that "race prejudice in individuals, or in churches, or in denominations, is a condition of spiritual infantilism which may be outgrown with divine assistance and conscientious effort." He holds out hope "that Southern Baptists will help to bring about the Christian way in race relations not by sponsoring legislative action or by fostering ecclesiastical fiats but by adopting, as individuals and as churches, the spirit and the mind of Christ in every phase of race relations."[1]

Although called to his new assignment on March 1, 1960, Valentine did not officially begin his duties until June 1, about a week after the 1960 Southern Baptist Convention concluded. Nevertheless, the Commission report did contain his input with respect to content. He noted he would be serving as a consultant to the White House Conference on Aging in 1961. He also related that at Brooks Hays' encouragement the Commission would be holding a leadership seminar on peacemaking at the United Nations in October 1960. Valentine managed to address the race issue at the 1960 Convention when he wrote, "The Commission urges our Southern Baptist people to make use of every opportunity to help Negro citizens to secure [equal rights] through peaceful and legal means and to thoughtfully oppose any customs which may tend to humiliate them in any way."[2]

After the Commission report was delivered by trustee Avery Lee, Valentine addressed the Convention with a passionate declaration of the Commission's responsibilities, attacking the twin enemies of communism and racism.[3]

Of particular concern for messengers this year was the fact that John F. Kennedy, the junior senator from Massachusetts, appeared to be the Democrat's presidential nominee in the fall election. Between his Roman Catholicism, pro-alcohol posture, and position on race, many rank-and-file Southern Baptists were concerned for different reasons. In the "Resolution on Christian Citizenship," messengers noted, "In all cases a public official should be free from sectarian pressures that he may make independent decisions consistent with the rights and privileges of all citizens."[4]

Of course, the great fear was that the Roman Catholic Church would exert undue influence on the decisions made by Kennedy should he be elected president of the United States.

It is not surprising, therefore, that Kennedy, who did indeed receive his party's nomination, requested the privilege of meeting with a group of Southern Baptist ministers. The selected venue was the

September 12, 1960, meeting of the Greater Houston Ministerial Association at which he hoped to dispose of the "religious issue once for all."[5]

In his address Kennedy affirmed his belief in the separation of church and state, his own patriotism, and his own independence. Kennedy stated, "I believe in an America that is officially neither Catholic, Protestant, nor Jewish—where no public official either requests or accepts instructions on public policy from the Pope, the National Council of Churches, or any other ecclesiastical source—where no religious body seeks to impose its will directly or indirectly upon the general populace or the public acts of its officials—and where religious liberty is so indivisible that an act against one church is treated as an act against all." He pleaded that these religious leaders review his record in Congress, "on my declared stands against an ambassador to the Vatican, against unconstitutional aid to parochial schools, and against any boycott of the public schools." He further stated, "I do not speak for my church on public matters—and the church does not speak for me."[6]

When the dust settled on election night in November, Kennedy won by a scant 118,574 votes, which gave him 303 electoral votes to 219 for Richard Nixon. Now Valentine had his hands full with a Roman Catholic headed to the White House. In the words of biographer Richard Reeves, "There could be no better answer to [the] innuendo that Catholicism was somehow un-American than the one Kennedy used: 'No one asked me my religion in the South Pacific (during World War II).'"[7]

Valentine came to his office at a volatile time in the nation's history. In addition to his concern about a Catholic in the White House, he would have to address increasingly the issues of race and Vietnam, the two hot-button issues of the 1960s.

Besides issues in the culture, Southern Baptists were beginning to express concern over the burgeoning theological liberalism in their schools, as well as the institutional bureaucracy that protected it. In 1959, Eric Rust, in his paper "The Challenge of Modern Science," had not only questioned but mocked the Genesis account of the creation and flood. Partially in response to Rust, but partially in response to the growing theological drift to the left, Ramsey Pollard, president of the Convention, in his 1960 president's address had declared, "If you don't believe the miracles and the Word of God, get out of our Seminaries."[8]

The SBC met in St. Louis in 1961, where seven years before Weatherspoon had assisted Southern Baptists to be on the right side of history and support the *Brown v. Board of Education of Topeka* decision. The civil rights movement was now in full swing with Freedom Riders protesting and people in the Southern cities resisting, sometimes with violence.

Instead of sounding off publicly, Valentine's early strategy was a letter-writing campaign. To Owen Cooper, he wrote saying that the Commission "should not bring agitation to our Convention. I have not developed a reputation as an extremist or an agitator. I realize that not all [Southern] Baptists have agreed with me, but in Baptist life fortunately that is not absolutely necessary." Besides race relations, Miller had also drawn criticism for becoming involved with labor-management relations and for championing the United Nations. Valentine assured Cooper that he did not intend to do anything that would "divide our people."[9]

At the Convention Valentine agreed to support a resolution offered by Homer Lindsay Jr. on race, which read:

> This Convention in years past has expressed itself clearly and positively on issues related to race relations. Today the solution of the race problem is a major challenge to Christian faith and action at home and abroad.
>
> Because Southern Baptists are the largest Christian group in the area where racial tensions between whites and Negroes are most acute, we feel an especially keen sense of Christian responsibility in this hour.
>
> We recognize that members of our churches have sincere differences of opinion as to the best course of action in this matter. On solid scriptural grounds, however, we reject mob violence as an attempted means of solving this problem. We

believe that both lawless violence on one hand and unwarranted provocation on the other are outside the demands of Christ upon us all.

We believe that the race problem is a moral and spiritual as well as social problem. Southern Baptists accept the teachings of the Bible and the Commission of Christ as our sole guide of faith and practice in this area as in every other area. We cannot afford to let pride or prejudice undermine . . . either our Christian witness at home or the years of consecrated, sacrificial missionary service among all the peoples of the world.

We therefore urge all Southern Baptists to speak the truth of Christ in love as it relates to all those for whom he died. We further urge that this Convention reaffirm its conviction that every man has dignity and worth before the Lord. Let us commit ourselves as Christians to do all that we can to improve the relations among all races as a positive demonstration of the power of Christian love.[10]

Other resolutions were "On Religious Liberty and Education," which addressed concerns about communism and Roman Catholicism, "On Taxation," which urged legislators not to appropriate funds to support private and parochial schools, "On Cooperation with Other Christians," which urged Southern Baptists to permit qualified students of any race to study at their seminaries and colleges, and "Concerning Communism," which argued the fundamental incompatibility between its philosophy and Christianity.[11]

At the 1961 Convention, the Executive Committee presented a revised program statement for the Christian Life Commission, asserting the Commission "shall assist Southern Baptists in the propagation of the Gospel" by helping them apply Christian ethics "in family life, human relations, moral issues, economic life, and daily work, citizenship, and related fields." It continued by spelling out the specific tasks expected from the Commission and concluded by authorizing it to "work diligently as a staff and service agency" with the Convention and all its agencies.[12]

In October 1961, the race issue in the country was heating up again when James Meredith, an air force veteran, enrolled at the University of Mississippi. In a power struggle Governor Ross Barnett opposed his matriculation to the university, but Kennedy sent federal troops and U.S. marshals to enforce his entrance. In the ensuing riots, two people were killed, forty-eight soldiers were injured, and thirty U.S. marshals were wounded. Meredith graduated in 1963, studied in Nigeria, and then received his law degree from Columbia University in 1968. Although he made several failed attempts to run for Congress as a Republican, he served for several years as a domestic advisor on the staff of United States Senator Jesse Helms. By his own testimony Meredith related that he saw himself as an individual American citizen who demanded and received rights properly extended to any American, "not as a participant in the U.S. civil rights movement."[13]

Meanwhile, things were heating up inside the Southern Baptist Convention with the Broadman Press publication of Ralph Elliott's *The Message of Genesis*. K. Owen White responded with a stirring essay entitled "Death in the Pot," in which he asserted that Elliott's book was "liberalism pure and simple." What matters about this is the growing mistrust of the Convention agencies, especially the seminaries, by rank-and-file Southern Baptists. It did get worse. In 1961, trustees at Midwestern Baptist Theological Seminary affirmed Elliott; but due to the fact that he would not withdraw his book from publication, his position at the Seminary was terminated the following year for insubordination.[14]

When the 1962 Convention met at San Francisco, the Commission gave its predictable glowing report. The big question, however, at this Convention was not communism or race but biblical truth. The "Genesis Controversy," as it was called, dominated the Convention. As an assurance to the Convention that the doctrinal lid was on, a committee was appointed to review the current doctrinal confession, The Baptist Faith and Message, 1925.

Resolutions at the Convention focused on keeping the Lord's day, concern over tax legislation that would affect church giving, and an affirmation that Christianity and communism were not compatible. The messengers did "affirm the Bible."[15]

Soon after the Convention in San Francisco, the Supreme Court announced its *Engel v. Vitale* decision (June 25), in which the practice of prescribed prayer in public schools was ruled "unconstitutional." Justice Hugo Black, writing the majority opinion, cited Jefferson's construct of a "wall of separation of church and state" for support. In its decision, the Court in Black's assessment that the Establishment Clause, "must at least mean that in this country it is no part of the official business of government to compose official prayers for any group of American people to recite as part of a religious program carried out by government." Potter Stewart, dissenting, wrote: "With all respect, I think the Court has misapplied a great constitutional principle. I cannot see how an 'official religion' is established by letting those who want to say a prayer say it. On the contrary, I think that to deny the wish of these school children to join in reciting this prayer is to deny them the opportunity of sharing in the spiritual heritage of the nation." As an attempt to correct what was perceived as so great an injustice, 147 bills were introduced through legislative and constitutional amendments, but to no avail. School prayer was out. Although most Southern Baptists were upset with the Court's decision, the Christian Life Commission was supportive.[16]

Besides the turmoil that had just spilled over from the Supreme Court, October (1962) brought the Cuban missile crisis, in which President Kennedy stared down the Soviet Union's bid to put nuclear weapons in Cuba. This proved to be a time of great anxiety due to communism's militancy. Curiously, it affected Southern Baptist agencies primarily due to the infighting that it generated.

Because communism was holding the attention of so many Southern Baptists, and Americans in general, particularly with the Castro coup in Cuba, the Southern Baptist Radio and Television Commission ran a front-cover article in that agency's *Beam* magazine entitled, "A Look at Communist Techniques and Practices." Valentine wrote to Porter Routh, head of the Executive Committee, pointing out that the Radio and Television Commission had stepped out of its program assignment and infringed on that of his Commission and that of the Sunday School Board. He expressed his wish that they could "avoid such serious problems in the future."[17]

Prior to the Convention's 1963 meeting in Kansas City, the civil rights movement continued to escalate. In April, Martin Luther King Jr. was arrested in Birmingham, a city he called "the belly of the beast." Three weeks before King was to lead a major demonstration in Birmingham, he was arrested for having "defied a court order that forbade marches, sit-ins and other peaceful protests," which was used to challenge institutional segregation. A group of white ministers sympathetic to King's long-term objectives disagreed with his tactics and called King's planned protest "unwise and untimely." In response to these religious leaders, King wrote his masterful "Letter from a Birmingham Jail," in which he referred to St. Augustine's distinction between just and unjust laws. In his letter he wrote, "I have no fear about the outcome of our struggle. . . . We will reach the goal of freedom . . . because the goal of America is freedom. . . . Our destiny is tied up with America's destiny. . . . The sacred heritage of our nation and the eternal will of God are embodied in our echoing demands."[18]

In May, when King led his promised protest against Birmingham's institutionalized racism, public safety commissioner Eugene "Bull" Connor had his firemen turn on fire hoses, his police turn loose their dogs, and treated the protesters with brutality. Because of the televised images, the nation's conscience was galvanized, and the civil rights movement moved forward.[19] These things transpired just before the Southern Baptist Convention was called into session in 1963.

Because of these incidents, it was surprising that the 1963 Convention was so low key with respect to race issues. It may be, however, that they were so preoccupied with the doctrinal issues that it simply did not find a champion or a platform at that time.

In his Commission report, Valentine only mentioned race one time, saying, "The aggressive projections of this program [of] Christian morality in the areas of family life, race relations, moral issues, daily work, and citizenship has been viewed by the Christian Life Commission as the greatest contribution it can make in the life of Southern

Baptists." The report reviewed a list of activities the Commission was involved in, had no recommendations, and was quickly accepted. In his address to the Convention, Valentine did not promote the race issue. Perhaps at that time he considered it too volatile.[20]

At the 1963 Convention, President Herschel Hobbs was the main attraction. He did not shy away from addressing the race issue. Although he had not been a strong supporter of Miller, Hobbs maintained that "it is impossible to solve [racial problems] by passing a blanket law, or by conducting a social crusade. . . . They must be dealt with on a spiritual and personal basis." Hobbs then recalled the Convention's approval of the 1954 Supreme Court decision, arguing that this posture was not enough. "Implementation must come at the local level, which places the responsibility . . . specifically upon the Christians in the community."[21]

Two days after this sermon, Hobbs presided over the adoption of the new Southern Baptist Confession, The Baptist Faith and Message of 1963.[22]

Later the Baptist Joint Committee, addressing the Convention through its Public Affairs Committee, reported on the controversial Supreme Court decision, *Engel v. Vitale*. The Committee reported to the Convention that it had taken a position supporting the ruling and had in fact submitted testimony, including resolutions from Baptist bodies, in favor of outlawing official prayer in public education. Surprisingly, the Convention accepted the report without much resistance. Nevertheless, many messengers left with great concern about where the nation and the Convention were headed.[23]

Before leaving the 1963 Convention, it is noteworthy to mention two resolutions. One, "On Human Freedom," seemed to be a veiled encouragement to address the emerging race issues from a Christian perspective. A second resolution, "On Federal Taxation," raised objections again to the notion "that Federal Public Funds be granted to church-related colleges and universities for the construction of academic facilities."[24]

Just a month after the Convention met, the Supreme Court ruled a second time on school prayer and Bible reading in *Abington Township v. Schempp* and the companion bill of *Murray v. Curlett*. The new ruling banned usage of both the Lord's Prayer and Bible reading. Writing the majority opinion, Tom Clark stated, "The place of religion in our society is an exalted one achieved through a long tradition of reliance on the home, the church and the inviolable citadel of the individual heart and mind." He explained that Americans "have come to realize through bitter experience that it is not within the power of government to invade that citadel." He then concluded that "in the relationship between man and religion, the State is firmly committed to a position of neutrality." In his solitary dissenting opinion, Justice Potter Stewart maintained that the Schempps' had, by their actions, infringed on the "free exercise" rights of the other students to pray and that the majority of the Court had established a "religion of secularism" in place of historic Christianity.[25]

Although legislators again offered bills which would overturn the Court's ruling, none gained enough traction to pass.

"I Have a Dream"

Meanwhile, the race issue continued to move front and center on the national agenda. On August 23, 1963, a massive march was held in Washington, D.C., calling for legislative action. On August 28, speaking from a podium in front of the Lincoln Memorial, King, addressing an audience of more than two hundred thousand in person and millions more watching by television, delivered his epoch-making "I Have a Dream" speech. Listeners heard King plead, "I have a dream that one day this nation will rise up and live out the true meaning of its creed: We hold these truths to be self-evident; that all men are created equal." Sadly, just two weeks later, the Ku Klux Klan bombed the Sixteenth Street Baptist Church in Birmingham on Sunday morning, September 15, killing four little girls: Denise McNair, Cynthia Wesley, Carole Robertson, and Addie Mae Collins. Riots erupted in Birmingham, resulting in the deaths of two more black students.[26]

The Executive Committee of the Convention met just a few days after the Birmingham bombing and high on its agenda was how to respond to the senseless slaughter of innocent human life. The Committee passed this resolution:

> Because racial strife has wrought tragedy and sorrow in many sections of our beloved nation and because this tragedy and sorrow lies heavily upon every Christian conscience, be it resolved . . . that we express our deepest sympathy to those families who have lost loved ones and to others who have been victimized by racial strife, [and] that we call upon members of our churches throughout the land to pray for a turning to and a sustaining of those Christian principles which alone can produce the balm of love that is sufficient to heal the rift in our world. We would pledge our prayers and our energetic efforts to this end.[27]

Like it or not, the race issue was demanding attention in the United States. And Southern Baptists of necessity were being called to take a stand for righteousness. How in the world could such an intolerable situation be permitted to go on? Could things get any worse? Yes, they could.

Two months later President Kennedy was scheduled to visit Texas. After a stop in San Antonio, he flew to Fort Worth and spent the night. On Friday morning, November 22, 1963, Kennedy spoke at a breakfast rally, then flew over to Dallas. The White House transcript of the day's events states: "After the breakfast at the Texas Hotel in Fort Worth the president flew to Love Field in Dallas. There he acknowledged greeters for a brief period and then entered an open car. The motorcade traveled down a 10-mile route through downtown Dallas on its way to the Trade Mart, where the president planned to speak at a luncheon. At approximately 12:30 (CST) he was struck by two bullets fired by an assassin." The president was declared dead at 1:00 p.m. at the Parkland Hospital in Dallas. In another hour Lyndon Baines Johnson, former congressman, former senate majority leader, and vice president was sworn into office. The nation mourned its dead president and experienced this event as yet another incident in a time of great uncertainty and high anxiety.[28]

In January 1964, the Twenty-fourth Amendment became law. In summary, Ward noted that "it tackles black disenfranchisement in the South by forbidding states to use payment of poll or other tax as a requirement to vote in federal elections."[29]

Two months before the next Southern Baptist Convention, the Supreme Court decided another landmark case in *New York Times Co. v. Sullivan*. The conclusion, in short, "established the actual malice standard before press reports could be considered to be defamation and libel; and hence allowed free reporting of the civil rights campaigns in the Southern United States." *The New York Times* argued that "the case against it was brought to intimidate news organizations and prevent them from reporting illegal actions of public employees in the South as they attempted to continue to support segregation." Justice William Brennan, writing the unanimous decision, viewed the case "against a backdrop of profound national commitment to the principle that debate on public issues should be uninhibited, robust, and wide-open, and that it may well include vehement, caustic, and sometimes unpleasantly sharp attacks on government and public officials."[30]

The 1964 Southern Baptist Convention met in Atlantic City, New Jersey, May 19–22. With the Christian Life Commission's budget increasing to $56,500, a third member, William Dyal Jr., was added to its staff. In his report to the Convention, Valentine asserted that the nation was experiencing a "crisis in morality." He pulled no punches relating to race at this Convention. He declared,

> We [Southern Baptists] have been part of a culture which
> has crippled the Negro and then blamed him for limping.
> Our failure to create a climate of Christian good will . . . has
> resulted in the racial protest movements which have been used
> for the redress of legitimate grievances.[31]

When the Commission offered recommendation two, which addressed the race issue, long and intense debate followed. The Convention accepted a watered-down version of the Commission's original recommendation and then rejected the Commission's further recommendation, which renounced the practice of capital punishment. The bottom line for the 1964 Convention was that the messengers were unwilling to follow blindly the leadership of Foy Valentine and the Christian Life Commission. Sadly, with respect to the race issue, not all churches were prepared to embrace an open-door policy for all races.[32]

Interestingly enough, as the Southern Baptist Convention was concluding, the president of the United States, Lyndon Johnson, delivered an epoch-defining address, "The Great Society," at the University of Michigan in Ann Arbor on May 22. What Southern Baptists were reluctant to embrace at this time, Johnson was busy promoting. In his address he stated, "The Great Society rests on abundance and liberty for all." He explained, "It demands an end to poverty and racial injustice, to which we are totally committed in our time." He went on to say, "So I want to talk to you today about three places where we begin to build the Great Society—in our cities, in our countryside, and in our classrooms." He then addressed each of these in turn. In short, he laid out a domestic agenda every bit as ambitious as Roosevelt's New Deal.[33]

By July 2, 1964, the Civil Rights Act of 1964 had become the law of the land. While "Kennedy's proposed civil rights legislation had been stalled in Congress by Southern Democrats," Johnson drove through "a much more radical Civil Rights Bill." The heart of the bill banned all racial discrimination in all public places and federal programs, and also in employment and union membership."[34]

Nevertheless, the civil rights movement met violent resistance in many places. A low point occured when, on August 4, three civil rights' workers in Mississippi, (two white and one black) were discovered buried in an earthen dam. James Chaney, 21; Andrew Goodman, 21; and Michael Schwerner, 24, had been working to register black voters in Mississippi. It was reported that when they went to investigate the burning of a black church they were arrested for speeding, taken to jail and "then released after dark into the hands of the Ku Klux Klan, who murdered them."[35]

As grievous as this crime was, it was buried in the headlines in the days that followed. On August 4, Johnson reported the North

Vietnamese had attacked without provocation two U.S. destroyers in the Gulf of Tonkin. This incident became the pretext for the "Gulf of Tonkin" resolution on August 7, which brought the U.S. into war with North Vietnam and the Viet Cong.[36]

In the fall of 1964, two events occurred that are worthy of mention. In October, Martin Luther King Jr. was awarded the Nobel Peace Prize for his leadership in America's Civil Rights Movement. On December 10, he delivered his acceptance speech in Oslo, Norway. Consider his sobering words:

> I accept the Nobel Prize for Peace at a moment when twenty-two million Negroes of the United States of America are engaged in a creative battle to end the long night of racial injustice. I accept this award on behalf of a civil rights movement which is moving with determination and a majestic scorn for risk and danger to establish a reign of freedom and rule of justice. . . .
>
> After contemplation, I conclude that this award which I receive on behalf of that movement is profound recognition that nonviolence is the answer to the crucial political and moral question of our time—the need for man to overcome oppression and violence without resorting to violence and oppression. . . .
>
> I accept this award today with an abiding faith in America and an audacious faith in the future of mankind. I refuse to accept despair as the final response to the ambiguities of history. I refuse to accept the idea that the "isness" of man's present nature makes him morally incapable of reaching up for the eternal "oughtness" that forever confronts him.

With King's acceptance speech, the civil rights movement in America was placed on the front burner of the world scene.[37]

Also, in the fall of 1964, Lyndon Johnson won his bid for reelection over challenger Barry Goldwater of Arizona. Goldwater's argument that "extremism in the defense of liberty is no vice" simply did not sit well with a nation still mourning Kennedy. Johnson won in a landslide with 61 percent of the popular vote and 486 to 52 in the nation's electoral college. Nevertheless, Goldwater's conservatism may well have prepared the way for Ronald Reagan's election in 1980.[38]

Meanwhile, the race issue continued to heat up across America. On December 14, the Supreme Court ruled in *Heart of Atlanta Motel v. United States*, concluding that "Congress did not unconstitutionally exceed its powers under the Commerce Clause by enacting Title II of the 1964 Civil Rights Act, which prohibited racial discrimination in public accommodations." This case represented the first comprehensive act by Congress on civil rights and race relations since the Civil Rights Act of 1875. It represented a major blow to the "separate but equal" mind-set that had for one hundred years left black Americans with inferior accommodations and service due to racial segregation. Justice Clark, writing for the Court's unanimous decision, asserted that "Congress may employ its commerce powers to legislate against 'moral wrongs' like racial discrimination."[39]

One month later the Supreme Court ruled in another civil rights related case, *Cox v. Louisiana*, on January 18, 1965. Describing the essence of the case, Irons and Guitton write:

> In December 1961, twenty-three black students were arrested in Baton Rouge, Louisiana, for picketing stores that maintained segregated lunch counters. The following morning, the Rev. B. Elton Cox led a march to the courthouse, where two thousand students gathered to protest the arrests. Cox urged them to conclude the demonstration with sit-ins in the segregated stores. The police immediately dispersed the crowd, using tear gas. Cox was arrested and convicted under laws against disturbing the peace, obstructing public passages, and courthouse picketing. He appealed his twenty-one-month sentence, claiming that his First Amendment rights of free speech and assembly had been violated. In 1965, the Supreme Court declared Louisiana's laws unconstitutional. "We affirm," Justice Arthur Goldberg wrote, "that our constitutional command of free speech and assembly is fundamental and encompasses peaceful social protest."[40]

In the context of a looming war in Southeast Asia and an ever intensifying civil rights movement, Southern Baptists' leadership was working diligently to cope and change. On the second Sunday in February 1965, the Convention's churches celebrated "Race Relation Sunday" for the first time. The sponsoring Christian Life Commission suggested a variety of program ideas to assist in implementing the goals of racial understanding and reconciliation.

On Sunday, February 21, 1965, Malcolm X, who was seen as second only to King in the civil rights movement's leadership, was gunned down in New York City by dissident Muslims. His murder seemed to harden hearts on both sides of the civil rights struggle and to make the Commission's efforts more difficult.

Meanwhile, the United States began its engagement in Vietnam by initiating its "Operation Rolling Thunder" bombing excursions against North Vietnam. During the first half of 1965, seventy-five thousand ground troops were sent to Vietnam; and by July, President Johnson announced that another one hundred seventy-five thousand would be deployed.

In the initial months of 1965, the civil rights movement shifted to Selma, Alabama. In the words of Greg Ward:

> The focus of the civil rights movement shifts in January to Selma, Alabama, a majority black city where only one percent of blacks are registered to vote. By February 1, Rev. Martin Luther King, Jr., and three thousand other demonstrators are in jail. After police shoot a black youth during a night-time demonstration in nearby Marion on February 18, a protest march from Selma to Montgomery on March 7 is violently broken up by state troopers. They also stop King leading another march on March 9. Prompted by these events, President Johnson presents a new voting rights bill to Congress on March 15, then federalizes the Alabama National Guard and sends in the Army to protect a third march, which completes the 54-mile route from Selma to Montgomery between March 21 and 25.

Nevertheless, the first march on March 7, which was aborted due to mob violence, became known as "Bloody Sunday" and marked another major turning point in the effort to gain the support of public opinion in the civil rights movement. National public outrage was aroused as the brutality was broadcast across the country.[41]

This was the national context of the June 1–4, 1965, Southern Baptist Convention as it met in Dallas. When it was his turn to address the Convention, Valentine commended the work of his Commission, acknowledging the circulation of almost three million tracts and literature pieces. Four state commissions had been started the previous year and the summer conferences at Glorieta and Ridgecrest on "Christianity and Race Relations" had drawn a record attendance of 3,290 people.[42]

After the intense debate over race and the churches' response and responsibility in 1964, the Commission addressed again the same subject. In Valentine's report to the Convention, he focused on three areas of moral concern, "The Moral Revolution," "The Challenge of Peace," and the "Racial Crisis." In his address he observed that "the whole world seems to be adrift in a vast sea of moral relativity. . . . We . . . reaffirm our conviction that while not all moral men are Christians, all Christians are moral men, called to be morally conformed to the mind of Christ."[43]

Valentine again spoke in opposition to militarism, which was set against the backdrop of U.S. Marine involvement in Vietnam and the Dominican Republic. "The strategy of saber-rattling and brinkmanship . . . will never solve the problems of world conflicts at their deeper levels and should not be considered as substitutes for Christian redemption and compassion."[44]

He next moved to the race issue, asserting that a "major turning point had been reached in race relations" since the 1964 Convention had met. "Throughout most of the nation there had been widespread compliance with the Civil Rights law, peaceful acceptance of desegregation in the public schools, a heartening move toward justice in job opportunities, housing and voting, and a steadily increasing extension of church ministries without racial restrictions." "Still," he maintained, "Southern Baptist witness for Jesus Christ continues to be challenged more seriously . . . by the racial crisis than by any other ideological movement or moral problem in our time. . . . Our foreign missionaries have joined . . . in the most moving and poignant pleas for Southern Baptists to reject racism . . . and by so doing to unchain their hands."[45]

Next Valentine no doubt offended those with a segregationist mind-set by calling on Southern Baptists to confess "that we have been guilty of the sin of conformity to the world [in race relations]. . . . In a spirit of true repentance, let us prayerfully rededicate ourselves to the Christian ministry of reconciliation between Negroes and whites and between segregationists and integrationists. . . . We earnestly hope [that more Southern Baptists will be] involved actively and redemptively in seeking specific cures for specific racial ailments as personal prejudice, unfair housing practices, discriminatory employment, unequal justice under law and denial of voting rights."[46]

Not surprisingly, Valentine steered clear of the much-publicized civil rights marches led by King in Alabama. Nor did he congratulate King for winning the Nobel Peace Prize. Ironically King, whom many viewed as a suspected communist sympathizer, was a virtual nonentity in speeches by Commission staffers to Southern Baptist audiences.

As usual, the Commission report was printed in the *Book of Reports* and, similar to 1964, was not well received by those who resisted attempts to disengage from the segregationist mind-set.

In the Thursday afternoon session, W. M. Nivens of Kentucky offered a resolution to abolish the Christian Life Commission. It was referred to the Committee on Resolutions where it died. Yet the effort pointed to more resistance ahead. After prolonged debate, a compromise was achieved that received the Commission report and a disclaimer that the Commission report was not binding on the local churches.[47]

Several resolutions worthy of note were passed at the 1965 Convention: One, "Concerning the Sunday School Board," expressed concern over the writers and speakers they had employed and confidence that its past mistakes would not be repeated. It was evident that denominational employees and rank-and-file Southern Baptists were not on the same page. Another resolution "On Human Relations" noted that "the progress made toward an easing of racial tensions and a Christian solution does not match the extreme urgency reflected in current crises." It went on to rededicate Southern Baptists "to a ministry of reconciliation among all men." It was amended, however, to add, "We deplore the open and premeditated violation of civil laws, the destruction of property, the shedding of human blood, or the taking of life as a means of influencing legislation or changing the social and cultural patterns." The move to amend was not surprising considering the growing violence associated with the civil rights movement. Other resolutions, including one condemning obscenity and the typical Baptist position on church-state separation, were also passed.[48]

In the aftermath of the Convention, Valentine and Commission chairman John Claypool spoke at a press conference, from which newspaper religion writers penned glowing stories on the influence of the Commission in helping Southern Baptists overcome the sin of racism.[49]

Two events occured in the remainder of the year that underscored the intensity of Southern Baptists' concern over racism and segregation. Race riots swept across America in a variety of locations. The worst was in the Watts section of Los Angeles in August, which left thirty-four people dead, more than one thousand injured, more than four thousand arrests, and more than $200 million worth of damage and destruction to property. In many places angry black voices began to echo the Black Power rhetoric of Stokely Carmichael. Due to the fear generated by the riots, particularly in Watts, hundreds of Southern Baptist churches passed rules instructing ushers not to seat Negroes and any other perceived civil rights agitators, or they simply reaffirmed old laws excluding blacks.[50]

A second event that characterized the times occurred on August 6 when President Johnson signed the Voting Rights Act, which abolished literacy tests as a prerequisite to voting. These laws had been used to disenfranchise black participation in the electoral process. These were days of incredible domestic tension throughout the country.[51]

Across the sea in Vietnam, the first military engagement against North Vietnamese regulars occurred at the Ia Drang Valley.[52] This was only a foreshadowing of the depth of the escalation of the American involvement in Vietnam.

As 1966 dawned, much tension existed inside the Southern Baptist Convention due to the Christian Life Commission's aggressive approach to racial reconciliation and the resistance from many of the die-hard segregationists. When the Commission requested an increase in its budget allocation for 1966 from $90,000 to $140,000, the Executive Committee offered $10,000 and no more. It did not help that Douglas Hudgins was chairman of the Executive Committee.

When the Executive Committee met, it recommended changes in some of the agency program statements. The proposed alteration for the Christian Life Commission was limited to two. First, they were to focus on Christian morality development with the objective briefly defined as "assist[ing]" the churches by "helping them understand the moral demands of the gospel." Second, they were to offer specialized service and coordination "with regard to world peace, counseling and guidance, and human welfare." Race relations were not even mentioned in the statements.[53]

At the Convention, which gathered in Detroit, May 24–27, the Christian Life Commission by design kept a low profile. In fact, the Committee on Order of Business scheduled the Commission report as the last item on Friday, when many messengers had already departed for home. From the introduction of Chairman Claypool to the motion to adopt the Commission's report and its second and approval, the process took less than one minute. At that point Claypool introduced Valentine for his remarks, which were minimal.

Resolutions at the Convention were both predictable and surprising. One on religious liberty urged against private entities and sectarian organizations seeking public funds. This was predictable. The first of the resolutions, which would run for ten consecutive years, was offered on Vietnam. This one simply expressed the hope that world leaders "may somehow be led of God together to find the high and honorable road to peace and gain together the wisdom and courage to walk it."[54]

One resolution "Concerning the Fellowship of Christian Athletes" was surprising. It was totally supportive of its presence, influence, and agenda, calling its work "a vital Christian witness to the young of America." What is surprising was that neither the Baptist Joint Committee nor the Christian Life Commission attempted to criticize its religious intention and presence on public school grounds. The silence was deafening, and one wonders why the issue of the absolutist position on separation of church and state was not raised.[55]

A second surprising resolution was about "Christian Attitudes in the Modern World." Acknowledging that ours is a pluralistic society, the resolution stated that "we also extend our goodwill and love to non-Christian bodies and pledge ourselves anew to the defense of full religious liberty for each of them as we claim it for ourselves in every part of the world." It concluded, "We find considerable encouragement to believe that the whole world may desire benefit from the fresh winds that give some promise of religious freedom for all religious bodies in all parts of the world." In light of the evangelistic imperative, one wonders what Southern Baptists were thinking at this point.[56]

The next month, racial tension intensified as James Meredith led a civil rights march from Memphis to Jackson, Mississippi. On June 6, he was wounded by a sniper's bullet. The picture of the fallen Meredith won the Pulitzer Prize for Photography the following year. Fortunately, Meredith recovered.[57]

As the year passed, race riots broke out in Chicago, Brooklyn, Atlanta, Cleveland, and many smaller cities. At the war protests, which were beginning to gain traction, students in Washington began the chant, "Hey, Hey, LBJ, how many kids did you kill today?" Needless to say, it was a sad time in America's history. Civil unrest was rife.[58]

The following year, 1967 saw only more of the same. On March 12, Senator Robert Kennedy of New York denounced Johnson's war involvement; and the antiwar movement, like the civil rights movement, continued to grow. Like Kennedy, King also denounced the war, insisting that the U.S. was there "to occupy it as an American colony."[59]

When the Southern Baptist Convention met in Miami, almost fifteen thousand messengers attended. Once again the Christian Life Commission was the target of disgruntled messengers upset with the agency's activist positions on race and war. Messenger Rufus Sprayberry of Texas made the motion that the Christian Life Commission be disbanded. The motion was debated and defeated.[60]

At the appointed time Valentine delivered his address and, acknowledging the defeat of the motion to do away with the Commission, he simply said, "Thank you for my annual call." He then turned his attention to Vietnam and his desire for peace. At that point he invited Senator Mark Hatfield, a leading dove in the Senate, to address the Convention. Needless to say, the "victory in Vietnam" messengers were not pleased with Hatfield's presence or with his message.[61]

Two typical resolutions were "On the Separation of Church and State" and "Peace." The former noted once again that "the state has no right to impose taxes for the support of any form of religion," while the latter maintained the need for the "Christian's pursuit of peace with the patriot's prosecution of defensive war."[62]

A third, somewhat interesting, resolution, "On Population Explosion," raised the spectre of "overpopulation and mass starvation," then commended the "judicious use of medically approved methods of planned parenthood and the dissemination of planned parenthood information." One wonders if this was a veiled suggestion for Christians to practice birth control or if it was the first discreet attempt to be supportive of abortion, which would surface as an issue in the near future. Did this resolution attempt to create an urgency that demands a solution?[63]

Four major events rounded out 1967. First, on June 12, the Supreme Court ruled on *Loving v. Virginia*, which did away with all laws banning interracial marriage. Chief Justice Earl Warren wrote for the unanimous decision, "There can be no doubt that restricting the right to marry solely because of racial classifications violates the central meaning of the Equal Protection Clause."[64]

Another major event occurred in Israel with its Six-Day War. Because Arab forces were massing on its border, the Israel Defense

Force launched a preemptive strike and in so doing extended its borders to include the Sinai Peninsula, the West Bank and the Golan Heights. Because of U.S. military and financial assistance, the surrounding Arab and Muslim nations became increasingly distant from the United States.[65]

A third major event occurred on October 2 when the grandson of slaves, Thurgood Marshall, was sworn in as the ninety-sixth justice of the Supreme Court. Marshall, who had argued and won the landmark *Brown v. Board of Education* decision in 1954, had won twenty-nine of thirty-two cases he argued before the High Court and now was its first African American. When President Johnson nominated Marshall to the Supreme Court on June 13, 1967, following the retirement of Justice Clark, he asserted that this was "the right thing to do, the right time to do it, the right man and the right place."[66]

A final major event in 1967 occurred October 21–22, when fifty thousand antiwar protestors marched on Washington, D.C. Needless to say, the civil rights movement was moving ahead, and the world was unsettled. Discontent was still rife across America.[67]

The year 1968 was one of crisis. In January, the *U.S.S. Pueblo* was captured by North Korea, which imprisoned its eighty-two member crew. In January the surprising Tet Offensive began as the North Vietnamese Regular Army launched an all-out assault on South Vietnam. When the war was over, it was clear the United States won the military conflict, yet the U.S. media led by Walter Cronkite had so demoralized the country, maintaining that the war was hopelessly lost and therefore unwinnable, that the United States government literally conceded its will to win. At the height of the conflict, almost a half-million soldiers were in Vietnam. On March 16, the My Lai massacre occurred in which Lieutenant William Calley and his men reportedly killed almost five hundred Vietnamese civilians. No doubt this further demoralized those who thought the war was justified to stop communist aggression.[68]

On March 31, President Johnson stunned the nation when he announced that he would not seek reelection. Appearing depressed, demoralized, and defeated, he told the nation that his address concerned peace in Vietnam and Southeast Asia, and for seven and a half pages of text that was his subject. Then in his conclusion he stated, "With America's sons in the fields far away, with America's future under challenge right here at home, with our hopes and the world's hopes for peace in the balance everyday, I do not believe that I should devote an hour or a day of my time to any personal partisan causes or to any duties other than the awesome duties of this office—the Presidency of our country." Then he revealed, "Accordingly, I shall not seek, and I will not accept, the nomination of my party for another term as your President."[69]

"I've Been to the Mountaintop"

Just a few days after Johnson's surprise announcement, on April 3, Martin Luther King delivered his "I've Been to the Mountaintop" sermon in Memphis. He prophetically told the crowd:

> It really doesn't matter what happens now. . . . some began
> to . . . talk about threats that were out—what would happen
> to me from some of our sick white brothers. . . . Like anybody,
> I would like to live a long life. Longevity has its place, but I'm
> not concerned about that now. I just want to do God's will.
> And He's allowed me to go to the mountain! And I've looked
> over, and I've seen the Promised Land. I may not get there with
> you. But I want you to know tonight, that we, as a people, will
> get to the Promised Land. And so I'm happy tonight. I'm not
> worried about anything. I'm not fearing any man. Mine eyes
> have seen the Glory of the coming of the Lord![70]

At 6:01 p.m. the next day, April 4, 1968, Martin Luther King was felled by an assassin's bullet as he stood on the balcony of the Lorraine Motel in Memphis, Tennessee. Friends ran out to the balcony to find that he had been shot in the throat. He died an hour later at St. Joseph's Hospital. The assassination led to riots in more than sixty cities.[71]

President Johnson declared a national day of mourning for the lost civil rights leader. More than three hundred thousand people attended King's funeral. Two months later James Earl Ray was arrested at London's Heathrow Airport, extradited to Tennessee, and charged with King's murder. Ray, who later pleaded innocent, was found guilty and given life in prison, where he died on April 23, 1998.[72]

On April 11, the Civil Rights Act of 1968 was signed by President Johnson. This Act, a follow-up to the 1964 legislation, prohibits discrimination in housing "concerning the sale, rental, financing of housing based on race, religion, national origin, sex (and as amended) handicap and family status." Civil rights workers were also protected in its provisions. This law added additional teeth and provided stronger guarantees that each citizen's civil rights would be protected.[73]

On June 4, 1968, the same day that the Southern Baptist Convention had its opening session in Houston, Texas, presidential candidate Robert Kennedy won the California primary for the Democratic nomination for president. After addressing his supporters early in the morning of June 5 in a ballroom at the Ambassador Hotel in Los Angeles, he exited through a crowded service area. A disgruntled Palestinian immigrant, Sirhan Sirhan, shot Kennedy in the head at close range. Although he was rushed to the Good Samaritan Hospital, Kennedy died from his wounds at the age of forty-two. Eulogizing his brother, Senator Edward M. Kennedy said, "My brother need not be idolized, or enlarged in death beyond what he was in life, to be remembered simply as a good and decent man, who saw wrong and tried to right it, saw suffering and tried to heal it, saw war and tried to stop it." Robert Kennedy was buried near his brother, John, at Arlington National Cemetery in Virginia.[74]

All of these events—the Tet Offensive, rumors of My Lai, President Johnson's decision not to seek reelection, the signing of the Civil Rights Act of 1968, and most importantly the twin assassinations of King and Kennedy—provided the incredibly emotional backdrop for the 1968 Southern Baptist Convention.

Foy Valentine's address on Wednesday of the Convention shared this observation, "Today's world is a strange, violent, disfigured world." He explained, "By an incredible distortion of logic it views immorality as a harmless exercise of the times, violence as a proper way of life, and racism as a divine right." No doubt Valentine captured the perception of the country and the Convention well.[75]

Valentine looked back on the previous March's Christian Citizenship Seminar on "Christian Action in a Disordered Society" held in Washington, D.C., March 25–27, just days before Johnson's announcement about not seeking reelection. At the seminar Johnson, who had spoken, said, "The only lasting solution to frustration and discontent and disorder will require a change in men's eyes—in the way they treat their neighbors." The seminar had featured other high-profile speakers as well.[76]

In his address Valentine stated, as he had before, that "no greater trouble has ever beset the church of Jesus Christ than that which issues from an arbitrary division of word and deed in an unwarranted fragmentation of evangelism and ethics. . . . In God's plan, faith and works are never divided; they are always united."[77]

Valentine then addresseed the sin of institutional racism when he stated, "Racism, the doctrine that one race is congenitally superior and all others congenitally inferior, is still a major premise in the world today and it should not have taken the report of the [Federal] Advisory Commission on Civil Disorder to tell us any of that." He then said quite honestly, "Although the church has struggled mightily with this evil spirit, it is still not exorcised."[78]

When Valentine finished his message, he received sustained applause, yet not unexpectedly some sat still in their seats.

When the time came for the election of president of the Convention, Owen Cooper and W. A. Criswell were nominated. Criswell won.

The major issue for the Convention was wrapped up in the proposed, "Statement Concerning the Crisis in Our Nation," to which Valentine, Clifton Allen, and others had contributed ideas leading to a collective document. C. R. Daley, editor of the Kentucky state paper, asked in an editorial, "Will Southern Baptists Fiddle While America Burns?" Prior to the Convention, widespread fear rumored that the

Convention would be disrupted by Baptist college students and others who were finally fed up with the old status quo.[79]

In the words of John Finley: "Across the convention, leaders were realizing that some kind of official SBC resolution, with broad representation and view was necessary. Daley again writes: 'Southern Baptists in Houston should . . . come forth with a loud and clear voice sounding our convictions on human rights. This voice should be so sharp and strong that no one hearing it could ever doubt where we stand.'" When the document was recommended, debated, and amended, it passed with a vote of 5,687 for and 2,119 against.[80]

The "Statement Concerning the Crisis in Our Nation," after its opening disclaimer that it expresses only the sentiments of the messengers meeting at the Houston Convention, nevertheless, proceeds to say:

> Our nation is enveloped in a social and cultural revolution. We are shocked by the potential for anarchy in a land dedicated to democracy and freedom. There are ominous sounds of hate and violence among men and of unbelief and rebellion toward God. These compel Christians to face the social situation and to examine themselves under the judgment of God.
>
> We are an affluent society, abounding in wealth and luxury. Yet far too many of our people suffer from poverty. Many are hurt by circumstance from which they find it most difficult to escape, injustice which they find most difficult to correct, or heartless exploitation which they find most difficult to resist. Many live in slum housing or ghettos of race or poverty or ignorance or bitterness that often generate both despair and defiance.
>
> We are a nation that declares the sovereignty of law and the necessity of civil order. Yet we have had riots and have tolerated conditions that breed riots, spread violence, foster disrespect for the law, and undermine the democratic process.
>
> We are a nation that declares the equality and rights of persons irrespective of race. Yet, as a nation, we have allowed

cultural patterns to persist that have deprived millions of
black Americans, and other racial groups as well, of equality of recognition and opportunity in the areas of education,
employment, citizenship, housing, and worship. Worse still, as
a nation, we have condoned prejudices that have damaged the
personhood of blacks and whites alike. We have seen a climate
of racism and reactionism develop resulting in hostility, injustice, suspicion, faction, strife, and alarming potential for bitterness, division, destruction, and death.[81]

After defining the crisis in the opening paragraphs, the document
moves on to articulate the efforts that had been made, voice a confession of guilt and repentance, declare the commitment of Southern
Baptists to correct past failings, and finally make an appeal to engage
in appropriate steps of action. The document concludes, stating, "We
believe that a vigorous Christian response to this national crisis is
imperative for an effective witness on our part at home and abroad."
Specifically, it states, "Words will not suffice. The time has come for
action."[82]

McBeth, assessing the significance of this statement, noted, "In the
midst of the racial crisis of the late 1960s, the Convention adopted [this]
statement . . . , and it was signed individually by the major Convention
leaders." He observed, "This is a courageous and prophetic declaration
by the most ethnically diverse denomination in America." Sadly not all
Southern Baptists were prepared to embrace this statement.[83]

When the Commission report concluded, and was received without rancor, Commissioner Wade Darby, speaking for the Commission,
said simply, "Your Christian Life Commission would like to thank
you for a greater degree of acceptance than this agency has ever experienced before." He then conceded, "To pay attention to the pressing
and often controversial issue is not always pleasant or popular." He
then gratefully acknowledged, "Our task would be impossible without
your encouragement, and we thank you."[84]

Reflecting back on the 1968 Convention, his presidential election, and the subsequent press conference, Criswell writes in his autobiography:

> In fact, most of those reporters didn't know a thing about me or about my values. They were surprised when I expressed my sympathies publicly to the entire Kennedy family upon young Bobby's tragic and untimely death. They were surprised when I informed them that First Baptist Church had black members already on its rolls. And they were surprised when the man they had labeled "an avid segregationist" signed the strong racial statement adopted by the Messengers.
>
> "Every Southern Baptist in the land should support the spirit of that statement," I exclaimed. "We Southern Baptists have definitely turned away from racism, from segregation, from anything and everything that speaks of a separation of people in the body of Christ."[85]

Before leaving the 1968 Southern Baptist Convention, it should be noted that most of the resolutions were consistent with those from previous years. One that was very appropriate for the moment was "On Violence, Disregard for the Law." No doubt this was of great concern to the messengers and served in the view of some as an appropriate complement to the "Statement."[86]

In the remainder of the year, besides the nation's ongoing racial strife and war protests particularly at the Democratic National Convention in Chicago, two events were noteworthy. First, in the November election, Richard M. Nixon was elected president with 31.8 million votes. Hubert Humphrey lost with 31.3 million votes, and George Wallace came in third with 9.9 million votes. The Democrats kept their majorities in both the House and the Senate.[87]

A few days after the election, the Supreme Court announced on November 12 its decision in the *Epperson v. Arkansas* case, finding in favor of Epperson. This case invalidated an Arkansas statute that prohibited the teaching of evolution, stating, "There is and can be no doubt that the First Amendment does not permit the State to require that teaching and learning must be tailored to the principles or prohibitions of any sect or dogma." The unanimous verdict concludes, "Plainly, the law is contrary to the mandate of the First, and in violation of the Fourteenth Amendment to the Constitution."[88]

Hopefully, 1969 would be more peaceful than the previous year had been both in the nation and in the Southern Baptist Convention.

On February 24, 1969, the Supreme Court announced its *Tinker v. Des Moines* decision, which ruled in favor of the plaintiff, Tinker. In the words of Justice Abe Fortas, "Students do not shed their Constitutional right to freedom of speech and expression at the schoolhouse gate." The high court "ruled that the Constitution guaranteed public school students a right to symbolic, nondisruptive political expression."[89]

Two months before the 1969 Convention in New Orleans, the Christian Life Commission held its annual seminar. This year's theme was "The Church's Mission in the National Crisis." This year's location was at the University of Chicago. Jesse Jackson, a keynote speaker, addressed the seminar on the subject "Black Power and the Church's Response." Gibson Winter, professor of ethics and society in the University of Chicago Divinity School, lectured on "Emerging Moral and Religious Themes in the Contemporary Crisis." In short, the seminar was far to the left philosophically and theologically from the average Southern Baptist.

At the 1969 New Orleans Convention, messengers were disgruntled over some of the resolutions proposed by the Baptist Joint Committee. For example, it lauded the past Supreme Court decisions in 1962 and 1963.[90]

Significant resistance came to Valentine's "Statement on Extremism—Left and Right." The perception was that he was more critical of the right than the left, and in fact he was. There was so much antagonism that Richard Barrett, a messenger from Mississippi, offered a substitute motion to the Christian Life Commission's report and recommendations, stating that the Convention thanked the Commission for its report and moved that it be received without adopting any of the recommendations. Barrett's motion was accepted by the Convention.

It was probably the best compromise that Valentine and the Commission could expect this year.[91]

As in past years the Convention again approved resolutions criticizing attempts to use public tax monies to support religious institutions and expressed its disapproval of the appointment of an ambassador to the Vatican. Advertising for cigarettes and liquor were criticized. A resolution on family life and sex education was adopted. This may have been promoted with the anticipation of the coming year's Commission-sponsored seminar. It did pass a resolution critical of the New Orleans Hospital for its slowness to integrate, entertained another motion concerning peace in Vietnam, rejected a resolution looking favorably on conscientious objectors to the war, and passed a resolution that categorically rejected the notion of paying reparations for past social injustices to minorities.[92]

One of the highlights of the 1969 Convention was the release of Criswell's *Why I Preach that the Bible Is Literally True*. This volume marked one of the rallying points for conservatives who were growing increasingly suspicious of the continual drift to the theological left. Things would begin to heat up in the next decade, and the Christian Life Commission would increasingly find itself out of step with its constituency, not because of the race issue but because of its stances on abortion and Scripture.

The remainder of 1969 hailed some significant events. On June 17, the Stonewall Riots in New York City initiated the homosexual rights movement in America. A month later Neil Armstrong walked on the moon, and by November massive antiwar protests were staged in Washington, D.C., and San Francisco.[93]

At the turn of the decade, unrest was still prevalent. By February the verdict was announced in the trial of the Chicago Eight. They were found innocent of conspiracy, which would have carried a weighty jail sentence, but five of them were convicted on crossing state lines to incite a riot, which carries a five-year jail sentence.[94]

The Christian Life Commission Seminar held in Atlanta on March 16–18 was entitled "Toward Authentic Morality for Modern Man." Little did Valentine know that he would receive a tremendous backlash for hosting such a conference. The rub, it seems, was due to the speakers who were invited to address the seminar. Set in almost a debate format, several leading proponents of less-than-biblical morality were invited to address the participants along with the biblical response. Critics reacted to the addresses by Joseph Fletcher, Anson Mount, Frank Stagg, and Julian Bond.[95]

Joseph Fletcher, professor of social ethics at the Episcopal Theological Seminary in Cambridge, Massachusetts, is best known for coining the phrase "situational ethics," which he advocated at the seminar. His approach to ethics is such that the situation or circumstances discerned by an individual or group determine the rightness or wrongness of any activity or moral choice. Henlee Barnett responded with his biblical critique.[96]

Anson Mount, manager of public affairs for *Playboy* magazine out of Chicago, addressed the participants on the subject "The Playboy Philosophy—Pro." Mount related that this magazine had become a leading forum in the reexamination of current ethical and social issues and moral values. Acknowledging that his magazine was read by an average of twenty million people each month, he pointed out specifically that it was read by half the men in America between the ages of eighteen and thirty-four. He went on to point out that they offered to their readers "a sort of substitute religion." He suggested that they did a better job influencing the culture than the church and then asserted their "religion is our love affair with life." Their goal, he argued, was to help redefine sexual norms in America. Bill Pinson offered the response.[97]

Two other addresses were by Frank Stagg and Julian Bond. Stagg's was a diatribe on "militarism," and Bond's was on "The Constructive Use of Black Power." Although Vietnam and race were not in the headlines, evidently Valentine believed it appropriate still to provide a venue to ventilate on these issues.[98]

Sadly Valentine had no idea the firestorm he created by hosting the speakers he did at this year's seminar. In a few months he found out.

As the spring passed, America experienced the drama and heroics of *Apollo 13*'s near tragedy and mourned with the families of the four slain students at Kent State University when a war protest turned into a riot and National Guardsmen, unprepared for the conflict, fired on the student protesters on May 4.[99]

Firestorm in Denver

June arrived and with it the 1970 Southern Baptist Convention's annual meeting, this year in Denver, June 1–4. The criticism the Christian Life Commission received in 1969 was mild compared to the firestorm in Denver. The Convention got off to a disturbing start Tuesday morning when a noisy group of professed black militants invaded the Convention hall. They stood yelling with their fists raised until ushers escorted them out. The appearance of the radicals only served to reinforce the belief of many conservatives that the Convention needed some change. Among other things, conservatives demanded that agency employees and even writers for the Sunday School Board sign their belief in biblical inerrancy.[100]

Many conservatives called for the Sunday School Board to withdraw volume 1 of the new Broadman Commentary, "because it is out of keeping with the beliefs of a vast majority of Baptists." No doubt this was the consensus of a group of Southern Baptist pastors and leaders who had met just prior to the 1970 Convention for an "Affirming the Bible Conference." At the conference, Joe Odle of Mississippi observed, "There is appearing in some of the literature, materials which are raising questions in the mind of a large segment of the Southern Baptist constituency." He explained, "A rumbling is being heard that will not be silenced. . . . No amount of reassurance from leaders has been able to stop it, nor can we expect it to ebb as long as objectionable materials continue to appear."[101]

At the Convention Gwin Turner challenged the doctrinal soundness of the Genesis-Exodus commentary and moved that its distribution be halted immediately and that the commentary be rewritten from a conservative perspective. A surprise to agency heads, his motion carried. An even larger outcry came from those who criticized the Christian Life Commission primarily for its spring seminar lineup of guest speakers. In fact, Michie Proctor of Texas moved to amend the Commission's budget recommendation by asking that the proposed $200,000 allocation to the Commission be canceled so that they only receive money designated by local churches. This motion failed, yet reflected the tone of the Convention.[102]

Valentine did not even mention the Atlanta seminar in his 1970 Convention report for the previous twelve months. He talked about new tract titles in the Commission's Issues and Answers series on the subjects of abortion, black power, civil disobedience, drugs, guaranteed income, totalitarianism, urban crisis, violence, law and order, and justice. But he never mentioned what was labeled the "Playboy" seminar.

Many of the Convention messengers were still angry over the seminar and could hardly wait for their turn at the microphone. Bertha Smith, retired missionary to China, called for the resignation of the entire Commission staff. California's Harold Coble moved that the Convention take note "that a great number of our people and our churches have been seriously offended by the Atlanta seminar." Altogether, five motions were made criticizing the Commission for hosting the seminar.[103]

The controversy over the Playboy seminar became so heated that four former Convention presidents caucused together and hastily drew up a statement that they hoped the messengers would accept. Ramsey Pollard, speaking for the group, read this statement:

> It is our sincere judgment, that the issues concerning the
> Christian Life Seminar in Atlanta have been fully exposed and
> nothing of real value can be contributed by additional discus-
> sion. Your convictions have been heard and they have regis-
> tered. . . . We would urge our boards . . . to be exceedingly
> careful in arranging future programs so that the
> harmony and cooperative spirit of the Convention not be
> destroyed. . . . We would also assure Foy Valentine and the
> Christian Life Commission of our concern and our prayers as
> they seek to lead us in a most difficult phase of our denomina-
> tional life.[104]

Pollard then moved that the five motions attacking the Commission be tabled. After more criticism of the Commission, the motions were voted on one at a time. The hand vote was ruled sufficient by the chair to table the motions critical of the agency.

Resolutions on race, Vietnam, law and order, financing education, extremism, the environment, and drugs and alcohol passed with little discussion.

Messengers left the 1970 Convention having accomplished nothing with respect to the needed corrections. The Convention voted to withdraw a book but did not change any policy which permitted the book's publication, criticized the format and content of the Christian Life Commission's seminar but accomplished nothing to correct the leadership which planned and promoted it, and expressed their concern over the doctrinal standards of our boards and agencies but did nothing to change them. In short, as Richard Land observes, "Conservatives, again, won in public and they ended up losing in private."[105]

Later, on June 24, Congress repealed the Tonkin Gulf resolution, which had provided the justification for the Vietnam War. It looked as though the end of the war was in sight, yet the unity of the nation appeared to be in shambles. Moreover, the growing discontent among Southern Baptists was not ebbing as Convention bureaucrats had hoped.

By the 1971 Convention meeting in St. Louis on June 1–3, things seem to have calmed down a bit for the Christian Life Commission. In fact, now sixteen months after the fact, Valentine finally mentioned the 1970 seminar, reporting simply that it had 379 registered participants and received national press coverage. Many wished he had just left it alone.

Valentine did not mention in his report that a special investigative committee had been selected from the Executive Committee to consider recommending to the Convention that the Commission be dissolved as an agency and its programs be reassigned to the Home Mission Board. The committee's work was supposed to be kept in confidence, but as so often happens, confidentiality was broken, and the press found out about it. In fact, a reporter from the Commercial Appeal in Memphis called requesting information from the Christian

Life Commission. Valentine was not happy, refused to comment, and hung up.

Valentine wrote to the chairman of the committee, E. W. Price Jr., with copies sent to the other fourteen committee members, irate that confidences had been violated. Once the story was out, however, the Commission's friends and supporters rallied; and the idea of the dissolution was dropped. The source of that leak is a mystery to this day, but it served the Valentine administration well.[106]

At the 1971 Convention in St. Louis, the Commission received no overt public criticism. It may have been partly due to the fact that the leaders and the Committee on Order of Business decided to combine all the reports of a dozen agencies between 2:50 and 4:00 on Tuesday afternoon. Valentine had less than five minutes to comment on the printed Christian Life Commission report. The productivity of the Commission seemed to be significant, and besides there was almost no time for questions. This, looking back, was purely intentional.[107]

The Christian Life Commission did work through the Resolutions Committee to offer a number of resolutions for the Convention's consideration and approval. The resolution "On Beverage Alcohol" sounded like something Barton might have written a half-century earlier. The one "On Prejudice" says, "There is something of the image of God in every man which should elicit from Christians understanding and love." No mention of race, however, was made. The resolution "On Peace" simply applauded efforts to finish the Vietnam War.[108]

The resolution "On Abortion," however, which appeared to uphold the sanctity of human life, was actually a pro-choice document and was subsequently used to help encourage the Supreme Court in its landmark *Roe v. Wade* and *Doe v. Bolton* decisions a year and a half later. The resolution reads:

> WHEREAS, Christians in the American society today are faced with difficult decisions about abortion; and
>
> WHEREAS, Some advocate that there be no abortion legislation, thus making the decision a purely private matter between a woman and her doctor; and

WHEREAS, Others advocate no legal abortion, or would permit abortion only if the life of the mother is threatened;

Therefore, be it RESOLVED, that this Convention express the belief that society has a responsibility to affirm through the laws of the state a high view of the sanctity of human life, including fetal life, in order to protect those who cannot protect themselves; and

Be it further RESOLVED, That we call upon Southern Baptists to work for legislation that will allow the possibility of abortion under such conditions as rape, incest, clear evidence of severe fetal deformity, and carefully ascertained evidence of the likelihood of damage to the emotional, mental, and physical health of the mother.[109]

When the resolution was presented, Hugo Lindquist of Oklahoma moved to amend it by deleting the last paragraph. His motion lost. Then James Garland of Kentucky moved to change the last paragraph by leaving out the words "and carefully ascertained evidence of the likelihood of damage to the emotional, mental, and physical health of the mother." Again, the attempt to amend was defeated. This resolution was carefully crafted, and its adoption was skillfully accomplished. Little did Southern Baptists know, or even realize, the implications of what they had just done. Southern Baptists had been deceived in the assessment of this historian into supporting the entire pro-abortion movement in America. In fact, this resolution would be used as part of the pro-abortion propaganda in the approaching debate and court cases on abortion.

What most Southern Baptists did not know is that Foy Valentine, the Christian Life Commission's executive secretary, was a member of the American Civil Liberties Union and that organization was definitely in the pro-abortion camp. The last paragraph of the 1971 abortion resolution from Southern Baptists essentially said abortion is acceptable under any circumstance and that Southern Baptists endorse a woman's right to choose to terminate her pregnancy. The problem was most Southern Baptists at that point had not thought much about the abortion issue, and the relatively few who did think about it considered it wrong with the exception of a small minority who controlled the Christian Life Commission, its policy and programming. Naylor was under the impression that the "resolution called for legislation that allowed for the possibility of abortion under carefully stipulated conditions." Like most messengers who trusted the Commission, he had no idea of the ramifications of this resolution and its precise wording for the days ahead.[110]

Also at the 1971 Convention in St Louis, questions continued to be raised about the doctrinal soundness of boards and agencies. Because two articles had been published in the *Baptist Program* that rejected the notion of biblical inerrancy, a motion was made requesting the Executive Committee and the editor of the *Baptist Program* to provide equal space for those who embrace inerrancy and biblical soundness. Naylor observed that "it is notable that the issue did not die." Because of the *Baptist Program* flap and the ongoing concern over the commentary, Naylor was more right than he realized.[111]

After the Convention, the Supreme Court again made headlines. On June 14, it ruled in the *Palmer v. Thompson* case, which challenged the closing of five swimming pools in Jackson, Mississippi, rather than integrate them. The Court ruled the closing was legal because it affected everyone the same. Justice Black wrote, "Nothing in the history or language of the Fourteenth Amendment persuades us that the closing of the Jackson swimming pools to all its citizens constitutes a denial of the 'equal protection of the laws.'"[112] Needless to say, this ruling did not sit well with those supporting the civil rights movement.

An even more destabilizing ruling came just two weeks later, the same day the Twenty-sixth Amendment gave eighteen- to twenty-year-olds the right to vote, when the Supreme Court ruled in the *New York Times Co. v. United States*, June 30, that it was legal for the *New York Times* to publish excerpts from what are commonly called the "Pentagon Papers." It concluded that freedom of the press is more sacred than the government's right to confidentiality and right to label documents as "classified due to national security." Summarizing the implications of this ruling, one historian writes:

The broader implications of this case at the time were that
the people of the United States were exposed to a history of
inner operations of the Executive with regards to the war, putting the Government under a level of public scrutiny it had not
known before. The *Times'* victory strengthened the notion that
it was not only the right of but also a central purpose of the
free press to scrutinize government.[113]

The notion that government and those in authority resided under
a cloud of suspicion did not help the Christian Life Commission, the
Executive Committee, or other boards and agencies of the Southern
Baptist Convention. Yet, this was the climate that developed in the
days when Vietnam was winding down and the civil rights movement
was advancing.

To make matters worse, the economy was in a period of economic
duress. The combination of inflation, unemployment, and the trade
deficit caused President Nixon to declare a 90-day wage and price
freeze. Coupled with the Organization of the Petroleum Exporting
Countries (OPEC) response and the revaluing of world currencies in
which the dollar was devalued by 8 percent, a new economic phenomenon occured in the United States called "stagflation," a combination
of high inflation and economic stagnation. The American people were
not happy.[114]

In February 1972, President Nixon visited China, meeting with
Mao Zedong and Zhou Enlai. Nixon, whose policy to this point recognized only Taiwan as the legitimate Chinese government, agreed to
recognize "Red" China's right to be represented at the United Nations.
Many hoped that this meeting, coupled with Nixon's trip to Russia in
May where two treaties were signed in an attempt to reduce and limit
the proliferation of strategic weapons, would play China against Russia
with the result that both would cease supporting North Vietnam.[115]

In March 1972, Congress passed the Equal Rights Amendment,
which on the surface looked innocent enough. It eventually was
ratified by thirty-five states but never reached the required thirty-eight
states to add it to the Constitution. The reason it was not ratified and

of Rights, no doubt due to the fact that messengers were meeting in Philadelphia. Other resolutions were adopted dealing with a litany of moral issues.[120]

Of particular interest was the resolution on Christian citizenship, which read, in part, that "we urgently call upon all Southern Baptists to carefully consider the vital moral issues in this year's campaigns, examining the moral positions of the candidates, scrutinizing the platforms of the political parties and the economic interests supporting the candidates, apply Bible truths and Christian insights in arriving at decisions related to politics, and prayerfully work for those who seem nearest to a responsible Christian position."[121]

The Convention for the most part was noncontroversial. Yet issues raised once again would simply not go away.

On June 17, local newspapers in the Washington, D.C., area noted that the Democratic National Committee Offices at the Watergate Hotel had been burglarized and that five men were arrested for the break-in. On June 22, Nixon denied any knowledge of the incident, yet by the time this scandal climaxed, it culminated in Nixon's resignation as president. In October future secretary of state, Henry Kissinger, announced that negotiations in Paris were going well and that "peace is at hand." In November Nixon won the presidential election in a landslide over Democratic challenger, South Dakota senator and war dove, George McGovern. Nixon took 520 electoral votes to McGovern's 17 in the Electoral College. Because peace talks broke down, Nixon renewed bombing North Vietnam over Christmas; nonetheless the war was coming to an end.[122]

As the new year, 1973, dawned, the most significant moral decision in the nation's history was being argued before the Supreme Court. In January two cases, *Roe v. Wade* and *Doe v. Bolton,* opened the door for legalized abortion on demand in the United States.

In these landmark cases, unlike the race issue, Southern Baptists inadvertently, and the Christian Life Commission intentionally, found themselves, to use Maston's terminology, on the wrong side of history. This case and this posture by the Convention's agency on moral concerns as much as anything led eventually to a change of administration and an incredible reversal of the Southern Baptist Convention's public policy position. And for those who would lead the fight, all of this would be a matter of conviction.

Notes

1. Foy D. Valentine, "A Historical Study of Southern Baptists and Race Relations, 1917–1947," a doctoral dissertation presented to the faculty of Southwestern Baptist Theological Seminary, 1949, 232–33.

2. 1960 *SBC Annual*, 273.

3. Radio and Television Commission tape of the 1960 Convention proceedings.

4. SBC Resolution on Christian Citizenship, 1960.

5. Paul F. Boller Jr. *Presidential Campaigns* (New York:Oxford University Press, 1985), 298.

6. John F. Kennedy, "Address to Southern Baptist Leaders," *The New York Times*, September 13, 1960.

7. Greg Ward, *The Timeline History of the USA* (New York: Barnes and Noble Books, 2003), 282–83; Richard Reeves, *President Kennedy: Profile of Power* (New York: Touchstone Books, 1993), 15.

8. Jerry Sutton, *The Baptist Reformation* (Nashville: Broadman & Holman Publishers, 2000), 6–7.

9. Foy Valentine letter to Owen Cooper, March 17, 1961.

10. 1961 SBC Resolution on Race.

11. 1961 SBC Resolutions.

12. 1961 *SBC Annual*, 60–62.

13. "James Meredith" in wikipedia.org.

14. Sutton, *The Baptist Reformation*, 9–11.

15. 1962 SBC Resolutions; Sutton, *The Baptist Reformation*, 9–11.

16. Peter Irons, *A People's History of the Supreme Court* (New York: Penguin Books, 1999), 410–11; Maureen Harrison and Steve Gilbert, eds., *Great Decisions of the U. S. Supreme Court* (New York: Barnes and Noble Books, 2003), 96.

17. John M. Blum, Bruce Catton, Edmund S. Morgan, Arthur M. Schlesinger Jr., Kenneth M. Stampp, and C. Vann Woodard, *The National Experience*, 2nd ed. (New York: Harcourt, Brace and World, 1963, 1968), 818–19; Letter from Valentine to Porter Routh, June 29, 1962.

18. Martin Luther King Jr., "Letter from a Birmingham Jail," April 16, 1963, reproduced in the U.S. Department of State's Bureau of International Information Program (usinfo.state.gov); see also "Daddy, why do white people treat colored people so mean?" in Erik Bruun and Jay Crosby, eds., *Our Nation's Archive* (New York: Tess Press, 1999), 854–57.

19. Ibid., Bruun and Crosby, *Our Nations Archive*, 854–57.

20. 1963 *SBC Annual*, 237.

21. 1963 *SBC Annual*, 92–93.

22. Sutton, *The Baptist Reformation*, 10–11, 39–40.

23. 1963 *SBC Annual*, 253.

24. 1963 SBC Resolutions; What was behind the latter resolution was the legislation, H.R. 10262, that would provide federal funding to nonprofits, i.e., schools with religious affiliation: "Make payment to any nonprofit institution engaged in health, education or welfare activities constructing or modifying approved public shelter space which meets shelter standards and criteria prescribed under the provisions of this Act." Its intention was to "authorize payment toward the construction or modification of approved public shelter space, and for other purposes." Translated, this was to help provide additional shelters in case of nuclear attack.

25. Irons, *A People's History of the Supreme Court*, 411–12.

26. Martin Luther King Jr., "I Have a Dream," in Bruun, *Our Nation's Archive*, 857–60.

27. Taken from the minutes of the administrative committee of the Executive Committee, SBC, September 18, 1963.

28. Reeves, *President Kennedy: Profile of Power*, 662.

29. Greg Ward, *The Timeline History of the USA* (New York: Barnes and Noble, 2003, 2005), 296.

30. "New York Times Co. v. Sullivan," in wikipedia.org; Irons, *People's History*, 419.

31. 1964 *SBC Annual*, 229.

32. Ibid., 73.

33. Lyndon B. Johnson, "The Great Society" speech given at the University of Michigan on May 22, 1964, the text may be found at americanrhetoric.com, or Bruun, *Our Nation's Archives*, 866–67 in its abbreviated form.

34. Ward, *The Timeline History of the USA*, 297.

35. "Civil Rights Timeline" at infoplease.com/spot/civilrights-timeline1.html.

36. Ward, *The Timeline History of the USA*, 297.

37. Martin Luther King Jr., "Acceptance Speech for the Nobel Peace Prize, 1964," Oslo, Norway.

38. Ward, *The Timeline History of the USA*, 298; Bruun, *Our Nation's Archive*, 870–73.

39. "Heart of Atlanta Motel v. United States" in widipedia.org; Irons, 419.

40. Peter Irons and Stephanie Guitton, eds., *May It Please the Court: The Most Significant Oral Arguments Made Before the Supreme Court Since 1955* (New York: The New Press, 1993), 105.

41. Ward, *The Timeline History of the USA*, 298; "Martin Luther King, Jr.," in wikipedia.org.

42. 1965 *SBC Annual*, 244–46.

43. Ibid.

44. Ibid.

45. Ibid.

46. Ibid.

47. Radio and Television Commission tape of the 1965 Convention proceedings.

48. 1965 SBC Resolutions.

49. *Georgia Baptist Index*, June 10, 1965, 5.

50. Ward, *The Timeline History of the USA*, 299; Howard Zinn, *A People's History of the United States* (New York: Harper Collins, 2003), 459.

51. Ward, *The Timeline History of the USA*, 299.

52. Stanley Karnow, *Vietnam: A History* (New York: Penguin Books, 1997), 493–94; Neil Sheehan, *A Bright Shining Life* (New York: Vintage, 1988), 573–79.

53. 1966 *SBC Annual*, 58.

54. 1966 SBC Resolutions.

55. Ibid.

56. Ibid.

57. Ward, *The Timeline History of the USA*, 300.

58. Ibid.

59. Ibid., "Martin Luther King Jr." in wikipedia.org.

60. 1967 *SBC Annual*, 69.

61. Radio and Television Commission tape of the 1967 Convention proceedings.

62. 1967 SBC Resolutions.

63. Ibid.

64. Irons and Guitton, *May It Please the Court*, 277.

65. Ward, *The Timeline History of the USA*, 302.

66. The Library of Congress, Today in History: October 2 at memory.loc.gov; "Thurgood Marshall" in wikipedia.org.

67. Ward, *The Timeless History of the USA*, 303.

68. Ward, *The Timeless History of the USA*, 304–06; Bruun, *Our Nation's Archive*, 904–06.

69. Lyndon B. Johnson speeches: "Remarks on Decision Not to Seek Reelection" at millercenter.virginia.edu (Scripps Library and Multimedia Archives at the University of Virginia).

70. "Martin Luther King Jr." in wikipedia.org.

71. Ibid.

72. Ibid.

73. "Civil Rights Act of 1968" in wikipedia.org.

74. "Robert F. Kennedy" in wikipedia.org.

75. Radio and Television Commission tape of the 1968 Convention proceedings.

76. 1968 Seminar Proceedings printed by the Christian Life Commission, Nashville, Tennessee.

77. Radio and Television Commission tape of the 1968 Convention proceedings.

78. Ibid.

79. John Finley, "The 1968 Statement Concerning the Crisis in Our Nation," *Christian Ethics Today*, February 2003.

80. Ibid.

81. 1968 *SBC Annual*, 66–69.

82. Ibid.

83. H. Leon McBeth, *A Sourcebook for Baptist Heritage* (Nashville: Broadman Press, 1990), 523.

84. Radio and Television Commission tape of the 1968 Convention proceedings.

85. W. A. Criswell, *Standing on the Promises: The Autobiography of W. A. Criswell* (Dallas, London: Word Publishing, 1990), 216; see W. A. Criswell's sermon, "Church of the Open Door," June 9, 1968.

86. 1968 SBC Resolution on Violence, Disregard for Law.

87. Ward, *The Timeless History of the USA*, 305.

88. Harrison, *Great Decisions of the Supreme Court*, 127–36.

89. Irons and Guitton, *May It Please the Court*, 121.

90. 1969 *SBC Annual*, 76.

91. Radio and Television Commission tape of the 1969 Convention proceedings.

92. 1969 SBC Resolutions.

93. Ward, *The Timeless History of the USA*, 306–10; Bruun, *Our Nation's Archive*, 906–08.

94. Ward, *The Timeless History of the USA,* 310.

95. Proceedings of the 1970 Christian Life Commission Seminar, "Toward Authentic Morality for Modern Man," Atlanta, Georgia, March 16–18, 1970.

96. Ibid.

97. Ibid.

98. Ibid.

99. Ward, *The Timeless History of the USA*, 310.

100. Sutton, *The Baptist Reformation*, 12–14.

101. Ibid., 13–14.

102. Ibid., 14.

103. 1970 *SBC Annual*, 67.

104. Ibid., 76.

105. Sutton, *The Baptist Reformation*, 17.

106. The entire body of correspondence can be found in the Southern Baptist Historical Library and Archives in Nashville, Tennessee.

107. 1971 *SBC Annual*, 209.

108. Ibid., 76, 79.

109. Ibid., 72.

110. Sutton, *The Baptist Reformation*, 309; Robert E. Naylor, *A Messenger's Memoirs* (Franklin, Tenn.: Providence, 1995), 167.

111. Naylor, *A Messenger's Memoirs*, 167; Sutton, *The Baptist Reformation*, 44.

112. Irons and Guitton, *May It Please the Court*, 291–304.

113. Robert S. McNamara, *In Retrospect* (New York: Times Books, 1995), 280–82; New York Times Co. v. United States in wikipedia.org, and "Pentagon Papers" in wikipedia.org.

114. Ward, *The Timeless History of the USA*, 311–12.

115. Ibid., 313–14.

116. See "The Equal Rights Amendment" at equalrightsamendment.org and "Memo on the Equal Rights Amendment 2000" at eagleforum.org.

117. Sutton, *The Baptist Reformation*, 44–45.

118. 1972 SBC Resolutions.

119. Ibid.

120. Ibid.

121. Ibid.

122. Ward, *The Timeless History of the USA*, 315–16.

CHAPTER

The Middle Years: Part 2 (1973–1988)

January 1973 marked an epochal month in America's history. In the space of a week and a day, the verdict of *Roe v. Wade* was announced, America's military involvement in Vietnam officially ended, and the Watergate trial concluded. Yet none of these verdicts, decisions, and agreements were really over. In fact, the fallout and aftermath was just beginning, with consequences lasting for decades.

In the *Roe v. Wade* decision and its companion *Doe v. Bolton*, the doorway was opened in the United States that legalized abortion on demand. Summarizing the case, Irons and Guitton write:

Some controversial issues in American society do not get
resolved by a judicial decision, as the continuing debate over
abortion illustrates. In 1970, an unmarried woman (Norma
McCorvey) in Dallas, Texas, learned that she was pregnant. She
immediately sought an abortion, which was denied under an
1845 Texas law prohibiting any abortion unless the woman's
life was endangered. Using the pseudonym of "Jane Roe," she
challenged the law, claiming that it violated her right of privacy
under the Constitution. In 1973, the Supreme Court struck
down state laws against abortion; the Fourteenth Amendment's
protection of liberty, Justice Harry Blackman wrote, is "broad
enough to encompass a woman's decision" whether or not to
terminate her pregnancy. But the Court recognized the state's
interest in protecting the "potentiality of human life" after the
first trimester of pregnancy, allowing restrictions on abortion.[1]

In his dissent William Rehnquist, the future chief justice of the
Supreme Court, begins by questioning the plaintiff's standing. Next
he asserts, "I have difficulty in concluding, as the Court does, that the
right of 'privacy' is involved in this case." He explains: "A transaction
resulting in an operation such as this is not 'private' in the ordinary
usage of that word. Nor is the 'privacy' that the Court finds here even
a distant relative of the freedom from searches and seizures protected
by the Fourth Amendment to the Constitution, which the Court has
referred to as embodying a right to privacy." Rehnquist goes on to
observe, "To reach its result, the Court necessarily has had to find
within the scope of the Fourteenth Amendment a right that was apparently completely unknown to the drafters of the Amendment."[2]

Irons and Guitton, assessing the case, state:

The central issue in the arguments, and the Court's opinion, focused on whether the fetus was a person and thus protected by the Constitution against depravation of life. "If this
suggestion of personhood is established," Blackmun said, Jane
Roe's case collapses. Sarah Weddington conceded as much on

reargument, he noted. On the other hand, Robert Flowers could cite no case holding that a fetus was a person. Consequently, the Court would only consider the rights of pregnant women to an abortion. But this right was not absolute. As the fetus grew toward viability, able to live outside the womb, the state had a legitimate interest in protecting it. Blackmun divided pregnancy into trimesters, or three-month periods. During the first, states could not interfere with the abortion decision. States could regulate abortion procedures during the second trimester. And abortion could be prohibited entirely during the last three months of pregnancy.

Justices Byron White and William Rehnquist dissented on Roe versus Wade. Rehnquist denied that the Constitution contained a privacy right. Abortion laws, he wrote, are the kind of social and economic legislation that elected lawmakers should vote on. White argued for fetal personhood and accused the majority of an exercise in "raw judicial power."[3]

Chief Justice Warren Burger provided his opinion on the Court's seven to two decision with what almost appears to be a disclaimer when he writes, "I do not read the Court's holdings today as having the sweeping consequences attributed to them by the dissenting Justices; the dissenting views discount the reality that the vast majority of physicians observe the standards of their profession, and act only on the basis of carefully deliberated medical judgments relating to life and health." He concludes, "Plainly, the Court today rejects any claim that the Constitution requires abortion on demand." Little did he realize the results of this one ruling.[4]

Many "what ifs" could have been addressed with respect to the Court's decision. Nevertheless, the decision was made, and the country was forced to deal with it as best it could. With this decision what has been called "the culture of death" was introduced into America's social landscape.

Besides the landmark *Roe* decision, January 27 marked the official conclusion to the Vietnam War when the future secretary of state,

Henry Kissinger, representing the United States, signed a pact in Paris with both North and South Vietnamese representatives. The immediate cease-fire was followed by the withdrawal of U.S. combat forces, which concluded on March 29. This was followed by the release of American prisoners of war on April 1. By the time the war ended, the United States had lost more than fifty-eight thousand combatants. One estimate suggests that the total death rate for all Vietnamese was in excess of a million. It would take a generation for the emotional wounds of Vietnam to heal.[5]

Meanwhile, back in the States, what appeared to be a simple burglary, arrest, trial, and conviction turned out to be a nightmare for the Nixon administration. Eventually, the break-in was traced back to the White House with devastating results.

The Christian Life Commission held its annual seminar on the theme, "A Future for the Family." Speakers for the conference came only from the moderate to liberal side of the theological spectrum. Sarah Frances Anders, sociologist, spoke on "The State of the Second Sex: Emancipation or Explosion." Anders related that she could not "really believe that men of my own [Baptist] faith are so insecure that they fear their own positions of leadership if women are elected or ordained to significant leadership places."[6]

David Mace, also a sociologist, spoke on "Abortion on Request— Implications of the Supreme Court Decision." In short he restated the obvious—that the nation had been forced to change almost overnight.

At the Christian Life Commission Seminar we find essentially an advocate for an egalitarian approach to women's issues and a commentary on the abortion issue, which does not assess the ruling in terms of sin or wrong. And this was a Christian Life Commission-sponsored event.

At the 1973 Convention in Portland, Oregon, most resolutions were repeats of the past and not intentionally controversial. One interesting resolution "On the Place of Women in Christian Service" was proposed by Mrs. Richard Sappington of Texas and may well have been a direct reaction to the Christian Life Commission's spring seminar:

> WHEREAS, The Scriptures bear record to the distinctive roles of men and women in the church and in the home, and
>
> WHEREAS, Christian women have made and are making a significant contribution to the cause of Christ, and
>
> WHEREAS, Christian women have been made exhorted to redig the old wells of mission promotion and education in our churches by Kenneth Chafin, and
>
> WHEREAS, There is a great attack by the members of most women's liberation movements upon scriptural precepts of woman's place in society, and
>
> WHEREAS, The theme of the Convention is "Share the Word Now" and this Word we share is explicitly clear on this subject.
>
> Therefore, be it RESOLVED, That we "redig" or reaffirm God's order of authority for his church and the Christian home: (1) Christ the head of every man; (2) man the head of the woman; (3) children in subjection to their parents—
>
> in the Lord.
>
> Therefore, be it further RESOLVED, That we "redig" or reaffirm God's explicit Word that (1) man was not made for the woman, but the woman for the man; (2) that the woman is the glory of man; (3) that as woman would not have existed without man, henceforth, neither would man have existed without the woman, they are dependent one upon the other—to the glory of God.[7]

What is noteworthy is that her resolution was referred to the Resolutions Committee, gutted and brought back to the floor later. From the floor she offered a substitute resolution, which was actually the original, and it was accepted by the Convention.

Cecil Sherman, the Christian Life Commission chairman, drew the messengers' attention to its report, acknowledged it had no recommendations, and moved its adoption. It was adopted. After Sherman said a few affirming words about the Commission he called on Valentine, who addressed the crowd. For the most part this was a quiet Convention.

As June 1973 moved to its conclusion, cracks began to develop in the Watergate cover-up. On June 25, John Dean testified that Nixon was involved. It continued to digress through the summer and into the fall.

On October 10, Spiro Agnew, vice president of the United States, resigned because of a corruption scandal unrelated to Watergate. Ten days later, an event called "The Saturday Night Massacre" occurred in which Elliott Richardson, attorney general, and his deputy, tendered their resignations rather than fire, at the president's instruction, Archibald Cox, who was the special prosecutor. The White House continued to fight, but the situation grew more difficult.[8]

All of this was set against the October 6–26, 1973, Yom Kippur War between Israel and a coalition of Arab neighbors. The war was launched on the Jewish holiday with a surprise attack by Syria and Egypt. Israel initially suffered losses due to the surprise but after two weeks and heavy causalities the Jewish state took control of the situation. The reason Israel did not make a preemptive strike was best summed up by Golda Meir, prime minister, in a meeting with her generals the morning the war was launched, "Israel might be needing American assistance soon and it was imperative that it not be blamed for starting the war." She acknowledged, "If we strike first, we won't get help from anybody." As the war began to conclude, both the Soviet Union and the Untied States were threatened and tempted to be drawn in. In the end the Soviet Union, deciding that initiating World War III was not in their best interest, was reconciled to the Arab defeat. On October 23, all sides agreed to accept the United Nations' brokered cease-fire. By October 26, all hostilities ceased.[9]

The principal fallout for the United States was that OPEC began to restrict its oil sales to the United States. This further impacted an already depressed economy.[10]

In December, Gerald Ford was sworn in as the new vice president under Nixon.

By the time the 1974 Convention met in Dallas, the nation was uneasy due to the Watergate scandal. When the Commission delivered its report, it recommended increased openness "as God speaks to us regarding race relations." It also called on agencies to resist racially selective evangelism, missions, and ministry. Two other recommendations called for "economic justice" and "integrity in government," no doubt expressing the concern for the present state of affairs in Washington.[11]

Although race did not evoke a strong reaction, the recommendations "Concerning Freedom for Women" did. The Commission asked that "we endeavor through religion, political, social, business, and educational structures to eliminate . . . discrimination [against women]." This would be done, it explained, by providing equal pay for equal work and "by electing women to positions of leadership for which God's gifts and the Holy Spirit's calling equip them."[12]

When the Commission then requested a bylaw change to establish a quota system to require 20 percent of trustees to be women, the debate ensued. The Commission attempted to have its support lined up by virtue of its previous conferences and speakers like Anders and Mace. They had not counted on the likes of Mrs. Richard Sappington resisting their leadership. When the debate was over and the vote was taken, support for quotas for women lost.[13]

The Commission was also challenged on its abortion position. Bob Holbrook of Texas asked that the Commission be instructed to "prepare and distribute to the churches updated materials on abortions, presenting the issue from all perspectives." Holbrook believed the action was needed "because of the confusing and oftentimes conflicting statements made public by Baptists in places of influence."

Ironically the request was assigned to the Commission, which to date had displayed only sympathy with the pro-choice, pro-abortion camp. When a follow-up motion "On Abortion and Sanctity of Human Life" was offered, the Convention at the Commission's lead merely reaffirmed the 1971 resolution. Bob Holbrook offered an amendment to strike all reasons for abortion except when the mother's life is in danger, but it failed. The Commission's nebulous language and pro-choice sympathies would come back to haunt them in the years ahead. The resolution's location on the ideological spectrum can best be understood by the third clause, which, after affirming the 1971 resolution, notes, "That resolution reflected a middle ground between the extreme of abortion on demand and the opposite extreme of all abortion as murder."[14]

President Nixon Resigns

On August 8, President Nixon resigned due to the Watergate scandal. Ford was sworn in as president and one month later, on September 8, pardoned Nixon, saying, "Our long national nightmare is over." He also announced in September that a conditional amnesty for draft dodgers and deserters during the Vietnam War was being granted. Not surprisingly, Democrats added to their House and Senate majorities in the mid-term elections.[15]

In the early months of 1975, in defiance of the Paris Peace Accords, North Vietnam invaded the South, captured Saigon and renamed it Ho Chi Minh City on April 30. The United States refused to intervene. With the images of people trying to get on helicopters and the desperate attempts to escape, it was hard to believe that the United States had actually achieved "peace with honor."[16]

By 1975, the Christian Life Commission had a professional staff of six and a Cooperative Program allotment of just under $250,000. The Commission seemed to churn out a steady stream of materials, interviews, and editorials from Valentine and other Commission notables, both to the secular and religious press. All of this brought a steady stream of correspondence, some criticizing, some praising, and others attempting to pick fights on controversial issues.

Besides race relations, abortion, and the role of women, two other subjects that generated strong emotions were capital punishment and gun control.

Whatever the topic, Valentine reminded the correspondent that he did not intend to speak for all Southern Baptists but spoke what he perceived to be the biblical position. Too often Baptists believed that he spoke out of his own social agenda and not from Scripture.

In the spring of 1975, the Commission hosted its seminar on "Integrity." Coming out of the Watergate scandal, this seminar received national attention, which Valentine loved. Consistent with the past, the program personnel came primarily from the religious, political, and philosophical left. For example, Senator George McGovern was a keynote speaker.

By this time in history, the Commission and the Committee on the Order of Business, as well as Convention leaders, were well aware that they could not control what messengers proposed or said at the annual Convention. To prevent parliamentary fights, Valentine and his staff customarily exercised caution in their choice of words and in deciding how and whether to make recommendations. At times, however, Valentine and his staff failed to recognize the extent of opposition on such sensitive subjects as quotas for women on boards.

From the opening prayer to the benediction, the annual Southern Baptist Convention was tightly programmed. Convention planners hoped for a jubilant meeting highlighting the familiar theme "Unity in Diversity." The SBC establishment, which now included Valentine, was still not fully aware of the intensity of concern among conservative Southern Baptists over biblical inerrancy and abortion.

The Bible question had not changed since the 1920s: "Is the Bible wholly true or does it merely contain truth?" By 1975, the conservatives had a newsmagazine called *The Southern Baptist Journal*, edited by Bill Powell, a former Home Mission Board field worker. By quoting from sermons and writings of suspected "liberals," Powell called attention to some teachers and agency staffers he was convinced did not believe the Bible was fully true. Many of Powell's subjects were frequent speakers at Commission-sponsored seminars. Although Powell could not pin Valentine down on his conviction about the Bible, he certainly kept readers aware of the Commission's pro-choice policy on abortion.

At the 1975 Convention, Bob Holbrook returned to offer a new resolution on abortion. The resolutions committee declined to release it, noting that the Convention had acted in 1971 and 1974 on the subject, presenting "a high view of the sanctity of all human life, including fetal life."[17]

At the conclusion of the Commission's annual report, a one-page response was offered detailing the agency's handling of the abortion question since the last meeting:

> The Christian Life Commission has given careful attention to the complex ethical issues related to abortion, and it will continue to do so. The many aspects of moral behavior in regard to abortion are being treated by the Commission in a variety of ways, including: distribution of carefully prepared, balanced, and updated materials; consultation with pastors and denominational agency representatives; channeling articles in [SBC] papers and magazines; and participation in state and Convention-wide conferences. The Commission will continue to point people toward the resources of the Christian faith as the best guide for dealing with abortion.[18]

When pro-lifers saw the Commission's nebulous response, which they interpreted as an attempt to minimize and marginalize their concerns, a quick response was forthcoming. After the Convention sermon that most perceived as an interruption of the abortion discussion, President Jaroy Weber proceeded to have the messengers vote on the Commission report one paragraph at a time. After considerable discussion Wade Jackson of Ohio moved that the "matter of reference," the response to Holbrook's request from the previous year, not be approved. Jackson held up a copy of the Commission's pro-choice position pamphlet on abortion and pointed out that the Commission had not done what the Convention requested—provide literature that was fair and balanced. When Valentine told the Convention Jackson was holding up out-of-date materials, he was informed the Commission had distributed these items in the previous thirty days.

After Bill Sherman spoke against Jackson's motion, the vote was taken and Jackson's motion passed.[19]

After the vote to delete the controversial paragraph, Valentine delivered his typical address without ever mentioning the abortion issue. Numerous resolutions on familiar themes were passed. One which stands out is a plea to assist refugees from Vietnam. The Commission was asked to study the public school curriculum for fifth and sixth graders, "Man: A Course of Study." And the Convention adjourned. The Commission staff returned to Nashville apprehensive about the year to come, and rightly so.

On August 1, the Helsinki Accords were signed by the United States, the Soviet Union, and thirty-one other nations. This document verified Europe's national borders as "inviolable," promised trade agreements along with proposing cultural exchange programs, and pledged respect for human rights.[20]

When the 1976 March seminar "On Christian Citizenship" lineup was announced, conservatives again complained that it was tilted to the philosophical left. Speakers included Hubert Humphrey, George McGovern, labor union activist Leonard Woodcock, and Edward Kennedy. It also leaned to the theological left with speakers like Harvey Cox of Harvard Divinity School, L. D. Johnson of Furman, and Bill Hull of Southern Seminary. Only in the specific area of the upcoming 1976 elections was there a pretense of balance. Howard Baker and John Tower were invited to speak for the Republicans, and Barbara Jordan and Andrew Young represented the Democrats. Assuming the accuracy of the transcripts, not a word was spoken about abortion.[21]

The Commission came under fire early at the 1976 Convention in Norfolk, Virginia, when Bryan Robison of Florida requested the Convention to instruct the Executive Committee to revise the Commission's program statement. His bottom line was that the Commission must make abundantly clear that they spoke for themselves and not for the Convention. Although the motion was ruled out of order, one wonders if the Commission was not speaking for the Convention which funded it, for whom did it speak?[22]

In Valentine's address, he offered no recommendations. Tensions did rise early when the Commission's assessment of the "Man: A Course of Study" curriculum was not condemned as un-Christian and unsuitable. H. A. Markham disputed the Commission's assessment, but in the ensuing discussion and debate, he lost the vote to reject the Commission's hands-off policy concerning the text.[23]

When the Resolutions Committee brought their recommendations, Chairman Andrew Tamplin confided that most of the resolutions offered to the committee addressed the abortion issue. When the resolution on abortion was offered, the last paragraph, explained as a compromise between pro-life and pro-choice sides, was discussed after messenger Jim Byington moved to delete it from the report. The paragraph reads:

> Be it further Resolved, that we also affirm our conviction about the limited role of government in dealing with matters relating to abortion, and support the right of expectant mothers to the full range of medical services and personal counseling for the preservation of life and health.[24]

For the record, this same paragraph was included in the 1977 and 1979 resolutions on abortion and affirmed in the 1978 resolution on abortion. What was extremely problematic was the fact that this paragraph, although written nebulously, was in fact a pro-choice statement asserting for those not enlightened enough to understand its intent that abortion is a woman's choice to be made in cooperation with her doctor and should not have legal limitations imposed by the government. After the discussion to delete the paragraph, the motion to delete lost partly because the messengers did not really know what it meant or was intended to mean.[25]

A second amendment was offered, which stated, "Whereas, Every decision for abortion, for whatever reason, must necessarily involve the decision to terminate the life of an innocent human being," and, "Be it further resolved that we reject as conflicting with Southern Baptist Convention doctrine and tradition any suggestion that Southern Baptists should become political activists in support of permissive abortion legislation." The minutes of the Convention are confusing at this point due to the fact that the minutes report that the motion to add the amendment failed, yet both of these clauses are included in the Convention's final draft of resolution 4, "On Abortion."[26]

Immediately after the adoption of the abortion resolution, the 1976 Convention voted in favor of a strong condemnation of the practice of homosexuality. Yet, in his assessment of the 1976 Convention, Naylor simply observes that "there was an expression of continued uneasiness with the Christian Life Commission."[27]

As the Convention came to a close, all eyes turned to the national political party conventions. Ford, as expected, received the Republican nomination, and Jimmy Carter, former Georgia governor and Southern Baptist, received the Democratic nomination. As the days led up to the national election, most Southern Baptist agency personnel were supportive of Carter, who testified to being "born again." The one notable exception to Carter's support came from W. A. Criswell, pastor of Dallas First Baptist Church, who endorsed Ford. The two strongest criticisms during the campaign were first of Carter for doing an interview with *Playboy* magazine and admitting his "lust" problem in print. The second was of Ford, who had pardoned Nixon and had thus let the guilty man go free.

When the dust settled and the votes were cast, Carter won the election forty-one million to thirty-nine million. In his sermon at Carter's presidential inauguration, friend Nelson Price preached from Colossians 3:23, "Whatsoever ye do, do it heartily, as to the Lord, and not unto men" (KJV). Price's closest allusion to social matters came when he counseled Carter, "Don't run from the inevitable complaints and criticisms of the people, but run to attain the commendation of the Lord."[28]

In Carter's inaugural speech, he called attention to the words of Micah 6:8. He acknowledged, "I have no new dream to set forth today but rather urge a fresh faith in the old dream." Then, he urged, "Let our recent mistakes bring a resurgent commitment to the basic principle of our Nation." He then observed, "We have already found a high degree of personal liberty, and we are now struggling to enhance equality of opportunity." Then added, "Our commitment to human rights must be absolute, our laws fair, our natural beauty preserved; the powerful must not persecute the weak, and human dignity must be enhanced." From a foreign policy perspective, he stated, "Because we are free, we can never be indifferent to the fate of freedom elsewhere." And he concluded by expressing his hope that at the end of his presidency, among other things, "that we had torn down the barriers that separated those of different race and region and religion, and where there has been mistrust, built unity, with respect to diversity."[29]

When the Carters moved to Washington, D.C., they joined First Baptist Church, where Charles Trentham, a former Christian Life Commission trustee, served as pastor. Not only did Trentham assist the Commission to have continuous access to the White House, but also this arrangement made the entire nation aware that the Southern Baptist Convention was a major denomination with a worldwide ministry.[30]

As we turn to 1977, it is important to recall that in 1972 the Supreme Court's ruling in *Furman v. Georgia* in effect called a moratorium on imposing the death penalty. The ruling of the Court was that because of a lack of uniformity in imposing capital punishment, it should be considered "cruel and unusual" in violation of the Eighth Amendment. In 1976, the Court ruled in *Gregg v. Georgia* that the death penalty was consistent with the Eighth Amendment on the condition that certain uniform guidelines are followed. As a result, the practice of imposing the death penalty was reinstated, with the majority opinion ruling that "capital punishment is an expression of society's moral outrage."[31]

As a result of the ruling in 1976, the death penalty was reinstated in numerous states. Headlines early in January out of Utah relate that Gary Gilmore, convicted murderer, was executed by firing squad on January 3, the first execution in the United States since 1967.[32] Since this was an issue upon which the Commission had expressed its opinion, it was only logical to anticipate something about the subject at the upcoming 1977 Convention.

In March the Commission hosted its annual seminar. That year's subject was entitled "Priorities," and similar to the past, an assortment of left-leaning speakers was scheduled. During the twenty-three addresses, abortion was mentioned only once, by Wayne Oates of Southern Seminary, and it was in keeping with past Convention sympathies.[33]

At the 1977 Convention, which met in Kansas City, abortion was not mentioned at all in the Christian Life Commission report. It did report on much that had been done the past year including the distribution of some two million pieces of literature on an assortment of topics. This year's major project had to do with producing a study and publishing results on the television viewing habits and assessments by Southern Baptists.

This Convention also saw an abortion resolution which began assertively by stating, "In view of some confusion in interpreting part of this resolution we confirm our strong opposition to abortion on demand and all governmental policies and actions which permit this." It did, however, conclude with the same "we support the right" wording as discussed before, exposing the pro-choice sympathies of the Commission.[34]

Despite its condemnation the previous year of homosexual behavior, the Commission did not comment on the subject in its report to the Convention in 1977. The committee on resolutions, however, believed it imperative to articulate clearly a Southern Baptist Convention posture on this growing movement and offered this resolution "On Homosexuality":

WHEREAS, The precipitous decline of moral integrity in American society continues at an alarming pace, and

WHEREAS, A campaign is being waged to secure legal, social, and religious acceptance for homosexuality and deviant moral behavior at the expense of personal dignity, and

WHEREAS, The success of those advocating such deviant moral behavior would necessarily have devastating consequences for family life in general and our children in particular, and

WHEREAS, The radical scheme to subvert the sacred pattern of marriage in America has gained formidable momentum by portraying homosexuality as normal behavior.

Now therefore be it RESOLVED, That the Southern Baptist Convention meeting in Kansas City, Missouri, June 14–16, 1977, reaffirm the firm biblical resolution on homosexuality passed in Norfolk, Virginia in 1976 and commend Anita Bryant and other Christians during the recent referendum in Miami, Florida for their courageous stand against the evils inherent in homosexuality.

Be it further RESOLVED, That we show compassion for every person in our society regardless of lifestyle, and earnestly pray for the redemption of all persons.[35]

After brief discussion, the resolution passed by a wide margin.

As a follow–up to the resolution on homosexuality, the committee offered an additional resolution "On Human Rights and Certain Misapplications." The heart of the resolution addressed the social agenda of the homosexual rights movement when it stated:

Be it therefore RESOLVED, That we reaffirm our belief in the free exercise of religion as determined by a free conscience, and that we oppose any discrimination, legal or otherwise, against any individual based upon race, age, gender, or nationality, and that in reaffirming our opposition to such discrimination, we also express our opposition to all governmental efforts to define discrimination in such a way that ridiculous extremes, repugnant to the Christian faith and life, become the law of the land, such as the legalization of homosexual marriages, permitting homosexual couples to adopt children, prohibiting father-son banquets or single-sex choirs, requiring sexually integrated housing and restroom facilities, requiring governmentally financed housing to be made available to persons living in adultery or fornication, prohibiting a draft law that applies to men only, and we urge all citizens to be active in opposing the adoption of such public policies.[36]

The major attention by Valentine at the 1977 Convention, again, had to do with the issue of television programming and Southern Baptist viewing habits. His desire was to challenge the immoral and applaud the family friendly with the intention of influencing not only the viewing habits of Southern Baptists but also the programming by the major networks. Surprisingly, nothing was mentioned concerning capital punishment.[37]

To this date in history, the Christian Life Commission had pulled Southern Baptists, with considerable resistance on the part of some, through the race crisis. The agency tried to be cautious in its assessment of homosexual behavior, criticizing the sin while expressing compassion for those trapped in its clutches. On the abortion issue the Commission held delicately to its pro-choice position while fending off as much as possible the pro-life advocates. All the while the Commission worked to reinforce its "unity in diversity" posture in cooperation with Convention and other agency heads. Part of the strategy that helped maintain the Commission's positions was the widespread practice of nominating new trustees selected and approved by the agency heads. This enabled Convention leaders to move people into leadership who, in general, agreed with prevailing agendas. This would be changing in the near future.

For conservatives who were concerned about the continued theological drift to the left, resolutions could be passed and motions could be made, but nothing changed. It seemed that those who embraced biblical inerrancy were the same constituents who supported the pro-life agenda.

In the late 1970s, Judge Paul Pressler of Houston, Texas, a political strategist, began working with Paige Patterson, a young theologian whose father served for many years as the executive director of the Baptist General Convention of Texas. Their deliberations—along with the influence of men like Bill Powell, Freddie Gage, LaVerne Butler, and Jim DeLoach, not to mention men like W. A. Criswell—coalesced into a coordinated movement among Southern Baptist pastors and laymen literally to change, or reform, the Southern Baptist Convention.[38]

began to experience significant resistance was its implications for both the abortion and homosexuality issues.[116]

The Southern Baptist Convention met June 6–8, 1972, in Philadelphia, Pennsylvania. Continuing concern was expressed over doctrinal integrity issues. A motion was made to withdraw the sale of the Broadman Bible Commentary, but it failed to pass. Convention President Carl Bates highlighted the difficulty of maintaining both denominational unity and doctrinal integrity simultaneously. No doubt this tension would escalate in the coming decade and climax in what is popularly called the "Conservative Resurgence."[117]

When the time came for the Christian Life Commission report, Valentine asked if there were any questions for discussion. When none were raised, he turned the report time over to Commission chairman Cecil Sherman. Nothing controversial was presented to the relief of everyone in attendance.

Resolutions at the 1972 Convention were somewhat subdued. One advocated welfare reform legislation, and another, tax reform legislation. A typical resolution was offered on religious liberty and the establishment clause. This one criticized the idea of tax policy that permits tuition tax credits and vouchers. One resolution on anti-Semitism recognized that "Baptists share with Jews a heritage of persecution and suffering for conscience sake."[118]

Surprisingly, a resolution was made on astronaut prayer stating, "We express our gratitude for the inspiring example of a number of our astronauts in regard to faith, prayer, and public testimony, and for a free society that guarantees this inalienable right of individual conscience." It was surprising that neither the Christian Life Commission nor the Baptist Joint Committee opposed this since the entire space program is a government operation. It seemed that issues related to nonestablishment should have been raised. And they might have been had this resolution not reflected the sentiment of a large number of Southern Baptists.[119]

Another resolution on prayer for China no doubt was a reaction to Nixon's recent visit. A typical resolution, too, was adopted about Vietnam. Interestingly, a resolution was adopted affirming the Bill

Bill Powell is credited for discovering the key to change in the Southern Baptist Convention, for he is the one who read and reread the Southern Baptist Convention's constitution and bylaws and discovered that the elected president has appointive powers to the Committee on Committees and the other standing committees. By electing the right president, through the appointive process, slowly and deliberately over time the makeup of the trustees on boards and agencies could be changed. And if trustees changed, the boards and agencies would follow suit; and, in turn, the Convention itself could change.[39]

Because James Sullivan was elected president in 1976 and Convention presidents as a courtesy are customarily given an automatic second year, Pressler and Patterson, along with their network of pastors and laymen, targeted 1978 to begin the intense effort to take back the Southern Baptist Convention from those who controlled it. Most saw this as democracy at work in its purest form. Surprisingly Sullivan served only one term. Jimmy Allen was elected in 1977; and as a result, conservatives waited until 1979 to make their move.

Valentine, it seemed, was also a political animal, knowing instinctively when to push controversial subjects and when to back off. Never was this more clearly practiced than when the 1978 Commission seminar on "Life-Style" was hosted in Nashville. Featured speakers were Chuck Colson, Southwestern Seminary professor William Hendricks, Leighton Ford (associate to Billy Graham), and Republican Senator Howard Baker. Guests spoke commendably about Valentine and his work.

One area of conflict, however, had to do with the role of women in the Convention. Carolyn Weatherford, president of the WMU, advocated "ordaining women for some areas of service." The most controversial speaker was Paul K. Jewett of Fuller Seminary, who decried the sexual hierarchy that he argued was an Old Testament construct. A close second to Jewett's was Henlee Barnett's address on "Homosexuality: A Christian Response." After arguing that homosexuality is a learned behavior, he stated, "It is incredible that the Southern Baptist Convention, which stresses separation of church and state, democracy, and freedom of religion, would call for the denial of basic rights of a minority group on the basis of sexual orientation." Barnett was one of the first Southern Baptists who attempted to assign to the homosexual practitioners a "minority" status.[40]

In some ways Valentine gave conservatives representation, yet most were not content with the constant leftward emphasis.

The Convention meeting in Atlanta in 1978 attracted more than twenty-two thousand messengers. Since Southern Baptists had last convened, the Panama Canal Treaty had been agreed to with the intention of turning the Panama Canal back to the Panamanians in 2000, Russia had invaded Afghanistan in April, and Proposition 13 had been adopted in California, which would limit the amount of taxation allowed in the state. Of course, the concern was the kind of precedent this would set for the rest of the nation. Each of these events, no doubt, help set the social context for Southern Baptists; yet still, the biggest concern had to do with the Convention's doctrinal integrity, which the majority perceived as slipping slowly and consistently away and to the left.[41]

The 1978 Convention was abuzz with talk of the conservative movement. Moderates thought it was a passing fad. The word was out that this would not be the year to challenge the incumbent, but rather 1979 would signal the beginning of the conservative movement.

Valentine announced that Barnett, Maston, and Texan Phil Strickland would be coming to work as consultants for the Commission, that the staff had been expanded to include William Tillman, that literature sales had had another banner year, and a major campaign to clean up television was being launched.[42]

The one recommendation from the Commission was a "Declaration of Human Rights" introduced by Commission chairman, Forest Siles, which received widespread approval.

When time came for resolutions, twenty-two were accepted. Most were typical of what Southern Baptists had affirmed in the past. Four, however, provoked pretty strong debate. One debate centered on the nation having a balanced budget. James Dunn, head of the Texas Christian Life Commission and future head of the Baptist Joint Committee, requested that the Equal Rights Amendment ratification time be extended. Charles Stanley spoke against his resolution and proposed that Southern Baptists go on record opposing the extension as well as the amendment. Stanley won and Dunn lost. A resolution asking messengers to reaffirm the 1977 abortion resolution was opposed because of the earlier resolution's lack of teeth to prevent abortions. After much debate the original motion passed. A final proposed resolution affirmed the Bible as inerrant and infallible. This resolution lost, but it was the last defeat for conservatives, who returned well organized and focused the following year. By this time many conservatives came to realize that the Bible resolutions were practically useless, dealt only with surface problems, and lacked any mechanism to affect change. All of this was about to change.[43]

By now hard questions were being asked about the Christian Life Commission and its connection to the Baptist Joint Committee. Both of these organizations were repeatedly taking stands with which a growing number of churches and messengers disagreed.

Meanwhile on the national scene and only a few weeks after the 1978 Southern Baptist Convention adjourned, the Supreme Court ruled June 28 in the *Regents of the University of California v. Bakke* case. Allen Bakke, an aerospace engineer, had twice applied for entrance to the University Medical School at Davis and twice had been rejected. When he learned the school had selected minority students with lower MCAT and grade-point averages, he sued for admission, arguing that the school's racial quota violated his Fourteenth Amendment rights to equal protection under the law. The Court ruled in Bakke's favor and ordered his admission. The Court also ruled that "race-conscious" admissions' policies were allowed by the Constitution. Commenting on the case, Thurgood Marshall wrote, "It is because of the legacy of unequal treatment that we now must permit the institutions of this society to give consideration to race in making decisions about who will hold the positions of influence, affluence, and prestige in America."[44] By declaring that affirmative action was not a standing requirement in all situations, old wounds of racial antagonism were reopened with this ruling. Nevertheless, it did reintroduce a measure of fairness into competitive academic markets.

The popularity of Jimmy Carter, who had been identified as the "human rights" president, began to drop among many Southern Baptists after he pardoned Vietnam War draft dodgers, signed the Panama Canal Treaty, and postponed production of the neutron bomb. Some believed he was surrendering America's vital interests. He did gain respect when he brokered the Camp David accords, establishing a peace treaty between Egypt and Israel. The left-leaning Commission and its staff, board members, and supporters maintained their loyalty to Carter through the presidential ups and downs, insisting that he was the greatest champion of traditional values in modern times.

The Conservative Resurgence

Among Southern Baptists, the old Convention establishment remained relatively unconcerned about a serious threat to its leadership. They had no idea that a conservative resurgence would within the next decade sweep Valentine and other old-line power brokers from their positions in America's largest Protestant denomination. The establishment had dealt with inerrancy, abortion, separation of church and state, and other volatile issues in the past. They were naively confident of maintaining control in the future.

At the beginning of 1979, two events on the national scene again caused anxiety in the Americas. In January the shah of Iran was deposed by the Ayatollah Khomeini, who established a militant Islamic regime. Demonstrators briefly took over the United States Embassy in Tehran on February 14. On March 28 a near catastrophe occurred at the Three-Mile Island nuclear reactor and brought to a conclusion the building of new nuclear power plants in the United States.[45]

When the 1979 spring Christian Life Commission seminar convened in March, its theme was "Help for Families." The seminar featured a lineup of speakers from the ideological left. Valentine, Cox, Anders, and Ken Chaffin were all repeats. Not surprisingly, some remarks of the speakers at the seminar were offensive to conservatives in the Convention. Some things never change. The difficulty

came when conservatives asked, "Why are we financially supporting seminars and conferences with our Cooperative Program dollars
when these very activities serve to undermine the very values we
cherish?"[46]

Meanwhile, conservative activists Pressler and Patterson were
preparing for the first round of the contest between newly motivated
conservatives and the old-guard Convention establishment. These men
had been traveling, talking, calling, and writing extensively for the
past six months. Their goal, simply, was to motivate enough conservative messengers to travel to Houston for the 1979 Convention that
they might elect a conservative president. This turned out to be Adrian
Rogers. If he was elected, they believed, he would make appointments
which would initiate a change of direction in the Southern Baptist
Convention.

A few state editors and other establishment figures were now taking the Pressler-Patterson coalition seriously. Oklahoma editor, Jack
Gritz, called the "maneuvering . . . an insult to the intelligence, integrity, and ability of the messengers who will be coming to the Houston
Convention." He argued, "This group should never be permitted to
take over the elected posts and organizational structure of the Convention." He then confided, "When I get to Houston, as soon as I find out
who the clique's candidates are—regardless of who—then I shall vote
for someone else."[47]

One part of the strategy utilized by the conservatives was to take
advantage of the Pastors' Conference to position key leaders in the
conservative movement. In fact, the high point of the 1979 Pastors'
Conference was when Criswell declared, "We have come to elect
Adrian Rogers our President!" Interestingly, Rogers was nominated
and elected president of the Southern Baptist Convention on the first
ballot with 51.36 percent of the votes even though there were five other
candidates.[48]

A second major conservative victory came when Larry Lewis
brought a resolution calling on agency trustees to employ only teachers "who believe in the inerrancy of the original manuscripts, the
existence of a personal devil and a literal hell, the actual existence of

a primeval couple named Adam and Eve, the literal occurrence of the miracles as recorded in the Bible, the virgin birth and bodily resurrection, and the personal return of the Lord Jesus Christ."

Before Lewis's resolution was scheduled for discussion and a vote, Wayne Dehoney, a past president of the Convention, offered a substitute motion that reaffirmed the Bible to be "truth, without any mixture of error." Rogers asked Dehoney to be "more specific in what he means by 'the Bible is truth, without any mixture of error.'" He then commented that if he meant the truth of the Bible is true, that his statement was nonsense. "The truth of everything is true," Rogers maintained. Rogers and Dehoney conferred briefly on the platform when Dehoney said his intention was to affirm that "in the original autographs God's revelation was perfect and without error—doctrinally, historically, scientifically, and philosophically. . . . I bring that to you [messengers] and ask you to support it." Lewis then withdrew his resolution on "doctrinal integrity." The Convention approved Dehoney's resolution.[49]

The agency reports were given as usual. The new Commission chairman, John Claypool, heaped high praise on Valentine for his twenty years of service. After Valentine's remarks, he asked if there were any questions. Joe Martin of Texas asked Valentine if he would clarify his stance on the abortion issue. Valentine responded that "we do not accept the Roman Catholic doctrine with regard to abortion." He attempted to explain himself by saying, "We do consider human life is sacred, and we so distribute the literature and make our speeches as we can, in that connection." Martin responded by saying, "In other words, sir, you have no plans to advocate the right to life of the unborn fetus." Valentine commented, "We have no plans to adopt the Roman Catholic position because the Convention has insisted on not adopting that position; it never has done so up to this point." When Martin said, "I would heartily wish that Southern Baptists would reconsider their stance," Valentine retorted, "Sir, they have reconsidered it about ten times and have never changed it."[50]

After fielding questions on capital punishment, further questions on abortion and Southern Baptist's name on abortion endorsements,

Convention time schedules mandated the next item of business be considered and Valentine's time expired.

After the vote for president, resolutions were presented. Because many conservatives came specifically to vote for Rogers, they left when that vote was concluded. As a result, the same typical outcome occured on the resolutions. The abortion resolution was a virtual repeat of past resolutions with all of their loopholes. When Gary Tebbets of Missouri offered a strong, pro-life amendment to the resolution, there were not enough conservative pro-life messengers remaining to sustain it, and the 1979 resolution was just like those in the past. Pro-lifers vowed to return in 1980 and they did.[51] It is interesting that Valentine and his kin blindly associated the pro-life position with Roman Catholicism and, therefore, seemed to reject it outright as a possible biblical position. His anti-Catholicism bent would be revealed in other decisions as well.

The old establishment won every vote in Houston except the presidency and the affirmation of the Bible. Nevertheless, the first steps were taken and the first shots fired in the battle identified as the Baptist Reformation!

In the remainder of the year, much unfolded on the national and international scene. Continued discussion abounded about the implications of the Three-Mile Island disaster. The Salt II Treaty was negotiated but never ratified, and the Marxist Sandinistas came to power in Nicaragua. Oil prices continued to rise due to OPEC's manipulation. On November 4 more than one hundred hostages were seized at the U.S. Embassy in Tehran, Iran, and only about half were released. On Christmas, Russia invaded Afghanistan. In short, the world once again was filled with tension.[52]

On the domestic religious scene, a flurry of activity was underway not only among Southern Baptists but also among the entire conservative spectrum of American Christianity. Within the Southern Baptist Convention, however, the old heads would be proven wrong. The year 1979, in retrospect, marked a dramatic turning point in its storied history. In less than a decade conservatives of the Pressler, Patterson, Rogers, and Criswell stripe would become the new establishment, one with a distinctly different philosophy, program, and public policy agenda on church and state and moral concerns than the Christian Life Commission and the Baptist Joint Committee fraternity had followed since the 1950s.

Southern Baptist conservatives had been slow in developing social ministries and for the most part had stayed out of secular politics. The pastors majored on evangelism in their churches. Many came to the annual Southern Baptist Convention meeting more for the Pastors' Conference than for Convention business. Conservatives had taken over the Pastors' Conference years before Pressler, Patterson, and kindred spirits showed them how to bring the Convention back to the bedrock biblical beliefs they held dear.

In recent years tension over race, the antiwar movement, the proliferation of the drug culture, abortion rights and homosexual rights, and the outlawing of prayer and Bible reading in public schools sent tremors and shock waves through people embracing traditional Christian values. Millions of citizens in conservative Christian America were searching for a solution to what was perceived as an era of national crisis. Answers began surfacing from Christian leaders who became identified as organizers of the religious right.

Most prominent among those leaders was Jerry Falwell, well-known preacher on The Old-Time Gospel Hour and senior pastor of Thomas Road Baptist Church in Lynchburg, Virginia. Falwell in many ways, particularly in influence, was the Charles Spurgeon of his day. He founded numerous ministries, particularly the world-famous Elim Home for alcohol and drug-dependent men and the Liberty Godparent Home for unwed mothers. He was not only the founder of his church (1956) but also the founder in 1971 of Liberty University, one of the premier Christian universities in America by the turn of the twenty-first century. With respect to influencing the American political scene, Falwell initiated the founding of the Moral Majority. Within two years of launching his media and mail campaign, he had an active mailing list of more than seven million.[53]

Also in this same time frame, other organizations were formed which helped establish what was identified as the religious right. Two early entries were the Eagle Forum (1972) and the National Right to Life Committee (1973). Focus on the Family started in 1977 and spun off the Family Research Council in 1983. In 1979, the same year that the Moral Majority was established, Beverly LaHaye along with her husband, Tim, incorporated Concerned Women for America; and Ed McAteer formed the Religious Roundtable. Each of these were part of a "we can change America" grassroots movement.[54]

Southern Baptist Convention conservatives began emerging from their separatist shells. By 1979, leading Southern Baptist pastors were beginning to ally with Jerry Falwell, Pat Robertson, and other leaders of the religious right. Jimmy Draper, Bailey Smith, and Adrian Rogers each agreed to serve on the Traditional Values Coalition founded by Louis Sheldon in 1980. This organization evaluated political candidates by ten basic concerns: A constitutional amendment to prohibit abortion headed the list, along with a public school prayer amendment, tuition tax credits for parents, a strong national defense against communism, and opposition to homosexual rights, pornography, and welfare programs that do not emphasize the work ethic.

The Christian Life Commission of the 1970s and much of the 1980s, while opposing pornography and much of the homosexual agenda, saw the Coalition agenda as reactionary and in some cases a violation of their understanding of the separation of church and state. The Christian Life Commission, along with the Baptist Joint Committee on Public Affairs, was more attuned to issues championed by more liberal organizations.

Moreover, the Commission and Baptist Joint Committee leadership, along with their civil libertarian comrades, also maintained their loyalty to Jimmy Carter, whose unstable political foundations were severely undermined by the taking and holding of fifty-two American hostages for 444 days in Tehran, Iran. Carter, in response to the hostage crisis, deported illegal Iranian students, froze Iranian assets, barred oil imports from Iran, and even attempted a disastrous hostage rescue mission on April 25, 1980. Due to the failure of that mission and the loss of eight military personnel, Secretary of State Cyrus Vance tendered his resignation. Meanwhile, the Christian Life Commission and the Baptist Joint Committee on Public Affairs held strong power bases among Southern Baptists, particularly in Texas, the home state of Pressler and Patterson.

Year after year the Commission and Committee continued to showcase left-leaning personalities and their viewpoints at national seminars paid for with Southern Baptist dollars. Speakers at the 1980 Commission seminar, "Ethical Issues for the Eighties," included environmentalist Barry Commoner, Attorney General Ramsey Clark, NAACP Executive Director Benjamin Hooks, and Special Assistant to the President Sarah Weddington, who argued the winning side in the landmark *Roe v. Wade* decision legalizing abortion. Again no Southern Baptist on the program was an identified conservative.

By the time the Convention met in St. Louis in 1980, conservatives had been networking to promote their agenda. Not surprisingly, this Convention drew the lowest registration in seven years primarily due to the fact that Rogers would almost automatically receive a customary second term as president. When he withdrew from running for reelection just prior to the Convention, Pastor Bailey Smith of Del City, Oklahoma, was the conservative choice. He won on the first ballot with 51.17 percent of the vote over Richard Jackson and James Pleitz.[55]

Rogers's appointments for the Committee on Committees were comprised of a list of solid convictional conservatives. The same was true of his appointment of the Resolutions Committee. Not surprising was the fact that no one on the Resolutions Committee had any connection with the Christian Life Commission or the Baptist Joint Committee.

When the Christian Life Commission made its report, it acknowledged appreciation for its $420,000 Cooperative Program allotment. It reported they now had seven full-time staffers and had produced a substantial amount of products and services over the previous year. It also reported that both Valentine and staffer Harry Hollis had been appointed to voluntary positions on government commissions and committees.

A New Direction

When time for the resolutions came, a total of fifty were proposed, and more than twenty were presented from the committee. Most were in keeping with previous resolutions. Two, however, marked a distinctive conservative stamp and met with resistance from Commission and old-guard bureaucracy sympathizers.

One resolution that attested to the new direction was "On Doctrinal Integrity." This resolution states:

> WHEREAS, Southern Baptists cherish our abiding conviction that the Bible is a perfect treasure of divine instruction which has God for its author, salvation for its end, and truth, without any mixture of error, for its matter, and
>
> WHEREAS, We believe freedom should be balanced with responsibility and doctrinal integrity, and
>
> WHEREAS, We acknowledge not only the right but the responsibility of this Convention to give explicit guidelines to the governing bodies of our various institutions,
>
> THEREFORE BE IT RESOLVED, That the Southern Baptist Convention express its profound appreciation to the staff and faculty members of our seminaries and other institutions who have persistently and sacrificially taught the truth with love—enriching our appreciation for the Bible as God's Holy Word and enhancing our ministry in Christ's name, and
>
> BE IT FURTHER RESOLVED, That we exhort the trustees or seminaries and other institutions affiliated with or supported by the Southern Baptist Convention to faithfully discharge their responsibility to carefully preserve the doctrinal integrity of our institutions and to assure that seminaries and other institutions receiving our support only employ, and continue the employment of, faculty members and professional staff who believe in the divine inspiration of the whole Bible, infallibility of the original manuscripts, and that the Bible is truth without any error.[56]

Yet the resolution that most marked an obvious and distinct change in the arena of moral concern was "On Abortion." In past years the Resolutions Committee had continued to recycle a statement on abortion that deplored abortion on demand but did nothing to request the Supreme Court to overturn *Roe v. Wade* or call for legislation that would reverse the decision. Although Valentine labeled himself pro-life, every association, decision, and comment stated otherwise. And every resolution to date included loophole words used to identify Southern Baptists as pro-abortion.

On Thursday morning of the Convention, the following resolution was presented and read to the Convention by Larry Lewis:

> WHEREAS, Southern Baptists have historically affirmed the biblical teaching of the sanctity of all human life, and
>
> WHEREAS, All medical evidence indicates that abortion ends the life of a developing human being, and
>
> WHEREAS, Our national laws permit a policy commonly referred to as "abortion on demand,"
>
> Be it therefore RESOLVED, That the Southern Baptist Convention reaffirm the view of the Scriptures of the sacredness and dignity of all human life, born and unborn, and
>
> Be it further RESOLVED, That opposition be expressed toward all policies that allow "abortion on demand," and
>
> Be it further RESOLVED, That we abhor the use of tax money or public, tax-supported medical facilities for selfish, non-therapeutic abortion, and
>
> Be it finally RESOLVED, That we favor appropriate legislation and/or a constitutional amendment prohibiting abortion except to save the life of the mother.[57]

When the prospective resolution was presented to the Convention, Lewis asked permission to speak in favor of its adoption. Lewis explained that in a local newspaper advertisement entitled "Religion Leaders Speak Out for the Right to Choose Abortion" the

Southern Baptist Convention was included right alongside the Union of American Hebrew Reformed Congregations and the Unitarian and Universalist Associations. Lewis explained that when he called to inquire about the reason for the Southern Baptist Convention's inclusion in the ad, he was told that that was the meaning of all past resolutions on the subject. Therefore, Lewis concluded, "This year, we felt as the [Resolutions] Committee that Southern Baptists needed to make a very strong statement, very explicit, that could not be misinterpreted by the news media or any of our own agencies or anybody else." Lewis went on to say:

> I think you will agree that this is a very strong concise statement, and surely identifies us as being opposed to any non-therapeutic abortion. We felt this pertinent issue of taxes and Medicaid funds being used to support abortion and in tax-supported facilities [called for] a paragraph: "We abhor the use of tax money and facilities for selfish non-therapeutic abortions."
> The final paragraph suggests that we favor "appropriate legislation and/or a constitutional amendment." It was the consensus of our committee that we wanted something done, . . . that we needed to fall in line behind those in Congress or whoever else wants something to be done. It's simply intolerable that a million and a half babies are taken every year. We must speak out against it. Something must be done.[58]

After Lewis spoke, William Hillis, a medical doctor from Maryland and former Resolutions Committee member, responded in opposition suggesting that those promoting this resolution had "a political axe to grind." He then offered a substitute resolution that affirmed the past resolutions. This led to a long discussion about past resolutions' intent, meaning, and perception. Lewis clarified the meaning of past resolutions' loopholes, which the culture interpreted as Southern Baptist support of abortion on demand. When the substitute resolution failed, the Convention again turned to the main resolution.

When the Convention returned to the main motion, the chair recognized messenger James Mann, also a medical doctor, who addressed the extent of the abortion industry's expansion in the United States since *Roe v. Wade*. After Mann, Welton Gaddy, former Commission staffer, moved that the last paragraph be deleted. Ralph Stewart responded by saying:

> We're being naïve if we think we can't influence our government. I've got an article in my hand that's called "A Call to Concern." The emphasis is to influence our government. One of the points is, "We call upon the leaders of religious groups supporting abortion rights to speak out more clearly and publicly." Now if that's not trying to influence our government, I don't know what is. And Dr. Foy Valentine, the chair of our Christian Life Commission, is a signatory of this article. I move we drop this amendment.[59]

When the votes were taken, the original resolution "On Abortion" passed by a strong majority. The press section emptied quickly as reporters hurried to file the story that the Southern Baptist Convention had made a dramatic turnaround on the abortion issue.

Other resolutions were scattered across the board. Some were compromises like the one "On Women," which advocated equal pay for equal work but refused to endorse the Equal Rights Amendment. Surprisingly, Harry Hollis, a Commission staffer, offered the resolution "On the White House Conference on the Family," which was critical of the Carter administration's support of abortion on demand and homosexuality. Although Hollis spoke for himself, this resolution suggested the Commission and the conservatives were not that far apart or that there was a breaking of ranks among the Commission's staffers. In Hollis's resolution, he suggested the Carter policy coming out of the committee of which he himself was a participant was "undermining of the biblical concept of the family." Not surprisingly, a resolution "On Homosexuality" was also affirmed by the Convention.[60]

The Christian Life Commission report was scheduled for Thursday afternoon, when many messengers had gone home. Valentine spoke briefly at his Commission's time slot noting that the report printed in the Book of Reports contained no recommendations. He noted, however, that it followed up on three referrals from the previous year, all of which were innocuous. In the words of one messenger, the Convention concluded with a whimper.

As summer came, President Carter fended off a challenge for the party's nomination from Edward Kennedy. Ronald Reagan received the Republican nomination. With hostages still captive at election time, inflation at 13 percent, unemployment at 7.5 percent, and the going interest rate at 20 percent, it was not surprising that Carter experienced the worst ever defeat of an incumbent president. To make matters worse for the Democrats, they also lost the Senate for only the second time in sixty years. Polls demonstrated that a majority of Southern Baptists voted for Reagan. On January 20, 1981, Reagan was inaugurated, and the hostages were released. Only two months later Reagan was shot by John Hinckley. In May the *New York Times* reported an unexplained health crisis, which would be identified in the next two years as HIV/AIDS.[61]

The Commission seminar in the spring continued to feature speakers from the left side of the spectrum. In fact, the keynote speaker, L. D. Johnson, a faculty member of Southeastern Baptist Theological Seminary who spoke five times, used each occasion to berate, criticize, and condemn the conservative movement in the Convention.

When Rogers's Committee on Boards' Nominations were announced, the agency heads knew almost none of them. So at the 1981 Convention, ten were challenged and replaced with moderates. Smith's appointments were similar to Rogers's and conservatives jumped on a fast learning curve to understand how the parliamentary game was played.

In violation of the unwritten rules of the customary second term for incumbent first-term presidents of the Convention, the moderates broke tradition and precedent by nominating Baylor University President Abner McCall. In urging messengers to vote for McCall, Ralph Langley pleaded for messengers to "come back to the middle with McCall, a latter-day Lincoln who can unify this Convention and bring us to the middle." The incumbent, Bailey Smith, won with a 60 percent majority.[62]

The 1981 Convention in Los Angeles belonged to the conservatives, who only lost two votes. First, Larry McSwain and Ken Chafin challenged five people on the Committee on Boards' report. And second, a resolution "On Affirming Religious Liberty and Separation of Church and State" passed. This resolution applauded the work of the Christian Life Commission and the Baptist Joint Committee. Unbeknown to conservatives, the final two paragraphs were a direct assault on the work of the growing religious right.[63]

No doubt the theological highlight of the Convention came when Herschel Hobbs moved to reaffirm the 1963 Baptist Faith and Message. When asked to clarify its intention, Hobbs noted the article on Scripture "meant that the whole Bible is truth not just that there is truth in the Bible." Hobbs clarified that the article's intention was that "every single part of the whole" was true.[64]

The Commission's report was again scheduled for Thursday afternoon. Valentine introduced David King and Patsy Ayres. The report was accepted with no recommendations, discussion, or debate. Valentine reviewed the many activities in which the Commission was involved and invited the messengers to stop by its booth in the exhibit hall and pick up a copy of *Light*, the newest issue of which addressed the new right and the Reagan presidency. Valentine turned over the microphone to staffer William Elden who proceeded to warn messengers of the grave danger of the new religious right. No doubt the folks at the Commission were greatly concerned about this emerging influence in America and rightly so, for it threatened their cherished presuppositions and exposed their loyalties.[65]

The Christian Life Commission and the Baptist Joint Committee were increasingly out of step with rank-and-file Southern Baptists. And the conservative leadership had every intention of both entities representing majority Southern Baptist values or not representing them at all.

Looking back at the spring of 1981, on March 15, James Dunn led the National Impact Briefing for the Baptist Joint Committee, which essentially was a broadside attack on the religious right. In his article "Reflections," published post April 24, Dunn severely criticized

President Reagan and the political proponents of tuition tax credits. Dunn clearly marked out his territory and was dead set against the religious right and the Reagan administration. But since key leaders of the conservative resurgence among Southern Baptists were part of the religious right, Dunn was actually squaring off against his principal financial support. This disparity would eventually lead to the Southern Baptist decision to defund their portion of the Baptist Joint Committee and redirect the resources ultimately to what would be the Ethics & Religious Liberty Commission.[66]

On September 21, 1981, Sandra Day O'Connor, a Reagan nominee, became the first woman Supreme Court justice in history.[67]

No doubt Reagan's election to the White House shook the staff of the Christian Life Commission. They were quickly assessing the situation and coming to the realization that the religious right was for real and was not going away. When Commission planners were preparing the 1982 national seminar on "Strengthening Families," they invited Jerry Falwell to speak. Even though he was the token conservative, his presence made an impact. Falwell followed Jimmy Allen late in the program and spoke on "Strengthening Families in the Nation." Allen brought up a litany of exceptions that should, in his opinion, be allowed for approving abortion. In contrast, Falwell identified abortion as America's national sin, comparing it to Germany's national sin of the holocaust. He declared, "I would agree with the Roman Catholics and many of our friends nationwide that the 10 to 12 million little babies who have died in this country since the *Roe v. Wade*, January 1973 Supreme Court decision have brought the wrath of God upon this nation."[68] Other speakers were virtually silent on abortion.

An interesting exchange of letters occurred in the spring of 1982. Maston wrote to Dunn observing:

> I recognize, of course, that I may be unduly concerned
> about the relation of church and state, but I definitely think that
> it is going to be one of the major issues that we will have to face
> up to in the years ahead. I recognize, also, that it is going to be
> extremely difficult to get anything done. My viewpoint is that if

we take it seriously we have to admit that our churches, pastors, and others, are violating our separation principles.[69]

Responding to Maston's letter, Dunn conceded, "It is possible, of course, that we need to restudy the whole matter of separation and determine if our theory needs to be updated." A few weeks later Maston again wrote to Dunn, encouraging him, "Please do what you can to keep the church-state issue alive. We have some very real problems which I think will be more serious in the years to come."[70]

Leading up to the Convention in June, the *Houston Post* carried an article entitled, "Baptists will tackle 'inerrancy' question." The article, written by *Post* reporter Jim Asker interviewed Ken Chafin, who said about the new conservative leadership, "They are basically stacking these boards with rightwing rednecks." He assessed, "Many are inexperienced, even hostile, to the goals of the boards." He then observed, "There are some nice people, but it's on accident." That same article goes on to say that rumor had it that the Baptist Joint Committee might find its funding removed.[71]

The 1982 Convention in New Orleans marked the fourth successive year of the conservative advance. New conservative trustees were showing up on boards and agencies. Clearly agency heads embraced a growing concern about the movement, and Valentine was as concerned as anyone.

At the Convention the biggest agenda item was the presidential election. Some attempted to draft Billy Graham to run since he was on the program. He graciously declined. Southern Baptist moderates backed Duke McCall. Conservatives put their hopes in Jimmy Draper. Two centrist candidates, both from Louisiana, were John Sullivan and Perry Sanders. McCall and Draper were in a runoff, which Draper won with 57 percent of the vote.[72]

Smith's appointments, consistent with previous years, were solidly conservative.

This year James Dunn addressed the Convention and spoke primarily on the issue of school prayer. He was particularly passionate in his opposition. Most know he was preparing the Convention for a resolution to follow on the same subject.

Valentine followed Dunn on the program. As usual, he referred messengers to the printed report. Of significance was the fact that four staff members resigned. David Sapp and William Elden took pastorates while Bill Tillman and John Wood returned to academia. Three new staffers included Larry Braidfoot, David Lockard, and Ron Sisk. Besides Valentine, Harry Hollis and Tim Fields were the two senior staffers.

Valentine noted the Commission had given two Distinguished Service Awards to J. B. Weatherspoon and Hugh Brimm, both post-humously. Valentine made no mention of A. J. Barton, probably the most conservative of the agency's past leaders. Valentine then recounted an impressive list of the year's accomplishments but had no recommendations.

The business of the Convention moved along smoothly until consideration of the resolution, "On Prayer in Schools." The debate was long and intense, but when the vote was taken, this resolution passed:

> WHEREAS, The first amendment to the Constitution of the United States of America clearly states that the Congress shall pass no law prohibiting the free exercise of religion, and

> WHEREAS, The same first amendment protects us against the establishment of religion, and

> WHEREAS, A constitutional amendment is pending wherein there is no violation of either of those ideals inherent in the separation of church and state, and

> WHEREAS, This proposed amendment neither requires nor restricts the vocal expression of individual or group prayer in public schools, and

> WHEREAS, Considerable confusion as to the rights and privileges guaranteed by the Constitution with regard to prayer in schools has been engendered by the Supreme Court decisions of 1962 and 1963, and

WHEREAS, Public school officials and lower courts have frequently misinterpreted these Supreme Court decisions as a ban on voluntary prayer, and

WHEREAS, For 170 years following the writing of the First Amendment, the right of prayer in public schools was a time-honored exercise and a cherished privilege, and

WHEREAS, Southern Baptists historically have affirmed the right of voluntary prayer in public places, and

WHEREAS, The proposed constitutional amendment reads simply, "Nothing in this Constitution shall be construed to prohibit individual or group prayer in public schools or other public institutions. No person shall be required by the United States or by any state to participate in prayer," and

WHEREAS, This proposed amendment does not constitute a call for government-written or government-mandated prayer.

Therefore, Be it RESOLVED, That we the messengers of the Southern Baptist Convention in session, June 1982, New Orleans, Louisiana, declare our support of the aforementioned proposed constitutional amendment.

Be if further RESOLVED, That we shall work continually to hold fast to our faith and to the freedoms in which we believe and by which we live.[73]

In response to the prayer resolution, Dunn called it "an incredible contradiction of our Baptist heritage." This demonstrated just how far the Baptist Joint Committee was away from rank-and-file Southern Baptists. It also foreshadowed the coming dissolution between the Convention and the Baptist Joint Committee.[74]

Another strong resolution was "On Abortion and Infanticide." This was the resolution which almost was not. After being introduced, it was placed "on the table" due to the fact that the Convention passed a strong pro-life resolution the year before. Concerned about perceptions, Larry Lewis walked to the pressroom and inquired as to how the "tabling" was being interpreted. Hearing that it was being perceived as a repudiation of the previous year, after lunch, Lewis requested it be taken off the table and voted on. It was and it passed.[75]

One interesting and even contradictory resolution was "On Tuition Tax Credit." The Convention essentially went on record opposing this Reagan initiative. Curiously, the same argument opposing the tuition tax credit could be used against tax deductions for charitable contributions to nonprofit organizations like churches. Also wrapped up in this was the fourth clause, which stated, "Whereas tuition tax credit legislation carries the potential of financing private education at the expense of public education." Some believed this smacked of class envy. Yet this resolution, promoted by the Commission and Baptist Joint Committee, curiously was accepted and approved by the messengers.[76]

Resistance to the Resurgence

After the Convention in New Orleans on into the summer, Maston wrote Dunn with two suggestions dealing with strategy. He noted: "It is possible, of course, that the heads of our boards and agencies will have to be rather careful about what they say and do. It seems to me that there are some very effective things that they can do without being too directly involved. For example, the Foreign Mission Board, the Home Mission Board, and the Sunday School Board could see that the fellows who are attempting to take over things do not have the kind of platform exposure that they have had in the past." He went on to write: "It strikes me that the Baptist Joint Committee may be able to speak out more openly and frankly about the contemporary situation than any of our Southern Baptist agencies. I do think that Foy's Christian Life Commission can speak out more frankly than is possibly wise for the heads of our Boards. I hate to think about what would happen to our whole Southern Baptist program if the ultraconservatives really win control."[77]

Maston suggested that moderates who still controlled boards and agencies use their positions to screen who did and did not address large audiences of Southern Baptists. Surprisingly he did not realize this had been going on a long time already. Also he realized the

Baptist Joint Committee, with less accountability, was in a position to challenge the present conservative movement in the Convention. He failed to realize that by embracing a "winner take all" approach, moderates would either lose their leadership, their financial support, or both.

The 1983 national seminar hosted by the Christian Life Commission was in Louisville, Kentucky. During the seminar there was evidence of a growing reaction on the left to the "Reagan Revolution" and the religious right. Present and involved in the seminar were members of the organization, People for the American Way (PAW), founded by media mogul Norman Lear in 1981. The singular purpose of the organization was to oppose the influence of the religious right. James Dunn was on their founding board of directors.[78]

Speakers at this year's seminar included Charles Swindoll and Robert Schuller, who were neither Southern Baptist nor politically connected. Other speakers, however, included Jim Wallis, Donald Shriver, and Gordon Kingsley. Not surprisingly, numerous critical remarks were made about the present state of affairs among Southern Baptists.

At the Convention in Pittsburgh, Draper, who was considered more conciliatory than Rogers and Smith, was reelected without opposition. Moderates gave up on the pre-Convention Pastors' Conference in Pittsburgh. It had long been as restrictive for speakers on the left as the Christian Life Commission seminar had been for conservative personalities on the right. Approximately nine hundred moderates held their own pre-Convention meeting at a local hotel.

When it was time for Valentine's report, he reviewed the previous year's work and referred messengers to the Book of Reports. When Vice President John Sullivan opened the floor for questions, several were forthcoming. Darrell Leslie from Oklahoma asked, "In your report you refer to the New Religious Right. . . . What do you mean by the term?" Lewis Garrett of Virginia asked, "Can you tell us what you believe about a woman's right to have an abortion?" Another messenger, Charles Blair of Kentucky, asked Valentine if anyone from the religious right would be welcome on his staff. To each question,

Valentine gave a safe answer attempting not to provoke any more messengers than was absolutely necessary.[79]

In James Dunn's report to the Convention, he was ecstatic over the recent government decision that entitled religious groups or companies to be granted "free access." This victory, he assured the messengers, was due to the diligence of the Baptist Joint Committee.[80] Next Dunn invited questions. Some were germane to the Committee's work; others were not. For most messengers nothing of real significance was reported.

Forty-five resolutions were offered to the Convention. Per protocol, these became the property of the Resolutions Committee, which would change them and recommend them back to the Convention, or let them die in committee. To understand the breadth of subjects, consider that resolutions were made, reported, and adopted on the following subjects: women, freedom and responsibility in Southern Baptist seminaries, religious liberty, black and ethnic involvement, pornography, peace with justice, the forced termination of ministers, gambling, the care of the environment, and alcohol. Other resolutions included an expression of appreciation to the people of Pittsburgh, the designation of 1984 to be the Year of the Bible, and resolutions on *The Reader's Digest Bible*, personal witnessing, and Bold Mission Thrust. Messengers agreed on many of the resolutions; however, some assisted in creating a line of demarcation.[81]

Moderates, who continued to support enthusiastically the work of the Commission and the Baptist Joint Committee, left the Convention with more disappointment. The balance on the Commission board was tilting less and less to a blind loyalty to Valentine and the left-leaning agenda. The change was incremental, slow, deliberate, and unmistakable.

Rudy Yakym, a new Commission board member, could not get the Commission staff energized on stopping what he perceived to be genocidal abortion, so he brought a motion "that the Southern Baptist Convention Executive Committee and the Christian Life Commission's board of trustees study ways in which the . . . Convention may take a more visible and positive stance against abortion and make a future report to the Convention." Interestingly, his motion was referred to the Convention's Executive Committee for consideration.[82]

Efforts to replace several nominated board nominees failed. One was Albert Lee Smith, a former congressman from Alabama. Smith, a staunch conservative, was nominated to the Public Affairs Committee, which linked the Convention to the Baptist Joint Committee. Smith's nomination was sustained by Convention vote.

The Pittsburgh Convention ended with conservatives another year closer to victory over the old denominational guard, to the capture and retooling of the Christian Life Commission, and to cutting ties with the Baptist Joint Committee.

In the post-Pittsburgh months, we again find an interesting exchange of correspondence between Maston and Dunn. Maston wrote, "I have not seen anything in any of the reports that would indicate that they made any progress in de-funding your agency or doing anything else that in any way would handicap your work." He acknowledged "that they did elect some folks as members of the Commission who could cause you some problems." He then concluded, "I would assume, however, that you have enough strength in other members of the Commission to resist successfully any attempt for them to seriously handicap your work."[83]

On the same day Maston wrote to Dunn, Dunn also wrote to Maston with his assessment of the Convention. He observed, "The SBC was mixed: Bad, very bad, killer board members, yet, new budget money, a prayer-religious liberty statement that's a great improvement."[84]

A few weeks later Maston again wrote to Dunn, "I knew that they did not defund you. I am glad of that." He then went on to say, "I hope that you have enough strength in your board that some of the fellows who were put on will not be able to carry much weight in trying to limit you." Maston went on to observe:

> From what I have heard about the convention, it seems to
> me that it was a considerable improvement over what we have
> been having. I know that some of the fellows, and you may

be among them, do not believe in Jimmy Draper but I do. I believe that he is trying the best he can to carry on what he has pledged to do. . . .

If it is true that we have a few on both extremes that I do not think are willing to accept what I think Jimmy and some of the others are trying to do. We must recover, in so far as we have lost it, the ability to differ and yet to work together agreeably.[85]

By August, Dunn again wrote to Maston mostly criticizing the direction of the Convention: "The guys that they put on our Committee are totally against us. They have one objective: to disagree, discredit. . . . Doc, some folks have no idea how mean and unprincipled this crowd really is. They are on a crusade. We are their enemy. What's true and fair and right doesn't matter. . . . Pray for us. I need wisdom, patients [sic], friends."[86]

Maston responded to Dunn's latest letter acknowledging the gravity of the situation, noting, "I would assume that the greatest possibility of something happening to undermine your work is through some action of the Convention. In other words, if the Convention really voted to defund your Commission, my understanding is that it would put you in a very tight spot." Maston went on to advise Dunn, "The best approach and that is most of the time [is] not to try to answer [your critics] but rather to ignore." Maston continued his advice, "You do know, also, that I could wish sometimes that you might say things with a little less sharpness or barb. May the good Lord give you the wisdom and grace and strength that you need."[87]

By briefly reviewing this correspondence, it is easy to conclude there was mounting concern about the impossibility of stopping the growing conservative resurgence. Of particular concern was how to respond to the new trustees and their agenda.

Meanwhile, in the country at large, eyes again turned to the Middle East. On October 23, suicide bombers attacked the U.S. Marine base in Beirut, Lebanon, killing 241 Marines and 58 French soldiers. Two days later the U.S. invaded Grenada. On November 2, Reagan signed legislation honoring Martin Luther King Jr. by establishing January 15 as a federal holiday. And by the end of November, the U.S. had deployed cruise missiles to the European Theater in support of NATO. After the turn of the year, Reagan announced all troops in Lebanon would be removed by the beginning of March.[88]

On the Southern Baptist scene, a growing moderate movement was organized to resist the new direction of conservatives.

Valentine, now in his twenty-fifth year as the Commission's executive director, provided no public hint that he was thinking of retiring. The workload remained steady, and the annual seminar continued to showcase an unmatched array of speakers for the most part resistant to Reagan and the religious right.

The 1984 seminar, entitled "Christian Citizenship: 1984," was held in Washington, D.C. Randall Lolley, embattled president of Southeastern Baptist Theological Seminary, spoke six times. Gardner Taylor likened the religious right to the novel by George Orwell, 2, and its manipulation of the naïve for political gain. It seems that this year's seminar was an overt exercise in political activity every bit as severe as its speakers accused conservatives of doing. Seminar speaker Helen Caldicott challenged the participants to join in the crusade for a nuclear freeze.[89]

Interestingly, the seminar invited two politicians to address the gathering. Jim Wright, a Democrat, spoke on the need to consider a gradual nuclear disarmament, and Bob Dole, a Republican, addressed the issue of the federal deficit.[90]

Meanwhile correspondence between Maston and Dunn continues to provide insight into what the denominational machinery was thinking and doing in response to the growing conservative influence. In response to several "letters to the editor" published in state denominational papers, Maston wrote one entitled "Baptist Joint Committee," in which he stated, "Withholding financial support by the SBC would cripple if not destroy the work of the Committee." This, of course, was the implication of withdrawing support. Maston then urged fellow Southern Baptists, "If changes need to be made, let us seek them from within the structure." Of course, conservatives found this almost impossible if past experience was any indicator.[91]

In early June, Maston again wrote to Dunn noting, "It is hard for me to believe, however, that a majority of the folks at Kansas City would vote to defund your commission." He then wrote:

> Let me give you two or three words of grandfatherly advice. Try as best you can to be kind and understanding of folks who oppose you. Tell them that one good thing about being a Baptist is the fact that we do not have to all agree but we should be agreeable about it. Be careful what you say and what you put in print, and particularly how you say it.[92]

As Convention time approached, both sides stayed busy on the speaking circuit, working to get out the vote. Moderates kept arguing the value of "unity in diversity," while conservatives kept responding with the need for "doctrinal integrity."

Moderates generally saw Jimmy Draper as the most tolerant among the present conservative leaders. Yet, with Draper unable to run again due to term limits, moderates viewed the 1984 election as a key opportunity. The "denominational loyalists" offered two well-known candidates, Grady Cothen and John Sullivan. Conservatives were supportive of Charles Stanley.

The 1984 Pastors' Conference featured Franky Schaeffer, son of Francis Schaeffer, Zig Zigler, and outgoing Convention president, Jimmy Draper. Draper, in his address, called, "Abortion, the gravest matter of our time."

At Kansas City, moderates launched their alternative to the Pastors' Conference, the SBC Forum. Their meeting drew about two thousand attendees, only 20 percent of those at the Pastors' Conference.

When election time came, Charles Stanley won with 52 percent of the vote on the first ballot. The new direction continued.[93]

Russell Dilday, in his Convention sermon, declared:

> Incredible as it sounds, there is emerging in this denomination, built on the principle of rugged individualism, an incipient

Orwellian mentality. It threatens to drag us down from the high ground to the lowlands of suspicion, rumor, criticism, innuendos, guilt by association, and the rest of the demonic family of forced uniformity.[94]

Many conservatives were convinced that his diatribe revealed more about Dilday than it did about the conservatives he vilified. Moreover, it served for the most part to push the two sides farther apart. When a winner-take-all mind-set exists, someone has to lose.

Budget planners in the Southern Baptist Convention Executive Committee recommended most agencies receive a 2.79 percent increase over the previous year's allocation. That would funnel $411,436 through the Public Affairs Committee to the Baptist Joint Committee and designate $729,843 for the Christian Life Commission.

For the first time a motion was made to cut the funding for the Baptist Joint Committee. Critics argued the Committee did not represent the Convention, loaded their programs with speakers critical of the Convention's positions, and then used Southern Baptist money to pay the honorariums. The vote failed narrowly, garnering 48.35 percent of the vote by messengers present.[95]

Later, attorney Joe Knott, messenger from North Carolina, made a motion that the Convention take steps "to establish a Southern Baptist presence in Washington, D.C., to address public and governmental affairs and that it be known as the Governmental Affairs of the Southern Baptist Convention." Following protocol, his motion was referred to the Executive Committee.[96]

When it came time for Dunn to speak, he labored to justify the work of the Baptist Joint Committee, recounting the many stands they had taken over the years that the Convention favored.

Valentine's presentation of accomplishments for the previous year was set against the backdrop of the Convention's proposed resolutions that the Commission be more forthright in opposing abortion. O. J. Peterson of Indiana requested the Commission "be directed not only to diligently pursue the study of the pro-life position against abortion on demand, but also to take positive action to both speak out and organize against the 'murder of the innocent unborn.'"[97]

When Valentine came to the platform, he did not address the abortion issue either in his report or in his remarks. When question time came, he was asked by messenger James Chandler from Virginia why the Commission's report was silent on the abortion issue. Valentine responded that he did not have the resources, time, or staff to address every issue that people felt strongly about. He went on to justify the Commission by saying, "We're doing all that we can within the limit of our strength."[98]

What Valentine did not say, but most messengers knew, was that he and the Commission fundamentally disagreed with what had come to be known as the pro-life position. Valentine was out of step with his constituency, and it was painfully obvious. Unlike the race issue, his position could not be justified by Scripture.

The resolution "On Abortion" was the strongest to date. An array of other typical resolutions was offered at the Convention. For the first time the Convention passed a resolution specifically "On Cigarette Smoking." And in the resolution "On Christian Citizenship," messengers approved the statement declaring, "That this assembly reaffirm the doctrine of our forefathers of separation of church and state which should not be interpreted to mean, however, the separation of God from government." No doubt this caused the absolute separationists no small amount of discomfort. More than likely this was an attempt in their eyes to legitimize civil religion and affirm the convictions of the religious right.[99]

For Southern Baptist conservatives, the 1984 Convention was another year of victory, and it meant that they were one year closer to bringing what they perceive to be honest changes facilitated through a democratic process.

Writing to Dunn in the post-Convention weeks, Maston commented that he was surprised that the Baptist Joint Committee was not defunded. Maston's perspective was still that Pressler and Patterson were manipulating a multitude of parties. Maston went on to observe,

"I really think that the strategy of the group trying to defund you this time might be the argument that they would make that we need a Commission just for Southern Baptists." He then noted, "Of course, if they did that, they would still have a problem of knowing what to do with you." No doubt most conservatives would consider this a small problem.[100]

In October, Dunn further alienated himself from Southern Baptist conservatives in his address at the "Faith and History Conference" sponsored by Southwestern Baptist Theological Seminary entitled "The Christian as Political Activist." He identified the religious right as a bunch of "extremists" and labeled their efforts "a pernicious plot." No doubt the support for Dunn and the Baptist Joint Committee was continuing to erode.[101]

On the national scene Walter Mondale received the Democratic nomination for president for the upcoming presidential election. Reagan was unchallenged for the Republican nomination. In November, Reagan was elected with 59 percent of the popular vote, winning the electoral college vote with a 525 to 13 victory.[102]

In March 1985, Mikhail Gorbachev was elected first secretary of the Soviet Communist Party and subsequently introduced the idea of *glasnost* (openness) and *perestroika* (reconstruction) that would eventually transform the Soviet Union and bring the collapse of communism's seventy-year reign of terror over the Russian people.[103]

Prior to the 1985 Convention in Dallas, the Christian Life Commission relocated to new office space in the seven-story Southern Baptist Convention Building adjacent to the Sunday School Board. Yet there was little time to celebrate. Since Kansas City the air had been thick with verbal missiles going back and forth over the present state of the Convention. Roy Honeycutt called for a "Holy War," which proved to be more talk than action.

At the 1984 Convention, a burning fuse on the abortion issue went virtually unnoticed by most messengers. Early at the Convention, David Blackney presented what appeared to be a harmless motion calling for designation of "the third Sunday in January as Sanctity of Human Life Sunday," beginning in 1985, and that the Christian Life

Commission promote its observance in the churches." As customary this motion was referred to the Calendar Committee that was scheduled to meet in January 1985. The designation of this day was because it marked the passage of *Roe v. Wade*.[104]

Not surprisingly Valentine attempted to offer an alternative date, the first Sunday in April, and an alternative name, "Concern for Life Day." Valentine was doing everything he could to keep Southern Baptists from being identified with the religious right.

When the committee rejected Valentine's request, he informed them he would appeal their ruling directly to the floor of the Convention in Dallas. No doubt the abortion issue was catching up with him.

At the 1985 Commission seminar entitled "Abortion: A Christian Perspective," Valentine shared some of his beliefs about abortion as "the most widely publicized, thoroughly politicized, emotionally charged moral issue in American life today." Valentine gave his assessment that most Americans were neither pro-life nor pro-abortion but somewhere in the middle. He then argued that a constitutional amendment to forbid abortion would be no more effective than the amendment on prohibition, concluding that the only way to prevent abortion was to stop unwanted pregnancy. Try as he might to persuade Southern Baptists to a relative posture, the ideal of the absolute sanctity of life was too deeply engrained in the hearts and minds of the majority of Southern Baptists.[105] Valentine was continuing to alienate himself from the Convention's majority.

When the 1985 Convention met in Dallas, a total of 45,519 messengers registered. Stanley was reelected with 55.3 percent of the vote. At Dallas the Convention adopted the proposal to form a Peace Committee to attempt to identify and resolve the outstanding issues.[106]

Control of trustee elections continued to be the critical issue. James Slatton of Virginia asked messengers "for the sake of peace and unity" to set aside the 1985 Committee on Boards as presented by Stanley's Committee on Committees and substitute two members from each state, the state convention president and the president of the state WMU. Stanley ruled Slatton's motion out of order and called for the vote on the Committee on Boards. It was approved. Moderate protests were long, loud, and fruitless.[107]

When time came for the Christian Life Commission report, chairman Charles Wade heaped praises on Foy Valentine for his twenty-five years of service and then presented him with the Commission's Distinguished Service Award. After referring messengers to the Book of Reports, a long list of activities from the past year was reviewed. The Commission then reported on three matters referred from the last Convention. The third matter concerned abortion and a renewed plea for the Commission to be more proactive. For the most part Valentine simply stated again what he had said in the past. He had no intention of changing anything. No doubt everyone's patience was growing thin, and the need for some resolution was growing more and more urgent.[108]

When Dunn delivered his report, he tried to be as optimistic as possible. When asked if he would welcome an additional Southern Baptist presence in Washington, he responded the only way he could, in the affirmative.[109]

When the Calendar Committee brought its report and recommendation, as promised, the Sanctity of Life proposal was challenged. Charles Wade, the Commission chairman, was the spokesman. Larry Lewis spoke against Wade's substitute motion. The discussion continued back and forth. Adrian Rogers was the last spokesman. He stated, "But it makes no difference when a little baby is being slaughtered, whether that is a Baptist baby, a Methodist baby, a Roman Catholic baby, or any kind of baby. . . . It's time to stand up against the slaughter of the unborn and do it worldwide if we can." When the vote was taken, Southern Baptists voted for January's third Sunday to observe Sanctity of Life Sunday.[110]

With the 1985 elections, conservatives were in sight of controlling the direction of the Convention's boards and agencies. The Christian Life Commission, as it had been led by Foy Valentine and associates, was now fighting for its ideological and organizational life.

In the summer Reagan tagged Iran, Libya, Cuba, Nicaragua, and North Korea as terrorist states. On into the fall Palestinian terrorists hijacked the *Achille Lauro*, killing one elderly American citizen. In November Reagan and Gorbachev met in Geneva. Although they disagreed over the Star Wars technology, they did agree to keep meeting. On January 28, 1986, a national tragedy occurred when the space shuttle *Challenger* exploded on takeoff. A few months later, on April 14, U.S. warplanes bombed Muammar al-Gaddafi's homes in Tripoli and Benghazi after it was confirmed that Libyans were behind the bombing of a Berlin building in which two U.S. servicemen were killed.[111] The world was still dangerous.

In March, Dunn released a two-page document entitled "On Government Infiltration of Churches," in which he identified a "disturbing pattern" concerning the government's infringement and intervention into the churches. It appeared to be an attempt to use scare tactics to rally support for the Baptist Joint Committee. Needless to say, Southern Baptists did not take the bait.[112]

Conservatives, albeit by narrow margins, had won every election since 1979. They were now within two years of having a majority on every agency board.

The Convention bylaws called for the Christian Life Commission to have thirty-six board members. Ten of these were due to be replaced at the 1986 Convention in June, bringing conservatives close to a majority. Six more board seats would change in 1987. This would presumably put conservatives in control of the Commission.

The Commission's March 1986 national seminar carried the theme "Recovering Moral Values." Most speakers, as usual, were from the left side of the spectrum. This year Roy Honeycutt used his platform to criticize the Convention conservatives, the religious right, and particularly Jerry Falwell.

Speaker Stanley Hauerwas irritated his "mainstream" colleagues by noting that "the mainstream" denominations succeeded in persuading Christians to become involved in public policy. However,

> Once politically inactive Christians became active, the causes they supported were not those the mainstream wanted supported. The temptation is to try to defeat the new [right

wing] political activism by using the slogans of the past—religion and politics do not mix or you should not try to force our religious views on anyone through public policy—but to do so is to go against the position the mainstream has been arguing for years.[113]

Most of the remainder of the seminar featured speakers critiquing the culture and particularly their perception of the mistreatment of children. Benjamin Hooks was critical of the pro-life crowd, whom he labeled as hypocrites, observing, "I question the sanity of some people who want to see every baby conceived born, but once they are born, they wouldn't give them a glass of milk to keep them alive."[114] The only speaker who gave a pretense at being pro-life was Ron Sider. "Why," he asked, "do many liberals and radical activists champion nuclear disarmament to protect the sanctity of human life and then defend the destruction of 1.5 million unborn each year?"[115] It is nice, while unusual, to read that one pro-life voice was in the Commission's lineup of speakers.

Nevertheless, Southern Baptist conservatives could only bide their time and keep urging like-minded church messengers to attend the upcoming 1986 Atlanta Convention.

As much as anything, the conservatives desired a new Christian Life Commission executive director. Valentine simply represented them on far too few concerns, especially abortion. When most Southern Baptists were pro-life, he was involved with the liberal Religious Coalition for Abortion Rights. Valentine was not only approaching retirement age; he was severely out of step with the majority of his constituency.

One of the last straws for many conservatives was when new trustees discovered that the Christian Life Commission had been forwarding $1,000 each month to John Buchanan, president of the liberal People for the American Way, which was created to oppose the very things for which conservatives stood. It was one thing for Dunn to be on their founding board of directors; it was another for the Commission secretly to fund the organization.[116]

Because of courtesy and tradition, the conservatives were willing to wait until 1988, when Valentine would reach retirement age and they would have plenty of votes to elect their choice of his successor. Then came the big surprise.

An Unexpected Transition

In April, two months before the 1986 Convention, Valentine informed his board that he had heart blockages and that his doctor advised him to seek a quieter life. Without setting a date for retirement, he urged the appointment of a search committee to begin looking for his successor.

Acting quickly, Commission chairman Charles Wade named himself and six other old-guard moderates to the search committee. No one on the committee was pro-life, and no one was sympathetic with the Convention's new direction. Conservatives took note of Wade's tactic, ventilated their frustration, and waited. Time was on their side. Of course, all the conservatives were suspicious of Valentine's motives.[117]

Meanwhile tensions were high in the Convention as the messengers looked to Atlanta for their 1986 meeting. The Peace Committee was hard at work, Stanley was being sued for his ruling as the chair in Dallas, and Winfred Moore, present first vice president of the Convention and the obvious moderate candidate for president, had his own peace plan which would transfer the president's appointive powers to state conventions.[118]

The Atlanta Convention in 1986 registered more than thirty-nine thousand messengers. When the presidential race came, Adrian Rogers, who had only served one term, 1979–1980, agreed to run again. As expected, Moore was the moderate candidate. When the votes were counted, Rogers received 54.22 percent. Conservatives cheered and moderates sat in stunned silence.[119]

At the Convention, Stanley read a letter from President Ronald Reagan. The Peace Committee gave its first report, and for conservatives things seemed to be on track.

Next to the concern about the seminaries, the two biggest issues in the Convention were the Christian Life Commission and the Baptist Joint Committee on Public Affairs. For the past two years speculation had been rife about what would happen to the Baptist Joint Committee and the possibility of having an exclusive Southern Baptist presence in Washington. Part of the discontent concerning the Committee was Dunn's other associations. Although he declined to accept a second three-year term on the board of People for the American Way, he was still a board member of Americans United for Separation of Church and State.

At the 1986 Convention, M. G. Daniels of Alabama moved that all ties between Southern Baptists and the Baptist Joint Committee be severed and that the Convention establish its own presence in Washington. This was referred to the Executive Committee after discussion.[120]

Resolutions this year were for the most part nonconfrontational and noncontroversial.

When the Commission report time came, Wade related nothing about Valentine's heart condition or request for the agency to seek a new executive director. Valentine commented that the full report was printed and mentioned briefly that resources had been prepared for the Sanctity of Human Life Sunday.

As part of his last report to the Convention, Valentine presented the Commission's Distinguished Service Award to former SBC president and Mississippi industrialist Owen Cooper. The audience responded with a standing ovation.[121]

Although nothing was said officially concerning Valentine's retirement, the information had been in most state papers and was common knowledge among the messengers. At the end of his presentation, Tony McDade of North Carolina expressed appreciation to Valentine for his twenty-five years of service. Messengers responded with warm applause.

The 1986 Convention concluded with the Commission receiving ten new trustees. Time was on their side.

Foy Valentine was the first agency head in the old denominational establishment to announce that he was stepping down. At the

Commission, Wade's tenure as chairman was up. Moderates backed Lynn Clayton of Louisiana while conservatives supported Coy Privette. Clayton won fifteen to thirteen.

The Christian Life Commission staff now included Foy Valentine, Larry Braidfoot, Tim Fields, David Lockard, Robert Parham, and Mary Elizabeth Tyler.

Nine months had passed without a nomination from the search committee. In January 1987, the moderate-leaning search committee called a full board meeting and presented their nominee, Larry Baker, vice president for academic affairs and faculty dean at Midwestern Baptist Theological Seminary in Kansas City. Prior to the meeting, Baker declined to answer any questions from conservative board members. When the board assembled, Chairman Wade announced that each trustee would be allowed to ask only one question.[122]

Baker was quizzed about his views on abortion, capital punishment, ordination of women, and other issues. He pledged to be a "team player" with the divided board. "Disagreement on some issues," he said, "does not preclude us from being sensitive and open."

Baker called abortion "a national tragedy." He did have a list of times when he believed abortion would be acceptable. He failed to speculate on when a fetus becomes a human being. Philosophically he was not pro-life. He did not believe capital punishment was justified in the American penal system. Neither did he believe the Bible precludes the ordination of women.

Everyone present at the interview was aware the 1987 Convention would bring five new trustees to the Commission. Soon the conservatives would have enough votes to overturn Baker's election.

When a trustee asked what would happen to Baker once the conservatives had a majority on the board, the newly elected chairman, Lynn Clayton said he was not under "any illusion or delusion." Baker was elected by secret ballot sixteen to thirteen. Then after intense debate, the board, by a seventeen to eleven vote, named Valentine executive officer for development until July 1988 when he would be sixty-five. Needless to say, Baker's employment and Valentine's reemployment upset many conservatives on and off the Commission.[123]

Baker's installation was in March 1987. He identified abortion as the most pressing moral issue in the country. He explained:

> The Commission simply will have to take assertive action. The distance between the polarities on the abortion issue is so great that we never will be able to have universal agreement, but it is possible to develop an approach that will have broad agreement and represent adequately Southern Baptists and their concerns.[124]

Pro-life conservatives hoped for a stronger stand from Baker. Conservative leaders across the country did not provide any support for Baker. Besides Valentine's retirement, Al Shackleford replaced W. C. Fields as director of Baptist Press, and William Tanner resigned as head of the Home Mission Board to accept the position of executive director of the Oklahoma Baptist Convention. After a conservative show of strength at the Home Mission Board, Larry Lewis was elected as its new president.

Registration at the 1987 Convention in St. Louis was down 40 percent from the previous year in Atlanta. Many moderates evidently gave up hope of stopping the conservative advance.

At the Convention a recommendation was made and approved that would transfer the majority of seats on the Public Affairs Committee away from agency heads to Convention-elected representatives. M. G. Daniels offered a follow-up motion requesting the newly elected committee work to replace the present leadership of the Baptist Joint Committee. His motion was referred.[125]

The Peace Committee also gave its report, presented its findings, and made suggestions. It confirmed what most messengers had believed all along—that the real issues were for the most part theological.

On Wednesday morning Commission Chairman Lynn Clayton introduced Larry Baker as the newly elected executive director of the Commission. At the podium Baker got straight down to business. First on his agenda was to present the Distinguished Service Award to Carolyn Weatherford, president of the WMU. Due to her advocacy of women's ordination, the reception was not overwhelming.[126]

In his report Baker acknowledged that Valentine had been its author and then proceeded to review the past year's accomplishments.

Next President Rogers recognized Commission trustee Hal Lane of South Carolina, who requested permission to offer a minority report prepared by twelve of the twenty-five trustees who had "continuing terms." The request was granted by the Convention. Lane reviewed the flaws in the system used to hire the new executive director as well as Baker's less than acceptable responses to conservative trustee questions. Everyone understood the proverbial handwriting on the wall.[127]

Between the 1987 Convention and the fall board meeting in September, Baker stayed busy speaking to numerous pastors' groups and conferences. Most people fully expected to see Baker fired at this meeting.

An informal caucus, held by fifteen conservative trustees the day before the September 14, 1987, meeting, was hosted by trustee Joe Atchison from Arkansas. They reviewed Clayton's committee assignments and, as suspected, found only moderates on the administrative committee that controlled the Commission. No one spoke harshly of Baker, and all agreed that he was an improvement over Valentine. They did want Baker out, however, because of the flawed process of his hiring and the positions he took on abortion, capital punishment, and women.

Reviewing the next day's agenda, they noticed that no time had been scheduled for miscellaneous business. When the meeting convened and minutes of the previous meeting were approved, Chairman Clayton moved the adoption of the supplied agenda. James Wood offered a substitute motion with a substitute agenda. It was accepted by a seventeen to nine vote.[128]

After Baker's report to the Commission trustees and a twenty-minute break, the Commission reconvened. Joe Atchison moved "that we dismiss Larry Baker immediately and that a new search committee be appointed by the new board chairman [successor to Clayton], and an interim director be named." The discussion continued for four hours. By secret ballot, the vote to terminate Baker was fifteen to fifteen. Chairman Clayton cast the tie-breaking vote, and Baker's dismissal was halted for the moment.[129]

At the full board meeting following the committee meetings, a majority approved a strong anti-abortion statement, ordered the withdrawal of the abortion and women in ministry pamphlets, directed the staff to prepare new materials condemning euthanasia and infanticide, and urged the board to recommend that the Convention call for a strong pro-life federal amendment that would prohibit abortion except to prevent the death of the mother.

Trustees also informed the Commission staff that they wanted input into the lineup of speakers for future conferences and seminars. Finally, in not an unexpected move, the slate of moderate officers proposed for the following year was overturned. Fred Lackey would be the new chairman. Joe Atchison would be vice chairman. And Rudy Yakym would serve as recording secretary.

The board meeting ended with conservatives having lost only one contested motion, the call to dismiss Baker. Defecting conservatives explained their voting saying they believed Baker deserved a chance to prove himself.

In 1986, the Commission board authorized renting office space in Washington, D.C. This was done on October 1, 1987, just two weeks after Baker narrowly escaped dismissal. Once the Washington office was up and working, the Commission board officers and the Public Affairs Committee members began promoting a merger. A great frustration existed due to the fact that Southern Baptists provided 90 percent of the denominational support to the Baptist Joint Committee's operating budget but had only a third of the seats of their trustees. With this ratio, change would never come, and Southern Baptists would continue to pay for those who opposed them.[130]

Officers of the Commission and the Public Affairs Committee met in Nashville on December 12, 1987, to discuss a possible merger. Baker believed the discussion was illegal and demanded its halt. Dunn called the idea an outrageous violation of well-established procedures. Because of the conflict being generated, the idea of the merger was shelved after the Executive Committee declined to act on the prospective merger. Nonetheless, trustees at the Commission and on the Committee knew that time was on their side.[131]

When the spring Commission seminar was convened on "Addressing the Nation's Agenda: Christian Citizenship '88," far more conservatives were on the lineup of speakers. Guests included Newt Gingrich, Cal Thomas, and Charles Fuller. Some interpreted the more balanced program as an effort by Baker to retain his job.

Yet, unknown to the Commission trustees, Baker was already talking to the pastor search committee at the First Baptist Church of Pineville, Louisiana, where Sarah Francis Anders and Lynn Clayton held membership. Because he realized he had lost the trust and confidence of the majority of his trustees, Baker proceeded to find another position, and began negotiating in April for a generous severance package from the Commission. Baker then announced on May 1, 1988, that he would be leaving, and in agreement with the trustees, his last day would be July 15, 1988. Robert Parham was elected by the trustees to serve as interim president.[132]

The 1988 Convention met in San Antonio on June 14–16. When election time came for president, the two major candidates were Richard Jackson, who represented the moderate constituency, and Jerry Vines, who championed the conservatives. Vines was elected with 50.53 percent of the vote. This was the closest the moderates would ever come to winning.[133]

The resolution of most interest to the Christian Life Commission was written by Kirk Shrewsbury, "On Pro-Life Actions of SBC Agencies," which strongly identified the Southern Baptist Convention with the pro-life camp. The most controversial resolution was "On the Priesthood of the Believer." The author of the resolution, Jerry Sutton, wrote it in response to the distortions of the doctrine being promoted by the doctrinal study produced by the Sunday School Board the previous year. In anger a large group of moderates led by Randall Lolley marched to the Alamo in San Antonio and burned the resolution.[134]

James Dunn complained that the priesthood resolution displayed a misunderstanding of the First Amendment. "The understanding of

Baptists [on separation of church and state]," he said in a press conference, "is not the understanding of [far right people like] Francis Schaeffer, Jerry Falwell, and Pat Robertson. . . . We believe separation of church and state is a two-way street; it guarantees free exercise and also guarantees no [religious] establishment. It protects the church from the state, but it also protects [from] domination of government by any religious group." Dunn saw definite "connections between far-right politics and some of the leadership in the Southern Baptist Convention. . . . Look at the associations . . . of several members of the Public Affairs Committee and the religious far right."

Dunn was painfully aware the Convention had cut $48,000 from the budget of the Public Affairs Committee as assigned to the Baptist Joint Committee and rejected an effort to increase the religious liberty allotment targeted for the Baptist Joint Committee. He did not seem to take seriously the much talked about proposal to transfer all Convention religious liberty funds from the Baptist Joint Committee to the Christian Life Commission.[135]

In Dunn's report to the Convention, he simply recounted the work the Committee did the previous year in publishing, lobbying, and conferences. Chairman Fred Lackey then spoke for the Commission. He noted Baker's imminent departure from the Commission. He also announced a committee had been appointed to make a careful search for God's person to become the next executive director. He then reviewed some of the past year's activities including the opening of a Washington office.

With respect to Commission literature, Lackey noted that "future pamphlets and publications will be more prophetic and biblically based." He elaborated, saying, "Some pamphlets have been removed . . . [while] others are being rewritten, with a greater emphasis on biblical authority." He then confirmed, "This will be in keeping with recent resolutions by this body."[136]

When time came for questions, Michael Haynes expressed his disappointment over Baker's departure and asked if other Commission jobs were in jeopardy. Lackey responded that the subject had not even come up.

Earlier in the Convention, the Executive Committee expressed gratitude to Foy Valentine on the completion of his twenty-eight years of service by adopting a resolution of appreciation. He was cited for his "faithful" service "in the field of applied Christianity in the general areas of family life, race relations, Christian citizenship, daily work, and special moral concerns." After citing his previous work, articles, and books, his notable accomplishments while serving with the Commission were acknowledged: chairman of the Baptist World Alliance's Commission on Christian Ethics; chairman of the American Civil Liberties Union's executive committee, and a long-term board member of the Baptist Joint Committee. The resolution did not note his membership with the Religious Coalition for Abortion Rights and that he had affiliated the Southern Baptist Convention with the National Abortion Rights Action League.[137]

The year 1988 was a defining moment for Southern Baptists and Christian Life Commission leaders. Only Barton had served longer than Valentine in a leadership capacity. Baker holds the record for the briefest tenure, only nineteen months. More than job resignations, however, the departure of Valentine and Baker marked the end of an era highlighted by conflict over race and abortion. The control of the Commission now transfered from moderate to conservative hands, whose views on abortion, Scripture, and religious liberty differed dramatically from their predecessors.

The leadership of the Commission, the Baptist Joint Committee, and the Convention had for a generation reflected the theological and philosophical left of center. Over the life of the Convention, issues transitioned in priority. Issues such as church and state, alcohol, race, and abortion held center stage at one time or another.

With respect to the church-state concerns, the old guard held to an absolute separation policy while the new administration would embrace an accommodation policy. It would not be so much a revision of approach, however, as it would be a clearer perception of the new realities. In short, the national culture and context were changing, and the absolutists were not. A philosophical vacuum was developing in the country that was being filled quickly with secularism and humanism, reinforced by a cultural elite in America that was preoccupied with removing every vestige of Christianity from the public square. Much of this was driven by rulings from the Supreme Court.

Although biblical inerrancy was the overriding concern in the Conservative Resurgence, the defining issue for the Christian Life Commission was undoubtedly abortion. In short, Commission leadership had been out of step with its constituency, and now was the moment to rectify the disparity. With respect to the Baptist Joint Committee, the overriding concern, besides the difference in understanding of church-state relations, was the fact that Southern Baptists supplied 90 percent of the financial support, yet had no proportionate influence on the trustee board and usually found itself paying the salaries of those who criticized its actions and intentions. And for those bringing change, it was strictly a matter of conviction!

Notes

1. Peter Irons and Stephanie Guitton, eds., *May It Please the Court: The Most Significant Oral Arguments Made Before the Supreme Court Since 1955* (New York: The New Press, 1993), 343.

2. Justice William Rehnquist, "Dissent to Roe v. Wade," January 22, 1973.

3. Irons and Guitton, *May It Please the Court*, 354.

4. Chief Justice Warren Berger, "Concurring Opinion on Roe v. Wade," January 22, 1973.

5. Ward, *The Timeless History of the USA*, 316.

6. 1973 Christian Life Commission Seminar Addresses, 44.

7. 1973 SBC Resolution on the Place of Women in Christian Service.

8. "Watergate Scandal" in wikipedia.org; Greg Ward, *The Timeless History of the USA* (New York: Barnes and Noble Books, 2001), 317–18.

9. "Yom Kippur War" in wikipedia.org.

10. Ward, *The Timeless History of the USA*, 318.

11. 1974 SBC Annual, 210.

12. Ibid., 209–10.

13. Radio and Television Commission tape of the 1974 Convention proceedings.

14. Ibid.; 1974 SBC Resolution on Abortion and the Sanctity of Life.

15. "Watergate Scandal" in wikipedia.org; Erik Bruun and Jay Crosby, eds., *Our Nation's Archive* (New York: Tess Press, 1999), 935–36.

16. Stanley Karnow, *Vietnam: A History* (New York: Penguin Books, 1997), 669.

17. 1975 *SBC Annual*, 80.

18. 1975 *SBC Book of Reports*, 201.

19. Radio and Television Commission tape of the 1975 Convention proceedings.

20. Ward, *The Timeless History of the USA*, 321.

21. 1976 Christian Life Commission Seminar on "Christian Citizenship," Washington, D.C., March 22–24, 1976.

22. 1976 *SBC Annual*, 39, 61.

23. Radio and Television Commission tape of the 1976 Convention proceedings.

24. 1976 Resolution on Abortion.

25. Ibid.

26. 1976 *SBC Annual*, 42, 56–58.

27. 1976 Resolution on Homosexuality; Robert E. Naylor, *A Messenger's Memoirs* (Franklin, Tenn.: Providence, 1995), 190.

28. Ward, *The Timeless History of the USA*, 321–22; Nelson Price, "Inaugural Sermon for President Jimmy Carter," January 20, 1977.

29. Jimmy Carter, "Inaugural Address," January 20, 1977.

30. See "The Daily Diary of President Jimmy Carter," White House, June 26, 1977.

31. Furman v. Georgia (1972), and Gregg v. Georgia (1976) in wikipedia. org; Irons and Guitton, *May It Please the Court*, 229.

32. Ward, *The Timeless History of the USA*, 322.

33. 1977 *SBC Annual*, 34.

34. 1977 SBC Resolution on Abortion.

35. 1977 SBC Resolution on Homosexuality.

36. 1977 SBC Resolution on Human Rights and Certain Misapplications.

37. 1977 *SBC Annual*, 55–56.

38. For a thorough treatment of the Conservative Resurgence among Southern Baptists, an interpretive history, see my volume, *The Baptist Reformation*; Paul Pressler's *A Hill on Which to Die* is an insider's autobiographical account of the resurgence; James Hefley's *Truth in Crisis* series and *The Conservative Resurgence* reflect a journalist's chronicling of events as they unfold.

39. Ibid.

40. 1978 Christian Life Commission seminar proceedings, 5, 12–13, 16–18, 34, 37, 60.

41. Naylor, *A Messenger's Memoirs*, 199; Ward, *The Timeless History of the USA*, 322.

42. 1978 *SBC Annual*, 183.

43. Ibid., 7, 64–65, 68.

44. Irons and Guitton, *May It Please the Court*, 305.

45. Ward, *The Timeless History of the USA*, 323.

46. 1979 Christian Life Commission seminar proceedings, 5, 23, 30, 43, 62.

47. Jim Hefley, "Southern Baptists Turn Toward Inerrancy," *Moody Monthly*, September 1979, 126–34.

48. Jerry Sutton, *The Baptist Reformation* (Nashville: Broadman & Holman Publishers, 2000), 91–102.

49. Hefley, "Southern Baptists Turn Toward Inerrancy;" Sutton, *The Baptist Reformation*, 45–46, 103–4.

50. Radio and Television Commission tape of the 1979 Convention proceedings.

51. Ibid.

52. Ward, *The Timeline History of the USA*, 323–25.

53. Jerry Falwell, *Falwell: An Autobiography* (Lynchburg, Virg.: Liberty House Publishers, 1997).

54. Each of these organizations has Web sites which provide information on its history.

55. Sutton, *The Baptist Reformation*, 113.

56. 1980 SBC Resolution on Doctrinal Integrity.

57. 1980 SBC Resolution on Abortion.

58. Radio and Television Commission tape of the 1980 Convention proceedings.

59. Ibid.

60. 1980 SBC Resolutions.

61. Ward, *The Timeline History of the USA*, 324–25, 330.

62. Radio and Television Commission tape of the 1981 Convention proceedings.

63. Sutton, *The Baptist Reformation*, 122; 1981 SBC Resolutions.

64. Sutton, *The Baptist Reformation*, 122; 1981 *SBC Annual*, 84.

65. William H. Elden III, "The New Right, 1981," *Light*, March 1983, 3–5.

66. "National Impact Briefing of the Baptist Joint Committee on Public Affairs," March 15, 1981; James Dunn, "Reflections" in Report from the Capitol, April 24, 1981.

67. Ward, *The Timeline History of the USA*, 331.

68. 1982 Christian Life Commission Seminar proceedings, March 22, 1982, 56, 61.

69. Letter from Maston to Dunn, March 4, 1982.

70. Letter from Dunn to Maston, April 18, 1982; Letter form Maston to Dunn, May 1, 1982.

71. Jim Asker, "Baptists Will Tackle 'Inerrancy' Question," *The Houston Post*, June 12, 1982, 6AA.

72. Sutton, *The Baptist Reformation*, 125–27.

73. 1982 SBC Resolution on Prayer in Schools.

74. Sutton, *The Baptist Reformation*, 124.

75. 1982 SBC Resolution on Abortion and Infanticide.

76. 1982 SBC Resolution on Tuition Tax Credit.

77. Letter from Maston to Dunn, August 5, 1982.

78. "People for the American Way" in wikipedia.org.

79. Radio and Television Commission tape of the 1983 Convention proceedings.

80. Ibid.

81. 1983 SBC Resolutions.

82. 1983 *SBC Annual*, 50–51.

83. Letter from Maston to Dunn, June 23, 1983.

84. Letter from Dunn to Maston, June 23, 1983.

85. Letter from Maston to Dunn, July 5, 1983.

86. Letter from Dunn to Maston, August 3, 1983.

87. Letter from Maston to Dunn, August 17, 1983.

88. Ward, *The Timeline History of the USA*, 333.

89. 1984 Christian Life Commission Seminar proceedings, Washington, D.C.

90. Ibid.

91. Maston, Letter to the editor on the "Baptist Joint Committee" mailed to state papers prior to the 1984 Southern Baptist Convention.

92. Letter from Maston to Dunn, June 1, 1984.

93. Sutton, *The Baptist Reformation*, 138, 141–43.

94. Russell H. Dilday Jr., "On Higher Ground," the 1984 Convention Address as printed in the *Baptist and Reflector*, June 13, 1984, 9.

95. 1984 *SBC Annual*, 32.

96. Ibid., 34.

97. Ibid., 53.

98. Radio and Television Commission tape on the 1984 Convention proceedings.

99. 1984 SBC Resolutions.

100. Letter from Maston to Dunn, June 20, 1984.

101. James Dunn, "The Christian as Political Activist," an address delivered to the "Faith and History Conference" at Southwestern Baptist Theological Seminary, October 19, 1984.

102. Ward, *The Timeline History of the USA*, 333–34.

103. Ibid., 335–36.

104. Report of the Committee on Denominational Calendar, 1985 *SBC Annual*, 233.

105. The Christian Life Commission Seminar proceedings, 1985, 31–39.

106. Sutton, *The Baptist Reformation*, 147–48.

107. Ibid., 148–49.

108. Radio and Television Commission tape of the 1985 Convention proceedings.

109. Ibid.

110. Ibid.

111. Ward, *The Timeline History of the USA*, 336. See "Muammar al-Gaddafi" in wikipedia.org.

112. "On Government Infiltration of Churches" by the Baptist Joint Committee on Public Affairs, March 4, 1986.

113. Stanley Hauerwas, "A Christian Critique of Christian America" in the Christian Life Commission seminar proceedings, 1986, 9, 20.

114. Ibid., 41.

115. Ibid., 50–53.

116. Personal conversation with ERLC President Richard Land.

117. Sutton, *The Baptist Reformation*, 312.

118. Dan Martin, "Committee Decries Political Excesses," *Baptist Press*, May 16, 1986.

119. Sutton, *The Baptist Reformation*, 150–51, 161.

120. 1986 *SBC Annual*, 68.

121. 1986 *SBC Book of Reports*, 310–18.

122. Sutton, *The Baptist Reformation*, 313.

123. Minutes of the Christian Life Commission Board of Trustees meeting, January 1987.

124. Larry Baker, "Installation Address," March 1987.

125. 1987 *SBC Annual*, 54.

126. Radio and Television Commission tape of the 1987 Convention proceedings.

127. Sutton, *The Baptist Reformation*, 313–14.

128. James Hefley, *Truth in Crisis*, vol. 3 (Hannibal), 112–13.

129. Ray Waddle, "Conservatives Fail to Oust Baptist Leader," *The Tennessean*, September 16, 1987, A1–2.

130. 1987 *SBC Annual*, 220.

131. Letter from Baker to Lackey, December 30, 1987; "Three SBC Agency Chiefs Criticize CLC-PAC Merger," *Baptist Press*, January 4, 1988.

132. Interview with Richard Land, May 7–8, 2007.

133. Sutton, *The Baptist Reformation*, 180.

134. Ibid., 189, 425–38. Kirk Shrewsbury worked closely with the Resolutions Committee in 1988, which the author chaired.

135. Press Conference, 1988 San Antonio Convention, June 16, 1988.

136. Taken from the videotape of the proceedings of the 1988 SBC annual meeting, Thursday morning, June 16, 1988.

137. Ibid., 61; Sutton, *The Baptist Reformation*, 309–12.

Arthur James Barton
Chairman, Social Service Commission,
1920–1942

Chairman, Committee on Temperance and
Social Service, 1914–1920

Chairman, Committee on Temperance,
1910–1914

Hugh Alexander Brimm
Executive Secretary,
Social Service Commission,
1947–1952

Acker Calvin Miller
Executive Secretary,
Christian Life Commission,
1953–1960

Foy Dan Valentine
Executive Secretary,
Christian Life Commission,
1960–1987

Nathan Larry Baker
Executive Secretary,
Christian Life Commission,
1987–1988

Richard Dale Land
Executive Director-Treasurer,
Christian Life Commission,
1988–1997

President, Ethics & Religious
Liberty Commission,
1997–Present

J. B. Weatherspoon was a professor of Christian ethics and sociology at the Southern Baptist Theological Seminary, 1929–1959, and served as chairman of the Social Service Commission, 1942–1947.

The ERLC's roots are in the temperance movement.

The Social Service Commission was renamed the Christian Life Commission in 1953.

A 1950s display at the Southern Baptist Convention

Foy Valentine (L) with former Executive
Secretaries, A. C. Miller and Hugh Brimm

Bill Moyers, seminar speaker,
"National Priorities and Christian
Responsibility," New York, 1971, with
James Dunn and Phil Stickland

Foy Valentine presenting the Distinguished Service Award to Billy
Graham, Orlando, April 13, 1988

Annual Seminar Speakers 1964–1999

President Lyndon B. Johnson, "Christian Citizenship," White House Rose Garden, 1964

Bayard Rustin, "Black Power: Phenomenon of a Disordered Society," Washington, D.C., 1969

Jesse Jackson, "Black Power and the Church's Response," Chicago, 1969

Annual Seminar Speakers 1964–1999

John Claypool, "The Uses of Power Inside and Outside the Church," Atlanta, 1970

Joseph Fletcher, the "father of situation ethics," Dialogue on Situation Ethics with Henlee Barnett, Atlanta, 1970

Sen. George McGovern (D-SD), "National Integrity and World Hunger," Louisville, 1975, "With Liberty and Justice for All," Washington, D.C., 1976

Andrew Young, "Race Relations in America: The State of Affairs," Dallas, 1981

Rosalyn Carter, "Family: A Personal Statement," Orlando, 1979

Sen. Edward Kennedy (D-MA), "National Health Security—A National Priority" Washington, D.C., 1976

Annual Seminar Speakers 1964–1999

Phyllis Schlafly and Harvey Cox, "The Women's Movement and Family Life: Two Views," Orlando, 1979

Martin Marty, Keynote Address: "Ethical Issues for the Eighties," New York, 1980

Ramsey Clark, "Personal Life Style: An Issue for the Eighties," New York, 1980

Sarah Frances Weddington, attorney who represented Jane Roe in the *Roe v. Wade* case, "Women in the Eighties," New York, 1980

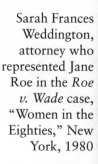

Tipper Gore, "Recovering Moral Values: Moral Responsibility in Popular Music," Nashville, 1986

Marian Wright Edelman, "Teenage Pregnancy: A Moral Indictment of American Society," Nashville, 1986

Annual Seminar Speakers 1964–1999

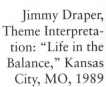

Jimmy Draper, Theme Interpretation: "Life in the Balance," Kansas City, MO, 1989

C. Everett Koop, "The Challenge of AIDS to American Families," Charlotte, 1987

Paige Patterson, "War of the Worlds: A Perennial Battle," Wake Forest, NC, 1995

William Bennett, "Church and the Culture," Washington, D.C., 1992

Fred Luter, "How the Church Can Minister to the Crisis in the Black Family in America," Del City, OK, 1994

Barbara O'Chester, "How to Build an Affair-Proof Marriage: Women," Del City, OK, 1994

Annual Seminar Speakers 1964–1999

Charles Colson, "The Struggle for the Soul of the Nation," Wake Forest, NC, 1995

E. W. McCall, "Transforming the Black Church in Surburbia," Washington, D.C., 1996

Rep. Charles Stenholm (D-TX), Washington, D.C., 1996

Jay Sekulow, "The Fight for Religious Liberty," Washington, D.C., 1996

Gov. David Beasley, "Public Policy and the Family," Charleston, SC, 1998

Gov. George W. Bush, Welcomes seminar attendees, Austin, TX, 1999

Richard Land during an interview with trustees in Nashville, September 1988, just prior to his election as CEO of the Christian Life Commission, now the Ethics & Religious Liberty Commission. Trustee chairman Joe Atchison is in the background.

Dr. Land's family joined him on the platform during his March 1989 installation service in Kansas City, MO. From the left are Dr. Spurgeon Gibbins and Mrs. Roland VanHooser (Becky Land's uncle and mother), Mr. and Mrs. Leggette Land (Richard Land's parents), Richard Land Jr., Rachel Land, Dr. Lamar Cooper (CLC staff), Jennifer Land, Dr. Rebekah Land, and Dr. Richard Land.

Richard Land leading in prayer at the National Right to Life
Committee's Rally for Life on the National Mall, 1990. Seated at Land's
left is Dr. John Willke, a founder of the NRLC.

Land with Cardinal O'Connor and other right-to-life advocates in the
National Right to Life Committee's 1995 March for Life in
Washington, D.C. To O'Connor's right is James A. Smith,
CLC Director of Government Relations.

Richard Land testifying before the U. S. Senate Foreign
Relations Committee, 1998

The Ethics & Religious Liberty Commission crest, adopted
when the name was changed as a part of the Covenant for a
New Century, 1997

THE ETHICS &
RELIGIOUS LIBER
COMMISSION
OF THE SOUTHERN BAPTIST CONVEN

Land with Adrian
Rogers and
Harold Harper,
Southern Baptist
Convention,
Orlando, 2000

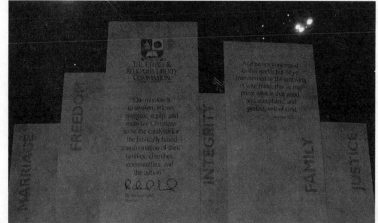

ERLC booth at the 2001 Southern Baptist Convention, New Orleans

Richard Land and Jimmy Draper, co-chairmen, presenting the report of the SBC's Task Force on Ministry to Homosexuals, SBC 2003, Phoenix

President George W. Bush greeting Richard Land in the Oval Office following the signing of the Partial Birth Abortion Ban Act, November 5, 2003

Richard Land speaking about the iVoteValues initiative at the 2004 SBC, Indianapolis

Land demonstrating the online voter registration procedure to SBC president Jack Graham, SBC 2004, Indianapolis

The iVoteValues truck leaving New Orleans Baptist Theological Seminary following a voter registration emphasis, summer 2004

Richard Land appearing at a press conference with President Bush in the Roosevelt Room of the White House after a meeting on immigration reform, Washington, D.C., March 23, 2006

Land addressing the Save Darfur Rally in front of the U.S. Capitol, April 30, 2006

Land and Morris Chapman greeting Condoleezza Rice prior to her address at the Southern Baptist Convention, Greensboro, NC, June 14, 2006

Richard Land and Sen. Joseph Lieberman (I-CT) at a U.S. Commission on International Religious Freedom press conference, Washington, D.C., February 8, 2007. Land was first appointed to the Commission by President George W. Bush (2001–2004), then reappointed by Sen. William Frist (R-TN, 2005–2007), and Sen. Mitch McConnell (R-KY, 2007–).

Land and Sen. Edward Kennedy (D-MA) talking after Land's testimony supporting FDA regulation of tobacco products before Sen. Kennedy's committee, March 29, 2007

Land speaking at the Free North Korean Refugees in China rally held in front of the U.S. Capitol, July 17, 2007

CHAPTER

The Latest Years of Engagement: The Final Days of the Christian Life Commission (1988–1997)

On the national scene, Michael Dukakis won the 1988 Democratic nomination over challenger Jesse Jackson in July. The Republicans selected Reagan's vice president, George Bush. Tagging Dukakis a tax and spend liberal and promising no new taxes, Bush won handily on November 8 with 54 percent of the popular vote and 426 to 111 in the electoral college.

Meanwhile, in Southern Baptist life, the Christian Life Commission elected Joe Atchison to chair the search committee to recommend a new executive director. Unlike the committee that recommended

Baker, conservatives, who now controlled the Commission's board, appointed two moderates along with six conservatives on the search committee, reflecting the board's makeup at this point in time.

The committee agreed that the nominee must have an earned doctorate, be an avowed inerrantist, a staunch pro-lifer, and a believer in capital punishment.

While the search was on, Robert Parham functioned as the interim executive director after Baker's July 15 departure.

On August 12, the committee had narrowed a list of eleven candidates to three. Atchison related to Baptist Press that while conservatives now outnumbered moderates twenty to eleven on the Commission's board, he anticipated the vote on the new executive director to be a strong majority due to the openness of the process. He also promised that all board members would receive far in advance both resumes and position papers prepared by the candidates.[1]

The committee's selection and subsequent recommendation to the entire trustee board of the Christian Life Commission was Richard Land, who at that time held the position at the Criswell College as vice president for academic affairs while serving a dual role as professor of theology and church history. More recently Land took a leave of absence from the college to serve as Texas Governor Bill Clements' senior advisor on church-state issues and public policy areas related to traditional family values from January 1987 to May 1988.[2]

Land, an outspoken and articulate elective member of the Convention's Public Affairs Committee, was closely attuned to disputes between Southern Baptist conservatives and the Baptist Joint Committee. Although a native Texan, Land holds three degrees from institutions outside the state. His bachelors degree is from Princeton University, *magna cum laude*. He holds a master of theology degree from New Orleans Baptist Theological Seminary, where he was student body president and named the inaugural recipient of the Broadman Seminarian Award as "outstanding graduating student." He also earned a doctor of philosophy degree from Oxford University in Great Britain.

In the interview process Land clearly articulated his understanding of the biblical positions he embraced and pledged to lead the Convention and Commission to express the same. He shared his pro-life convictions, his position on women and ministry, capital punishment, race relations, alcohol, pornography, family, affirmative action, welfare, and "just war" philosophy. In all of his answers, the majority of trustees were pleased.

Land modeled the priority of family. His wife, Rebekah, also a New Orleans Seminary graduate, had an earned doctorate and worked as a Christian psychotherapist. They had three children, Jennifer, Richard Jr., and Rachel. Two of the children, Richard and Rachel, went on to earn degrees at Southeastern Seminary.

The committee made a unanimous recommendation to the board. Atchison, who mailed Land's position papers to the board in July, recommended him to the full board for a vote in September. In his presentation to the board, Atchison said, "Nobody [from the conservative movement] got on the phone to try to sway us." They brought a unanimous recommendation, he explained, because "we believe he is the best qualified man among Southern Baptists for this job."[3]

Holding up his Bible, Atchison stated, "Richard Land is a man who believes this Book." He went on to say, "His moral ethics come from this Book and his principles are scriptural principles." He further noted, "He would give us . . . leadership that is theologically and philosophically sound."[4]

After being introduced to the full board and their guests, Land was asked to recount his conversion, call to ministry, and ministry experience. He then fielded a variety of questions to the majority's satisfaction. When asked about his relationship to the Commission's board, Land stated,

> I believe very strongly in the Southern Baptist system of organization and in board and trustee governance. We are the Christian Life Commission of the Southern Baptist Convention and the Convention elects the commissioners of this agency. . . . It is the responsibility of those commissioners [trustees] to make

certain through their administrative supervision that the executive director and the staff are performing the program statement of the Christian Life Commission.[5]

When asked about his vision for the Commission, Land explained:

> [The Christian Life Commission] needs to raise the awareness of Southern Baptists concerning applied Christianity. . . . There are probably more born-again believers in American society now than [ever before], but at the same time there is less adherence to the cultural mores of Judeo-Christian beliefs than ever before in our history. . . . When people don't have societal values, then they pick whatever values suit them. . . . So, I think that [there has] never been a more important time for us to know why we believe what we believe and to know the truth that the Bible is true, not just on Sunday, not just in our personal lives, but true in the workplace, the study hall, the neighborhood, and everywhere, and we need to try to apply it everywhere.
>
> I see the essential mission of the Commission as two-pronged. One is educational and evangelistic, educational in that we are to seek to speak to and talk with and discuss with Southern Baptists the social and ethical moral issues of the day, and to raise their awareness on these issues. I think that we must always have an evangelistic content. . . . We have an obligation to Jesus to make it very clear to people why we believe what we believe and that we are motivated by love for them and love for victims, because they are people for whom Jesus Christ died and are thus of incalculable value.
>
> The second prong is to seek to influence and inform legislators concerning Southern Baptist concerns on legislative issues that would impact moral and ethical concerns other than First Amendment issues. That's sometimes a tricky call because these are increasingly going to be issues that are very difficult to categorize as one or the other.

It's important for the largest Protestant denomination in
the United States to have an office in Washington. . . . That
presence ought to be expanded. . . . We need to network with
other groups [with which] we share similar concerns. We are
mandated by the Baptist Faith and Message (1963) . . . to work
with people of goodwill on issues of moral concerns. It probably has never been more important than it is now and for the
rest of this century [to work in Washington] because we are
going to be faced with issues which . . . were [only] moral issues
15 or 20 years ago and are now both moral and legislative
issues.

In 1969, when I graduated from college, for all intents and
purposes abortion was illegal in this country except under very
limited circumstances. Let's remember that homosexuality was
a crime that was being prosecuted. Pornography was not what
it is called today—a victimless crime. I am incredulous that
even a presidential commission could conclude that pornography is a victimless crime when you have the exploitive display
of undraped women. The woman is a victim first and foremost.

Land went on to comment on the future of the Christian Life
Commission in a Convention that was at that point in history clearly
divided:

There is more unity on the issues with which we deal in
our program statement than there are on many other issues in
the Southern Baptist Convention. For instance, on abortion. I
was moved and gratified by the response when Adrian Rogers
commented on abortion during his [San Antonio] Convention
sermon. When [I saw] the Southern Baptist Convention [rise
and applaud, that's] one of the few times in my life that I was
speechless. To see the extent of consensus that there is now in
the Convention on abortion was very moving to me.

There is [also] a very strong consensus in our Convention
on racial equality and racial justice, especially when it is made

clear that this does not include affirmative action or reverse prejudice.

[But] we do have profound disagreements in our Convention [on] the extent of theological diversity, how much there is, and how advisable it is to have it, and what are the parameters of it. . . . The Peace Committee ought to be commended for saying that there was theological diversity and to the extent there has been political activity, it has been motivated by genuine doctrinal and theological concern.

The second thing that I feel strongly about is that personally. . . I have been deeply hurt and offended by agency heads of Southern Baptist institutions who have intruded themselves into the process of the selection of our Convention presidents. I will not do that.[6]

After a lengthy question-and-answer period and a time for trustees to give their thoughts and perceptions, Search Committee chairman Joe Atchison requested and was granted a secret ballot. The vote was twenty-three to two in favor of Land, and he was officially hired on September 12, 1988.[7]

In the aftermath of Land's election, Curtis Caine, a medical doctor and a trustee, made some disparaging remarks about Martin Luther King Jr. and world hunger that came across as prejudicial at best. When the press picked up on his comments and put them in print, it proved to be an embarrassment to Land and the rest of his staff and trustees. Sadly it gave some of Land's detractors an opportunity to be critical of his administration from the start. In all honesty some people did not like Land or the conservatives that recruited him to the office, and they were looking for something, for anything, which might undercut Land's credibility.[8]

Richard Land took office on October 24, 1988. To his dismay he found the Commission was over $90,000 in debt, with many bills far behind and $50,000 due in the form of a bank note within six weeks of his arrival. In Land's words:

Looking at the state of the situation when I came to the office, it's difficult to imagine that Larry (Baker) was not at least on some sub-conscious level, if not a conscious level, trying to bankrupt the agency prior to his exit and he very nearly succeeded. We were in terrible shape in May of the year he resigned. He had dumped all the special gifts and all the designated gifts into the general fund to mislead the trustees into believing there was more money in the general fund than there was. Of course, this was done by the administration without the knowledge of the trustees.

Land went on to state:

When I came into the agency, we were about four months behind on most bills. We had a rather significant certificate note due at the bank in about six weeks and I was hamstrung completely in what I could do for the first six months I was here. I was trying desperately to plow all the Cooperative Program money that was coming in back into paying off the debts so the agency did not go bankrupt.

The other thing I did of course was that I wrote notes to all the people who had their designated gifts dumped into the general fund telling them this had happened, that we had discovered it. Of course, this was illegal and if they wanted their money back we would send it back to them. Otherwise, we would redesignate those gifts. Graciously, none of the people wanted the money back. They were grateful for being informed, and they were pleased that it went back into designated gifts.[9]

Land's early days at the Commission were less than ideal. Cleaning up a messy financial situation, Land promised trustees and staffers, especially the Commission's bookkeeper, Jean Davis, the Commission would never be in this shape again. Under Valentine's administration some former leaders were "in" while others were not. Land recounted:

Dr. [A. J.] Barton was very prominent in Southern Baptist life and was a nationally prominent prohibitionist. If you look at the *Southern Baptist Encyclopedia*, you will find that Barton had a prominent role in national assemblies and conferences of the prohibitionist movement. He was very much involved as a temperance leader in Southern Baptist life and beyond Southern Baptist life to the nation.

Yet he was loathed and detested by Foy Valentine. When I came to this position, we had portraits, oil paintings, of our previous executive directors starting with Hugh Brimm and then A. C. Miller and then Foy Valentine. I discovered from talking to Mary Tyler, who had been secretary to Foy and had worked for the Commission for many years, that there was an oil painting of A. J. Barton, but it was in a closet in the basement. Foy had banished it down there and evidently didn't want any reminders that Barton had been so prominent in the agency. So I had the staff rummage around in the basement, and they found Barton's portrait.

I brought it up from the closet in the basement to a position of prominence on our floor in the SBC building.[10]

Land went on to note that now portraits of all past and present leaders of the Commission were prominently displayed, commenting that "Barton was really the man who delivered each year the Social Service Commission report and was very much identified with the Temperance movement." And as such he was an influential Christian leader who represented the best of our Southern Baptist heritage.[11]

When asked about Valentine, who was Land's predecessor (note that Baker was essentially a transitional figure who exercised little leadership for the Commission), Land reflected:

In many ways Foy Valentine and the Christian Life Commission redeemed the honor of Southern Baptists by taking a biblical and Christian stand on race. As he had earlier when he was pastor at First Baptist Church, Gonzales, Texas, and then as head of the Texas Christian Life Commission, from 1954 to 1960, when it was positively dangerous, physically dangerous, to take the positions that Foy was taking, slamming and standing up against the Jim Crow segregationist system.

We in the Southern Baptist Convention owe an uncountable debt of gratitude to Dr. Foy Valentine for his courageous and biblical stand and his courageous, biblical, uncompromising stand on racial equality and condemnation of segregationism and the segregation system. It was truly something which saved our honor as Christian men and women during the fifties, sixties, and early seventies.

Foy was about as wrong as you could be on a lot of other issues. He was a liberal. . . . He was an active member of the ACLU. . . . He also was a member of the Americans United for Separation of Church and State. In fact, after his retirement he chaired the committee which hired Barry Lynn to be its executive director.

Foy and his staff did everything they could to keep us from having a Sanctity of Human Life Sunday on the denominational calendar. They claimed that it [abortion] was a Catholic issue. They tried to play on anti-Catholic bigotry, went to the committees, went to the meetings of the committees that were deciding this issue . . . and fought hard to not have a Sanctity of Human Life Sunday. . . . Then, when it was apparent that we would have it, he pleaded that it be on another day besides the Sunday in late January. Due to this decision by the Convention, Foy saw the handwriting on the wall so to speak and began to consider early retirement. He did have a heart condition, but this is the issue that led him to step down early so that the moderate trustees could replace him with one of their own before conservatives had a majority of trustees.[12]

Land began his tenure as executive director of the Commission on October 24 of 1988. First on his agenda, besides cleaning up the finances and initiating a change in the Commission culture, was to bring a refocus on the need for racial reconciliation. In fact, Land recalled:

One of the first things I did is propose a conference on racial reconciliation. We had a meeting here, a private meeting of leaders to talk about African-American Southern Baptist leaders and white Southern Baptists leaders to talk about the issue in preparation for a conference which we had in January. . . .

After we had had this consultation, and it was out of that consultation and in conference that the idea was formulated in my heart and in my mind that resulted in the 1995 Southern Baptist Convention resolution in which we apologized for the Convention's support of slavery, segregation, and racism and in which we asked our Southern Baptist African-American brothers and sisters to forgive us, and we apologized to them and asked for their forgiveness.[13]

At the January board meeting, Land added Lamar Cooper of the Criswell College and Louis Moore to his staff. He also added Mattie Lee Massey as administrative assistant.

Interestingly enough, the Conference on Race, held in January at Nashville's First Baptist Church, was a defining moment for Land's leadership. He invited Valentine to be one of the speakers. Both men were criticized, Land by his friends and supporters for inviting Valentine, whom they consider a theological heretic, and Valentine by his friends for being willing to speak on Land's program. Yet both agreed that race was not an issue of right or left but of right and wrong.

Land recalled, "I told Foy that *my* friends did not want me to invite him and his friends did not want him to come, but that the issue of racial reconciliation was bigger than our respective friends—he agreed."

Valentine spoke and in all of this, Land proved to be his own man. Land noted, "While there may be many issues that were conservative-moderate issues, the issue of race was not one of those issues."[14]

Meanwhile the events in the world in some ways seemed bigger than life. Domestically, at the same time Land began at the

Commission, the government passed the "Indian Gaming Regulatory Act" legalizing gambling on reservations. In December 1988, Gorbachev told the UN that he would greatly reduce the Soviet military presence in Eastern Europe. After Bush was inaugurated in January, he traveled to China in February. March brought the Exxon Valdez oil spill in Alaska. In June, just prior to the 1989 Southern Baptist Convention in Las Vegas, the pro-democracy protests in Tiananmen Square were brutally crushed by the Red Chinese Army in Beijing. The issues of gambling, communism, China, human rights, and the environment are all prominent as messengers made their way to the Convention.[15]

In many ways the 1989 Convention was a complex intermingling of a variety of interests. Many of these would affect the Christian Life Commission. Three distinct groups were involved in the public policy arena. The Christian Life Commission dealt with moral issues. The Public Affairs Committee represented Southern Baptist interests in matters of religious liberty and separation of church and state. The Baptist Joint Committee on Public Affairs was the larger body of which the Public Affairs Committee members held board representation constituting about one-third of their trustees while financing approximately 90 percent of its denominationally supported budget. As such, the Convention heard reports from Richard Land, Sam Currin, and James Dunn, who represented each entity, respectively.

The ongoing tension between the Public Affairs Committee and the Baptist Joint Committee was obvious. Southern Baptists were increasingly disillusioned with the Baptist Joint Committee's leftward posture. Moreover, they were frustrated that Southern Baptists financially sustained the Baptist Joint Committee while it often opposed the issues the majority of Southern Baptists hold dear.

In fact, going into the Convention, the Executive Committee of the Convention prepared a recommendation, which was subsequently postponed to 1990, to create for Southern Baptists its own Religious Liberty Commission as a substitute for the Baptist Joint Committee. This recommendation was delayed due to a request from Convention president Vines. In the meantime, Rudy Yakym of Indiana brought a motion to the floor of the Convention, which was referred to the Executive Committee for later consideration. He requested that the program statement and budget of the proposed Commission instead be assigned to the Christian Life Commission.[16]

Meanwhile, the Public Affairs Committee announced in the Executive Committee's report that it was launching a quarterly newsletter, *Southern Baptist Public Affairs*, dealing with subjects germane to its assignment and by implication countering the Baptist Joint Committee.[17]

Also at the Convention, the resolution of the *Crowder et al. v. Southern Baptist Convention and the Executive Committee* lawsuit was announced. The suit brought by Robert and Julia Crowder complained about Charles Stanley's ruling of the chair in the 1985 Convention in Dallas. The lawsuit was decided in favor of the Convention when the district court of the northern district of Georgia ruled that "the Court holds that this dispute is one involving questions of internal church affairs and governance over which this Court has no jurisdiction." The ruling was based on the First Amendment. When appealed to the Eleventh Circuit Court of Appeals, the ruling was sustained. And upon final appeal to the Supreme Court, by its refusal to hear the case, the rulings of the lower courts were sustained and the matter was finished. Those who embraced an absolutist separation posture would not see the irony or even the hypocrisy of attempting to correct through the courts what the majority of messengers approved on the floor of the Convention.[18]

Also brought to this Convention was a "memorial" from the Baptist General Association of Virginia. A "memorial" is defined as "an overture to another based on a summary or presentation of facts." In short, the memorial complained conservatives had moved to a position of prominence in the Convention and had subsequently controlled the direction of the Convention. The memorial requested that conservatives give up the power they had gained by the ballot. A conservative response followed that essentially called the memorial "sour grapes." The Executive Committee requested the memorial and response both be printed in total in the 1985 SBC Annual. It was.[19]

Another issue brought to the Convention was a formal complaint made by the Executive Committee in response to Bill Moyers' PBS special, "God and Politics," which criticized the conservative resurgence in the Convention. The heart of the issue was the fact that "Federal tax dollars [were spent] to support one faction in the Southern Baptist Convention controversy through the use of the Public Broadcasting System." One wonders why the Baptist Joint Committee did not seem concerned about this. They were somewhat selective over which issues needed to be addressed.[20]

The Executive Committee supported the decision for the Convention to establish its own Religious Liberty Commission that would replace the Baptist Joint Committee as Southern Baptist's representative in Washington on church-state concerns. As noted earlier, the issue would not be addressed until the 1990 Convention in New Orleans.[21]

In the Christian Life Commission report, Land reviewed the previous year's work, calling special attention to the January 1989 "Southern Baptists and Race" conference. It was a modest beginning for Land, and conservatives were pleased.[22]

The Public Affairs Committee report was more contentious as chairman Sam Currin pointed out the ongoing difficulty of working with the Baptist Joint Committee. The report concluded by stating:

> Finally, the Public Affairs Committee and the Baptist Joint
> Committee continue to have unresolved differences regarding
> institutional and financial ties, as well as disagreements on
> issues. This ill serves our Convention at the very time we need
> to be restoring our nation to biblical principles. The Public
> Affairs Committee, however, feels the proposed establishment
> of a Religious Liberty Commission—solely accountable to the
> Southern Baptist Convention—will provide the overdue solution
> to the current impasse.[23]

In contrast, the Baptist Joint Committee report provided, not surprisingly, a strong affirmation of the value and importance of the committee's work. It asserted, "Freedom's task requires special expertise for work in Washington, D.C." And explained, "The Baptist

Joint Committee on Public Affairs has the distinctive perspective, the specialized staff, the established relationships, the well-deserved reputation, and the distinguished history needed to do the job." It then proceeded to recount a summary of the year's activities.[24]

Ironically the names of representatives posted at the conclusion of the committee's report are the same names as those posted at the conclusion of the Public Affairs Committee report advocating the drastic decision to discard the Joint Committee and establish a unique Southern Baptist voice.[25] A final resolution would come in the next few years.

At the Convention, resolutions were typically conservative. Of special interest was the resolution "On China and in Support of Chinese Christians." Interestingly, messenger David Waugh attempted to amend the China resolution with a substitute motion to include a condemnation of South Africa. The amendment failed. The resolution was adopted.[26]

The Convention concluded with much unresolved tension that would resume in New Orleans.

On the national and international scene, life continued to move at a dramatic pace. In August, Colin Powell became the first black chairman of the Joint Chiefs of Staff for the United States military. In Poland, Solidarity was ushered in as the ruling party in the government. In November the Berlin Wall came down, signifying the collapse of the old Soviet Union. In a conference held December 2–3, Bush and Gorbachev announced that the Cold War had ended. On December 20, the U.S. invaded Panama; Noriega was deposed and arrested the following week.[27]

In Southern Baptist life, the Executive Committee met in September 1989. At this gathering Convention president Vines expressed appreciation for deferring the vote on the Baptist Joint Committee's status, saying he "believes the time has come to settle the issue of the Baptist Joint Committee on Public Affairs." His request was to bring the issue to the New Orleans Convention in 1990. At the Executive Committee meeting, Dunn requested a 15 percent increase in the allocation made for the Baptist Joint Committee. Also, the recommendation to create a Religious Liberty Commission was rescinded and the request was made to expand the Christian Life Commission's assignment to include religious liberty issues. Needless to say, Dunn was not happy with the Executive Committee's intentions. Wisely, Land stayed above the fray but hoped the intentions would become reality in the next Convention.[28]

James A. Smith, who was Director of Communications for the Republican Study Committee of the U. S. House of Representatives, was named the Commission's first full-time staff member in Washington, D. C., by trustees in the fall of 1989. He had graduated with a degree in political science from Dallas Baptist University in 1987.

In the February 1990 meeting of the Executive Committee, plans were finalized with the recommended budget allocation for the Baptist Joint Committee at only $50,000. The balance of funds would be reallocated to the Christian Life Commission. As before, the Public Affairs Committee was allotted only a small budget by comparison.

The spring seminar hosted by the Commission was entitled "Addictions and Family Crisis," addressing a variety of issues.

Meanwhile both conservatives and moderates were preparing to attend the June Convention in New Orleans. Moderates would promote Don Vestal while conservatives would rally around Morris Chapman.

Early 1990 saw Nelson Mandela finally freed from his South African prison. In Nicaragua the Sandinistas were peacefully voted out of power. In early June, Bush and Gorbachev agreed to a nuclear and chemical weapons reduction. Yet the world continued to be a volatile place.[29]

The 1990 Convention's opening session was on June 12, and Morris Chapman was elected president. The conservative resurgence continued. This Convention proved to be important for the Christian Life Commission. The budget recommendation proposed an increase of funding for the Commission from $897,508 to $1,262,836 and a Baptist Joint Committee reduction from $391,796 to $50,000. The budget recommendation made by the Executive Committee was adopted by the Convention.[30]

Earlier the Christian Life Commission's program statement was revised to include religious liberty concerns, and the Public Affairs Committee's program statement was deleted. Making the motion for the Executive Committee was Bill Harrell of Georgia. His principal argument was that Southern Baptists were requesting "a distinctive Southern Baptist voice in Washington, D.C., to address not only the social and moral issues of our day but the Religious Liberty issues as well." He also argued that "a body consisting of nearly 15 million people should have a distinctive voice of its own speaking in a unique way." He further noted that "the revised program statement will solve some of the problems of recent years regarding funding and accountability." He explained that the Funds for Religious Liberties would go to an agency which was solely responsible to this Convention, with all Commissioners elected by the SBC. The motion passed with approximately 70 percent of the vote. The budget allocation was also passed to support the previous decision by the Convention.[31]

Surprisingly, the Executive Committee believed it was important to provide a rationale for its proposed budget allocations. Noting that Southern Baptists provided about 90 percent of the Baptist Joint Committee's denominational funding, it then pointed out that the other eight Baptist bodies collectively supplied only 10 percent. It then related the interesting statistic that the American Baptist Churches, USA, while giving only $21,817 to the committee, provided eight times that amount, $163,620, to fund their own Washington office. And this had been their ongoing pattern and policy. Moreover, the American Baptists, USA, were also partners with the National Council of Churches and were represented, likewise, by them. Executive Committee writers pointed out that this did not seem to be problematic for the Baptist Joint Committee. In short, the Executive Committee, which reflected the majority opinion of Southern Baptists, was simply tired of what they perceived as an obvious double standard.[32]

Besides this issue, which was one among many, the Executive Committee pointed out that various problems with the Baptist Joint Committee were ongoing. It voiced concerns about the unresponsiveness of committee personnel to Convention concerns, affiliations of its executive director—particularly his position on the board of the People for the American Way—and the fact that the Baptist Joint Committee was far to the left of most Southern Baptists on public policy issues. It concluded its report and rationale by stating, "By properly funding the CLC Washington office, the Southern Baptist Convention will be doing only that which the American Baptist Churches, USA, have been doing for years."[33]

The Executive Committee did recognize that the Baptist Joint Committee, through its executive director, Dunn, had taken a stance on the abortion issue. In 1983, Dunn criticized conservatives, stating, "The complex issue of abortion is reduced to the simple cry of 'infanticide' by Mr. Reagan, who would redress 'a great national wrong' in the name of civil religion, making it virtually impossible for mothers to make their own decision in this very private, very religious matter." Dunn's position on the abortion issue was clearly out of step with the people he claimed to represent.[34]

Following the Executive Committee's "Reasons" document, a "Minority Report," prepared by moderates on the Executive Committee, pleaded to retain the status quo. Both of these "reports" were included in the 1990 SBC Annual. When the votes were taken, the Executive Committee's recommendations were approved by the Convention.[35]

An interesting phenomenon occurred with respect to recommendations from the Committee on Resolutions. The first two, "On Possession of Child Pornography" and "On Environmental Stewardship," were easily adopted. Later, when the time for business resumed at the conclusion of the Convention, not enough messengers return to constitute a quorum, so all the other resolutions were offered for information purposes by Resolutions Committee chairman, Mark Corts, and were not adopted.[36]

At the New Orleans Convention, the Christian Life Commission, the Public Affairs Committee, and the Baptist Joint Committee presented their reports. The Commission's report was consistent with past reports. The Public Affairs Committee reported its work and how it contrasted with the Baptist Joint Committee's. And the Baptist Joint

Committee argued that it needed and deserved the funding consistent with past levels of support. Its plea fell on the majority's deaf ears.[37]

When the 1990 New Orleans Convention adjourned, Southern Baptists were one giant step closer to having a single agency represent it for both ethics and religious liberty concerns.

Land was not one to gloat for the Christian Life Commission. He spoke in a conciliatory tone at a press conference. "Before [New Orleans] we could not address the religious liberty and church/state separation issues." Considering where Southern Baptists had presently arrived, he commented, "Now we can and this frees us to work more closely with the Baptist Joint Committee on joint statements." Clearly Land perceived this point as a transitional stage and foresaw the day when the Commission alone would represent Southern Baptists in the realms of public policy.

Concerning the difference between his "accommodation" posture and Dunn's "absolutist" posture with respect to church and state issues, Land explained,

> Another area where I was committed was to begin to espouse a position which I believe is more in accord with Baptist heritage and with the Baptist message than the position that was being espoused by the Baptist Joint Committee. Identified as the "accommodation view," we agree with the Supreme Court's decision of 1962 and 1963, but we disagree vehemently with what has been done with them by subsequent courts and subsequent attorneys and subsequent opinions, that we did not want the government to sponsor religion, but we didn't want the government to censor religion either. We didn't want the government to sponsor religion. We didn't want the government to suppress religion. We wanted the government to accommodate itself to the people's right to express their convictions in the public square. So we began to move toward that goal of helping Southern Baptists understand their heritage in this area.[38]

During this post-New Orleans period, several changes of note were made. The Baptist Press office heretofore located at the Baptist Joint

Committee office was transferred to the Christian Life Commission's Washington office. Upon Larry Braidfoot's departure from the Commission to William Carey College in Mississippi, Land hired Michael Whitehead to work with James Smith in Washington. Whitehead, who joined the staff on October 1, 1990, was a partner in the firm that argued the pivotal equal access case, *Widnar v. Vincent,* before the U. S. Supreme Court in 1980.

At the same trustee meeting that Whitehead, an attorney from Raytown, Missouri, was named the Commission's General Counsel and Director of Christian Citizenship and Religious Liberty Concerns, the board also approved the hiring of Tom Strode.

Strode, who was named Director of New Information/Washington, was formerly staff journalist at Bellevue Baptist Church in Memphis. He earned his bachelor of journalism from the University of Missouri at Columbia and an M.Div. from Mid-America Seminary in Memphis. Strode, who had worked at the *Arkansas Gazette* in Little Rock, also filled the position of *Baptist Press* bureau chief in D.C. when he joined the CLC staff.

At this time, the only Valentine/Baker holdover was Robert Parham.

The Commission now had more money, an expanded staff, and as the public policy arm of America's largest non-Catholic religious body, more clout with the White House, Congress, and hopefully with the courts.

On October 30, 1990, Land and Morris Chapman along with sixteen other evangelical leaders met with President George H. W. Bush. During the meeting Land expressed concern over the White House's willingness to invite homosexual activists to attend bill-signing ceremonies, the administration's failure to seek restrictions on controversial grants given by the National Endowment for the Arts, and the need for stronger and more visible leadership from the president on abortion concerns.

Reflecting on the meeting, Land conceded, "It was better than I expected but worse than I had hoped." He noted that the president made no promises other than agreeing to consider their requests.[39]

The post-New Orleans world was tense. Because of the perceived economic crisis, Bush conceded to tax increases that by the next election would be remembered as a broken promise. In August 1990, Iraq invaded Kuwait. The Iran-Iraq War, which killed more than a million men, had only concluded in 1988, and the region was again in conflict. In a matter of months, the United States and the world would enter the conflict. In the fall election Democrats picked up seats in both the House and the Senate. The prevailing fear in Washington was that Iraq was close to developing or obtaining nuclear weapons. By the end of 1990, more than 100,000 Americans had died of AIDS, and former President Reagan expressed regret for the slow response to the growing health crisis.[40]

In response to the Iraq invasion of Kuwait, Bush sent 200,000 troops to Saudi Arabia in a protective move known as Desert Shield. On January 12, 1991, the Senate voted fifty-two to forty-seven to authorize the president to use force to counter Iraq's invasion of Kuwait. On January 17, 1991, the First Gulf War, known as Desert Storm, began with an air assault. The land invasion was launched on February 24. The Iraqi casualities exceeded 100,000 while the United States lost 79 dead with another 213 wounded.[41]

When the invasion occurred, the National Council of Churches immediately called for an end to the war on grounds that it violated the principles of a "just war."

In order to explain his decision and also gain an understanding of the whole notion of "just war," President Bush received papers from Land and also Daniel Heimbach on the subject. Bush used these reports as he justified his decision to go to war in a major speech given to the National Religious Broadcasters on January 28, 1991. After Leigh Ann Metzger left her post at the White House, where she served as a liaison to evangelicals, she cited Land's contribution as extremely helpful to the president.[42]

Land also used his influence with the president to request stronger action against child pornographers.

Land's influence nationwide took a step forward when he was invited to speak at the 1990 Convention of the Concerned Women for America. Addressing the gathering, he stated, "Abortion, as awful as it is, is the thin end of the wedge, . . . the camel's nose under the tent. . . . We are fighting a culture war over the definition of the nature and value of human life and whether human life is indeed distinct from other life." He reiterated, "We are in a war, literally to the death."[43]

Land asserted, "The biblical view is that all human life is sacred and begins at conception, and the right to life is a sacred act." He further explained, "Both before and after the Fall, from Genesis to Revelation, God always deals with human beings differently from the way he deals with all other life." Land went on to say:

> The idea that human beings are no different than other animals has a consequence. What it boils down to is, if we do not put this evil genie back in the bottle we are going to end up not only with the wholesale slaughter of unborn children, we are going to deal with the termination of children who don't have a high predictability of productivity and success. And for those in the nursing home and in intensive care, the "quality-of-life" either will be applied to them, which means, "Are you healthy enough, are you normal enough to justify your continued existence? If not, we're going to pull the plug."
>
> If this "quality-of-life" standard is not reversed, dire consequences will occur in the near future. We are already seeing an increasing percentage of elderly persons in the United States, a development partly due to the legality of abortion and the resultant decrease in population growth among the young.
>
> Christians have the right, the responsibility, and the obligation to speak boldly on this issue, and if we won't stand in the gap, who will? If we won't stand on this, on what issue will we? And if we won't stand now, when will we start?

Land paused again, wiped his brow, and concluded, after relating a personal testimony,

> So you can understand, ladies, that I feel an obligation to speak for those who are not fortunate enough to have a

Christian mother like mine, for those who can't speak for themselves; but if they could they would say, "I want to live!"[44]

Early in 1991, the Commission and Land's influence took another
step forward with the launching of a new publication, *SALT*. The first
issue was released in May and featured articles that addressed taxpayer funding of obscene art by the National Endowment for the Arts,
a preview of the *Lee v. Weisman* case, which the Supreme Court would
hear in 1991, Land's meeting with President Bush, and information on
how to contact government officials with concerns.[45]

Defunding the Baptist Joint Committee

The 1991 Convention in Atlanta proved to be a defining moment
for the Christian Life Commission. Although the Executive Committee had recommended continuing the $50,000 funding for the Baptist
Joint Committee, Fred Minix of Virginia made the motion that "the
Southern Baptist Convention Operating Budget . . . be amended by
reducing the amount designated for the Baptist Joint Committee on
Public Affairs from $50,000 to $0." James Dunn, of course, spoke
against the motion to amend. Debate ensued and the motion received
a proposed amendment, which was rejected. Convention president
Chapman called for a ballot vote. When the results were announced,
the motion carried by 52.97 percent of the vote. The Baptist Joint
Committee was no longer officially supported by the Southern Baptist
Convention.[46]

In the Commission report, Land presented an update on the
year's activities. He expressed his pleasure at receiving the religious
liberty assignment from the Convention and pointed out that with
the expanded staff in Washington the Southern Baptist influence in
Washington would be stronger. He also related that several *amicus
curiae* "friend of the court" briefs involving abortion, pornography,
and religious liberty had been filed. Of particular importance was the
Rust v. Sullivan case. Not surprisingly, the Commission would now
find itself periodically on the opposite side of issues with the Baptist

Joint Committee, People for the American Way, Americans United for the Separation of Church and State, and the American Civil Liberties Union. Land summarized the spring Commission conference, "Christians and the Environment: Finding a Biblical Balance between Idolatry and Irresponsibility."[47]

In response to the ongoing debate about government funding of obscene art, Land requested that the Committee on Resolutions sponsor a resolution "On Government Sponsorship of Obscene and Offensive Art." The resolution states:

> WHEREAS, God has organized government to do good works; and
>
> WHEREAS, Southern Baptists have historically supported the constitutional rights of free speech and have opposed undue censorship; and
>
> WHEREAS, Regulation of government funding of art or certain types of expression claimed to be art is not censorship of the arts; and
>
> WHEREAS, The Supreme Court recently stated in *Rust v. Sullivan* that government may regulate expressive activity to conform to public policy as a condition for obtaining public funding; and
>
> WHEREAS, The National Endowment for the Arts (NEA) has, increasingly in recent years, demonstrated a pattern of support for obscene, offensive, morally repugnant, and sacrilegious "art"; and
>
> WHEREAS, The Chairman of the NEA, who is appointed by the President, has demonstrated a clear lack of sensitivity to the concerns of evangelical Christians and others regarding the funding abuses of the NEA; and
>
> WHEREAS, Last year, despite pleas from evangelical Christians and others, Congress and the President failed to support legislation which would have placed meaningful restrictions on what the NEA is permitted to fund but instead

adopted an ineffectual standard calling for "general standards of decency"; and

WHEREAS, Since last year's ineffectual action by Congress, additional homoerotic, pornographic, and sacrilegious "art" has been funded by the NEA with the explicit approval of its Chairman; and

WHEREAS, Some members of Congress and the President continue to oppose content restrictions on NEA funding; Now, therefore,

BE IT RESOLVED, That we the messengers to the Southern Baptist Convention meeting in Atlanta, Georgia, June 4–6, 1991, recognizing the influence which the NEA has on our culture, deplore the lack of initiative by the President and Congress in addressing the continuing abuses of the NEA; and

BE IT FURTHER RESOLVED, That we urge the President to act immediately to remove the current Chairman of the NEA and replace him with an individual who will stop funding obscene, offensive, morally repugnant, and sacrilegious "art"; and

BE IT FURTHER RESOLVED, That we call on Congress and the President to set standards which will prevent the funding of obscene, offensive, morally repugnant and sacrilegious "art," or, if that is not done, to cease funding the National Endowment for the Arts.[48]

Needless to say, the resolution was approved by a healthy majority of the Convention's messengers. Other resolutions of note supported the United States and its role in Desert Storm, advocated the right of families to have a choice in education, "which include proper tax incentives for families," equitable taxation for families, and a host of resolutions related to morality—especially a new resolution "On Sanctity of Human Life."[49]

The Public Affairs Committee presented what proved to be its last report to the Convention. Chairman Albert Lee Smith, former congressman from Alabama, who along with Judge Samuel Currin was one of the two strongest leaders of the committee, concluded his remarks by stating, "Eternal vigilance is the price of liberty, particularly religious liberty." He then pleaded, "Southern Baptists, wake up and be counted." His words would be well heeded.[50]

Likewise, the 1991 Convention would be the last for the Baptist Joint Committee and James Dunn. In his report Dunn pleaded for additional funding because of the significance of their work. One wonders why he was incapable of understanding why he was so out of touch with the majority of Southern Baptists.[51]

With acclamation Morris Chapman was reelected president of the Southern Baptist Convention. The conservative resurgence continued, and messengers left with one voice speaking for them on moral, religious liberty, and church-state issues. In the unspoken struggle for leadership in the Southern Baptist Convention, the Christian Life Commission had come out on top and Richard Land was its principal spokesman. Land would not disappoint his constituency.[52]

At this juncture in the history of the Christian Life Commission, its trustee chairman, Nolan Phillips, summarized well the present state of affairs when he said, "The salt has never been saltier, and the light has never been brighter."[53]

A month after the Convention, Parham submitted his resignation to Land. It turned out that he had been working with W. C. Fields and others to create an alternative ethics agency sponsored by the Cooperative Baptist Fellowship, a renegade convention within the Convention consisting of disgruntled and disaffected moderates. One criticism from the moderate crowd was that the new Christian Life Commission placed too much emphasis on abortion. In response Land stated, "It's true we have emphasized the abortion issue." He then provided his assessment, "If we are being charged with putting a major emphasis on what is the most crucial and defining issue of our time, we plead guilty."[54]

When the Baptist Joint Committee was defunded by the Convention, one untied, loose end was a question of $300,000 designated to the Public Affairs Committee in 1964. Both the Baptist Joint

Committee and the Public Affairs Committee laid claim to the funds. Because Porter Routh, a previous executive director of the Executive Committee of the Southern Baptist Convention, had instructed the Southern Baptist Foundation, with whom the funds resided, to pay earnings to the Baptist Joint Committee, the committee laid claim to the principal.

At their September 1991 board meeting, Commission trustees asked the Executive Committee to allocate the money to them for the purchase of a permanent office on Capitol Hill. In response, Buzz Thomas, general counsel for the Baptist Joint Committee, charged the Commission with "pilfering our account." Thomas called the Commission request both unethical and illegal. At stake was $381,927.53, including the accrued interest as of August 1, 1991. Public Affairs Committee members who served on the Commission's trustee board countered, arguing the funds should come with them to the Commission.[55]

When Parham resigned, his position was filled by ethicist Ben Mitchell, who had served as a trustee of the Commission from 1987–1991. Not only did he assume Parham's duties but brought with him an expertise in biomedical issues.

At the September board meeting, the Commission adopted a 1991–1992 budget of $1,538,898 anticipating the reception of the Foundation funds. Also, a new Religious Liberty Award was established; in addition, Carl F. H. Henry, the nation's most prominent evangelical theologian, was awarded the agency's Distinguished Service Award. The Commission also made the decision not to send representatives to the Baptist Joint Committee on Public Affairs' board meeting but to authorize a Commission staffer to attend as an observer. It would take the 1992 Convention in Indianapolis for all ties to the Baptist Joint Committee to be severed officially.

A major issue up for serious debate in late 1991 and 1992 was the proposed Religious Freedom Restoration Act. One particular issue wrapped up in the debate was how it would affect the abortion debate. Some believed that the pending bill would attempt to guarantee abortion as part of religious liberty. Land believed that abortion need not be considered under the free exercise clause, and Dunn had gone on the record previously as saying it did. Dunn had argued along with his predecessor James Wood that abortion should be protected by the free exercise clause because anti-abortion legislation was a form of government interference in religion. Now Dunn maintained that the "Baptist Joint Committee has never suggested abortion as a free exercise right, nor have we addressed the issue of abortion in any fashion." As a result of Dunn's latest statement, Land decided to support the Religious Freedom Restoration Act, arguing that along with its benefits, "It need not advance an abortion agenda." Because of the vigorous debate in committees of both the House and Senate, it would not be signed into law until 1993.[56]

During this same time frame the Commission, the U.S. Department of Justice, and many others believed the U.S. Supreme Court should modify its current test for determining whether a government activity was a constitutional establishment of religion. As a test case, *Lee v. Weisman,* on school prayer, was working its way through the court system and was argued before the Supreme Court in November 1991. In short this case involved the legality of a rabbi's offering a prayer at a public school commencement ceremony. The plaintiff, Daniel Weisman, complained that he was offended by the mention of "God" at the ceremony. Complicating the matter was the fact that the school's principal had given the rabbi a pamphlet on composing prayers for public occasions.[57]

The *Lemon v. Kurtzman* decision from June 28, 1971 was at stake. The outcome of this case was the "Lemon test," which defines the government's requirements in order to address First Amendment issues with respect to religion. It consists of three "prongs." First, "the government's action must have a legitimate secular purpose." Second, "the government's action must not have the primary effect of either advancing or inhibiting religion." And third, "the government's action must not result in an 'excessive entanglement' with religion." From the Court's perspective, "if any of these three prongs is violated, the government's action is deemed unconstitutional under the Establishment Clause of the First Amendment to the United States Constitution."[58]

Matt Staver, dean of the Liberty University School of Law, pointed out that the Lemon test was not consistently used by the courts and in the *Lee v. Weisman* decision, June 24, 1992, opted for a so-called "coercion" test. At times the court even prefers no test at all and surmised that the original intent of the First Amendment was adequate.[59]

The Christian Life Commission sent a mass mailout explaining its position on this latest round of church-state debates. Land wrote, "We have urged the Court to replace Lemon with a test which will avoid the concept of 'secularization' while retaining the historic principle of benevolent neutrality in government's relation to religion, a principle central to historic Baptist church-state separation." Land was concerned to preserve the strengths of Lemon without leaving and conceding to what he considered its fatal flaw, the elevation of abject secularization.[60]

The Commission, Land, and General Counsel Whitehead supported a test adopted from a law review article by University of Chicago Law Professor Michael McConnell, which suggests:

> (1) Does the official accommodation facilitate the exercise of religious beliefs and practices, adopted through private, family, church, and community influences, independent from state influence, rather than inducing or coercing beliefs and practices acceptable to the government?
>
> (2) Does the accommodation interfere with the religious liberty of others by forcing them to participate in religious observances?
>
> (3) Does the accommodation use the government's taxing power, or its expenditure of public funds structured so the effect will be (a) to induce, coerce, or distort individual religious choice, or (b) to interfere with the religious autonomy of a religious institution, or (c) to promote a religion, or discriminate against a religion, by providing direct subsidy to religious indoctrination of belief?[61]

Commenting on the principal's "composing prayer" pamphlet, Justice Kennedy, who rejected the constitutionality of such prayers, writing the majority opinion, noted that "the principal directed and controlled the content of the prayers." He continued, stating, "It is a cornerstone principle of our Establishment Clause jurisprudence that it is no part of the business of government to compose official prayers for any group of the American people to recite as a part of a religious program carried on by government, and that is what the school official attempted to do." He went on to conclude, "As we have observed before, there are heightened concerns with protecting freedom of conscience from subtle coercive pressure in the elementary and secondary public schools." He further explained, "Our decisions in [Engel] and [Abingdon] recognize, among other things, that prayer exercises in public schools carry a particular risk of indirect coercion."[62]

In this decision, which in its application was perceived to rule out even voluntary prayers in public arenas, Justice Scalia wrote the dissenting opinion. Concerning this five to four decision, he stated,

> In holding that the Establishment Clause prohibits invocations and benedictions at public school graduation ceremonies, the Court—with nary a mention that it is doing so—lays waste a tradition that is as old as public school graduation ceremonies themselves, and that is a component of an even more longstanding American tradition of nonsectarian prayer to God at public celebrations generally. As its instrument of destruction, the bulldozer of its social engineering, the Court invents a boundless, and boundlessly manipulable, test of psychological coercion.[63]

Although the strengths and weaknesses of various interpretations of the First Amendment were once again visited, the ruling for the most part satisfied no one completely except maybe the secularists.

At this same time Clarence Thomas was gingerly proceeding through the Senate's confirmation process to become the next associate justice on the Supreme Court. In time he would be confirmed and, as a rule, embrace a more strict constructionist posture than other justices. Often he voted with Anthony Scalia.

Although the Commission was consistently at odds with the Baptist Joint Committee, periodically they did agree on issues of common interest. When the Bush Treasury Department proposed that churches become responsible for reporting contribution records to the government, both the Commission and Committee were quick to express their opposition. Needless to say, this proposal was quickly retracted.

During this same period of time, Planned Parenthood, which had received millions of dollars as an abortion provider, decided to spend between $3 and $5 million to overturn Title 10 regulations, which prohibit federally funded clinics from doing abortion counseling, promotions, and referrals as part of its family-planning program. The regulations sustained in the *Rust v. Sullivan* decision were challenged by pro-abortion lobbyists. Land and other pro-life advocates worked diligently to sustain the regulation. Although some parts were overturned, the regulation that forbade the use of federal funds for abortion remained.[64]

Just weeks prior to the 1992 Indianapolis Convention, the nation was again engulfed in racial strife. The media captured on tape the beating of a black man, Rodney King, by four white policemen in Los Angeles, California. When the jury acquited the policemen on charges of police brutality, the city erupted in riots, which saw forty-four people die and eighteen hundred injuries.[65]

Through the end of 1991 and early 1992, Land and the Commission stayed busy with a variety of issues. When the Convention met in Indianapolis from June 9 to 11, one item of business abruptly addressed was Recommendation 5, which terminated the Convention's participation in the Baptist Joint Committee. It was adopted. When the Baptist Joint Committee requested the Convention to enter into binding arbitration concerning the funds in question, the Convention declined and eventually negotiated a settlement acceptable to all parties in general and no one specifically.[66]

The Convention also saw the adoption of the revised program statement for the Christian Life Commission. At this meeting, for the first time the Christian Life Commission was unequivocally the exclusive representative for Southern Baptists in the areas of ethics and morality and also religious liberty concerns.[67]

Of interest at this Convention was the motion adopted by the Convention to exclude as an active participant in the Convention any congregation demonstrating approval of homosexual behavior.[68]

In Land's report to the Convention, he reviewed the status of representing Southern Baptists in the additional area of religious liberty and noted, especially, that they had filed an *amicus curiae* "friend-of-the-court" brief in the *Lee v. Weisman* case. Land explained, "In our brief we have asked the Court to overturn a lower court order prohibiting invocations and benedictions containing the word 'God' at public school commencement exercises." He further noted, "We have also asked the Court to revise the 'Lemon' test and we have suggested a new test to replace Lemon, a test which is premised on the principles of government accommodation of religious practices which exist independently of government action and are not induced or coerced by government." He concluded by stating, "We believe students must have the right to free exercise of their religious liberty while in school. They must have the right to associate voluntarily with one another during lunch, recess, and free periods to pray, to study their Bible, and to discuss religious issues with each other, without government control or censorship."[69]

The 1992 Convention adopted a number of resolutions. Of particular interest were the ones on "Free Exercise of Religion in Public Schools," "On the Right of Religious Freedom for All Human Beings," "Fetal Tissue Experimentation," and "Euthanasia and Assisted Suicide." Each of these reflected issues the Christian Life Commission was addressing.[70]

Twelve days after the conclusion of the 1992 Convention, President Bush vetoed a medical research bill that would have lifted the ban on federal funding of the use of fetal tissue in medical research from induced abortions. Bill Clinton, who would be the presidential contender for the Democratic Party, issued a statement in response denouncing Bush for "playing politics by turning what would have been an important step forward in the fight to save millions of lives [of sick people] . . . into an ugly bow to the far right. I urge Congress to override the President's veto."

Land replied quickly to the aspiring Clinton. "This is not a question of right or left, but of right and wrong. As a nation, we decided not to use medical research obtained from human experiments on prisoners in Nazi death camps, even if it proved to be beneficial. The source of the information so contaminated it that it was unusable by civilized society. The same is true of using fetal tissue from elective abortions. The source—voluntarily taking a baby's life—is unacceptable in civilized society."[71]

Congress sustained Bush's veto in supporting the ban on the use of fetal tissue. Yet the excitement generated by the victory was short-lived because of the June 29 Supreme Court decision of *Planned Parenthood v. Casey*. By a five to four margin, the justices reaffirmed the 1973 *Roe v. Wade* ruling. Three of the four justices voting to reaffirm *Roe v. Wade* were Reagan-Bush nominees.

Whitehead, speaking for the Commission, stated, "Pro-life America's hopes that Roe will be reversed . . . have been dashed by so-called pro-life justices. Reversing Roe will require another, real pro-life justice to help Rehnquist, White, Scalia, and Thomas who remained committed to stopping the convenience killing of pre-born babies." Land was scalding in his criticism of the one-vote margin in putting the high court's stamp of approval on *Roe v. Wade*.[72]

During these days issues addressed by the Commission were getting more varied and complex.

In the aftermath of the Indianapolis Convention, the nation experienced a terrible national disaster as Hurricane Andrew hit Florida. Thirty-eight people were killed, two hundred fifty thousand people were left homeless, and the damage in property loss was estimated at more than $30 billion.[73]

When Ross Perot entered the presidential race in the summer of 1992, it created a three-man race. Democrat Bill Clinton won the election in November with 43 percent of the popular vote. The Democrats also held on to both the House and Senate. Land, commenting on the election's exit polls, concluded that the majority of voters considered the economy as their top priority. He stated in a post-election press release that "this is an economic, not a social values mandate." He insisted, "There is no mandate for sweeping value changes." After the election Clinton announced on November 11 that he would allow homosexuals to serve in the military, reversing the country's long-standing policy.[74]

On November 12, Land sent an open letter to President-elect Clinton. After addressing issues which he considered vital to Southern Baptists, Land wrote:

> In 1785 Thomas Jefferson said, "To compel a man to fur-nish contributions of money for the propagation of opinions which he disbelieves is sinful and tyrannical." Pitting govern-ment policy [alluding to the NEA's financing of obscene and anti-Christian art] against religious-based conscience violates the church-state principles which our Baptist forbears cherished.
>
> Therefore, we earnestly plead with you to prayerfully reconsider your stated positions on abortion on demand and special civil rights status for homosexuals. We urge you to affirm those moral values which have made America great. We appeal to you to be tolerant of all people, but not tolerant of wrong-doing. Accord dignity to all, but do not dignify sin and vice, no matter how common. Please do not treat immoral human behavior as being of equal worth to right conduct and virtue. America needs moral conviction, not moral neutrality. America's children need a model of leadership committed both to excellence and to virtue. May God bless you, Mr. President, and make you that leader. And may God bless America![75]

Interestingly, only three weeks later, Land sent Clinton another letter in which he said, "I am writing to ask you to strike a blow for these great principles [religious liberty and the separation of the insti-tutions of church and state] by redressing a wrong done by President Reagan in 1984 when he appointed an ambassador to the Vatican." He concluded, "President Reagan and the U.S. Senate acted erroneously in deciding this matter in 1984." Needless to say, Land's requests to Clinton fell on deaf ears and proved to be the typical reception and response during the Clinton presidency.[76]

On December 17, outgoing President Bush signed the North America Free Trade Agreement; and on January 3, Bush and Boris Yeltsin signed the START II Treaty, which promised to cut the United States and Soviet arsenals by two-thirds.[77]

Five days after his inauguration, Clinton signed an executive order that wiped out Bush's pro-life policies. On social and moral issues, Clinton was no friend of conservatives.[78]

Just weeks after assuming the presidency, Clinton, on February 26, 1993, was faced with the first attack on the World Trade Center. In the assault seven were killed, and more than one thousand were injured. The attack's mastermind, Ramzi Yousef, was arrested and subsequently received a sentence of life in prison. Just two days after the New York assault, on February 28, four federal agents were killed in Waco during the assault on the Branch Davidian compound outside of Waco, Texas. Its aftermath and climax on April 19 left eighty-one dead and a host of questions about why it ever happened. In ensuing months Clinton raised taxes. By May he officially canceled the Strategic Defense Initiative (SDI) introduced by former President Reagan. Also in May, Clinton convened a universal health care task force chaired by the first lady, Hillary Rodham Clinton. The initiative eventually ended in failure.[79]

More germane to the Commission's concerns, on March 10, David Gunn, an abortion doctor, was shot and killed by an abortion protestor. The pro-abortion lobby, with all the hypocrisy it could muster decried the taking of this "innocent" life. Of course, the pro-abortion lobby was quick to associate this with all "religious intolerance." Wisely Land issued a quick statement to the press stating, "The Christian Life Commission continues to oppose and deplore acts of violence against all human beings, born and unborn."[80]

On the heels of the Gunn killing, the president announced two initiatives. First, he proposed to weaken the Hyde Amendment that had hindered abortions being provided at taxpayer expense. Then he proposed the Freedom of Choice Act, which according to Smith in the Commission's Washington office "would invalidate virtually all meaningful state regulations and restrictions on abortion."[81]

The 1993 seminar, under the theme "Life at Risk: Crisis in Medical Ethics," attempted to address the implications of the new proposed legislation. Speakers included Carol Everett, former abortion provider turned right-to-life advocate. Her bottom line was that "abortion is about money." Other speakers included Thomas Harris, a Vanderbilt University professor of biomedical engineering, and Francis Collins, who soon became the director of the National Center for Human Genome Research.[82]

When the legislative dust settled, the Hyde Amendment survived, giving the pro-choice White House and supporters on Capitol Hill a major defeat. The Freedom of Choice Act was postponed; and, according to the National Right to Life Committee, it "faded from view after Republicans took control of the House of Representatives in the 1994 election."[83]

Leading up to the 1993 Convention, the Commission also continued its resistance to Clinton's pro-homosexual agenda. In another matter it expressed its opposition to Joycelyn Elders, the president's nominee for surgeon general, due to her avid pro-abortion posture.

In response to the major homosexual rights march on Washington in late April, Land wrote in *SALT*:

> Despite attempts to camouflage [the gay march] as a civil
> rights movement, their real goal is to "normalize" homosexual-
> ity as healthy, acceptable in mainstream America. Simply put,
> the homosexual movement wants not toleration of what society
> considers deviant behavior among consenting adults in private,
> but public acceptance of its sexual preference and lifestyle by
> both adults and children. Exposing six-year-olds to Heather
> Has Two Mommies and Daddy's Roommate as part of the pro-
> homosexual curricula in numerous public schools epitomizes
> such efforts.[84]

Clearly the moral agenda being peddled to the American people under Clinton's leadership was out of touch and out of step with where most Americans and most Southern Baptists were at this time in history.

When the Southern Baptist Convention gathered for its annual meeting in June 1993, the conservatives were soundly in control. When Michael Hamlet of South Carolina nominated Edwin Young of Texas for the Convention presidency, there were no other nominations.

The Executive Committee announced it had negotiated a settlement with the Baptist Joint Committee on the disputed funds and authorized a settlement of $100,000, which would be paid out of reserve funds of the Executive Committee.

Most resolutions addressed concerns in the culture. In fact, eighteen were submitted addressing Clinton's public policy and moral concerns. The second resolution "On President William Jefferson Clinton" brought attention to some of the concerns:

> WHEREAS, On his third day in office, January 22, 1993, the twentieth anniversary of the landmark *Roe v. Wade* Supreme Court decision, which made abortion on demand legal throughout the United States, President Clinton signed executive orders repealing pro-life policies of the two previous presidential administrations; and
>
> WHEREAS, At the direction of President Clinton, the Food and Drug Administration is attempting to make certain abortion pills available in the United States; and . . .
>
> WHEREAS, The President has requested funds from Congress to pay for elective abortions in the federal Medicaid program; and . . .
>
> WHEREAS, President Clinton has asked the Congress to repeal the Kemp-Kaston Amendment so that money we give to the United Nations might be used to support nations that require abortions, namely the "coercive abortions" of China; and
>
> WHEREAS, President Clinton on January 29, 1993, requested the Department of Defense to present to him by July 15, 1993, a draft executive order repealing the policy which

bans openly declared homosexuals from serving in our nation's armed forces; and. . . .[85]

And this was not the entire resolution, only a portion. Clearly Southern Baptist messengers were greatly alarmed at President Clinton's moral and social agenda.

Other resolutions included one "On Homosexuality, Military Service and Civil Rights"; one "On the Freedom of Choice Act, Hyde Amendment and Other Abortion Policies"; one "On Racial and Ethnic Reconciliation"; one "On Accommodation of Religious Expression in Public Schools"; and one "On Diplomatic Relations with the Vatican." Each of these bore the influence of the Christian Life Commission and Richard Land.[86]

The Christian Life Commission report reviewed the numerous issues that were being addressed and especially the progress being made in the area of religious liberty. With particular concern over the present political party's presidential public policies, Southern Baptists were grateful Land was at the head of their Christian Life Commission.[87]

At this juncture in its history, the Christian Life Commission's professional staff included Land, Lamar Cooper, Louis Moore, Ben Mitchell, Michael Whitehead, Tom Strode, and James Smith. Even with this exceptional team of professionals, the workload was almost overwhelming.

As the year transpired, international concerns once again grabbed headlines. On September 13, 1993, the Israeli prime minister, Yitzhak Rabin, met at the White House with the Palestinian Liberation Organization's Yassar Arafat, where they signed a draft peace agreement previously and confidentially negotiated in Oslo, Norway. A month later, in Somalia, on October 3, a U.S. Black Hawk helicopter was ambushed by armed militia, and eighteen U.S. soldiers were killed when they attempted to capture a Somali "warlord."[88]

At the turn of the year, the NAFTA went into effect. In the Ukraine the Trilateral Statement between the United States, Russia, and the Ukraine provided the dismantling of the latter's nuclear weapons.

In Haiti, due to the political turmoil, the U.S. imposed an economic blockade beginning in May.[89]

When June arrived, former President Carter traveled as Clinton's emissary to North Korea for the purpose of negotiating an agreement, which was signed with considerable pomp and fanfare. The outcome would be North Korea's empty promise not to develop nuclear weapons.

In late 1993 and early 1994, the Christian Life Commission continued its work on a variety of fronts. Race relations remained high on Land's agenda. Ben Mitchell worked diligently on what were considered the "Brave New World" topics.

Late in 1993, the Christian Life Commission purchased a permanent office facility in Washington, D.C. The narrow three-story building was named the John Leland House in honor of the famous Virginia "apostle of liberty." Providing insight into the acquisition of the facility, Land related:

> Leland House: In 1967, the Convention voted to have the Joint Committee give $400,000 to build a building for the joint use of the Joint Committee and the Washington, D.C., convention. Well, instead of doing that, they totally ignored it and used the interest to pay for a lease on office space in the Veterans of Foreign Wars offices. So they never did what the Convention asked them to do. When they transferred the money to us, we within eighteen months did what the Joint Committee didn't do in over three decades. We purchased a property. We used about half of the money to renovate it and the other half as a down payment for the mortgage. We took out a twelve-year mortgage, which is now paid off. Interestingly enough, when we went from being a leaser of office space in the Hall of States to being a property owner, that home, the row house we bought, had been a private residence so it was on the tax rolls. The financially strapped District of Columbia government said, "We're not going to give you a tax exemption because you are not a ministry, you're a lobbying group." We said, "No, we're

not. We're a ministry and a public policy advocacy group." And they denied our petition and kept us on the tax rolls. We went into court in the District of Columbia arguing that we paid our taxes under protest, that we were not a lobbying group, that we were a ministry and a public policy advocacy group. We found out later that we were their stalking horse. If they had been able to do that to us, and we had rolled over and taken it, they were going to go after every ministry in the District for tax revenue. We fought them. We won. We got all our taxes back. Every time the Associated Baptist Press calls us a lobbying group, we just mention that according to the judge in the District of Columbia where there was a trial about this we are not. Now, my trustees wondered if we really wanted to fight this much over $5,500 a year. I told them it was a matter of principle. If we lose in the District of Columbia, we are going to federal court. This is a First Amendment case. We won in the District of Columbia.[90]

In September, James Dunn arranged a meeting of religious leaders with President Clinton and his staff. Not surprisingly Land was not invited. Eleven days later, Rex Horne, Clinton's Little Rock pastor, arranged a brief visit between Clinton, Al Gore, Convention President Young and Executive Committee President Chapman, and another pastor. According to Young nothing was accomplished.

Land, continuing his criticism of Clinton's policies, wrote an article in *SALT*, "Does Character Matter?" and particularly expressed his opposition to Clinton's proposed nationalized health care plan. As was often the case, the sticky point was the abortion on demand planks and the expectation that tax money would help provide for them. In a Commission-sponsored consultation on health care (both Hillary Clinton and Al Gore were invited but declined to attend), Land confessed that "our medical delivery system is in significant need of reform" because "significant numbers of people are not now covered by medical insurance."[91]

Following the Health Care Consultation, the Commission prepared two documents, "Health Care Reform: A Moral Preamble" and "Health Care Reform: A Statement of Concerns." In short, Land drew a line in the sand and declared that we will not budge on the abortion issue.

Perhaps it was divine sovereignty or good planning or both when the esteemed Mother Teresa of Calcutta was invited to address the Presidential Prayer Breakfast on February 3, 1994. She proceeded to deliver in a gracious manner a scathing critique of any culture that willingly sacrifices unborn children on the altar of convenience.[92]

In 1994, Land wrote "An Open Letter to Evangelical Leaders Visiting the White House" in which he challenged these Christian leaders to be truthful and forthright with the president on moral concerns. Alluding to the February Prayer Breakfast, he wrote:

> As I have said before, Mother Teresa of Calcutta's speech at the National Prayer Breakfast last February [1994] has given Christian leaders everywhere a sterling example of what it means to be truly prophetic in the presence of Caesar. One can only pray that all of those who are in Caesar's presence in the future will be both inspired and instructed by her example.
>
> Why did Mother Teresa's speech have such impact? First, she attacked policies, not persons. Second, she came not as a Democrat nor as a Republican, but as a person of faith who lives what she preaches. Third, Mother Teresa was neither impressed or inhibited by the trappings of secular power and privilege. Fourth, she sought no favor and brought no endorsement to Caesar, but instead sought only to speak the truth as it had been revealed to her.[93]

Mother Teresa's words and Land's counsel addressed both the abortion issue and also the Christian's responsibility to stand for righteousness in the public arena. Abortion was an issue that would not go away.

Meanwhile, more turmoil again came to the Southern Baptist Convention. In March 1994, the trustees at Southwestern Baptist

Theological Seminary dismissed Russell Dilday as president of the institution. Many Southwestern alumni brought their disappointment and even anger over the incident to the Convention in Orlando.[94]

As time approached for the Convention, the Commission was involved in attempting to override a workplace guideline being proposed by the Equal Employment Opportunity Commission, which in effect would prohibit employees from sharing their faith in the work environment. Sharing one's faith might be construed as practicing "religious harassment." This provision was subsequently dropped due to the outcry of public opinion.[95]

In May the Commission's staff met, laid out an agenda, and established goals that would carry them into the twenty-first century. The rule of thumb was to expand the organization to expand the influence. If one keeps score, the Commission won the confrontation with the EEOC but lost the vote to deny Elders the surgeon general position.

When the Convention gathered in Orlando in 1994, Jim Henry, pastor of Orlando's First Baptist Church, was elected president of the Convention. In business sessions some motions were made criticizing the trustee action at Southwestern Seminary. None were accepted.[96]

When resolution time came, issues addressed were health care reform, the RU 486 French Abortion Pill, the relationship between Southern Baptists and Catholics due to the "Evangelicals and Catholics Together" document which needed clarification according to the messengers, the EEOC Guidelines on Religious Harassment, AIDS, and the True Love Waits campaign. All of these at one point or another reflected on the work of the Christian Life Commission.[97]

Tying Up Loose Ends

In the Executive Committee's report to the Convention, they presented a "Proposed Charter Amendment" for the Christian Life Commission. It was approved, and as a result the messy loose ends of past entities, the Public Affairs Committee and the Baptist Joint Committee on Public Affairs, were finally organizationally resolved.[98]

In Land's report to the Convention, he expressed his appreciation for their support, related the events and activities of the past year, and projected what the "journey ahead" would entail. For the record it should be so noted that the Executive Committee went on record approving the purchase of the Leland House and its repayment arrangements.[99]

In the days after the Orlando Convention, a major backlash developed against President Clinton and his policy agenda. Capitalizing on this, Congressman Newt Gingrich of Georgia helped formulate what was identified as the "Republican Contract with America" in which they "offered a detailed agenda for national renewal." Their goal was to bring the "end of government that is too big, too intrusive, and too easy with the public's money." It also aspired to be "the beginning of a Congress that respects the values and shares the faith of the American family."[100]

Because the legislative agenda was nationalized in the "Contract with America," Republicans seized both houses of Congress. From a moral perspective, much of Clinton's agenda and social engineering was brought into check with this historic election.

In July 1994, abortion doctor John Britton and a volunteer escort were gunned down as they arrived at the Pensacola (Florida) Ladies Center. Those who supported a woman's right to choose to end the life of her unborn child used the tragic incident to cast all those in the pro-life movement as being complicit in these murders, as well as earlier assaults on abortionists, their staffs, and property.

In response, Richard Land and the CLC organized a consultation meeting to draft a formal statement, entitled the "Nashville Statement of Conscience," which decried the violence directed at these individuals but affirmed "that acts of *nonviolent* civil disobedience related to abortion, though not morally *obligatory* for Christians, may be seen as morally *permissible*."

The statement, which was released September 18, 1994, asserted that "killing abortion doctors is not a moral option for Christians" and that such behavior "does not constitute a meaningful defense of unborn life." The document continued, "We believe that Christians are, nevertheless, morally obligated to oppose legalized abortion on demand."

Land was joined on the drafting committee for the statement by Mark Coppenger, then-vice president for convention affairs with the SBC's Executive Committee; David Gushee, who was an assistant professor of christian ethics at Southern Baptist Theological Seminary at the time; Daniel Heimbach, professor of ethics at Southeastern Baptist Theological Seminary; C. Ben Mitchell, who was then a consultant on biomedical and life issues for the Commission; and Albert Mohler, president of Southern Baptist Theology Seminary.

In the aftermath of the 1994 Orlando Southern Baptist Convention, which elected as vice presidents, Simon Tsoi and Gary Frost, an Asian American and an African American, respectively, Land found wise allies as he caucused and developed a strategy to accomplish a major goal he had embraced and envisioned in the area of race relations.

In the post-Orlando months Land particularly spent time with Gary Frost as the two together worked on shaping a resolution on racism and reconciliation for the 1995 Southern Baptist Convention in Atlanta. Speaking at the spring Commission seminar entitled, "The War of the Worlds: The Struggle for America's Soul," Frost provided this observation: "The paralyzing sin of pride manifested in racism has in many cases rendered the witness of the corporate church almost totally ineffective. Until this racism is biblically and publicly dealt with among believers, there is no hope of a sweeping revival of the magnitude that is necessary to save our cities." Frost went on to acknowledge that "some are arguing that corporate repentance is unbiblical. Yet I read in the Old Testament of three great leaders—Daniel, Ezra, and Nehemiah—who in their return from Babylonian captivity all offered prayers for repentance for national sins they had not committed."[101]

After caucusing with other seminar participants, Land and Frost together decided to host a consultation on the issue of race. The group consisted of fourteen invited pastors, half of whom were African American. They met in Nashville on May 22, 1995, for dialogue and prayer with the purpose of crafting a statement which all could support when introduced at the upcoming Atlanta meeting, which would mark the 150th anniversary of the Southern Baptist Convention. As a backdrop to the meeting, in recent weeks arsonists had attacked a number of black church facilities. The discussion was honest and pointed. Someone noted that debate over racism had been divisive and rancorous at the 1968 Convention and feared that a replay of the dynamics might be damaging to the Convention. Yet another responded it simply was not the same Convention it had been in those days. Discussion reached far into the night, but in the early hours of the next morning, a consensus was achieved and a resolution was penned.

All participants affirmed the completed document. Land believed that if embraced by the Convention, it had "the potential for healing old and hurtful wounds, and for laying a firm foundation for a bright future for multi racial fellowship, cooperation and ministry." Maston would have been proud.[102]

Of course, the Committee on Resolutions, this year chaired by Charles Carter of Birmingham, would have the final say on what would be presented to the Convention. Because of the importance of this particular resolution, they began their work on Saturday preceding the Convention so that it would be ready for release on Tuesday morning of the Convention.

When Land was able to join the committee on Saturday evening, he noticed that the phrase "particularly inhumane nature of American slavery" had been removed. One committee member argued against leaving it in the resolution, believing that it was "needlessly inflammatory." Land responded, "No, the phrase taken out is essential and informative." He explained, "If you don't put it in, people will say 'the Bible teaches the American kind of slavery.'" He continued, "What the Bible has is different from what America had before the Civil War." He then stated bluntly, "American slavery dehumanized people and reduced them to the level of property." As a result of Land's stand, the phrase was reinstated, and the resolution was presented as drafted in the May consultation.[103]

The anniversary meeting of Southern Baptists convened on June 22, 1995, in Atlanta. The backdrop of the Convention was Gingrich's election in January as Speaker of the House of Representatives, President Clinton's new inability to offer almost any policy initiatives, and most shockingly, the April 19 bombing of the Oklahoma City Federal Building where 168 innocent people were killed. On the international scene the conflict in Bosnia continued to degenerate as Serbs carried out a systematic plan of genocide and ethnic cleansing.[104]

Of particular importance to this Convention was the recommendation from the Executive Committee to adopt the proposed "Covenant for a New Century." This plan consolidated the number of agencies from nineteen to twelve. The Christian Life Commission underwent a name change to the Ethics & Religious Liberty Commission in keeping with its program assignment.[105]

The mission of the Ethics & Religious Liberty Commission would be that it "exists to assist the churches by helping them understand the moral demands of the gospel, apply Christian principles to moral and social problems and questions of public policy, and to promote religious liberty in cooperation with the churches and other Southern Baptist entities." In broad strokes it would embrace a fourfold ministry:

1. Assist churches in applying the moral and ethical teachings of the Bible to the Christian life.

2. Assist churches through the communication and advocacy of moral and ethical concerns in the public arena.

3. Assist churches in their moral witness in local communities.

4. Assist churches and other Southern Baptist entities by promoting religious liberty.

With respect to its relationships, "the Ethics & Religious Liberty Commission will work within the Southern Baptist Convention agency relationship guidelines approved by the Inter-Agency Council and the Executive Committee and printed in the Organizational Manual of the Southern Baptist Convention."[106]

The Executive Committee's recommendation was adopted by a 64 percent majority. If accepted at the next Convention in New Orleans, it was to be implemented the following year.[107]

On Tuesday afternoon of the Convention, Jim Henry was reelected president of the Convention by acclamation after being nominated by Johnny Hunt of Georgia. When the "time of business and resolutions" came, Charles Carter recommended the adoption of the "Resolution on Racial Reconciliation on the 150th Anniversary of the Southern Baptist Convention."[108]

After short discussion, the resolution was adopted by a near unanimous vote. The resolution states:

> WHEREAS, Since its founding in 1845, the Southern Baptist Convention has been an effective instrument of God in missions, evangelism, and social ministry; and
>
> WHEREAS, The Scriptures teach that Eve is the mother of all living (Genesis 3:20), and that God shows no partiality, but in every nation whoever fears him and works righteousness is accepted by him (Acts 10:34–35), and that God has made from one blood every nation of men to dwell on the face of the earth (Acts 17:26); and
>
> WHEREAS, Our relationship to African-Americans has been hindered from the beginning by the role that slavery played in the formation of the Southern Baptist Convention; and
>
> WHEREAS, Many of our Southern Baptist forbears defended the right to own slaves, and either participated in, supported, or acquiesced in the particularly inhumane nature of American slavery; and
>
> WHEREAS, In later years Southern Baptists failed, in many cases, to support, and in some cases opposed, legitimate initiatives to secure the civil rights of African-Americans; and
>
> WHEREAS, Racism has led to discrimination, oppression, injustice, and violence, both in the Civil War and throughout the history of our nation; and

WHEREAS, Racism has divided the body of Christ and Southern Baptists in particular, and separated us from our African-American brothers and sisters; and

WHEREAS, Many of our congregations have intentionally and/or unintentionally excluded African-Americans from worship, membership, and leadership; and

WHEREAS, Racism profoundly distorts our understanding of Christian morality, leading some Southern Baptists to believe that racial prejudice and discrimination are compatible with the Gospel; and

WHEREAS, Jesus performed the ministry of reconciliation to restore sinners to a right relationship with the Heavenly Father, and to establish right relations among all human beings, especially within the family of faith.

THEREFORE, be it RESOLVED, That we, the messengers to the Sesquicentennial meeting of the Southern Baptist Convention, assembled in Atlanta, Georgia, June 20-22, 1995, unwaveringly denounce racism, in all its forms, as deplorable sin; and

Be it further RESOLVED, That we affirm the Bible's teaching that every human life is sacred, and is of equal and immeasurable worth, made in God's image, regardless of race or ethnicity (Genesis 1:27), and that, with respect to salvation through Christ, there is neither Jew nor Greek, there is neither slave nor free, there is neither male nor female, for (we) are all one in Christ Jesus (Galatians 3:28); and

Be if further RESOLVED, That we lament and repudiate historic acts of evil such as slavery from which we continue to reap a bitter harvest, and we recognize that the racism which yet plagues our culture today is inextricably tied to the past; and

Be it further RESOLVED, that we apologize to all African-Americans for condoning and/or perpetuating individual and systemic racism in our lifetime; and we genuinely repent of racism of which we have been guilty, whether consciously (Psalm 19:13) or unconsciously (Leviticus 4:27); and

Be it further RESOLVED, That we ask forgiveness from our African-American brothers and sisters, acknowledging that our own healing is at stake; and

Be it further RESOLVED, That we hereby commit ourselves to eradicate racism in all its forms from Southern Baptist life and ministry; and

Be it further RESOLVED, That we commit ourselves to be doers of the Word (James 1:22) by pursuing racial reconciliation in all our relationships, especially with our brothers and sisters in Christ (1 John 2:6), to the end that our light would so shine before others, that they may see (our) good works and glorify (our) Father in heaven (Matthew 5:16); and

Be it finally RESOLVED, that we pledge our commitment to the Great Commission task of making disciples of all people (Matthew 28:19), confessing that in the church God is calling together one people from every tribe and nation (Revelation 5:9), and proclaiming that the Gospel of our Lord Jesus Christ is the only certain and sufficient ground upon which redeemed persons will stand together in restored family union as joint-heirs with Christ (Romans 8:17).[109]

After the resolution was adopted, Gary Frost "responded to the resolution and led the convention in a prayer of forgiveness and reconciliation."[110] Frost prayed:

Father, our nation is rotting from the core, in hatred and anger and bitterness and violence. Father, you've called the church to be the salt of the earth and the light of the world. . . . Father, we believe that applies to us, and you told us Father, "If my people who are called by my name will humble themselves and pray, and turn from their wicked ways, then shall I hear from heaven and forgive their sin and heal our land." Father, it is our prayer, our desire that you forgive us of white racism and

black racism. . . . Father, we believe that you're going to do a
great work, and we're asking that you'll bring . . . millions into
the body of Christ.[111]

Richard Land observed, "At every Convention, you'll notice scores
of black people busy working at lunch stands and counters along the
corridors. Usually they pay no attention to what's happening on the
Convention floor. This time, they stopped whatever they'd been doing,
moved over to the entranceways and stood stock still, watching and
listening with great attention."[112]

The passage of the resolution "On Racial Reconciliation" marked
one of the greatest victories in the history of the Christian Life Commission and a turning point for Southern Baptists.

Students of history left their Georgia meeting thinking of another
day, a Thursday in April 1845, when the divided board of the American Home Mission Society met, with Southerners splitting away
to start their own Convention. The reason was that the Northern
majority would not accept a Baptist slaveholder as a missionary. Over
the past 150 years, the Southern faction had grown to be the largest
Protestant denomination in the nation. Slavery was dead, but it had
taken the Convention, meeting in a corporate session, 150 long years
to apologize and ask for forgiveness for the evils practiced by many of
their white forefathers.

A new door had been opened, a door that Richard Land, Gary
Frost, Jim Henry, and other far-seeing Southern Baptists would enter
to lead Southern Baptists into a new day.

Looking back on the passage of the resolution, Land observed,
"The progress we have made on racial reconciliation and on including
African Americans in Southern Baptist life has advanced exponen-
tially from the point that we did that particular resolution in which
we apologized and which we took responsibility for the actions of
our forefathers and we apologized and asked for forgiveness of our
African American brothers and sisters." With great satisfaction Land
concluded, "It had a tremendous healing effect."[113]

Another resolution passed in Atlanta focused on the nomination for Henry Foster to be surgeon general. Because he was pro-abortion, he was unacceptable to Southern Baptists. Other resolutions addressed religious liberty, support of a constitutional amendment on prayer and religious expression, gene patenting, and dismay over the Oklahoma City bombing.[114]

Land's report recounted the year's victories and accomplishments and expressed great anticipation for the future. In his heart he left rejoicing over a resolution that corrected an age-old wrong. To the Convention Land said, "We have dealt with unfinished family business," and noted, "Southern Baptists black and white have given a witness to the reconciling work of the gospel of our Lord and Savior, Jesus Christ."[115]

As an exclamation mark to the historic Convention, at the meeting's close Land led a tour of historic civil rights sites in Georgia and Alabama, which included wreath-laying ceremonies at Dr. Martin Luther King's tomb in Atlanta, the Civil Rights Memorial in Montgomery, Alabama that honors the achievements and memories of those who lost their lives in the Civil Rights Movement, and the Sixteenth Street Baptist Church in Birmingham, where a bombing in September 1963 killed four little girls in the church building.

When the Commission board met in September, Land brought up the issues of pornography and obscenity, noting particularly the importance of opposing the growing availability of pornography on the Internet. He also expressed, again, his concerns about the sanctity of human life, which should be stressed from conception to natural death. He was concerned, moreover, with ensuring the distinction between human and all other life.[116]

Staff members presented their reports as well. Bill Merrell, who replaced Louis Moore, who had moved to work at the Foreign Mission Board, reviewed the new products available from the Commission. Ben Mitchell reviewed the biomedical issues that were being addressed. James Smith detailed what was happening in Washington, while Mike Whitehead recounted the status of some major cases before the Supreme Court. Sadly Lamar Cooper, who had served with Land for six and a half years, announced his resignation to assume a new position at Midwestern Baptist Theological Seminary along with Whitehead. Smith also left for another assignment. Also, Merrill accepted a new position with the SBC Executive Committee. As a result Land hired Will Dodson, an attorney and judge from Lubbock, Texas, to join the Commission staff and began his search for other competent replacements. [117]

One of the most shocking and serious issues emerging in the culture was the practice of partial-birth abortions. A baby would be delivered breech (feet first), and before the head emerged, it would be penetrated by a pair of scissors and its brain would be sucked out by a suction device. Planned Parenthood, NARAL, People for the American Way, NOW, and other groups insisted this procedure should be protected under *Roe v. Wade*. When Congress passed legislation outlawing the barbaric procedure, President Clinton vetoed it.[118]

The March 1996 Commission seminar addressed the issue of "Christians in the Public Square: Faith in Practice?" Land was the opening speaker and addressed the attendees with a message out of Jeremiah 6:15. In this address he held up a new book published by the Commission and written by theologian Carl F. H. Henry entitled *Has Democracy Had Its Day?* The volume's thesis, Land communicated, was that "Democracy as we know it cannot survive without a moral cleansing and renewal." He went on to observe about present-day America that "there is little evidence that faith has penetrated the public square of ideas and public policy." Land argued the "litmus test for public policy was whether or not it squared with Scripture."[119]

Other speakers included Charles Roesel, Gary Bauer, Jay Sekulow, Charles Fuller, O. S. Hawkins, David Gushee, Dee Jepsen, E. W. McCall, and Gary Frost. Three congressmen—Tony Hall, Charles Stenholm, and Chris Smith—were also on the lineup. In conjunction with the seminar, Land announced the addition of Dwayne Hastings to his staff. Land pointed out that "Dwayne won the Distinguished Service Award in Christian Ethics when he graduated from

Southeastern." Upon meeting Hastings, Land noted "the Lord led me to add him on to our staff."[120]

Two months after the spring seminar, two pawns in the infamous *Roe v. Wade* and companion decision *Doe v. Bolton* returned to challenge the pro-abortion culture of death. Norma McCorvey, who was Jane Roe, and Sandra Cano, who was Mary Doe, were both, then, pro-life advocates. Both had become Christians since their notorious court case. Their testimonies certainly strengthened the pro-life position in the public arena. Of interest was the fact that both women could not go through with their abortions, carried their children to term, and gave them up for adoption.[121]

In the meantime Land was working with Congressman Chris Smith and Nina Shea, director of Freedom House, to address issues of Christian persecution, especially in China, which was then—and now—notorious for its human rights abuse. Although pushed by a coalition of evangelicals to address this issue forthrightly, President Clinton in effect did very little.[122]

The Southern Baptist Convention gathered in New Orleans in 1996. Tom Elliff, nominated by Fred Wolfe, was elected president-elect with no opposition. The "Covenant for a New Century" was adopted by the Convention and would therefore go into effect at the conclusion of the 1997 Convention in Dallas. The challenge now was with the Implementation Task Force, chaired by Bob Reccord, as it attempted to facilitate a smooth transition.[123]

Tuesday afternoon Land presented his Christian Life Commission report. As usual Land reviewed the past year's activities. He commented on how a federal court of appeals had just struck down a law forbidding assisted suicide. He concluded that we as a nation must decide if we are going to embrace a culture of death or life. He also announced the Commission was giving its Religious Freedom Award to theologian Carl F. H. Henry. Finally, he again addressed the importance of appropriately funding the Commission. As his predecessors had often said and as had been the case all too often, the Commission was still underfunded when the stakes were so incredibly high.[124]

On Wednesday morning the Committee on Resolutions presented its recommendations. Several were supportive of the Commission's work. In response to the malicious arson attacks on a number of black church buildings, a resolution was adopted, "On the Arson of African-American Churches." Messengers also stopped to collect an offering for those congregations, which totaled more than $281,000. A resolution was passed "On Disney Company Policy," which was a harbinger of a future call for economic action against The Disney Company for its anti-family, pro-homosexual agendas.

Another resolution addressed the president's veto of the bill banning partial-birth abortion as a "shameful decision" and encouraged Congress and the President to reverse their decision. Convention President Henry had sent a letter on June 7 to President Clinton asking him "to repent of your veto." Ten former Convention presidents signed the letter; however, Jimmy Allen, Carl Bates, and Wayne Dehoney declined. Still another resolution addressed the issues related to the persecution of Christians overseas. The longest resolution, "On Homosexual Marriage," spanned four pages in the Convention Annual. Still other resolutions addressed issues of assisted suicide, gambling, parental choice in education, and support of hunger and relief ministries.[125]

The national scene dominated the time frame after the New Orleans Convention. On July 27, an explosion killed two people in a park near the site of the Atlanta Summer Olympics. In August the Congress passed sweeping welfare reforms. In November, Bill Clinton was reelected president over Kansas Senator Bob Dole and business tycoon Ross Perot with 49 percent of the popular vote. In December, President Clinton nominated Madeleine Albright as the first female secretary of state. In January, Gingrich was reelected Speaker of the House of Representatives.

At the September Commission board meeting, Land introduced new staff member Barrett Duke, a theologian and public policy specialist, and Steven Nelson, who would primarily work on hunger concerns. Both were elected by the board with a unanimous acceptance. According to Land, Duke brought an intense concern for the culture with him when he came to the ERLC in 1997. His years growing up as a teenager without Christ in New Orleans, Louisiana, during the 1960s and 1970s and more than a dozen years as founding pastor of the Cornerstone Baptist Church in the largely secular Denver, Colorado, metroplex gave him an acute understanding of the important role the ERLC needed to play in the culture war. His writing added theological and scholarly weight to the ERLC's efforts to engage the minds and hearts of Southern Baptists. Nelson's position was a joint venture with the Foreign Mission Board and the Home Mission Board. These two entities supplied $60,000 to support his position. Considering the fact that he assisted Southern Baptists to raise multiple millions of dollars each year for world hunger, the investment in this position was one of the wisest decisions with respect to stewardship. When the International Mission Board decided to withdraw Nelson's funding, Nelson was forced to pick up other program assignments at the Commission. Eventually, Nelson took a leave of absence to run for political office. Land commended Nelson for the outstanding results he achieved while at the Commission.[126]

Another major piece of legislation which had now passed the Congress was the Defense of Marriage Act. Instead of vetoing the bill, President Clinton signed it into law to the surprise and applause of Southern Baptists. And he did it in spite of the intense homosexual lobby. But, of course, he was facing reelection in November, and that may have swayed his decision.

In spite of all the Commission could do, it was still hampered by a lack of funds. The allocation from the Cooperative Program at that time was just shy of 1 percent. In order to communicate the need, Land held a press conference in January 1997 requesting the Executive Committee to increase their funding. Chapman commented that this was unusual, and yet it was only natural for Land and his trustees to make their requests known.

The March 3–5 Commission seminar held that year in Louisville, Kentucky, was cast as the fiftieth anniversary seminar in Baptist Press and featured a stellar lineup of outstanding speakers.[127]

When the Convention met in Dallas, June 17–19, an air of expectancy was present due to the adoption of the "Covenant for a New

Century" and its implementation. In keeping with the changes, the Commission would have authorized an amended and restated charter as well as an official name change. It should be noted that its Cooperative Program budget allocation increased over the previous year from $1,437,455 to $2,207,958. With the increased funding, Land was finally able to establish an Executive Leadership Team that would be instrumental in helping him map out a vision for strategic growth and would influence the direction that God would use for decades to come. Yet even with the increased support, financial limitations restricted the full potential impact of the Commission.[128]

In Land's final Christian Life Commission report, he reviewed the past year's work. Of interest is the fact that they developed a Web site, www.erlc.com. He responded to matters referred to them by the Convention and then projected on the journey ahead, stating that he, his trustees, and his staff "look forward with excitement and anticipation to becoming the Ethics & Religious Liberty Commission (ERLC) on June 19, 1997, as part of the implementation of the Convention's Covenant for a New Century." Yet the highlight of the Convention for Land and the new Ethics & Religious Liberty Commission was the honor given Land to deliver the Convention address. This message would set the tone and direction for the years to come.[129]

This year's resolutions addressed issues close to the Commission's concerns. They included resolutions on religious persecution, moral stewardship and the Disney Company, world hunger, displaying the Ten Commandments in public buildings, genetic technology and cloning, issues related to "domestic partners," home-schooling, drug abuse, and gambling. Each of these involved a moral or religious liberty concern being addressed by the Commission.[130]

The resolution on moral stewardship targeted "entertainment providers including, but not limited to, The Disney Company, [that] are increasingly promoting immoral ideologies such as homosexuality, infidelity, and adultery, which are biblically reprehensible and abhorrent to God and His plan for the world that He loves." In approving the resolution messengers encouraged "Southern Baptists to refrain from patronizing any company that promotes immoral ideologies and practices."

Concerning the call for families to consider a boycott of Disney's products and places, the amazing facts to the story were that Land not only supported the boycott but defended it with full force because that is what the Convention voted to do. Reflecting on his role, Land said:

> The larger story is that the leadership of the Convention
> including myself were ambivalent about the prospect of the
> Disney boycott. We saw all kinds of problems about getting
> the message out. In terms of how do you measure it. I argued
> strenuously for a limited boycott—limited in terms of the target
> and limited in terms of time. I argued that we should do a "tar-
> geted" boycott of two years on Disney stores. That is where we
> could have the most measurable impact. If the sales dropped off
> at the Disney retail stores, we could claim credit for that and
> probably that was the most exposure Southern Baptists had to
> Disney in localities. It was not the theme parks. I argued for the
> Disney stores and possibly the theme parks and for only two
> years. But that was also the year I preached the Convention
> sermon. While I was getting ready to go over to the Convention
> to preach the Convention sermon, a young woman got up and
> made the impassioned appeal; and the Convention voted to do
> the boycott. Well, at that point in time, whatever my reserva-
> tions were, whatever my concerns were, they were irrelevant.
> The Convention had spoken. And they had made us the point
> people. I had a choice. I could either be very self-serving and
> get up and say, "Well, I argued for a limited boycott, a targeted
> boycott, limited in time duration; but since the Convention has
> spoken, I'll go through the motions." Or, I could say, "I work
> for the SBC, and the SBC has overwhelmingly expressed this
> opinion, and we're going to do our very best to do what South-
> ern Baptists have called us to do which is what I did, and which
> is what I think a denominational servant should do unless he in

conscience could not. My objections were not objections of con-science; mine were pragmatic. It is important for the Convention to know that. The fact that I had pragmatic reservations and that I had proposed a targeted and a time-limited boycott would be news to a lot of Southern Baptists."[131]

The following year and in concert with Broadman & Holman, Land released *Send a Message to Mickey*. The book addressed the concerns many Americans had with Disney's corporate practices and entertainment offerings.

When the Convention came to an end, so did the old Christian Life Commission. The next day it became the Ethics & Religious Liberty Commission with the same staff, an expanded budget, and a renewed vision still led by people who saw its work not just as a job but as a matter of conviction.[132]

Notes

1. Dan Martin, "CLC Search Narrows Exec. Field to Three Candidates," *Indiana Baptist*, August 24, 1988, 8.

2. Richard Land vita, Ethics and Religious Liberty Comission.

3. Minutes of the September 1988 board meeting of the Christian Life Commission. Land, commenting on the search process, shares the following observations:

It's important to note that when I went into the interviews, I was aware that there were two other men being interviewed, and my impression was that they both started out in a higher post position than I. This was subsequently confirmed to me, that I was seen as just "too controversial" even by this search committee. What will happen if we bring in a movement conservative? Larry Lewis was sympathetic to the conservative resurgence, but he wasn't part of it. There was no denying that I was an integral part of the conservative resurgence having worked in the bowels of the headquarters of the conservative resurgence. So I was the first person openly identified with and integral to the conservative resurgence to be elected as an agency head. Even these conservatives were worried about the possible backlash of this.

Three weeks prior to the interview, George W. Bush came to my office. He was the liaison to evangelicals for his father's campaign. He came to the office to try to enlist me to support his dad and to help with the campaign and if his father were elected to consider going to Washington with the new administration. I told him that I was being interviewed in three weeks by the search committee of the CLC and I didn't think they would pick me. But if they did, I would have to take that as a sign of divine providence and that if they did I would accept that position; but if they didn't, I would call him back. I was going to support his dad. Whether I would work in the campaign or whether I would consider going to work in the new administration would depend on what happened.

I went into the interviews and later found that I was correct in my perception that I started out. . . . The other two guys both thought they had the job. One guy had put his house up for sale before he came to the meeting. In the interview process God worked. It was clear to me when I left the interview that they were far more favorable to me than they had been when I went in. They ended up voting unanimously to recommend me to the full board. It didn't start out that way. I took it as a sign from the Lord that He wanted me to do that.

The qualifications set by the search committee were above those expected of most Southern Baptists in qualifying for an office. This was especially true in finding true conservatives. The process finally came down to three men. Each was brought before the board to make their presentation for the position and answer questions from the full board. As a result, the trustees by secret ballot (twenty-three to two) overwhelmingly affirmed my election. It should be noted that through this whole process, the committee was pressured by moderates to elect a moderate. The reason being this agency had been one of their strongest voices in the denomination. In the view of many, this was the first entity that the resurgence was able to change.

When I was presented to the board as the elected president, the chairman of the Commission voiced to the trustees that this board was standing on a mountain in the history of this denomination which will mark a new turn back to biblical morals and ethics.

My critics were especially hostile to my leadership over the fact of my association with Criswell College and Paige Patterson. Land Interview, May 7–8, 2007.

4. Ibid.

5. Ibid.

6. Ibid.

7. Ibid. According to Land, a second vote on his leadership was taken early in his tenure. The board, it seemed, was in a turf war around Land's leadership and the philosophy of board involvement. Some trustees wanted to micromanage the activities of the Commission. A decisive vote on board leadership was taken, and Land was reaffirmed as the leader of the agency. From that point forward, Land was able to carry out his task assignment with the necessary freedom. Land interview, May 7–8, 2007.

8. Ken Camp, "Texas CLC Rejects Views," *Baptist Standard*, September 28, 1988, 4.

9. Personal interview with Richard Land, January 2, 2007 and May 7–8, 2007.

10. Ibid.

11. Ibid.

12. Ibid.

13. Ibid.

14. Ibid.

15. Greg Ward, *The Timeless History of the USA* (New York: Barnes and Noble Books, 2003), 338–39.

16. 1989 *SBC Annual*, 42.

17. Ibid., 67.

18. Ibid., 68–69.

19. Ibid., 68–73.

20. Ibid., 74.

21. Ibid.

22. Ibid., 182–83.

23. Ibid., 205–6.

24. Ibid., 215–17.

25. Ibid.

26. Ibid., 56–57.

27. Ward, *The Timeless History of the USA*, 340.

28. "Executive Committee Changes Direction of Religious Liberty," *Word and Way*, September 28, 1989, 7.

29. Ward, *The Timeless History of the USA*, 340–41.

30. 1990 *SBC Annual*, 61–62.

31. Ibid., 47–55. Land provides additional insight into the behind-the-scenes dynamic at play between the Christian Life Commission and the Public Affairs Committee:

When the Convention voted to subsume the PAC into CLC, part of that solution was the PAC members became a part of our board as temporary board members until their current terms of service were up, which means that Norris Sydnor became one of CLC trustees for a short but painful period of time. He basically accused me of undermining the PAC. He said I was the person who thwarted the PAC. These people did become members of our board, and they were trustees of our board until their terms of service ended, and they were not replaced. (The board temporarily expanded to include Albert Lee Smith. His widow is on the present board.) There was a difference of opinion. Some of the members of PAC wanted a Religious Liberty Commission (RLC). Jerry Vines was president of SBC, and I think Jerry was the one who said we couldn't afford it. Why are we going to create a new commission when we can merge this into the ERLC which already exists and which already has a Washington office? Prior to 1987, we were in a bind in that we were supposed to talk about citizenship and being involved as Christian citizens, but we were forbidden from talking about religious liberty issues because of the Baptist Joint Committee. The SBC gave permission to talk about the issue of religious liberty in 1987–88–89 and the full-fledged assignment was given in 1990–91. Where was the demarcation between the proposed RLC and the CLC?

Before I became the head of the CLC, when I was a member of the PAC, as an elected commissioner, I argued for a merger of the two program assignments. In other words, taking the program assignment and putting it into the CLC program statement. Before I ever had a personal interest, I said it was a far better exercise of stewardship, but there was some ill feeling among some of the PAC members because they wanted a Religious Liberty Commission. It was a philosophical and pragmatic disagreement. As far as I am concerned, it was mostly amicable. Land Interview, May 7–8, 2007.

32. Ibid., 81–86, and the manuscript of the Executive Committee recommendation by Bill Harrell of Georgia.

33. Ibid.

34. Ibid., 84.

35. Ibid.

36. Ibid., 63–65, 68.

37. Ibid., 216–19, 240–43, 251–54.

38. Jerry Sutton, *The Baptist Reformation* (Nashville: Broadman & Holman Publishers, 2000), 316–17.

39. Tom Strode, "Land Joins Evangelical Leaders for Meeting with Bush," CLC News, November 2, 1990.

40. Ward, *The Timeless History of the USA*, 339–40.

41. Ibid.

42. Carey Kinsolving, "Bush Aide Linked White House, Evangelicals," *Baptist Press*, November 5, 1992.

43. 1991 *SBC Annual*, 232.

44. Richard Land, "Keynote Address," 1990 Concerned Women for America Convention.

45. 1991 *SBC Annual*, 95.

46. Ibid., 33, 39.

47. Ibid., 230–32.

48. 1991 SBC Resolution on Government Sponsorship of Obscene and Offensive Art.

49. 1991 *SBC Annual*, 73–84.

50. Ibid., 254–56.

51. Ibid., 263–66.

52. Ibid., 42.

53. Radio and Television Commission tape of the 1991 Convention proceedings.

54. Darrell Turner, "S. Baptist Moderates Organize New Ethics Agency," *Religion News Service*, July 29, 1991.

55. Herb Hollinger and Louis Moore, "CLC Trustees Seek Funds Held by SBC Foundation," *Baptist Press*, September 12, 1991. See 1964 *SBC Annual*, 55–56; 257 and 1968 *SBC Annual*, 120.

56. Randy Frome, "New Cases Test Limits of Religions Freedom," *Christianity Today*, October 7, 1996, 82.

57. Lee v. Weisman in wikipedia.org; Peter Irons, *A People's History of the Supreme Court* (New York: Penguin Books, 1999), 412–13.

58. Lemon v. Kurtzman in wikipedia.org.

59. Matthew Staver, *Faith and Freedom*, 2nd ed. (Orlando: Liberty Council, 1998), 83–85.

60. Tom Strode, "Supreme Court Hears Argument in Lee v. Weisman Case," CLC News, November 7, 1991. Richard Land provides some insight into the behind-the-scenes dynamics with these observations:

In the *Lee v. Wiseman* decision on school prayer, Justice Kennedy wrote the majority opinion which rejected the constitutionality of such prayers. Scalia wrote the dissenting opinion. This is one of those cases where we filed a friend of the court brief on one side and the BJC filed on the other side. We lost. The BJC had five justices on their side, and we had four.

There were two decisions that so classically show the difference between where the Joint Committee was going and where we were going. The first was the *Lee v. Wiseman* decision where we filed on one side and they filed on the other. They had five justices on their side and we had four. The other decision was the Rosenberger decision. The Rosenberger decision came out in the 1990s as well.

Concerning the Rosenberger decision: The University of Virginia (UVA) decided they wanted to foster free speech on campus. And they were going to give contributions in kind to student newspapers, and then they rejected an Evangelical newspaper. They gave contributions in kind to Jewish and Muslim papers but rejected the Evangelical newspaper edited by a guy named Rosenberger because it was religious. The Jewish and Muslim ones were cultural but this was religious. Rosenberger filed against the university saying they were discriminating against him and against Christianity. Rosenberger's argument and our argument was this: Nobody says UVA has to give these contributions in kind to student newspapers; but if they choose to do so, they can't then say the only ones they won't give it to are religious newspapers. We won five to four. We filed a brief on one side, the winning side, and the BJC filed on the other side. That's a key illustration in the whole accommodation issue—that the government is accommodating. You can't just say the government is going to give this assistance, but it can't go to religious groups. That's just discrimination against religion, and it's part of the definition of the strict separationists' position. Land Interview, May 7–8, 2007.

61. Ibid.

62. *Lee v. Weisman.*

63. Ibid.

64. Tom Strode, "CLC Asks Congress to Support Pro-Life Rules," CLC News, July 19, 1991.

65. Ward, *The Timeline History of the USA*, 343.

66. 1992 *SBC Annual*, 40, 42, 148.

67. Ibid., 47–52, 155–59.

68. Ibid., 80.

69. Ibid., 279–82.

70. Ibid., 86–95.

71. Tom Strode, "Clinton's Criticism of Veto Strikes at Own Denomination," CLC News, June 29, 1992.

72. Tom Strode, "Court Reaffirms Roe, Stings Pro-Life Movement," CLC News, July 6, 1992.

73. Ward, *The Timeline History of the USA*, 343.

74. Ibid., 343–44; "Richard Land Comments" [The Day after the 1992 Presidential Election], CLC News, November 4, 1992.

75. Open Letter from Richard Land to Bill Clinton, November 12, 1992.

76. Letter from Land to Clinton, December 2, 1992.

77. Ward, *The Timeline History of the USA*, 344.

78. "Southern Baptist Official Decries Clinton's Pro-Abortion Acts," CLC News, January 22, 1993.

79. Ward, *The Timeline History of the USA*, 344–45.

80. CLC News, March 11, 1993.

81. Tom Strode, "Pro-Lifers Decry Clinton's Plan to Repeal Hyde Amendment," CLC News, March 31, 1993; James A. Smith, "Dr. Abu Hayat and FOCA: Reality Over Myth," *CLC Ethics Commentary*, April 7, 1993.

82. Jon Walker, "Former Abortion Provider Details Her New Lifestyle," CLC News, March 1, 1993; Linda Lawson, "Human Genome Project Offers Breakthroughs, Ethical Concerns," CLC News, March 2, 1993.

83. "Pro-Abortion Senators Propose Bill to Invalidate Limits on Abortion," NRLC, February 4, 2004.

84. Richard Land, "Oval Office Meeting, March Push Homosexual Movement into Limelight," *SALT*, vol. 3, no. 3, 1993.

85. 1993 *SBC Annual*, 95–96.

86. Ibid., 96–103.

87. Ibid., 277–80.

88. Ward, *The Timeline History of the USA*, 345.

89. Ibid., 346.

90. Land Interview, May 7–8, 2007.

91. Tom Strode, "CLC Sets Health Care Consultation, Slams Abortion in Clinton Plan," CLC News, October 14, 1993; Ferrell Foster, "Land Lists Key Issues Facing Americans in 1994," *Baptist Press*, December 15, 1993.

92. The author was in attendance at the 1994 National Prayer Breakfast as the guest of Tennessee Congressman Bob Clement.

93. Richard Land, "An Open Letter to Evangelical Leaders Visiting the White House," 1994.

94. Sutton, *The Baptist Reformation*, 363–80.

95. Tom Strode, "EEOC Guidelines May Stifle Christian Witness, Some Warn," CLC News, February 11, 1994.

96. Sutton, *The Baptist Reformation*, 224–32.

97. 1994 *SBC Annual*, 100–12. Early in 1995, both Lewis and Land requested to have their names withdrawn from the document. Both concluded that the misunderstanding was not worth the benefits.

98. 1994 *SBC Annual*, 40–42, 155–58.

99. Ibid., 304–7, 129.

100. The Republican Contract with America, 1994.

101. Proceedings of the 1995 Christian Life Commission Seminar; Dwayne Hastings, "Racism Renders Church Ineffective in Struggle for Cities," CLC News, March 1, 1995.

102. Bill Merrill, "Consultation Yields Historic Document," CLC News, May 25, 1995.

103. From personal notes of Jim Hefley, January 1997.

104. Ward, *The Timeline History of the USA*, 348–50.

105. 1995 *SBC Annual*, 151–76.

106. Ibid., 170–71.

107. Ibid., 47.

108. Ibid., 64, 79.

109. Ibid., 80–81.

110. Ibid., 79.

111. Radio and Television Commission tape of the 1995 SBC Convention proceedings.

112. Personal notes of Jim Hefley, June 1995.

113. Personal interview with Richard Land, January 2, 2007.

114. 1995 *SBC Annual*, 80–97.

115. Ibid., 300–3.

116. Minutes of the CLC September board meeting, September 12–13, 1995.

117. Ibid.

118. "Brutal Abortion Procedure Protected Under FOCA," *Light*, September–October, 1995, 15.

119. Dwayne Hastings, "Land: Growth of Evangelicals Fails to Stem Moral Decline," CLC News, March 4, 1996.

120. Dwayne Hastings, "Congressman Takes Aim at Failed Policy on Religious Persecution," CLC News, March 5, 1996; Land Interview, May 7–8, 2007.

121. *Christianity Today*, September 11, 1995, 70; *Christianity Today*, June 17, 1996, 62.

122. Tom Strode, "White House Plan on Persecution Inadequate, Evangelicals Say," CLC News, June 4, 1996.

123. 1996 *SBC Annual*, 36–50.

124. Ibid., 298–301.

125. Ibid., 83–99.

126. Ibid., See also Letter from Rankin to Land, October 14, 2003.

127. Tom Strode, "Christians Need to Change First to Revive U.S., CLC Speakers Say," *Baptist Press*, March 7, 1997.

128. 1997 *SBC Annual*, 74, 130.

129. Ibid., 262–65. See Land's convention address in the appendix.

130. Ibid., 89–100.

131. Land Interview, May 7–8, 2007.

132. Ibid., 265.

CHAPTER

9

The Latest Years: Richard Land and the Ethics & Religious Liberty Commission (1997–2006)

With the Christian Life Commission having its name changed to the Ethics & Religious Liberty Commission (ERLC), and the Southern Baptist Convention transitioning through a major reorganization plan, Richard Land brought the agency responsible for moral concerns and First Amendment issues into its most fruitful and prominent days. Land and his supporters were convinced that the Commission's greatest influence lay ahead. With the Convention's reorganization came increased funding for the Commission. In Land's words,

We got the rocket fuel and the rocket took off. There was this huge explosion of growth—the radio ministry, more vice presidents, and the addition of our Research Institute. The impact of all that was made possible by the funding increase. The Convention gave us rocket fuel and we tried to fire off rockets with it.[1]

When the name and identity was changed, Land's team included Mattie Lee Massey, Dwayne Hastings, Ben Mitchell, William Dodson, Tom Strode, Barrett Duke, and Steve Nelson. This core leadership team worked with Land to make every effort possible and conceivable to influence the culture in a direction of public righteousness.[2] What was astounding about this comparatively small agency was the amount of work that it produced and the impact it made with such a relatively small team. On a consistent basis, Land and his team monitored the public policy movements both within the nation and worldwide, provided commentary and direction, wrote numerous articles, interacted with decision-makers, conducted conferences and seminars, and provided clear leadership for Southern Baptists.

Immediately following the 1997 Convention, three important decisions came out of the Supreme Court in Washington, D.C. On June 20, the government settled its lawsuit with the U.S. tobacco companies. For a settlement of $385.5 billion, they were granted immunity from further legal action. This settlement, to be paid out over twenty-five years, would be used to settle claims by smokers and state health authorities who had made claims for compensation due to tobacco-related illnesses and the related expenses.[3]

On June 25, the Supreme Court struck down part of the Religious Freedom Restoration Act. This legislation, which originally attempted to reinstate the "Sherbert Test," mandated that "strict scrutiny be used when determining if the Free Exercise Clause of the First Amendment . . . guaranteeing religious freedom had been violated." It required the government first establish if a sincere religious belief was present, and then whether government action created a "substantial burden on the person's ability to act on that belief." If those two elements were

present, then "the government must prove that it is acting in furtherance of a compelling state interest and that it has pursued that interest in the manner least restrictive." This law was overturned because
the Supreme Court concluded Congress had overstepped its power of
enforcement.[4]

Land believed the Court's decision was wrong and called it, "the
worst religious liberty decision of the last 50 years." Land saw clearly
that the law's overturning meant that government intrusion into the
citizens' free exercise of religion had lost its safeguards.[5]

The next day, the Supreme Court ruled again, this time in its
Washington v. Glucksberg decision that "a right to assistance in com-
mitting suicide was not protected by the Due Process Clause." Land
commented on the court's decision by providing some historical context. Citing a recent article from the *Journal of the American Medical
Association* on the Dutch experience, Land recounted what had been
the slippery slope of euthanasia, "from allowing doctors to assist with
suicide, to pressuring doctors to assist with suicide, to then allowing
doctors to kill patients without their permission." Land concluded,
"We must do all we can to assure that there is never a first time in the
United States."[6]

Besides commenting on cases and filing *amicus curiae* briefs in
the Supreme Court, Land also kept his hand on the pulse of what was
happening in the executive branch. He commented favorably on the
"Guidelines on Religious Exercise in the Federal Workplace." According to *Baptist Press,* "The 15-page directive requires all non-military,
federal agencies and their officials to allow to the 'greatest extent
possible' personal religious exercise, to not discriminate on the basis
of religion and to 'reasonably accommodate' religious practices by
employers." Here, Land believed, Clinton did something right.[7]

Land also had every intention of influencing as much as possible
the House and Senate. In fact, on August 28, 1997, he sent a two-page
memorandum to members of the Congress with suggestions for items
to be placed on their "legislative agenda." His list included a plea for
them to address issues related to the sanctity of human life, religious
liberty, and empowering families. He encouraged them to incorporate

his suggestions as part of their "immediate legislative priorities." Of particular concern for Land was the House's consideration of the Religious Freedom Amendment. Congressman Ernest Istook originally introduced the proposed amendment just prior to the 1997 Convention, on May 8. The first draft raised red flags for Land because it appeared to provide government endorsement of religion. During the Convention, Land helped write the resolution, "On the Display of the Ten Commandments in Government Buildings," which among other things addressed Istook's proposed constitutional amendment. Through the influence of this resolution and ongoing communication with Representative Istook, Land was able to have Istook's proposal altered to include "according to the dictates of their conscience," so that it became clear that it was not advocating government-sponsored acknowledgment, but rather advocating the government protecting citizens' right to their acknowledgment, which was Land's accommodation position. It would be the following June before a House vote, 224 to 203, fell short of the necessary two-thirds vote. Land promised to make this a future campaign issue.[8]

Land's interests, however, were not restricted simply to domestic issues. Testifying before the House of Representatives International Relations Committee, he joined others endorsing the "Freedom From Religious Persecution Act." The bill's effect would be to create a White House office to monitor religious persecution and recommend appropriate steps which might be taken by the administration. The bill was sponsored by Frank Wolf from Virginia in the House and Arlen Specter of Pennsylvania in the Senate. After much maneuvering, it was eventually passed and signed into law by President Clinton on October 27, 1998.[9]

With its new name and increased budget, the Ethics & Religious Liberty Commission made several major advances in its September trustee meeting. First, it added King Sanders and Harold Harper to its staff. Sanders, a trustee of the ERLC, was already heavily engaged in public policy issues in New Mexico. Harper had worked with mega-church pastors and was deeply committed to strengthening families. Trustees also approved and announced plans to launch a national radio program, *For Faith and Family*. This daily 30-minute show would feature Land, Harper, and others as it addressed pressing issues of the day. Commenting on this strategic step forward, Land said, "For years Southern Baptists have been asking when we were going to have a radio program to deal with the moral issues we face as a nation." He then related, "We are all excited that we will soon have such a program because of the generosity of Southern Baptists in investing a significant increase in financial resources in the ministry of the ERLC." One other long-overdue decision was to award posthumously the Distinguished Service Award to A. J. Barton, who for many years carried the agency on his shoulders.[10]

Launching a broadcast element of the ministry changed the ability of the Commission to impact the culture by providing Land a daily mass media voice. Finally, Land had a platform to address real-time issues. What was most gratifying was the manner in which the work of three separate entities converged to make it a reality. First, the ERLC's trustees committed to make the radio media become the Commission's top priority. Second, LifeWay Christian Resources agreed to be a financial partner by providing $100,000 a year for three years as startup capital. And finally, the Executive Committee gave its blessing and then provided space and built the radio studio at a cost of approximately $50,000 in the Convention's Executive Building. The launching of the radio ministry demonstrated a significant level of interagency cooperation which signaled a new day for Southern Baptists.[11]

A week after the fall trustee meeting, Land joined forty-six signers as they endorsed a document entitled, "We Hold These Truths: A Statement of Christian Conscience and Citizenship." According to the document, numerous judicial decisions had increasingly taken the "people's ability to govern themselves" away. It states, "The great threat to the American experiment today is not from enemies abroad but from disordered liberty." It elaborates, "That disorder is increasingly expressed in a denial of the very concept of moral truth." It further opines, "Increasingly, law and public policy will be pitted against the social and moral conviction of the people, with the result that millions of Americans will be alienated from a government that they no longer recognize as their own." It concludes, "We cannot, we must not, let this happen." In short, this collection of conservative academicians was extremely concerned about the runaway courts usurping the power of the legislatures and legislating *de facto* from the bench.[12]

In line with Gore's advocacy, Michael Eisner, Disney's CEO, called his critics "nuts," orchestrated a gloss job about Disney on *60 Minutes*, and denied, with a mountain of evidence to the contrary, that Disney had embraced a pro-homosexual agenda. Each time, Land called his hand.[14]

In January of 1998, Eisner was still defending Disney's pro-homosexual agenda and immoral movies, and the majority of Southern Baptists were lamenting the sad state of affairs that ever allowed the passage of *Roe v. Wade*. Concerning the upcoming twenty-fifth anniversary of the landmark decision, Land stated that it was "one of the saddest and most tragic anniversaries in the history of the American nation."[15]

Between the full court press to normalize homosexuality and the reminder that abortion on demand was essentially forced on the American people, it was not surprising that the Commission opted to theme its 1998 spring seminar, "The Family and Human Sexuality: Reaffirming God's Design." Commenting on the subject matter, Land observed, "The number one battle line now, and for the next decade, for the soul and conscience of America is the struggle over sexuality." Land went on to say, "The issues are clear and compelling," explaining, "We must either reassert Judeo-Christian sexual values or be submerged in a polluted sea of pagan sexuality." Concerning the present cultural mores, Land argued America had "lost its moral compass" and was "wandering aimlessly in dangerous, uncharted territory."[16]

The highlight of February came on the sixteenth when the Commission's daily radio show, *For Faith and Family,* was launched and changed the work of the Commission in a major way. Harper was more than cohost of the program; his work beyond the scenes made the program a quick success. Land expressed his vision for the program, relating, "We hope and pray that *For Faith and Family* will help listeners develop a Christian worldview which will enable them to fully understand and address the critical social, moral and public policy issues facing our nation." At last the Commission had a daily media outlet that permitted Land to address real-time issues in a real-time venue.[17]

In March the spring seminar went flawlessly and major issues were addressed with competence and conviction. Speakers included, besides Land, Ed Young Sr., Joe McIlhaney, Linda Keener, Wade Horn, Michael and Harriet McManus, Hal Lane, David Beasley, Paul House, Barrett Duke, Dorothy Patterson, Michael Johnston, and Rick Stanley. Probably the most poignant statement was made by Duke when he said, "I understand that we must love the sinner and give him time to repent, but I also know that while we are being patient the very attitudes and lifestyles that these people are promoting are stealing our children, and it must stop."[18]

During the remainder of March, Land was extremely busy speaking in a number of different venues on a variety of moral issues. In less than three weeks, he delivered major addresses on medical ethics, pornography, racism, and world hunger.[19]

As April and May rolled around, Eisner was still criticizing the Southern Baptist boycott, calling his critics a "splinter group" of Southern Baptists with "Nazi leanings." The following month, leaders in the homosexual community announced plans for a nationwide "buycott" to support Disney. Commenting in a radio conversation with Don Wildmon of the American Family Association, who was also a prime mover in the Disney boycott, Land said that the homosexual community understood what was at stake in the boycott. He contended, they

> Understand the emotive power of Disney. They understand
> the value of wrapping themselves in the images of Mickey
> Mouse and Donald Duck and they understand what a boycott
> means.[20]

Dwayne Hastings, editor of the ERLC's *Light* magazine, wrote: "When messengers to last year's SBC annual meeting approved the resolution calling for punitive economic action against Disney and other companies that 'promote immoral ideologies,' homosexual advocacy groups responded by buying Disney-themed toys and donating them to hospitals and other children's organizations." No doubt, this was a war of ideas and wills.[21]

Leaders of the Religious Right, in the meantime, were growing impatient with what they perceived as a lack of moral leadership in the Republican Party. In February, James Dobson threatened to withdraw his support because the party was ignoring the pro-life and pro-family principles and roots. As a result, a three and a half-hour meeting was arranged between key congressional leaders and key religious leaders at the Library of Congress on May 8. Land was included in this somewhat confrontational meeting. At the meeting, Land stated, "Our constituents want moral leadership," explaining, "We want you [Congress] to care as much about moral issues as you do about tax issues." At the conclusion of the meeting attended by Newt Gingrich, Tom DeLay, Dick Armey, and Robert Livingston, along with a small but powerful group of religious leaders, the congressmen promised to elevate the pro-life and pro-family issues. Concerning the political leaders, Land said afterward, "They must stand for and articulate the right principles and values because evangelical Christians are looking for parties and candidates that endorse their own values."[22]

Land went on to state, "Christians need to be involved in the political process and influence the selection of candidates in both political parties." He explained:

> If enough Christians do this at some point issues like abortion will no longer be partisan in nature because both parties will agree in principle, and the differences will be over the best way to achieve the goal of protecting life from conception onward. That has already happened on the race issue. Both parties are committed to racial reconciliation and oppose racial prejudice. The disagreements come over how best to achieve those goals, not whether they should be the nation's goals.[23]

The 1998 Southern Baptist Convention was held in Salt Lake City, Utah, the heart of Mormon country. In his report to the Convention, Land noted that the Commission now had a Web site, www.erlc.com.

He explained this too would be another tool to keep Southern Baptists and other Christians "updated on matters of concern on public policy and legislation in our nation's capitol." He then proceeded to review the past year's busy agenda and accomplishments. He expressed his gratitude to his staff for all their assistance in getting the *For Faith and Family* broadcast program off the ground. With principal leadership from Harper, Land's vision for a creative, interactive radio program was brought to life. The launch of the broadcast ministry, along with a continued emphasis on publishing, allowed Land to bring the work and concerns of the ERLC to America's living rooms and automobiles. It was during this Convention that Land released *Send a Message to Mickey,* a book describing the many family-unfriendly activities of Disney.[24]

Messengers to the 1998 Convention approved the recommendation of a special committee selected by then-Convention President Tom Elliff[25] to add an Article on the Family to the Convention's statement of faith. Land joined other committee members in drafting the new section for the Baptist Faith and Message, which reads in part, "God has ordained the family as the foundational institution of human society. It is composed of persons related to one another by marriage, blood, or adoption."

The article, which was adopted overwhelmingly by the Convention, also says, "Marriage is the uniting of one man and one woman in covenant commitment for a lifetime."

The vote caused a stir among many in the press and society-at-large who lampooned the idea of wives by necessity submitting to their husband, as the article relates: "A husband is to love his wife as Christ loved the church. He has the God-given responsibility to provide for, to protect, and to lead his family. A wife is to submit graciously to the servant leadership of her husband even as the church willingly submits to the headship of Christ."

Yet Land and others stressed the article was thoroughly biblical, mirroring the teaching of God's Word, particularly Ephesians 5, and not the ways of the world.

Resolutions at that year's Convention reflected issues of high priority to the Ethics & Religious Liberty Commission. Four resolutions were particularly noteworthy. First, it should be no surprise that one was offered "On the True Christian Gospel," which affirmed the traditional historic Christian faith and the unique authority and sufficiency of Scripture. A second resolution of note was "On Public Funding of Anti-Christian Bigotry." This resolution once again cited the hypocrisy of the National Endowment for the Arts funding exhibits and artists who attack Christianity. Why in the world would the federal government sponsor anything that belittles religious faith? Is this not a clear violation of the Establishment Clause of the First Amendment? A third noteworthy resolution was "On the President's Executive Order on Homosexual Federal Employees." The resolution pointed out that what was parading as "civil rights" had been traditionally viewed as morally bankrupt behavior which is unacceptable to a moral society, and if not rescinded by the president should be challenged by the Congress. It is not surprising that a fourth resolution addressed the issue of the moral character of public officials.[26]

After the Southern Baptist Convention, it was back to Washington, D.C., for Land. Speaking to a U.S. Senate Committee on June 17, Land declared, "The worst thing Congress could do with respect to the issue of religious persecution overseas is to take no action." Here, Land again lent his support for the Freedom From Religious Persecution Act. About a week later, Land was called to testify before the U.S. Senate Judiciary Committee concerning a different bill. Referring to the overturning of the Religious Freedom Restoration Act, known as the *Boerne* decision, Land confided, "I believe it is one of the worst decisions rendered by the Supreme Court in its long history." The Senate was considering a new law, the Religious Liberty Protection Act, which attempted to restore the "compelling interest" test struck down previously. This bill "would protect religious expression from government interference by prohibiting the government from placing a substantial burden on religious practices unless it is the least restrictive means of furthering a compelling interest such as health and safety." In time, this bill went through several major changes and compromises before President Clinton finally signed it into law on

September 22, 2000, as the Religious Land Use and Institutionalized Persons Act of 2000.[27]

This bill was eventually sustained as constitutional after a legal challenge that reached all the way to the Supreme Court. In its May 31, 2005, *Cutter v. Wilkinson* decision, the Court ruled "the Religious Land Use and Institutionalized Persons Act was not facially unconstitutional but was instead a permissible accommodation of religion under the First Amendment." The Court's opinion was unanimous.[28]

Meanwhile, as the summer of 1998 neared a close, terrorists struck U.S. facilities. The U.S. embassies in Kenya and Tanzania were bombed. As a response, President Clinton ordered the military to strike alleged terrorist training camps in Afghanistan and what was believed to be a weapons plant in Sudan. The terrorist problem would grow larger in the days ahead.[29]

On the domestic scene, the fall brought a crucial vote on a gruesome activity. The Senate, by a vote of 64-36 on September 18, failed to override President Clinton's veto of the Partial-Birth Abortion Ban Act by three votes. For the record, the House voted 296–132 and had enough votes to override the veto. Land's assessment was that "Clinton bears sole responsibility for the continuation of this barbaric practice." He explained, "By his repeated veto of legislation ending this barbaric practice, he has assumed sole responsibility for this continued slaughter. . . . I continue to pray for the president, both because I am commanded to by Scripture and because some day he will answer to a far higher authority than the court of public opinion for his despicable actions in this matter."[30]

In October, Land delivered a major address at a conference hosted at Union University in Jackson, Tennessee. The conference theme was "Christian Faith and Public Policy: Where do we go from here?" Speaking about the abortion issue, Land noted that "the abortion issue's divisiveness shouldn't convince Christians to avoid the pro-life effort, but rather, give them hope and encouragement to continue the struggle for hearts and minds." Explaining "we've won in some respects," Land commented that "most of America is uncomfortable with abortion today." Land noted that people have a choice to make,

"They can choose to emphasize individual rights (such as those of the woman) or emphasize the human life which God has created." He concluded, "For those who say we cannot legislate morality, I say explain the civil rights movement."[31]

Serving as a backdrop to the entire U.S. political arena in 1998 was President Clinton's alleged affair with White House intern Monica Lewinsky. In a January 30 Baptist Press article, Hastings wrote, "As allegations of salacious and possibly criminal acts swirl out of Washington, and into America's homes through newscasts and the morning paper, parents are left wondering how to explain to their youngsters the news reports of rumors involving a 20-something government intern and the nation's chief executive."[32]

In May, Land, along with Gary Bauer, wrote, "Not only has the president's personal life completely captured the public's attention, lowered respect for political leadership and threatened his hold on office, but his penchant for deception and double talk has bled over into our relationship with foreign powers, with fatal results," speaking of the president's lack of moral authority in dealing with China. By August, Land was stating publicly that the president should "just tell the truth." By the latter part of August, Clinton was expressing his regret for his "critical lapse of judgment." Al Mohler noted that the lack of discipline in the church enabled Clinton to live a double life. By September, Clinton was telling religious leaders he had repented and was asking for forgiveness. Yet, the issue would not go away.[33]

In a November article, Kenneth Woodward, of Watergate fame, suggested that the president's behavior and cover-up could not be understood "without grasping the nuances of his Baptist upbringing." Tom Strode, the ERLC's journalist in their Washington, D.C. office, offered the following assessment of Woodward's ideas: "Baptist moderates laid [the] groundwork for Clinton morality." Land commented, "I think it is true that the liberal antinomianism represented by James Dunn, Glenn Hinson and Foy Valentine is partially responsible for producing people with the tragically flawed moral compass of a Bill Clinton."[34]

Impeaching President Clinton

By December, the Republican-dominated Congress was ready to impeach the president. Charges were not for immorality but because he had perjured himself in denying his behavior, which was subsequently proved. As a result, Land called for Clinton's resignation, but the plea, as expected, was ignored. The president, rather, called the entire matter an exercise in the "politics of personal destruction."[35]

When the new year, 1999, came the president's impeachment was not the only issue on Land's mind. In an address to the Baptist World Alliance, Land provided his assessment of the state of race relations in America. In summary, he confessed, "I am disappointed, sometimes even depressed, that . . . we have not come farther as Americans in our quest for a racially reconciled society."[36]

Of even greater concern to Land was the recent announcement by the National Institutes of Health (NIH) that it intended to fund research on "pluripotent stem cells." Pro-life advocates immediately responded to the announcement calling it "unethical and illegal, because stem-cell research required the destruction of human embryos." Commenting on this, Ben Mitchell, a renowned bioethicist and the ERLC's consultant on bioethics, stated, the announcement

> means that our tax dollars will be used to fund the exploitation
> of the tiniest of human beings for the benefit of others. . . . This
> is the kind of utilitarian ethic we have been warning about.
> Human beings, including human embryos, are to be treated
> with dignity and respect and are not to be used as a means to
> someone else's ends. . . . Increasingly, efforts will be made to
> experiment on and commercialize human embryos. Those who
> respect human dignity can neither remain ignorant nor silent.
> We must speak for those who cannot speak for themselves.[37]

In light of the intensity of what had been termed the culture wars, the Interfaith Alliance chaired by former Southern Baptist pastor and Christian Life Commission staff member, Welton Gaddy, called for a series of meetings and discussions on "civility in public discourse." Land was invited to speak to the first meeting in Washington, D.C.

Addressing the group, Land acknowledged the country was "in the midst of having a very necessary and a very important debate about where America should go in the future." He further noted the debate was often facilitated in a "very unnecessary and very destructive manner, and I think there's enough blame to go around." The consensus of the deliberations was that people should at least be agreeable in their disagreements and conduct themselves with a modicum of civility in the public arena.[38]

In February, the Congress ruled in its decision of President Clinton's impeachment. The trial, lasting 21 days, was resolved on February 12 with the decision falling for the most part on party lines. The charges of obstruction of justice and perjury arising from the scandal surrounding Monica Lewinsky fell short of the two-thirds majority required for conviction and removal from office under the Constitution. The aftermath of the failed impeachment, however, brought the wrath of Federal District Judge Susan Webber Wright as she found Clinton guilty of contempt of court, which eventually brought a suspension of his Arkansas law license and a fine.[39]

A few days after Clinton's acquittal, Paul Weyrich, president of the Free Congress Foundation and a long-time political strategist in Washington, as a reaction to the congressional verdict, wrote to his constituency lamenting from his perspective that those who embrace the Judeo-Christian culture had "probably lost the culture war." In his assessment, "Politics failed because of the collapse of the culture." Writing to his conservative base, he lamented:

> The culture we are living in becomes an ever-wider sewer.
> In truth, I think we are caught up in a cultural collapse of historic proportions, a collapse so great that it simply overwhelms politics . . . [while] we have been fighting and winning in politics, our culture has decayed into something approaching barbarism.[40]

Land, with his usual positive outlook, countered, saying, "Nothing is finally and totally lost or finally and totally won, because there is always the next election and the next moral crisis." He maintained that the battle is "won or lost every generation." Land went on to exhort fellow believers by stating the biblical mandate, "If we are going to heed the call of the Lord Jesus to be salt and light, we cannot withdraw" from cultural engagement. Land also observed that his own evangelical perspective was different from that of Weyrich, who is Catholic. He explained,

> Catholic social conservatives are more disappointed and depressed than evangelical Protestants at the current moral state of the nation. . . . There is a long Catholic social-issues tradition which has historically placed more confidence in government and societal institutions' ability to effect moral change in the culture than would be the case among evangelical Protestants. Evangelicals historically have had a profound mistrust of such institutions and certainly have never expected as much from them in terms of real moral change in society. Evangelicals have known from the beginning that unless there is a heaven-sent revival, spiritual awakening and reformation, America as we have known and loved her was doomed.[41]

The entire discussion was a sober wake-up call for Southern Baptists. Neither should anyone be surprised that only a few days later, SBC President Paige Patterson and Commission President Land, along with others, were meeting to pray with congressional members and discuss with them, face to face, issues of concern. Among other things, each member of Congress was given a copy of the Ethics & Religious Liberty Commission's legislative priorities.[42]

As the spring came, one issue that was strongly debated in Congress was the concept of hate crimes. In March, Land, in the shadow of the hate-crimes debate, said, "The greatest threat to America's liberty in the next 20 to 30 years . . . will be over governmental suppression of free exercise." He warned, "If we are not careful, we are going to lose our right to preach what we believe and say what we believe in the public square." Citing the recent push for strengthened hate-crime punishments, Land noted, "Those who are attempting to normalize homosexuality and affirm it as a healthy lifestyle are intent on abnormalizing and stigmatizing those who stand for biblical truth." He further explained that the hate-crimes movement is an attempt to silence those who embrace traditional morality. The following month, Land asserted, "President Clinton's recently announced effort to include homosexuality in hate-crimes legislation and tolerance training in public schools is an attack on biblical values and parental rights."[43]

What occurred on April 20, 1999, brought the nation to a standstill. Two students, Eric Harris and Dylan Klebold, walked into Columbine High School in Littleton, Colorado, and with a planned approach began a killing rampage that left fifteen people, including themselves, dead. Up to that time, "it is considered the deadliest school shooting in United States history." Upon hearing of the tragic massacre, Land released the following statement through *Baptist Press:*

> The problem exposed by this terrible tragedy in Colorado is not guns. We've had guns readily available in our culture for generations and we did not have this kind of insane mayhem and grotesque violence.
>
> We must ask ourselves what is different today than a generation ago, not what's the same. The things that are different are a lack of parental involvement and supervision, an absence of adult and societal boundary-setting and the barbaric glorification of violence on the Internet, in video games and the entertainment industry generally. . . .
>
> You can only imprint so many obscenities on a person before they begin to malfunction.
>
> Just like any other exposure to toxic waste, the younger the person exposed the greater the potential for serious damage. These two boys [accused killers in Littleton, Eric Harris, 18, and Dylan Klebold, 17, who committed suicide after killing 13 and wounding more than 20 others in a siege of the school with guns and homemade bombs] were obsessed with extremely violent video games provided by an entertainment industry with its eye on the bottom line, willing to pimp for violence and to become pushers of mayhem in order to line their own pockets.

The connection between the glorification of violence against human beings in the entertainment industry and the increasingly violent activities by children and young people can be convincingly made by anyone who has eyes to see and ears to hear. . . .

Increasingly children like these two youngsters grow up in relative material affluence but emotionally malnourished and spiritually deprived. They get little, if any, involvement from their parents and little, if any, discipline, structure or boundary-setting by society. A generation ago, any students who showed up at a public school dressed in black trench coats and knee-high black leather boots sporting swastikas mirroring the grotesque appearance of Marilyn Manson, would have been severely disciplined and sent home, if not expelled. Their parents would have been called in to explain why they allowed such a thing to happen in their home.

Obviously, this school, like most other schools, did not exercise such wise oversight. . . . How many episodes like this must we endure before we realize how grievously we have failed our children as parents, as adults and as a society? And how many more children have to die before we understand that the pimps and panderers of media violence either will not or cannot regulate themselves? The people's elected representatives must intervene to insist that this emotional toxic waste be kept out of the hands of children and adolescents.[44]

Much soul searching followed the massacre including debates over gun control, school cliques, and bullying, the influence of violent movies and video games, and the breakdown of the home. If nothing else, Columbine provided a glimpse into the alienation and spiritual vacuum that many of the day's students experience with chilling implications for a culture that seems to make no place for God.

The following month, the president's National Bioethics Advisory Commission announced that it would recommend that the federal government should provide grants to fund research on embryos discarded by fertility clinics. Its rationale was that benefits of seeking a cure of disease would outweigh the ethical problems of destroying embryos. The draft report argued, "This research is allied with a noble cause, and any taint that might attach from the source of the stem cells diminishes in proportion to the potential good which the research may yield." Land provided his assessment stating, "When you cut to the bottom line, what the president's advisory commission is advocating is publicly funded research which will develop technology that will allow us to kill human babies and cloned embryos of ourselves in order to harvest their cells to make treatments to improve our health." He concluded,

> That is nothing less than biotechnical cannibalism in which we literally devour our young to sustain and improve our own health. To call that barbaric is to insult barbarians. To seek to force to make the American public to pay for that research is totally and completely unacceptable.[45]

Several weeks later, the 1999 Southern Baptist Convention gathered in Atlanta, Georgia. In his report to the Convention, Land reviewed the Commission's accomplishments in the past year and noted a new addition to its strategy of being "salt" and "light." The report read, "The Commission has also launched a daily one minute radio commentary on the news, 'Faith and Family Insight,' which is heard on an additional 115 stations around the nation." Land also provided a scathing critique of Barry Lynn and the Americans United's misinformation campaign.[46]

Most of this year's resolutions were a reflection of domestic and international events over the past year. These included resolutions on school violence, on the American Psychological Association's bulletin minimizing the impact of pedophilia, the need to halt the genocide and ethnic cleansing in the Balkans, the need to prohibit human embryonic stem cell research, concern about youth violence in the media, the need for Christians to participate in public discourse and its guarantee by the Free Exercise Clause, and a sound criticism of Clinton's Gay and Lesbian Pride Month proclamation.[47]

Between the Southern Baptist Convention and the fall trustee meeting, Land and the Commission found themselves addressing three important issues. In the aftermath of the Convention, the first issue, which was discussed earlier, addressed "ten reasons" to oppose hate-crimes legislation. Besides being a lead story in the *Salt* newsletter, *Baptist Press* also picked it up and provided greater distribution of its information.[48]

A second important issue concerned the blocking of Ohio's voucher program. In order to assist low-income families to provide better education, the state created the program so that parents could have a wider array of choices for their child's education. The assistance would be $2,500 a year and would help about four thousand underprivileged students attend one of fifty-six private schools, many of them religious. The day before Cleveland's public school started, Judge Solomon Oliver issued an injunction stating that the vouchers appeared to have the primary effect of advancing religion.[49]

Land provided a scathing critique of the judge's ruling. He argued that "the real issue is whether poor people, working-class people, lower-middle-class people are going to continue to be trapped with no alternative economically but to send their children to the public schools no matter how dissatisfied they may be with the public schools, no matter how much they feel their values may be assaulted in those public schools." Land continued, "All that vouchers do is give back a portion of the taxes that these people pay so that they have the choice of either using that tax money to support public schools or, if they feel their children's need would be better served in a private school, to send them to a private school and even up to and including a school that is religiously affiliated." He further noted that "the people who control public schools understand that far too often they are putting out a product that is so subpar that unless they have a captive audience that they can't afford fair and equal competition." In short, Land declared, "This is an outrageous decision." Needless to say, the issue of school choice was a growing concern among many Americans.[50]

A third issue addressed in the days leading up to the fall trustee meeting concerned the content of network television's prime time programming. Commenting on the latest report of the Parents Television Council, Land stated, "Anyone who examines the study can come to no other conclusion than that the broadcast networks are totally impervious to the concerns of parents, grandparents and other Americans who are rightfully appalled by the cesspool into which American television has sunk." Of particular concern was the prime-time content of the FOX network. This problem continued to escalate.[51]

The fall trustee meeting was held September 14–15, 1999, in Nashville. One obvious concern was the desire to reinforce the Disney boycott even during the 2000 Convention, which would meet in Orlando. A second item was the transformation of the quarterly *Salt* newsletter to an electronic format, *e-Salt,* and the decision to release it monthly. Also at this meeting, the decision was made to move ahead with establishing the Research Institute, which would provide valuable assistance in matters of culture, moral issues, and public policy matters. Land's vision for the Research Institute was far-reaching.

The Institute serves three main functions: (1) to provide a professional organization where conservative, evangelical scholars can discuss current trends in American culture; (2) to apply biblical truth to moral, public policy, and religious liberty issues in order to transform American culture; and (3) to develop a comprehensive worldview model to equip Christians to evaluate and interact with the moral and religious liberty issues confronting families in the modern culture. The fellows who work in the Institute include university and seminary presidents, academic deans, professors, lawyers, doctors, theologians, and other evangelical scholars. Founding members of the Institute along with Land and Barrett Duke, who served as the Director of the Institute, were Carl F. H. Henry, Paige Patterson, Albert Mohler, David Dockery, Timothy George, Russ Bush, Danny Akin, Steve Lemke, Ben Mitchell, and Don Buckley. The trustees also promoted Barrett Duke, Harold Harper, and Dwayne Hastings, granting to each vice-president status in their respective assignments.[52]

The Commission also hired Bobby Reed as director of administration in the Nashville office, and Shannon Royce as legislative counsel and director of government relations in the ERLC's Washington, D.C., office. When he joined Land's executive team, Bobby Reed immediately took on the mission of integrating organization-wide operational effectiveness and worked to improve the organizational structure. Because of his expertise in information technology systems, he actually created programs to accomplish tasks that heretofore had been impossible.[53]

Shannon Royce was the first female to serve in a leadership capacity in the Washington office. In fact, her hiring placed her in the forefront of female leadership involvement in the Southern Baptist Convention. With her extensive experience in D.C. politics, including legislative advocacy for Concerned Women for America and serving on the staff of Iowa Senator Charles Grassley, Royce was the perfect person to head up the Commission's D.C. advocacy work. Under her leadership, the Commission's Washington office secured its foothold as a major presence in the nation's Capitol. She brought insight into how Washington works as well as an outstanding network of both congressional and White House contacts.[54]

The rest of the year found Land and the Commission extremely busy addressing a number of high-profile issues.

Although the next presidential election was a year away, both parties had candidates who were already vying for their party's nomination. As a result, pro-family groups working in concert created "The Presidential Candidate Pledge on Marriage," which was drafted by the Americans for Truth about Homosexuality organization based in Washington, D.C. The pledge signers agreed to "vigilantly defend this age-old institution against any effort—judicial or legislative—to redefine it." It also stated, "I will oppose all judicial and legislative efforts to place children in homosexual households, which are motherless or fatherless by design." Its primary pledge was to uphold "the sacred institution of marriage as the lifelong union of one man and one woman" and to resist any attempt to alter or redefine its meaning to encompass homosexual relationships. When the pledge was printed in the *Des Moines Register* just prior to the GOP straw poll, Texas Govenor George W. Bush's campaign for president sent a statement endorsing the pledge but conceded it was unclear about some of the gay rights agenda and domestic partnership laws.[55]

In contrast to the strong Republican support, Al Gore and Bill Bradley, leading Democratic candidates, simply refused to sign the pledge. Responding to the candidates' choices, Land commented:

> As I talk with people of faith, I find little, if any, comprehension of an acceptable reason why any candidate seeking to be a "pro-family" candidate would hesitate to take this pledge to uphold "the sacred institution of marriage as the lifelong union of one man and one woman. . . . There is no social or public policy issue which is of more concern to Southern Baptists and other people of faith than the radical homosexual rights agenda. . . . The "homosexual agenda" is being foisted upon them by efforts of radical homosexual activists and the often weak and ineffective response of political leaders. . . . Nothing symbolizes that concern more than the assault on the institution of marriage through the efforts of the radical homosexual activists to both devalue the sanctity of marriage and to affirm and normalize their homosexual lifestyle through gaining marital status for same-sex relationships.[56]

The report on the Marriage Pledge, which came out in October, was followed the next day with a review of the U.S. Senate vote to ban the partial-birth abortion procedure. The Senate vote was sixty-three to thirty-four to uphold the ban. It fell short of the two-thirds vote necessary to veto-proof the bill. The House was expected to pass the ban with enough votes to override the anticipated veto. Land, again, asked for prayer for the president that he might have a change of mind and heart when the bill finally reached his desk.[57]

In November, two more moral issues came to the forefront. The first had to do with the ruling of a federal judge in New York City, which required taxpayers to subsidize an objectionable exhibit. In short, an art exhibit from the Charles Saatchi "Sensations" collection was coming to the Brooklyn Museum of Art at taxpayer expense. Not only was much of the exhibit pornographic in nature, but also some of it was a desecration to Christianity. Richard Land commented, "Multitudes of believers are outraged by the museum's decision to display this blasphemous work by rightly protesting that the public should not be asked to subsidize through public tax money portrayals which denigrate and desecrate symbols of their deepest religious convictions." He continued, "It is outrageous for the museum's defenders to try to hide behind the First Amendment freedom of speech protections, when in actual fact what they are really doing is reaching into the public's money, to subsidize an obvious assault on people of faiths' beliefs." He then noted, "This kind of Christian bashing will continue until we demand it stop" explaining, "There is such a thing as accountability to the public trust."[58]

A second even more serious issue came to the public's attention a few days later. It had recently been brought to some congressmen's attention that abortion clinics were selling aborted fetuses and, at times, particular body parts to researchers. Ben Mitchell's assessment was that "commodifying, commercializing and marketing aborted babies is almost too grotesque to imagine." He then asked, "Have we created an American research culture without a conscience?" Land commented, "I applaud the Congress for calling for hearings, and I pray they will take place at the earliest possible opportunity." He then noted, "This highly lucrative but barbaric business that is being supplied from the tiny victims of partial-birth abortion must be stopped."[59]

A similar issue was addressed in December when the National Institutes of Health announced its proposed guidelines that would recommend government funding for embryonic stem-cell research. As a loophole, it recommended that private funding be used to acquire the embryonic stem cells. Ben Mitchell critiqued this recommendation stating that these NIH guidelines "represent government-funded biotech cannibalism." He explained, "Derivation of stem cells cannot be separated from the use of those cells." His assessment was that "the decision to kill embryos taints whatever use the cells may have." He further commented: "Deriving stem cells from human embryos or aborted fetuses sacrifices one group of human beings for the use of other human beings. This is grotesque and unconscionable." In response to the NIH's proposed guidelines, a document signed by one hundred specialists in law, ethics, medicine, science, and theology was released calling for a halt to the proposal. Land was one of several Southern Baptist leaders to affix his signature.[60]

Later in December, Land and others shifted their attention from domestic to international concerns and requested President Clinton work for peace in Sudan. Noting that approximately two million people had already died in the conflict, the letter asked the president to take a "visible, personal stance on the genocide now taking place in Sudan." It urged, "Your voice above all others—declaring to the world the reality of Sudan's agony—will be heard and heeded." The letter went on to say, "Either America leads the way towards peace at this crucial historic juncture, or an unspeakable catastrophe evident to all will take its final, dreadful toll in a century already defined too fully by indifference and genocide."[61]

As Christmas approached, and with it Southern Baptists' emphasis on world missions through its Lottie Moon Christmas Offering, a clear request was communicated for Southern Baptists to pray for and share the Gospel with Jews, Hindus, and Muslims. President Clinton's press secretary, Joe Lockhart, was asked about this and responded, "I think the President has made very clear his view from any quarter, no matter what quarter it comes from, his views on religious tolerance, and how one of the greatest challenges going into the next century is dealing with intolerance, dealing with ethnic and religious hatred, and coming to grips with the long-held resentments between religions." He concluded, "So I think he's [Clinton] been very clear in his opposition to whatever organization, including the Southern Baptist, that perpetuate ancient religious hatred." Needless to say, a litany of responses came from Southern Baptist leaders. All of them were critical and justifiably so.[62]

With the new millennium and new year, the Ethics & Religious Liberty Commission addressed numerous issues, some new and some old. One issue that introduced the year was Land's concern for the human trafficking of women and children. In a letter dated January 7, 2000, to Mrs. Clinton, who served as co-chair for the President's Interagency Council on Women, Land with several cosigners communicated his strong concern about the mounting crisis. The letter concluded, "We are determined and morally committed to end today's slave trade in women and children and ask you to join in this effort." In a Baptist Press article a few days later, Tom Strode clarified the Clinton letter's intent noting that the present policy trajectory of the administration was "to liberalize international sanctions against the sexual exploitation of women and children." It decried the assumption that "voluntary prostitution is a legitimate career option for women" and warned if this were adopted at an upcoming summit in Vienna, "[it] would create the loophole long sought by those [traffickers] and will effectively insulate them from criminal prosecution." In an article a month later, Baptist Press quoted Shannon Royce, Commission legal counsel in Washington, D.C., concerning Senate hearings on the trafficking travesty. She stated, "I was just horrified that this kind of trade in women and children even exists in our world today." Senators resolved to craft a complementary bill with the House's "Trafficking Victims Protection Act." White House officials noted they would be reluctant to add or enforce economic sanctions to U.S. policy.[63] The ERLC became a major force behind the eventual passage of this landmark legislation to end the modern day slave trade.

Of equal concern, and especially because 2000 was an election year, was the entire homosexual rights issue and how it was playing out on the national political stage. Coming out of Vermont was a tirade of homosexual rights proposals. Early in the year, a government panel recommended the adoption and legitimizing of same-sex unions or partnerships, stopping short of calling it marriage. Throughout the spring this became a growing issue. California surprisingly adopted a definition of marriage as only "between a man and a woman." Commenting on this approval of "Proposition 22," Land observed that it was more than a religious issue; it was a moral issue. And he was pleased that the voters in California approved it.[64]

In the course of the spring, Dr. Laura Schlessinger received incredible criticism for her resistance to homosexuality. Land, among many others, came to her defense. Defending her right to express her views, Land stated, "Dr. Laura has every right to express her views and

Americans have every right to hear them." Toward the end of April, Land and a group of other evangelical leaders requested to meet with candidate Bush after he met with a group of homosexual Republican leaders on April 13. The joint letter from Land and others stated, "You will find that homosexual activists will not be satisfied with the civil rights all Americans enjoy. . . . They do not want tolerance; that's what they have. They demand acceptance of their lifestyle and protection for their practices. . . . They seek nothing less than the ability to mandate teaching to schoolchildren that homosexuality is normal and healthy, and to hem in dissent on this issue with a thicket of legal and social penalties." Needless to say, the homosexual rights debate would get hotter as the days went by and would force itself onto the national agenda, especially when national party platforms were written in the summer.[65]

One highlight for the Ethics & Religious Liberty Commission came in the inaugural meeting of its Research Institute. Of special significance was the inclusion of renowned Christian theologian Carl F. H. Henry as a founding fellow of the Institute. Speaking to the fellows, Henry stated, "Instead of total disengagement from the culture, Christians should challenge it. . . . The time has come for America again to exhibit to the world the moral leadership and integrity that exhibits and commends ethical democracy to the world." Introducing Henry, Land noted that Americans "owe Dr. Henry a tremendous and incalculable debt of gratitude for his strong and uncompromising stance and his willingness to apply academic rigors to the issues that have been so seminal in the last half of the 20th century." Commenting on the birth of the Institute, Land confessed, "It is my hope this will be the beginning of the marshalling and focusing of the resources that God has put at our disposal as Southern Baptists . . . to invigorate the church to be that counter-culture which offers an alternative of hope to a contemporary culture that offers no real hope." Land further stated, "We must seek to revive, rearm and reawaken God's people, to inoculate them against what is looking alarmingly like a fully blown pagan culture." Land then expressed his vision that in creating the Institute, it might "gain a synergy in gathering some of the best thinkers available to address critical moral and ethical issues."[66]

Playing in to the political climate was a speech given by Republican hopeful John McCain, who called Pat Robertson and Jerry Falwell "forces of evil" with an "evil influence" over his party. Commenting on what was perceived as McCain's cheap shot to neutralize the Christian right's influence on Republican policy, Land remarked, "I don't agree with Pat Robertson and Jerry Falwell about many things, but to compare them to Louis Farrakhan and Al Sharpton, who are racists and hate-mongers, and then to follow it up by calling these two ministers an evil influence is disgraceful behavior by someone who claims the title of being a uniter and not a divider." Land, like many Evangelicals, was deeply incensed by McCain's remarks. In this case, Evangelicals had a long memory.[67]

Along with all the other activities Land and the Commission were involved in, two *amicus curiae* briefs were filed on their behalf with the Supreme Court. One asked the Supreme Court to reverse the lower-court decision that struck down a ban on partial-birth abortion, and the other supported the Boy Scouts in its ban on homosexual leaders.[68] These were but a couple of many briefs the Commission would sign onto with the nation's highest court, voicing Southern Baptist convictions and concerns.

At the end of March, another issue came from a judicial decision with long-reaching ramifications. A Florida judge ruled that the state legislature's school-voucher program was unconstitutional. Land commented that this was "one more example of raw judicial power thwarting the clearly expressed will of the people." The ruling, which permitted students attending failing public schools to receive vouchers to attend a school of their choice, was overturned. Again, Land noted, "As is often the case, the people who are most hurt are among the weakest and most defenseless—children who had been attending public schools where it was manifestly evident they were not being taught to read and write and count." He then observed the decision "raises the question how long the American people will put up with being ruled by these judicial czars in black robes." The issue of school vouchers was another one that would not go away.[69]

A particularly disturbing incident that occurred in the spring was the arrival in America of refugee Elian Gonzalez. Because his mother died in their escape from Cuba, custody became an issue. In late April, a Gestapo-type raid took Gonzalez out of his Florida home and returned him to Cuba. Many, including Land, were not happy with this action nor the precedent that it set.[70]

In late April, Land had an opportunity to return to his collegiate alma mater, Princeton University. In his address, entitled, "The American Religious Experiment: Avoidance, Accommodation, and Acknowledgment," Land addressed the role of Christianity and religion in the public arena. In his address, he identified what to many conservatives would be the most important issue in the upcoming presidential and senatorial election, noting that, "the next president of the United States will name two or three justices to the U.S. Supreme Court, making this election the most important since Civil War Reconstruction." In his address, Land described the moral backbone and the courageous role that ministers, especially Baptist ministers, had played in shaping America and challenged the students attending to embrace such character and embody such courage.[71]

There were still other issues that Land addressed in the spring, including his concern for human rights in China and America's corresponding foreign policy, and the prospect of the French import, RU 486, and the Food and Drug Administration's ruling on its prospective approval.[72] During that same month, Barrett Duke testified before the Bureau of Alcohol, Tobacco, and Firearms in Washington, D.C., disputing the alcohol industry's claims of health benefits of alcohol use.

In June the 2000 Southern Baptist Convention held its annual meeting in Orlando, Florida, on June 13–14.

Messengers at the Convention adopted a proposed revision of the SBC's 1963 version of its statement of faith, with a reported 90 percent of those voting in approval of what became the 2000 Baptist Faith and Message.

"We have sought to clarify the intention of both previous editions [1925 and 1963] of the Baptist Faith and Message. We have made the total truthfulness and trustworthiness of the Bible even more explicit.

And we point to Jesus Christ as the focus of divine revelation," explained Adrian Rogers, who was the head of the committee that drafted the revised statement, as well as the pastor of Bellevue Baptist Church in Cordova, Tenn., at the time.[73]

Land was on the Baptist Faith and Message Study Committee[74] that prepared the 2000 BFM. It was indicative of the growing influence of the Ethics & Religious Liberty Commission that its president—Richard Land—was the only person to serve on the committee that drafted the 1998 addition of the Article on the Family and on the committee that wrote the 2000 revision of the SBC's statement of faith.

Following the adoption of the 2000 BFM, Land, Al Mohler, president of Southern Baptist Theological Seminary, and Chuck Kelley, president of New Orleans Baptist Theological Seminary, authored a commentary on the new version of the Baptist Faith and Message.

In his report to the Convention, Land recognized eight Southern Baptists whom he deemed "champions of the faith," who had dared "to step out from within their high-walled sanctuaries" and "with a rich legacy of courage and conviction" had along with our fore-fathers lived out "the purifying power of God's Word as 'salt' and 'light.'" Land's report featured a video vignette of these eight different champions.[75]

In his printed report, Land reviewed in general terms an overview of what the Commission accomplished in the previous year. He drew attention to the fact that *Salt* was now *e-Salt* and increased its release from six times a year to twelve. He also responded to five motions referred to the Commission from the previous year. Of interest was motion number 4 that requested the ERLC provide churches more information on the legislative process and issues. Land responded in print that they were doing all they could at the present funding levels.[76]

When resolutions were presented, several were reflective of issues addressed by the Commission in the past year. The resolution "On Religious Freedom and Evangelism in a Pluralistic Society" addressed the debate over hate crimes. Another addressed human rights issues in Sudan and China. Still another condemned the trafficking of women and children for sexual purposes. Another defended the Boy Scouts against the present climate of judicial assaults. Of particular interest were the resolutions "On Human Fetal Tissue Trafficking" and "On Capital Punishment." The following June, Duke served on a panel of the Pew Foundation for Religion and Public Life in D.C., describing the Convention's biblical position on capital punishment. Each of these represented highly visible issues in the culture at large.[77]

The remainder of the summer of 2000 found Land and his team addressing a litany of moral and cultural issues. When the group working on genetic mapping was introduced at a White House ceremony and its potential was optimistically applauded, Land and Mitchell responded with their assessment that "the bad news is this science is being conducted in a moral dark age." They explained, "Those who make public policy about such matters cannot agree that unborn babies are human persons who deserve at least a right not to be unnecessarily harmed. They cannot agree that human beings and their body parts should not be owned through the patent process. They cannot agree that the disabled, infirm and aged should be cared for in a dignified and humane manner rather than being discarded via euthanasia." Minimally, they were skeptical because of the lack of moral norms and ethical parameters.[78]

At the end of June, the Supreme Court released a quartet of decisions with moral implications. It decided the Boy Scouts could restrict homosexuals from being troop leaders. It overturned the Nebraska law prohibiting partial-birth abortion. It ruled that federal government aid could be used by religious schools to purchase instructional equipment. And it upheld a Colorado law restricting pro-life workers near abortion clinics.[79]

Also in the summer, Land sent a letter to each senator and each congressman urging the passage of the compromise bill, "The Religious Land Use and Institutionalized Persons Act of 2000." It passed and was eventually signed into law by President Clinton.[80]

In Oregon, a citizens' petition featuring 83,281 signatures challenged the teaching of homosexual behavior as normal in the public schools. Land supported the effort to resist this "normalizing" of homosexuality and applauded the initiative of the concerned parents who created this Oregon ballot initiative.[81]

In the middle of July, Land was forced to counter Barry Lynn's criticism when he featured an interview with Jerry Falwell on his *For Faith and Family* radio program. Lynn believed that Land gave in to his pressure tactics to edit out some of Falwell's remarks. Land responded they always edit their program and that Lynn was "evidently a legend in his own mind."[82]

By August, the National Institutes of Health released its guidelines with respect to embryonic stem cell research. As with the gene mapping announcement, Mitchell and Land pointed out the shortcomings and flaws of the ruling. This became a dividing point among many between Bush and Gore as they received their party's presidential nominations. Not surprisingly, the subject of biotechnology and the disconnect between faith and learning in Christian higher education became a dominant theme at the fall meeting of the Commission's Research Institute.[83]

In October of 2000, the Commission added Kerry Bural to its executive team. Bural immediately set out to build a more robust and intentional media relations effort to set the stage for the coming years as he attempted to provide a greater platform from which Land and the Commission might speak. According to Land, "Bural is extremely creative and capable, always thinking outside the box and in numerous dimensions."[84]

The major issue in the fall was the U.S. presidential election. When the Commission completed its non-partisan comparison of the two political party platforms, the two parties' values, beliefs, and convictions stood in marked contrast. When the Associated Baptist Press accused Land of endorsing Bush, he responded clearly, "I do not endorse candidates. . . . I do . . . tell (people) they should vote their values, beliefs and convictions." Land went on to say, "Nor am I encouraging ministers to do anything other than inform voters and encourage them to vote their values, beliefs and convictions."[85]

After the November 7 election, which remained in limbo for over a month, Richard Land debated Brent Walker, who was the executive director of the Baptist Joint Committee on Public Affairs. In the debate held at Southwestern Baptist Theological Seminary, Land stated, "I think the greatest threat to religious freedom is government suppression of the free exercise rights of American citizens to express their religious convictions and to bring their religious convictions to bear on the public policy issues of the day." In his assessment of the Baptist Joint Committee, he believed their overemphasis on the no-establishment clause was the greatest distinction between the two entities.[86]

When the Supreme Court finally denied Gore's suit for a recount of thousands of disputed ballots in Florida on December 12, Bush was declared the winner of the presidential election. Land commented the decision was "the correct one, that you can't have votes being counted by different standards in different counties and even [at] different tables in the same canvassing board room." Land continued, "We don't insist on perfect elections in this country, but we must have fair elections." And, he noted, "We have some work to do."[87]

On December 22, Bush announced he would nominate former Missouri senator, John Ashcroft, who was an evangelical Christian, to be the next attorney general. Said Land, "I could not be more pleased with the nomination of John Ashcroft." After confirmation hearings, the Senate confirmed Ashcroft on February 1, 2001, by a vote of fifty-eight to forty-two, but not without a lot of criticism, primarily for his religious convictions. In a surprise move, Land endorsed Ashcroft's nomination while labeling his critics "religious profilers." Land also commented that he was offended by the "outright religious bigotry being spewed at John Ashcroft's nomination."[88]

Even before his inauguration, President-elect George Bush received from Land a list of requested policy initiatives which included asking Congress to send him a bill banning partial-birth abortion, taking initiative to regulate bioethics research, taking initiative to work with Congress to reform election procedures, improving education, changing the tax code to provide relief for families, and taking steps to restore the military.[89]

Ten days after his inauguration, Bush established a White House Office of Faith-Based and Community Initiatives. Land recommended caution.[90]

Responding to moderate critics that he had not represented the views of Southern Baptists in his endorsement of Ashcroft, Land responded that he did not presume to speak for all Southern Baptists, just the majority of them. Again calling the criticism of Ashcroft "anti-evangelical bigotry," Land added, "The only way it can succeed is if we cower into silence, and we are not going to be made to be quiet!" Responding to critics accusing him of advocating that God is a Republican, Land responded that "you can't reduce God to any merely human construction, particularly a political party." Then he asserted, "But trust me—God is pro-life!"[91]

At the February 20, 2001, SBC Executive Committee meeting in Nashville, construction of the broadcast studio was complete, and a ribbon-cutting ceremony was held with SBC President James Merritt doing the honors. More than 100 guests were in attendance for the ceremony that signified the opening of the studio that Land described as a "living monument to interagency cooperation."[92]

In a letter to Bush on March 2, 2001, Land and Mitchell urged Bush to clarify as quickly as possible his "administration's position on human embryonic stem cell research." They strongly recommended that he alter the present policy advocated by the NIH, to which he agreed.[93]

On March 15, Land delivered a far-reaching address at the Freewill Baptist Bible College's annual Bible Conference in Nashville, Tennessee. In his message he stated, "If America perishes, she will die from self-inflicted wounds." He went on to say, "We face a far greater peril from our own immorality and our own degradation and our degeneracy than we ever faced from the Japanese navy or the German air force or the soviet missile command." After a lengthy address, Land concluded:

> One of the reasons America is in such a sorry state is that
> we have allowed the world to tell us we don't have the right
> to be involved in public policy. That's plain wrong. Christians
> have just as much right as any other citizen to be involved, and
> we have a command from the Lord as well, for we are the salt

of the earth and the light of the world. You have a right and a command from on high to bring your moral perspective to bear on public policy.[94]

In May, Land wrote a first-person editorial for Baptist Press on pornography, which he labeled "a ravenous cancer destroying modern society." Noting it was an $8 billion a year industry, he declared, "Despite assertions to the contrary, pornography is not a victimless crime or simply harmless entertainment." He pointed out "the painful trail left by pornography is reflected in increased incidents of child molestation, rape and sexual violence, transmission of sexually transmitted diseases, and societal values and attitudes that condone and even encourage dissemination of soft-core pornography."[95]

Also in May, Land addressed the upcoming nominations Bush would make for the federal judiciary. He noted "President Bush is doing what he was elected to do—put strict constructionists on the federal bench at every level who interpret the Constitution, not rewrite it to reflect their own views and perspective." No doubt the issue of judicial nominations would create a great deal of political wrangling. Left-leaning interest groups stood to lose more here than anywhere else.[96]

Less than a month later, the Southern Baptist Convention met in New Orleans on June 12–13. Land's printed report was essentially an update from the year before with no new items, other than to respond to questions about the Disney boycott and messenger Fred Steelman's 2000 request that Commission employees not be required to sign the Baptist Faith and Message of 2000. Land politely responded that "The Ethics & Religious Liberty Commission expects all program staff to affirm the Baptist Faith and Message and to minister from the perspective of its doctrinal foundations and theological tenets." Like the previous year, Land recognized "Champions of the Faith" from the past year.[97]

Most resolutions reflected major issues that had been addressed during the previous year by the Commission. Concern about the family was expressed in a resolution "On Covenant Marriage." The stem cell issue was addressed in a resolution "On Human Cloning." Concern was expressed about the genocide in Sudan and the need to give to alleviate world hunger. Alarm was raised about "the plague of Internet pornography." Life issues were addressed in the resolution "On Euthanasia in the Netherlands." Finally, the rights of believers were reinforced through two resolutions, "On Discrimination Against Military Chaplains" and "On Protecting Free Speech in Campaign Finance Legislation."[98]

June, July, August, and early September seemed almost to be business as usual for Land and the Commission. The White House announced a ban on human cloning. Land followed up with a first-person editorial on "The Power of a Presidential Promise." In August, Bush delivered less on the stem cell issue than hoped in an attempt to craft some kind of a compromise with his critics. In August, Land once again addressed the issue of Internet pornography and lottery concerns. In early September, the Commission and others made a strong plea for support of pro-life justices. Then, the unthinkable occurred.[99]

When Terror Fills the Skies

On Tuesday morning, September 11, 2001, the United States was attacked by a group of nineteen Islamic terrorists, most from Saudi Arabia, but all from the Middle East, who hijacked four airliners and turned them into guided missiles. Two planes were flown into the Twin Towers of the World Trade Center. Over three thousand people were killed. Another plane crashed into the Pentagon in Washington, D.C. A fourth plane crashed in Pennsylvania when passengers fought back and attempted to regain control. September 11 was the worst terrorist attack in U.S. history.[100]

Later in the day, Land released this statement to the press:

> As believers, we need to trust in the promises of God, that He is indeed our Shepherd. We can rest in Him and trust in Him. We need to understand that what the devil has intended for evil, God can use for good.

This terrible tragedy that evidences a callous disregard for human life will prompt many Americans to think about eternal things in a way that they don't on a daily basis.

I hope that all Christians will join me in praying that the Holy Spirit will use this, and use us, to reach out to Americans who are concerned about their spiritual futures in a new and more sensitive way that they may come to know the peace and assurance that can only be found in Jesus Christ.

Even in the midst of this tragedy, we need to pray that God will give us the faith to obey His commandment to love our enemies and that we would not harbor a spirit of vengeance against the perpetrators of these atrocities. We are commanded to pray for them, to pray knowing that God loves them and God wants them to come to know Jesus as Savior as well.

Let us pray that God will convict them and that they will have the calluses removed from their heart and the blinders from their eyes that they may see that God, who is the Father of our Lord Jesus Christ, is the one true God.[101]

The next day, Land shared his thoughts on his *For Faith and Family* radio program. He made the observation that this had been "an attack on civilization, not just America." He also stated Americans must insist that they "are not going to allow our way of life to be threatened by these barbarians." He then noted, "These threats must be eliminated," acknowledging, "We have the power" and asking, "Do we have the will?" He then declared, "We must declare war against terrorism." And on a personal note, he suggested parents love, hug, touch, and read to their children and reassure them things would be better. Of great significance was the fact that through these events God opened multiple major doors for Southern Baptists to share a Christian worldview. ERLC staffers worked with journalists and producers from a host of news networks, including CNN, FOX News, and MSNBC, as well as many international media outlets. Opportunities increased dramatically for speaking engagements in university settings, panel discussions, forums, and other venues.[102]

Under the radar screen and almost unnoticed, a few days later Land was appointed by President Bush to the U.S. Commission on International Religious Freedom (USCIRF). In response to his nomination, Land admitted, "It will be a privilege to labor alongside the other eight members of the USCIRF to spotlight and monitor repressive regimes and nations that are denying basic human rights to those within their boundaries."[103]

On September 20, President Bush addressed the joint session of Congress and the American people with a major policy address. He highlighted the role of Al-Qaeda, Osama Bin Laden, and the Taliban, which harbored the former in Afghanistan. He declared, "Our war with terror begins with Al-Qaeda, but it does not end there." He expanded, "It will not end until every terrorist group of global reach has been found, stopped and defeated." He then declared to every nation in the world that "either you are with us, or you are with the terrorists." Not surprisingly, when the Taliban refused to hand over Bin Laden, Afghanistan was invaded on October 7, 2001.[104]

In September, Land released his assessment of the state of the nation and made it very clear the United States had every justification to enter into this "just war." After detailing components of a "just war," Land stated:

> This is a defensive war. We've been attacked, and our citizens have been slaughtered, and they will continue to die in the hundreds if not thousands unless we attack these terrorists and remove their safe havens and places of refuge. It's not a question of whether people are going to die; it's a question whether innocent citizens are going to die as opposed to perpetrators of this evil and trained soldiers, sailors and airmen who have volunteered to put themselves in harm's way to defend our nation. . . . Unless we deal with this problem, we can expect biological, chemical and even nuclear attacks against our civilian population.[105]

Throughout the remainder of the year, the Commission and Land continued to address moral and religious liberty issues, yet the war on terror and how to cope in this new environment seemed to be foremost on the minds of the American people.

The new year, 2002, brought a number of issues which the Commission had to address. Not surprisingly, the religiously and morally conservative posture of the Commission was not embraced by everyone. In fact, early in the new year, Land found it necessary to respond to a new Democratic tactic, that of comparing the "religious right" to the Taliban. Land commented, "It appears that the Democrats are willing to say if you are not going to favor special rights for homosexuals or the continued killing of a baby every 20 seconds, then you are the American Taliban." It seemed Democrat strategists were attempting to form a mental link between religious extremism and intolerance in Afghanistan and at home. Land, very simply, called the plan, "outrageous" and noted, "the only way they (the Democratic operatives) can get away with it is if we take it lying down." Land maintained that this was being driven by "secular fundamentalists" who, he maintained, "want to silence and stigmatize everyone who disagrees with them."[106]

Criticism also came from those who were pushing the cloning of human beings. Their argument was that religious conservatives were attempting to "impose their moral code." Land commented, "We are not trying to impose our beliefs at the point of a gun." He explained, "We are out with information and ideas rooted in Scripture, and in the United States, if you can convince a majority of citizens you are right, you have the right for your view to prevail." Land concluded saying, "A human clone is a human being."[107]

The worst form of criticism of religious conservatives came when, in the U.S. Senate Judiciary Committee, Judge Charles Pickering was rejected as being qualified to sit on the Fifth Circuit Court of Appeal. His flaw? He was a conservative Southern Baptist judge who had in fact served as president of the Mississippi Baptist Convention at one time. Land's assessment was that "Judge Pickering believes in the rights of the unborn; he seeks to interpret not change the law; and he refuses to follow the radical homosexual agenda and subvert the will of the American people who are, for example, adamantly opposed to homosexual marriage. . . . This was a party-line rejection of a good and decent man."[108]

Pro-life and pro-family issues were quite demanding during the first part of 2002. Early in the year, both Norma McCorvey and Sandra Cano were featured in pro-life television commercials. The president's proposal that health care benefits be extended to the unborn received severe criticism. Land characterized the critics as those who continued to embrace the "pro-death agenda." Later in the spring, the U.S. House again passed the Child Custody Protection Act, which would ban the transport of underage girls for abortions across state lines. When this bill was passed before, however, the Senate had killed it by inaction.[109]

Four times, Land addressed the issue of the homosexual agenda and the drive for its normalization. In the discussion of the "American Taliban," John Walker Lindh, Land pointed out that part of what this young man rejected about American life was his father's departure from the family and leap into the homosexual lifestyle. Land also addressed the seriousness and wrong-headedness of the American Academy of Pediatrics' new support of adoption rights for homosexuals. Asked about the strife within the Roman Catholic Church over pedophile priests, Land commented that "the welfare of children, not the restoration for the clergy, should be the priority in dealing with sexual abuse by church leaders." Later in the spring, Land endorsed the House's consideration of a constitutional amendment to define marriage as a union between a man and a woman exclusively.[110]

In March, Land wrote to President Bush and asked him to veto the campaign finance reform bill. When the bill was examined closely, it had some components that would limit the free speech rights of citizens and attempted to limit non-profit groups from using advertising to promote or oppose issues prior to campaigns.[111]

In the spring, Land also criticized the Supreme Court's ruling that invalidated portions of the Child Pornography Prevention Act. If the images on a computer were computer-generated and not "real," then they were not criminal, the Court ruled. Land commented, "This decision by the Supreme Court marks a dark day for the court and an even darker day for the nation's children." Hypocritically, Representative Mark Foley stated, "I'm deeply disappointed the high court sided with pedophiles over children."[112]

In April, Land sent a letter to Bush asking him to use his influence to continue fighting the trafficking of women and children, especially in some of the Eastern European countries. When a new report from the U.S. State Department was released on the same subject, Land expressed his displeasure and ERLC staffer Shannon Royce noted it was a "deplorable shirking of responsibility."[113]

Leading up to the 2002 Convention, Land also addressed issues of anti-Semitism, concern over Arafat's credibility, and offered his assessment of the state of affairs concerning the Second Amendment. All in all, the winter and spring kept Land and the Commission extremely busy with speaking engagements, interviews, press statements and press conferences. In fact, Bural informed Land that in the eleven-month period after 9/11, Land had been the focus of 936 interviews.[114]

Yet, no doubt the highlight for Land leading up to the 2002 Southern Baptist Convention in St. Louis was the launch of his new Saturday talk show, *Richard Land Live!*, on June 8, 2002. The program airs noon to 3 p.m. Eastern Time on the Salem Radio Network and the Bott Radio Network. It features Land at his best as he addresses contemporary spiritual, social, moral, and religious liberty issues, and interacts with callers from across the country. About the show, Land said, "It is my prayer that *Richard Land Live!* will aid listeners in examining issues in light of the presuppositions of a Judeo-Christian worldview and help them integrate such a process in their everyday lives." He summarized, "In short, we want to help listeners think 'Christianly' about the issues of the day."[115]

Perhaps a close second to the launch of *Richard Land Live!* was the release of his new book, *For Faith and Family: Changing America by Strengthening the Family*. The thesis of the book is that change comes from the inside out; and if only we can build strong families, those strong families can help build America. In the course of the book, Land addresses the enemies that are attacking the family, and offers sound guidance on how to be victorious. Of greater significance, however, is the fact that this volume marked the birth of a publishing strategy, spearheaded by Bural, with which the Commission would repeatedly address major moral and cultural issues.[116]

The Convention met in St. Louis on June 11–12, 2002. In his written report, Land pointed out that President Bush appointed him to the U.S. Commission on International Religious Freedom. The launching of *Richard Land Live!* was so new that it was not even mentioned in the report. The report did address two motions referred from the 2001 Convention on faith-based initiatives essentially expressing that Southern Baptists exercise caution. A third motion referred to the Commission proposed forming a task force to facilitate ministry to those who struggle with same-sex attraction. Land responded that his intention was to work with LifeWay to make it happen.[117]

In his verbal report, Land stated the "culture is locked in a fierce battle over whether humans will continue to be defined as unique creations of God." Addressing the issue of genetic manipulation, Land said, "Whether man is going to continue to be as God created him to be or we are going to allow man to play God and manipulate human genetic structure and clone human beings for their own profit is what is at stake." He urged fellow believers to contact senators who were working to "provide a firewall against the cloning of human beings." He encouraged Southern Baptists to get involved in the political process.[118]

As expected, resolutions reflected much of the year's concerns of the Commission. The first resolution, not surprisingly was "On Terrorism." The Convention also adopted resolutions on the sexual integrity of ministers, the sufficiency of Scripture in a therapeutic culture, on the support of timely reviews for judicial nominations, on the martyrdom of Martin Burnham (a New Tribes Missionary in the Philippines), and on partial-birth abortion.[119]

The rest of the summer found Land and the Commission addressing a truckload of issues. As technology and communications had improved, the capacity to influence Southern Baptists and U.S. public policy was escalating at an exponential pace. All the issues addressed earlier in the year had their follow up in the summer. Working with the Commission's research staff, Barrett Duke compiled an on-line package of articles on "Just War," with Land's article as its main piece, to help interested people understand the issue.

In the fall, Land addressed issues related to Just War theory, which brought him once again onto the national stage. On the one-year anniversary of the terrorist attacks on America, Land articulated the components of a Just War. Reviewing what had occurred to date, Land stated, "If you are looking for just cause, we have already passed that threshold," speaking of the prospects of going to war with Iraq.[120]

In a letter to President Bush written by Land and signed by Chuck Colson, Bill Bright, James Kennedy, and Carl Herbster, Land articulated the components of Just War theory. These include a just cause, a just intent, that it be as a last resort, that it be by a legitimate authority with limited goals, that it be with the intention of noncombatant immunity, and that it have appropriate proportionality. With the components of Just War laid out, Land assured President Bush that he had the prayers and support of a vast number of Southern Baptists and other fellow Americans. If ever the president needed wisdom, it was in the days immediately ahead.[121]

As the New Year approached, war with Saddam Hussein and Iraq appeared more and more likely. Although Land and the Commission were involved in numerous domestic issues, the prospect of the impending war was the darkest cloud on the horizon.

In the new year, 2003, Land and the Commission again faced a long list of issues each demanding attention. On January 7, Land wrote to Bill Frist, then-Senate majority leader, and Dennis Hastert, then-Speaker of the House of Representatives, asking both of them to support comprehensive bans on cloning. The ERLC provided educational support for this issue by producing a major paper on cloning and posting it and numerous other articles on the Commission's web site. Other legislative priorities offered by Land were the confirmation of pro-life judges and a plea to support other pro-life legislation. Other pro-life issues addressed by Land during the first few months of 2003 included revisiting the notorious *Roe* decision from thirty years earlier and the stark confession that 42 million American babies had died. Providing his assessment, Land stated,

> As a culture, we have chosen to ignore the value God places on each human life. . . . We have strict federal laws in the Endangered Species Act that protects the snail darter fish and the spotted owl. In California it's a crime to disturb a seagull's nest because the unhatched eggs represent the potential for life. And yet abortion remains legal and commonplace in this country thirty years after *Roe v. Wade.* . . . Sad as it seems, this news doesn't even make a ripple in the public debate anymore.[122]

Land was grateful when the House of Representatives approved a comprehensive bill banning cloning. Late in February, the Supreme Court voted eight to one in the combined *Scheidler v. NOW* and *Operation Rescue v. NOW* to rule that abortion protesters cannot be prosecuted under federal anti-racketeering laws. Land considered this a great victory for those dependent on free speech and freedom of assembly to let their voice be heard.[123]

Land also addressed the issue of capital punishment. Citing a January 2002 study by Emory University, he pointed out that "legal change allowing executions beginning in 1977 has been associated with significant reductions in homicides" in a study of 3,054 U.S. counties between 1977–1996.[124] The ERLC continued to hold to the biblical teaching on this issue, and Barrett Duke wrote an article on capital punishment for the new *Holman Bible Dictionary*, published by B&H Publishing Group.

When a new set of guidelines was released by the Department of Education on what is and is not a proper display of religion in public schools, Land expressed his appreciation to President Bush and secretary of education, Rod Paige, "for clarifying and re-emphasizing the freedom of students to express their religious beliefs and convictions while on public school property." He then noted, "We need to consistently remind school administrators and radical secularists that the Supreme Court has made it clear . . . that students do not leave their First Amendment rights of speech, assembly and worship at the boundaries of public school property."[125]

At the end of February, Land again joined a cadre of other evangelical leaders in addressing the president. This time, it was to commend him for addressing the HIV/AIDS crisis in Africa. The letter, also signed by numerous others, recommended a strategy that these Christian organizations believed would work best to alleviate the suffering.[126]

March and April of 2003 were overshadowed by the U.S. and its allies invading Iraq. The air war was launched on March 20; and by April 9, the land war had taken Baghdad. Time would prove that winning the peace would be much more difficult than winning the war. One gratifying event during these tumultuous days occurred when the U.S. Senate passed a partial-birth abortion ban.[127]

During this time, Land made the strategic decision to relocate Barrett Duke to Washington, D.C., with the express intention of bringing greater influence on public policy decisions. Concerning the move, Land said, "Integrating our research and public policy teams into one unit is a move I have contemplated for some time. . . . God opened the door for such an organizational change and the shifting of resources to our Washington office. . . . I am grateful He has provided Barrett Duke to oversee this new approach." Part of Duke's responsibilities was to pick up the load from Shannon Royce, who moved into a consultant role with the Commission. Land viewed Duke's move to Washington as providential. Land noted that Duke built off Royce's work and actually increased the visibility and effectiveness of the Washington, D.C., office through his involvement in the many policy discussions on Capitol Hill and his numerous coalition-building activities, which included starting a broad-based coalition to address human rights and religious freedom in the U.S. and around the world.

Duke also focused on developing an active national grassroots network of Southern Baptists that is prepared to act to help influence public policy decisions, using the Internet as a key medium for this strategy. Assessing Duke's transition, Land commented,[128]

> When Shannon announced that she would be leaving our
> employment full time, I decided to ask Barrett to move to

Washington. I felt it was important at this time to have someone who understood us in a way that only someone who had
worked in Nashville and who was a pastoral person and who
was also committed to the culture could. The more I thought
about it, I'm looking for someone and he is right under my
nose. It was a considerable sacrifice for Barrett. He was settled
here (Nashville), but he was willing to pray about it and willing
to do it, and we are profoundly grateful.[129]

At the same time that Duke was reassigned to Washington,
D.C., Land made another strategic move that had far-reaching consequences. Land recommended to his trustee executive committee that
Harold Harper be assigned the newly created position of executive
vice president. The principal responsibilities included the coordination
of the work of the other vice presidents and acting as the team leader
directly answerable to Land. The recommendation was unanimously
approved. Reflecting on Harper's promotion, Land said:

We were working well together. We came to the place
where it became apparent to me that instead of talking to each
vice president I had to have one person, a choke point, and
the choke point was one person the VPs could go to and one
person I could go to. It fits my management style. My management style is very consciously Ronald Reagan. I believe that you
find the best possible people you can find that are in sync with
your vision, and you give them clear parameters about what
you want them to do, and then you depend on them and let
them do it unless there is a problem. My philosophy is that if
someone else in the organization can do it, then I shouldn't be
doing it which then leaves me free to do those things that only
the president can do. I also believe in instantaneous feedback.
I do not believe in annual reviews. I believe in instantaneous
feedback—negative and positive. If somebody does a great job,
I'm going to tell them they did a great job; I'm going to tell
them why I thought they did a great job. If they did something
that should have been done better, I'm going to give them

instantaneous feedback right then so they can learn from it and not wait for an annual review. We don't do annual reviews; we do continuous, instantaneous reviews. I am not a microman- ager. One of the things I have to take into consideration when I hire people—I have to have self-starters. I can't have people just waiting around waiting to be told what to do because that's not my management style. My management style is: This is what we need to get done; this is what I expect you to do. Now, I'm not going to look over your shoulder until it doesn't get done. Then we're going to have a conversation. I'm a forest kind of guy, which means I need lots of tree counters around me.

Harper is the chief tree counter for Land. Continuing his thought, Land related, "Another part of my philosophy includes my personnel policy. I believe that you find God's man or God's woman and then you write the job description. Tom Landry had a system and he fit players into the system, and Bum (Phillips) had players and he fit the system around the players. I'm a Bum Phillips' guy."[130]

Meanwhile, in two public addresses and one corporate letter sent to President Bush, Land commended the president for his step against Iraq but reminded him of the importance of supporting Israel.[131]

Leading up to the Southern Baptist Convention, Land and the Commission's D.C. office were heavily engaged in pressing for passage of the Partial-Birth Abortion Ban. The U.S. House, on June 4, passed its version of the Partial-Birth Abortion Ban by a vote of 282–139. The Senate's vote was sixty-four to thirty-three. When the conference resolved the two versions, it was sent to President Bush for a certain signature.[132]

On June 10 in Canada, an Ontario Appeals Court changed Canada's definition of marriage from "a union of one man and one woman" to "the voluntary union for life of two persons to the exclu- sion of all others." In a *Baptist Press* article, Michael Foust wrote, "America's social conservatives fear that a cultural battle is on the horizon, the likes of which could rival even the debate over abortion." All of this formed the backdrop to the 2003 Southern Baptist Conven- tion in Phoenix, Arizona, June 17–18.[133]

The Commission's printed report included the standard updates on a variety of issues, yet the opening in this year's report was distinctly different. Land reviewed the ministry assignment, which is, "To assist churches by helping them understand the moral demands of the gospel, apply Christian principles to moral and social problems and questions of public policy, and to promote religious liberty in cooperation with the churches and other Southern Baptist entities." He continued by sharing the results of his executive team's retreat in which together they hammered out the nuances of the Commission's newly articulated vision and mission statements:

> As we have reflected on this ministry assignment, God has given us a vision for America that has energized every facet of our work. Our vision is: An American society that affirms and practices Judeo-Christian values rooted in biblical authority. A society like this would not only respect the values that undergird our lives as Christians; it would live by those values. This society would honor those things that honor God and create a place where all people can achieve their highest possible potential. In this society all men would be treated as equals, and every life would be valued; morality, honor, integrity, and justice would be national virtues. Such a society would enjoy marvelous blessings from God, and be a source of inspiration for all the world.[134]

Land went on to write that the mission statement embodying this vision and now adopted by the Commission was, "To awaken, inform, energize, equip, and mobilize Christians to be the catalysts for the biblically based transformation of their families, churches, communities, and the nation." Land continued to explain that the "starting point for this transformation is obvious." He noted, "We believe the Southern Baptist Convention has identified the key to changing America: The key to healthy people, healthy churches, and a healthy nation are healthy families." Land next expressed the fact that his two foundational concerns would be worldview issues and the relations of the family to the broader culture. Land expounded on his premise by describing the building blocks that the Commission would use to address these issues.[135]

When Land addressed the Convention, he talked about the importance of strong families. A Baptist Press report stated, "Land cited a 10-year Duke University study that revealed it was not only the absence of fathers in a household but also the timing of their departure that made a critical difference in their daughters' future behavior." He further cited the alarming statistic that "girls reared in a home where the biological father left before their sixth birthday were five times more likely to become sexually active before turning fifteen than girls whose fathers were still in the home." He then focused on the importance of putting a priority on family.[136]

When resolution time came, the Convention adopted eight resolutions and two of them addressed the family. The first was "On Kingdom Families" and a later one was "On Same-Sex Marriage." Of critical importance, because of its timing, was the resolution, "On the Liberation of Iraq." A resolution that carried implications for Iraq and Afghanistan, too, as well as the U.S., was "On Religious Liberty." Coupled with these was a resolution "On Anti-Semitism," which decried "all forms of bigotry, hatred, or persecution." Still another resolution, which was supported by the work of the Commission, was "On the Global AIDS Crisis."[137]

Of particular note was the resolution, "On Thirty Years of *Roe v. Wade*," which in many ways rejected what the Southern Baptist Convention might have said in the past to support abortion and made a forthright declaration of what the Convention now, with clarity and conviction, embraced:

> WHEREAS, Scripture reveals that all human life is created in the image of God, and therefore sacred to our Creator (Genesis 1:27; Genesis 9:6); and
>
> WHEREAS, The Bible affirms that the unborn baby is a person bearing the image of God from the moment of conception (Psalm 139:13–16; Luke 1:44); and

WHEREAS, Scripture further commands the people of God to plead for protection for the innocent and justice for the fatherless (Psalm 72:12–14; Psalm 82:3; James 1:27); and

WHEREAS, January 2003 marked thirty years since the 1973 United States Supreme Court Roe v. Wade decision, which legalized abortion in all fifty states; and

WHEREAS, Resolutions passed by the Southern Baptist Convention in 1971 and 1974 accepted unbiblical premises of the abortion rights movement, forfeiting the opportunity to advocate the protection of defenseless women and children; and

WHEREAS, During the early years of the post-Roe era, some of those then in leadership positions within the denomination endorsed and furthered the "pro-choice" abortion rights agenda outlined in Roe v. Wade; and

WHEREAS, Some political leaders have referenced 1970s-era Southern Baptist Convention resolutions and statements by former Southern Baptist Convention leaders to oppose legislative efforts to protect women and children from abortion; and

WHEREAS, Southern Baptist churches have effected a renewal of biblical orthodoxy and confessional integrity in our denomination, beginning with the Southern Baptist Convention presidential election of 1979; and

WHEREAS, The Southern Baptist Convention has maintained a robust commitment to the sanctity of all human life, including that of the unborn, beginning with a landmark pro-life resolution in 1982; and

WHEREAS, Our confessional statement, The Baptist Faith and Message, affirms that children "from the moment of conception, are a blessing and heritage from the Lord"; and further affirms that Southern Baptists are mandated by Scripture to "speak on behalf of the unborn and contend for the sanctity of all human life from conception to natural death"; and

WHEREAS, The legacy of Roe v. Wade has grown to include ongoing assaults on human life such as euthanasia, the harvesting of human embryos for the purposes of medical experimentation, and an accelerating move toward human cloning; now, therefore, be it

RESOLVED, That the messengers to the Southern Baptists Convention meeting in Phoenix, Arizona, June 17–18, 2003, reiterate our conviction that the 1973 Roe v. Wade decision was based on a fundamentally flawed understanding of the United States Constitution, human embryology, and the basic principles of human rights; and be it further

RESOLVED, That we reaffirm our belief that the Roe v. Wade decision was an act of injustice against innocent unborn children as well as against vulnerable women in crisis pregnancy situations, both of which have been victimized by a

"sexual revolution" that empowers predatory and irresponsible men and by a lucrative abortion industry that has fought against even the most minimal restrictions on abortion; and be it further

RESOLVED, That we offer our prayers, our love, and our advocacy for women and men who have been abused by abortion and the emotional, spiritual, and physical aftermath of this horrific practice; affirming that the gospel of Jesus Christ grants complete forgiveness for any sin, including that of abortion; and be it further

RESOLVED, That we lament and renounce statements and actions by previous Conventions and previous denominational leadership that offered support to the abortion culture; and be it further

RESOLVED, That we humbly confess that the initial blindness of many in our Convention to the enormity of Roe v. Wade should serve as a warning to contemporary Southern Baptists of the subtlety of the spirit of the age in obscuring a biblical worldview; and be it further

RESOLVED, that we urge our Southern Baptist churches to remain vigilant in the protection of human life by preaching the whole counsel of God on matters of human sexuality and the sanctity of life, by encouraging and empowering Southern Baptists to adopt unwanted children, by providing spiritual, emotional, and financial support for women in crisis pregnancies, and by calling on our government officials to take action to protect the lives of women and children; and be it further

RESOLVED, That we express our appreciation to both houses of Congress for their passage of the Partial-Birth Abortion Ban Act of 2003, and we applaud President Bush for his commitment to sign this bill into law; and be it further

RESOLVED, That we urge Congress to act swiftly to deliver this bill to President Bush for his signature; and be it finally

RESOLVED, That we pray and work for the repeal of the Roe v. Wade decision and for the day when the act of abortion will be not only illegal, but also unthinkable.[138]

After the Convention, Land stated, "It's never too late to say you're sorry." He then confessed, "We need to express our sorrow and our grief over the fact that for a time our convention was officially, through its resolution process, on the wrong side of this issue." Land concluded the interview asserting, "Southern Baptists [now] stand with other Bible-believing people as the last line of defense against the culture of death."[139]

No sooner had the dust settled from the Phoenix Convention than the Supreme Court announced its notorious landmark decision on the *Lawrence v. Texas* case on June 26. In the six to three decision, the Court ruled "a Texas law prohibiting homosexual sodomy violated the privacy and liberty of adults, under the Due Process Clause of the Fourteenth Amendment, to engage in private intimate conduct." Just seventeen years earlier in the *Bowers v. Hardwick* case the Court stated it could not find "a constitutional protection of sexual privacy."

Conservatives were dumbfounded and the homosexual rights crowd was ecstatic.[140]

Anthony Scalia offered a scathing rebuke in his dissent; Rehnquist and Thomas joined him. In short, Scalia accused the majority of fabricating law to conclude their predetermined ends, and in effect, castigated them for opening a proverbial Pandora's Box which quite likely would never be shut.[141]

As the summer passed, Land and the Commission addressed numerous issues that were emerging on the cultural landscape. He was critical, and rightly so, of the Episcopal Church's ordination of Gene Robinson, a practicing homosexual, to be the bishop of New Hampshire. In Land's words, his election was an expression of the church embracing a "deadly theology."[142]

At the end of August, Land's assessment of all the "10 Commandment" concerns were that they were expressions of a runaway judiciary which needed to be checked and balanced. To him, it was "further evidence of an ongoing pattern of attempts by judges to impose a secular bias on public places."[143]

On October 16, the case of Terri Schiavo became front-page news and Baptist Press ran the first of almost 150 stories on the subject. At this point, the severely brain-damaged woman's family, the Schindler's, had been waging a five-year court battle with Terri's husband, who subsequently had moved in with his lover and fathered children with her. After collecting a court settlement in a medical malpractice lawsuit, he reportedly said he remembered after the fact that Terri had said she would not want to live like that so he had petitioned the court to withhold food and water until she died from starvation and dehydration. This became a nationwide story that set in marked contrast the culture of life and the culture of death. This clear case of euthanasia was fought in legislatures, executive offices, and the judiciary. Its eventual outcome caused many to ask, "How could that happen here in the United States?"[144]

The one bright spot in the latter weeks of 2003 occurred on November 5, when President Bush signed into law the Partial-Birth Abortion Ban Act, "the first restriction on a particular procedure since the Court legalized abortion 30 years ago." After meeting with the president in the Oval Office, Land said, "Today is a landmark day in the long struggle to rekindle the vibrant flame of the sanctity of life ethic upon which this nation was founded." He went on to express his belief that "Passage of this bill is the best of news for all Americans— first, for the unborn, who will have at least some marginal protection at the moment before birth, and second, for all citizens, since God is not going to bless a nation that countenances the barbaric and heinous act of partial-birth abortion."[145]

Although 2003 was filled with great turbulence on the moral and social front, not to mention the international front, Land and the Commission did everything within the limits of their power to motivate and speak for Southern Baptists and the greater Christian community. Of all the addresses, interviews, articles, and product Land and his team produced, this author believes there is none more poignant and timely than his address in the fall to the Commission's trustees. Land stated:

> If not for the United States, religious liberty would not
> be an issue of concern for most countries or the United
> Nations. . . . The only reason anybody in the world goes to
> bed at night with any degree of freedom and dignity is because
> of the United States of America and its citizens' willingness to
> stand up not only for their own rights and liberty but for the
> lives, dignity and liberty of others. . . . It is a universal, inherent
> longing of the human heart that, given the opportunity, people
> want freedom and the right to follow their conscience. . . . If we
> lose our will to stand for that, a lot more is at peril than just
> the freedom of Americans.[146]

Land, like his trustees, staff, and Southern Baptist constituency, understood the crucial and even providential role the United States has played in world affairs. And closer to home, they realized the critical role that Southern Baptists play in shaping America.

Perhaps the low point of the year came in the death of former Commission staffer King Sanders on October 30. About King, Land and his trustees said: "Your perseverance has inspired us and your concern for the local church has instructed us. Your enthusiastic and effective ministry among us has blessed us. We are grateful for your resolve to do God's will no matter what the cost." King, who died of heart failure, was only 54.[147]

When the New Year, 2004, came so did a slate of challenges for the Ethics & Religious Liberty Commission. On January 4, New Jersey Governor James McGreevy signed into law a bill that authorized therapeutic human cloning and approved for parents with unwanted embryos to donate them for research. A few days later, Democratic presidential hopeful, Howard Dean, announced his endorsement of homosexual unions due to his religious beliefs. He stated: "From a religious point of view, if God had thought homosexuality is a sin, he would not have created gay people. . . . My view of Christianity . . . is that the hallmark of being a Christian is to reach out to people who have been left behind. So I think there was a religious aspect to my decision to support civil unions."[148]

Between the major issues still hot from the previous year like the Terri Schiavo case, or the debate in courts over partial-birth abortion, or the headlines from the previous week, on his *Richard Land Live!* show Land felt compelled to spell out his perception of what was unfolding in the culture. The "contemporary culture is home to two very disparate civilizations: Judeo-Christian civilization, which is based on the sanctity of all human life, and the neo-pagan civilization, which zealously promotes a relativist quality-of-life." He explained, "When these two totally antagonistic worldviews come up against each other, it makes a real difference in people's lives because real people die when the quality-of-life ethic usurps the sanctity-of-life ethic." He went on to say, "The only hope is for the people of God to stand up and say enough is enough."[149]

Of primary concern in 2004 was the consideration of the Federal Marriage Amendment. Over the course of the winter and into the spring, headlines read, "Land, others encourage Bush to support Marriage Amendment;" "Bush to endorse Marriage Amendment, leaders say;" "President Bush backs Marriage Amendment, says 'activist' judges, officials warrant action;" "Marriage initiative, along with welfare reform, halts in Senate;" "Marriage Amendment needs grass-roots outcry, Land says;" "Same-sex marriage no longer make believe;" "Psychologists' OK of same-sex unions called 'gay-agenda;'" "Federal Marriage Amendment: Far from dead;" "Land: Marriage debate is over society's 'basic building block;'" "Marriage amend. falls short of 290, but receives majority vote;" and "Thousands rally in nation's capitol for traditional marriage."[150]

As anyone can tell from reading these headlines, a major debate in the culture, sadly, was over the definition of marriage. If ever there was a need for Christians who believe in the traditional construct of marriage to stand up and let their voice be heard, it was at this time over this issue! The Research Institute responded to this need by publishing an FAQ on homosexuality for the Commission's Web site. When completed the project provided answers to twenty-two frequently asked questions about homosexuality, including questions about theology, genetics, culture, and ministry.

When Believers Vote Their Values

Because this was an election year, Land and others who were passionate about the culture created a venue for Christians to express their convictions at the ballot box. On February 17, Land, speaking to Southern Baptists' Executive Committee, announced that "he is spearheading a voter education and registration drive to encourage Americans to vote their values, not their pocketbook or their political party." The initiative adopted the "iVoteValues" moniker, established an *iVoteValues.com* Web page, and did everything possible to encourage voters to vote their values.[151]

The genesis of the iVoteValues campaign was, in Land's words, "a miracle." While attending a Washington, D.C., meeting with leaders of conservative grassroots organizations, one person looked at Land and said concerning the 2004 elections, "Richard, if we're going to mobilize the grassroots, you're going to have to do it." Harper, who was with Land, commented after the meeting that he was "in shock—nothing like pressure!" Upon their return to Nashville, Harper met with Kerry Bural and related the conversation along with Land's concern that people not vote their party or pocketbook but their values and Land's desire to create a strong voter registration campaign. At that point, Bural gathered his creative team and they coined the tagline, "iVoteValues."[152]

The following month, Land, Harper, and Bural were in Colorado Springs in a series of meetings. Harper and Bural visited the offices of Focus on the Family to inquire of their plans to mobilize voters. Their contacts said FOTF did not have a game plan but expressed interest in the Commission's ideas. At that point, Bural pulled out sketches of the iVoteValues campaign. From out of the blue, the Focus representatives offered to partner with the Commission and Southern Baptists. And almost immediately the Family Research Council (FRC), an organization spun off Focus on the Family, requested to partner as well. In Harper's words, "This whole meeting was a God thing." In order to maintain a strict separation of organizations, the Commission retained the iVoteValues.com URL while giving iVoteValues.org to Focus and the FRC.[153]

A further component in the campaign was the availability of the Sid Yochim family's eighteen-wheeler, which became a moving advertisement for the campaign as well as a mobile center for voter registration. Yochim and his family lived in Middle Tennessee. A final factor in the launch of the campaign was a nationwide simulcast from Bellevue Baptist Church in Memphis on Sunday, July 11, 2004, (7:00–8:30 p.m.) Overall, as 2004 unfolded and with it the election cycle, the iVoteValues campaign and the mobilization of the values voters proved to be a major factor in the reelection of a pro-life president, which eventually resulted in the nomination and confirmation of conservative jurists John Roberts and Samuel Alito to the Supreme Court, not to mention the maintaining of Bush's pro-life and pro-family policies, which for the most part were a manifestation of the Christian voters' values.[154]

As the spring progressed, one highlight was the passage of the "Unborn Victims of Violence Act," strongly supported and promoted by the ERLC. In short, "The bill treats an unborn child as a crime victim when he or she is injured or slain during the commission of a federal offense against a pregnant woman." Land commented that this was a significant step forward in reasserting the legal rights of human persons to the unborn. He went on to say, "It is yet one more indication that we are slowly but surely winning the battle for the hearts and minds of the American public when it comes to the personhood of unborn human beings. . . . We should draw inspiration from this victory to strengthen our resolve to move forward and not rest until every unborn child has the same protection under the law that each of us possess."

Not surprisingly, Gloria Feldt, president of the Planned Parenthood Federation of America, stated, "It is part of a deceptive anti-choice strategy to make women's bodies mere vessels by creating legal personhood for the fetus." Many may better remember this law as "Laci and Conner's Law," after Laci Peterson and her unborn son who were found murdered.[155]

While all these issues were swirling about, the ERLC determined it must end its hunger needs partnership with the North American Mission Board and the International Mission Board. This project, originally planned to last three years, lasted for more than seven. When the two SBC mission boards decided they were no longer able to assist with financial support of the ministry, the ERLC was forced to reassign Steven Nelson, the entity's director of hunger concerns, to additional duties.

Later in the spring, Land was awarded two significant citations. A Nashville-based magazine identified him as one of Tennessee's "power elite," calling him "the chief ideologue at the Southern Baptist Convention," noting that "he leads the self-proclaimed war on behalf of all Christendom against homosexuality, amorality and foreign religions." A few weeks later, Land was recognized by the *National Journal* as one of the ten top church-state experts "politicians will call on when they get serious about addressing important public policy issues."[156]

In the weeks just prior to the 2004 Southern Baptist Convention meeting in Indianapolis, Land sent two very important letters in two very different directions. On May 18, he sent a letter co-signed by concerned supporters from around the world to leaders of the Czech Republic. Land expressed in gravest tones and terms his great concern about their announced intention to legalize prostitution. A second letter, sent on June 9 to House Speaker Dennis Hastert, encouraged him in his efforts to restore the free speech rights taken from the churches in 1954 when then-Senator Lyndon Johnson led Congress to prohibit 501(c)(3) organizations "from participating in or intervening in any political campaign on behalf of any candidate for public office." Land expressed his concern over a portion of the bill that seemed to give the IRS latitude to meddle in the internal affairs of churches.[157]

Both of these letters, as with the citations in the previous paragraph, served to demonstrate that Richard Land, representing Southern Baptists, was an extremely influential figure whose positions, convictions, opinions, and suggestions carried considerable weight. Due to this perception of Land, it was not surprising to find him giving a major policy address at Rice University on "Global Security and U.S. National Interests: Why Religious Freedom Matters."[158]

At the same time the Southern Baptists met in Indianapolis, June 15–16, Land released his latest book, *Real Homeland Security*. Echoing lectures, addresses, and commentary from recent years, Land painted a vivid word picture of the kind of America God would bless and steps necessary to receive those blessings. This call to renewal was a hope-filled vision of what America could be and a practical challenge to every believer on what their part should be.[159]

When the Convention was in session, Land in typical fashion and according to historical precedent referred messengers to their printed report in the SBC *Book of Reports*. This provided an update on the Commission's impact. Of particular interest was the development of printed materials and the entity's media exposure, which Land credited as the divine Hand of God. The report stated:

> Dr. Land and other ERLC staff were interviewed nearly
> 500 times by local and national television, radio, and print
> news organizations, addressing the whole range of ethical and
> moral issues, from embryonic stem cell research to faith-based
> initiatives to religious persecution:

For the third consecutive year, God has granted Dr. Land unparalleled opportunities to communicate the ERLC message through various radio, print and television interviews. His television exposure increased by 1,260 percent since September 1, 2002, his significant radio exposure held steady, while his print exposure increased by 1,181 percent. We have also seen a significant increase in international exposure. The potential listening, viewing, and readership audience surpassed 500 million people.[160]

When Land delivered his verbal report to the Convention, he focused on the necessity of Christians being involved in the nation's electoral process. He announced the Commission was partnering with the Family Research Council and Focus on the Family to produce three satellite-borne simulcasts on issues critical to America. He commented that it was "a disgrace that 33 percent of the members of an average Southern Baptist Church are not even registered to vote." He then declared, "It is every Christian's responsibility to be registered to vote, to be an informed voter, and to vote their values, beliefs and convictions." He went on to explain:

We are to be obedient for conscience's sake in a participatory republic like the United States. That means we get involved in the public policy process. It is not enough to say that we look forward to a day when decisions are made in our homes, in our states, in our churches, and in our nation's capitol that are totally in accordance with biblical principles. We have not only to work for that, to pray for that, and to seek God's blessing for that, we have to help people, confront people and equip people and give them an opportunity to do it. . . . The culture faces issues of titanic importance that demand that Christians respond. This is a life-changing election cycle in the history of the United States. We have converging visions and they are contrasting visions for America's future. We need to make our voice known about which direction we want God to lead our country. Now is the time we must make our voice heard in the body politic in the United States. . . . Same-sex marriage will become the law of the land; it will be forced upon us unless the people of the United States stand up and say no.[161]

When resolution time came, the first one proposed and adopted, not surprisingly, was "On Supporting the Federal Marriage Amendment." Other resolutions included those recognizing the secularizing of our culture, on the need for Christian citizenship, on appreciating those who serve in the military, gratitude for twenty-five years of conservative resurgence, and one expressing appreciation for the life and leadership of President Ronald Reagan who had passed away a few days before the Convention met in Indianapolis.[162]

In the days following the Convention, Land and the Commission spent time addressing key issues of hate crimes, embryonic stem cells, and the Federal Marriage Amendment. On top of this, they maintained a steady focus on promoting the iVoteValues initiatives as well. By this time, Bural was leading and coordinating a team of over fifty staff and freelancers to promote the iVoteValues initiative.[163]

When the 2004 Democratic national platform was completed and published for popular review, Land was not surprised to find it affirming, "We support full inclusion of gay and lesbian families in the life of our nation and seek equal responsibilities, benefits, and protection for these families." It also stated, "In our country, marriage has been defined at the state level for 200 years, and we believe it should continue to be defined there." It continued, "We repudiate President Bush's divisive effort to politicize the Constitution by pursuing a Federal Marriage Amendment" and concluded, "Our goal is to bring Americans together, not drive them apart." Quite obviously the homosexual agenda embraced by many on the left stood in marked contrast to the vision of America embraced by the majority of Evangelical Christians.[164]

In the days preceding the election, Land was incredibly busy. In a Pew Forum on Religion and Public Life-sponsored symposium, Land with several others discussed the role and restrictions on churches in the public arena in a September 28 meeting. Commenting on government-imposed restrictions, Land stated, "We don't think that churches ought to be getting involved in partisan political activity, but we think that ought to be a decision made by the church, not the government."[165]

On October 15, Land spoke to the tens of thousands of people gathering on the National Mall at the "Mayday for Marriage Rally" in Washington, D.C., along with Ken Hutcherson, Chuck Colson, James Dobson, and others. Land gave this challenge:

> It is the prophetic leadership of pastors in churches that puts calcium in the backbone of the churches and the people of faith across America. This is the critical moment to stand in the gap as prophets and to call our people to be salt and light that God has called us to be. It is time to be salt and to stop the sexual paganization of America. It is time to be light to penetrate the darkness and to boldly proclaim what God's intention is for man and woman in the confines of holy matrimony as God designed it. . . . The United States is at a cultural fork in the road. Make no mistake about it. If we allow same-sex marriage to be foisted upon us by an imperial judiciary in the Untied States, God will not bless this nation. That's what's at stake.[166]

And just a few weeks after this, Land, meeting with his Research Institute in Nashville, held a forum on stem cell research at Lipscomb University in Nashville and prepared a "Statement on Human Stem Cell Research," which clearly identified the major issues involved.[167]

On November 2, the American voters traveled to the polls and reelected George Bush over challenger John Kerry by three million-plus votes. Reviewing the results, the undeniable conclusion was that values voters made the difference. In each of eleven states where a marriage amendment was on the ballot, it passed. Land provided this assessment:

> The underlying story, of course, is the culture war being quietly waged in communities across America. It is a story the national news media can't be blamed for overlooking. Most of

them live in the "blue" counties where the predominant culture is comfortable with the maxim "anything goes." Yet a majority of Americans recognize the agenda of those who want to redefine what marriage looks like and who justify the killing of pre-born children to serve the needs of others. And on Election Day, they made their views known.[168]

In the aftermath of the national election, Land was interviewed on *Meet the Press*.[169]

The national discussion over the cause and the impact of the national election carried on until the day after Christmas when an undersea earthquake caused a tsunami that killed over three hundred thousand and left more than five million people homeless in Indonesia and the surrounding area. Overnight, this became the world's top story. Southern Baptists immediately shifted into relief mode, raising millions of dollars and sending thousands of volunteers to minister to people whose lives had been devastated by this disaster.[170]

As customary, Land released his "legislative agenda" early in January of 2005 for what appeared to be a very promising year. His agenda included a desire to pass the Child Custody Protection Act, the Unborn Child Pain Awareness Act, a ban on human cloning for research or reproductive purposes, a constitutional amendment to protect marriage as a union of a man and a woman, and a bill designed to help bring an end to dictatorships and to promote democracy in other countries without the use of the armed forces. Other goals included promoting religious freedom, confirmation of conservative judges, restoring a degree of morality to the entertainment industry, and helping to bring to an end the trafficking of women and children. All of this and more proved to be a very ambitious legislative agenda.[171]

It would seem that life would slow down some since the election cycle had passed, but if anything, it appeared to bring a heavier workload.

In 2005, Land presented major addresses at Bucknell, Harvard, Wheaton, Georgetown, Vanderbilt, and Princeton Universities, not to mention speaking at several Southern Baptist seminaries. He was a featured speaker on the Town Meeting at Two Rivers Baptist Church when it hosted *Hardball with Chris Matthews*, was invited to do a repeat appearance on *Meet the Press*, and delivered a major address at the Council on Foreign Relations. It was little surprise that *Time* magazine named Land one of the 25 Most Influential Evangelicals in America. He joined other Southern Baptists—Rick Warren, Chuck Colson, and Tim and Beverly LaHaye—in receiving this recognition. Again, it was not surprising that he was reappointed to the U.S. Commission on International Religious Freedom.[172]

Of all the multiple issues in early 2005, none was more prominent or important than the life and death struggle for Terri Schindler Schiavo. After a war of ideas in the media, the courts, legislative and executive branches on both a state and national level, she was slowly killed, finally dying on March 30, 2005. President Bush, responding to the news of her death, stated, "I urge all those who honor Terri Schiavo to continue to work to build a culture of life, where all Americans are welcomed and valued and protected—especially those who live at the mercy of others. The essence of civilization is that the strong have a duty to protect the weak. In cases where there are serious doubts and questions, the presumption should be in the favor of life."[173]

Richard Land commented on her death, confessing it was "a sad day for America." He elaborated, saying, "It's a particularly sad day for anyone who is physically or mentally handicapped, or seriously and debilitatingly ill, and those who love them." He continued, "The judiciary at the state and federal level condemned Terri Schiavo to death by dehydration and malnutrition on the hearsay evidence of a husband who was cohabiting with another woman whom he introduced as his fiancée and with whom he fathered two children." Land went on to elaborate, saying:

> This was done in spite of the heart-wrenching pleas of
> Terri's parents, who have loved and nurtured her throughout
> her life and have repeatedly volunteered to take over respon-
> sibility for her care. It's really hard for millions of American
> parents to accept the fact that the judicial system in the United
> States of America has told a mom and a dad they cannot feed

their child. . . . I pray that this terrible tragedy will be a wake up call for the American people to stand up and insist on the reassertion of the sanctity-of-life ethic upon which this nation was based in the Declaration of Independence, which holds that all human beings have the inalienable right to life because they are human beings—born, unborn, healthy, unhealthy, young, old, handicapped or incurably ill.[174]

The pro-life community was clearly shaken by what the U.S. courts had allowed and directed to happen to Terri Schiavo.

The same-sex marriage debate continued to rage in 2005. With legislation and rumors abounding, the ERLC's Research Institute sought to speak some biblical sense to the issue. In March they released "The Nashville Declaration on Same-sex Marriage," which identifies four key aspects of biblical marriage and demonstrates the ways in which same-sex marriage falls short of these.

Leading up to the summer's Southern Baptist Convention, which would meet in Nashville, June 21–22, concern was expressed about legislative filibusters with respect to judicial nominations. Of course, with Supreme Court Justice Sandra Day O'Connor's announced retirement set for July and Rehnquist's unexpected death in September, this became an extremely important issue.

The Southern Baptist Convention's written report presented by Land reviewed the impact of the past year's work. The iVoteValues campaign was seen as extremely successful. In Land's words, "The values voters showed up." Land also applauded the signing of the partial-birth abortion ban. He pointed out the Commission had sent out 24 action alerts on multiple issues and was grateful for the release of his latest book, *Imagine! A God-Blessed America.* In short, it was a busy product year.[175]

In his verbal report, Land reviewed the impact of the iVoteValues campaign. He summarized his assessment stating, "Last November . . . they heard loud and clear that there is a new force loose in America and it is people who are going to vote traditional religious values, be they evangelical, be they Catholics or be they Jewish. . . . We did all we could

to help you vote your values, beliefs and convictions." Land acknowledged that without the Convention's additional funding, the media ministry and iVoteValues campaign would have been impossible.[176]

Resolutions offered at the Convention, as usual, reflected many
of the major concerns of the Commission. These included resolutions
on educating children, affirming adult stem cell research, denouncing
the judicial temptation to legislate from the bench, promoting religious
freedom and freedom of speech, the need to reduce teen smoking and
an expression of appreciation of our military and our president. Perhaps the most interesting resolution was the one that announced the
official conclusion to the Disney boycott launched in 1997. For the
most part, the Convention was smooth and revolved around President
Bobby Welch's theme, "Everyone Can," about sharing the Good News
of Jesus Christ.[177]

The two big issues in the post-convention months were about the
Gulf Coast and the Supreme Court.

On August 29, Hurricane Katrina hit the Gulf Coast with devastating force, affecting the coastal population from Alabama to Texas.
The Mississippi Gulf Coast and the city of New Orleans were particularly hard hit. The storm killed more than thirteen hundred people
and displaced another 1.5 million. Sadly, local, state, and federal government emergency preparedness was for the most part a failure. In
contrast, Southern Baptist disaster relief was at its best with millions
of dollars and thousands upon thousands of volunteers. Recovery was
long and slow.[178]

On September 29, John Roberts was confirmed as the successor to William Rehnquist as chief justice of the Supreme Court. The
ERLC's Washington office used all its weight and influence in this
effort, including personal contacts, letters, action alerts, and public
demonstrations. They also opened the ERLC's building to help provide logistical and personal assistance to Roberts supporters who had
come to D.C. to help gain his confirmation. Because of his judicial
philosophy, many Evangelicals, including Land, were extremely grateful for his confirmation. Land commented that Roberts "possesses the
judicial philosophy, intellect and dedication to be one of the great chief

justices in our history." The greater challenge, Land agreed, would be over the next judicial nominee who might tip the balance of the Court in a more conservative direction.[179]

During the rest of the year, the Commission continued to address multiple issues on multiple fronts. It was still pro-life, pro-family, pro-traditional values, and pro-Israel. Yet, not surprisingly, support for the war with its mounting casualties and uncertain resolution continued to be a major and growing concern for the American people.

Early in December, Land, speaking at Princeton University, was asked to provide his explanation for the growing engagement of Evangelicals in public policy concerns. He responded with an issue and an inspiration. The issue was abortion and the Supreme Court's *Roe v. Wade* decision in 1973, and the inspiration was theologian and author Francis Schaeffer. Land expanded his thoughts, saying:

> What happened would not have happened without Roe
> v. Wade and 1.5 million abortions a year. There were a lot of
> other complicating factors, but without that, what happened
> wouldn't have happened. . . . Had the Republican Party not
> welcomed pro-life evangelicals and Catholics in the 1970s,
> it may not have survived. . . . If there is a crisis in the United
> States in which neither of the two parties will accommodate
> itself to a social movement that has reached critical mass, then
> the weaker of those two parties will die and it will be replaced
> by a new party. . . . I firmly believe that if the Republican Party
> in the wake of Watergate, as vitiated as it was, had not accom-
> modated itself to a pro-life movement that had reached critical
> mass in the period between 1976 and 1980 and had not put
> a pro-life plank in their platform, [it] would have died and it
> would have been replaced by a new party, a central part of
> which would have been its pro-life beliefs.[180]

At the end of the year, Land and a host of others sent another letter to President Bush asking him to please sponsor a constitutional amendment to protect marriage in America.[181]

The year 2006 held some surprises, some good, some bad. Early in the year, former executive director of the Commission Foy Valentine died in Dallas on January 7. Commenting on his predecessor, Land noted, "While Dr. Valentine and I had significant differences of opinion on many issues, all Southern Baptists will be forever in his debt for his courageous and prophetic stance on racial reconciliation and racial equality in the turbulent middle third of the 20th century."[182]

January always brings a reminder of life issues due to the anniversary of *Roe v. Wade*. When the news media communicated the percentage of abortions dropped to its lowest level since 1976, some people rejoiced. Land responded that still way over a million abortions had occurred and that there was "little cause to celebrate." In essence, the nation was still getting sicker, just at a slower rate.[183]

If there was no cause to celebrate the abortion rate, there was cause to celebrate the Senate's confirmation of Justice Samuel Alito on January 31. He became the 110th justice to serve on the Court and brought with him a judicial philosophy that Land and other conservatives applauded.[184]

The next month introduced what some perceived as a "showdown" with political correctness gone amuck. Evangelical chaplains were increasingly being instructed not to use Jesus' name in their prayers. This was brought to the attention of congressmen and the president. The navy issued directives that "inclusive and non-sectarian prayers" be offered at certain settings. This gave the appearance the government was violating the Free Exercise Clause and by directive the Establishment Clause. The air force and army appeared to be following suit. This would need to be addressed.[185]

In a completely different vein, the environmental issue was forcing its way on the Evangelical table. On February 6, eighty-six Evangelicals signed the Evangelical Climate Initiative (ECI) that affixed responsibility for global warming or climate change on human behavior, which could be corrected through reducing carbon dioxide emissions. Among the signees were Rick Warren, David Dockery, Timothy George, and David Gushee. Other Evangelicals, however, were not so certain of the cause or severity of the problem. At the Greensboro Convention in June, a resolution "On Environmentalism and Evangelicals" was adopted, which stated in part, "Environmentalism is threatening to become a wedge issue to divide the evangelical community and further distort its members from the priority of the Great Commission."[186]

In July, a more cautious group of Evangelicals, the Interfaith Stewardship Alliance, issued a different statement on the environment. Interestingly, Barrett Duke, Ben Mitchell, James Borland, Michael Salazar and Gregory Thonbury signed on with the other 110 signatories. A follow-up conference was held in November to further address the issues and featured David Gushee and Calvin Beisner. This seemed to be an issue that was gaining an increasingly higher profile.[187] Indeed, the Research Institute devoted a significant portion of its Spring meeting to understanding this complex issue.

Meanwhile, back to March 2006, the Commission released its legislative agenda. Six items were priority in the agenda. The first two were passage of the Unborn Child Pain Awareness Act, and the Child Custody Protection Act. The next two addressed the issues of prohibiting human cloning and passage of the Marriage Protection Amendment. This proved to be an ambitious agenda.[188]

As the springtime approached and arrived, much energy was expended on international issues. Land and others criticized Saudi Arabia for human rights violations. The immigration issue from Mexico repeatedly came up as an item of concern. The Darfur genocide was cast as "the worst humanitarian crisis today" as Land addressed a rally of thousands of concerned citizens on April 30 in Washington, D.C., on the front lawn of the U.S. Capitol. Religious freedom concerns were identified in both Afghanistan and Iraq.[189]

On the domestic scene, Al Gore delivered a keynote speech at a fundraising dinner in Los Angeles for the Human Rights Campaign, the nation's largest homosexual activist organization. This organization, which raised at least $20 million per year for homosexual lobbying purposes, was a prime mover towards "gay marriage." Affirming their ultimate goal, Gore said in his address:

You know that what you are engaged in is the furtherance
of a vision that is true and just and it does require the evolution
of consciousness along a pathway that is a logical extension
of what the United States of America has always promised to
humankind. You shall know the truth, and the truth shall set
you free. And the United States of America will, at some point
say, "What you are asking is what you shall receive."[190]

Needless to say, Gore's vision for America and choice of words
seemed strangely out of place and insulting for most conservative
Christians.

Just prior to the Convention, which met in Greensboro, North
Carolina, June 13–14, and after much encouragement from Land and
others, President Bush urged Congress to put the Federal Marriage
Amendment into the hands of the American people. Bush stated,
"Marriage is the most fundamental institution of civilization, and it
should not be redefined by activist judges," explaining, "An amendment to the Constitution is necessary because activist courts have left
our nation with no other choice." He further noted, "When judges
insist on imposing their arbitrary will on the people, the only alternative left to the people is an amendment to the Constitution, the only
law a court cannot overturn." Commenting on the president's plea,
Land said, "If we allow the federal judiciary to redefine it [marriage],
it will shatter the definition beyond recognition, and it will have disastrous effects on marriage, on children and on society."[191]

When the 2006 Convention arrived, Land's report communicated the difficulties of the day. Hurricanes, war, euthanasia,
embryonic stem cell research, and judicial nominees were the subject
of his opening written report. He reiterated the need for Christian
people to be involved in "the nation's public policy process." And he
reminded Southern Baptists of the Commission's vision, "a society
that affirms and practices Judeo-Christian values rooted in biblical authority." His report delved into more detail this year with
respect to specifics that he deemed critical to the safety, security, and
stability of the nation. He also reviewed the extensive reach of the

Commission's work. He drew attention to the renamed publication, *Faith and Family Values*. He concluded stating, "Much work remains to be done" before responding to four items referred from the 2005 Convention.[192]

In his verbal remarks, Land confided, "While the future of the nation looks bleak, hope is rising." Besides the spiritual indicators, Land cited the change in the Supreme Court, explaining, "Instead of having four liberal votes, three conservative votes, and two swing votes on the Supreme Court, we now have four conservative votes, four liberal votes, and one swing vote." He added, "All we need is one more and you will see some changing going on at the Supreme Court level that you haven't seen in your lifetime or mine." Commenting on the abortion issue, Land said, "We are winning the struggle for hearts and minds when it comes to the issues of abortion, for the first time since the Supreme Court decision in *Roe v. Wade* a minority of the American people support the decision." Land also addressed strongly the need for a Federal Marriage Amendment, along with other critical issues.[193]

Resolutions at this year's Convention addressed, as usual, many of the issues that Land and the Commission had prioritized. The desire for a marriage amendment and for an end to resisting the president's nominees for judges, the still great concern of alcohol use, the danger of human species-altering technologies, environmentalism, public schools, and disaster relief were domestic issues addressed. International issues adopted dealt with China's treatment of North Korean refugees, conflict in Darfur, illegal immigration, and prayer for the president and the military.[194]

Overall, from the Commission's perspective, this was a peaceful and uneventful Convention with the exception of the floor debate on the alcohol resolution.

The remainder of the summer brought two disconcerting events, one international and the other domestic. On the international scene, Israel went to war in Lebanon against the Hezbollah militia for two reasons. One was because of the kidnapping of Israeli soldiers, and second was because of the incessant launching of rockets into the northern parts of Israel. Supposedly, the war was fought to a stalemate. According to one employee at the Knesset, if the politicians had permitted the military to fight this as a war, the outcome would not have been uncertain. Any additional conflict in the Middle East brought concern to Christians.

A second event was domestic. The president, as promised, vetoed the Stem Cell Research Enhancement Act, which would have authorized Congress to pay for embryonic stem cell research. Explaining his decision, Bush stated, "I made it clear to Congress that I will not allow our nation to cross this moral line."[195]

As the fall arrived, ethical issues continued to demand attention. European researchers published a study in the September issue of *Science Journal* describing how new technology demonstrates that a woman perceived to be in a "persistent vegetative state had the capacity to understand and respond to verbal commands." On September 11, Princeton Ethicist Peter Singer reiterated his position that he would kill a disabled baby "if that was in the best interest of the baby and of the family as a whole." This was labeled as "a logical extension of the culture of death." Al Mohler commented that "the very fact that Singer and others seriously make such arguments about the value of human life indicates that the culture of death is growing in assertiveness."[196]

The Commission's trustees met in mid-September. To them, Land recounted the significance of recent days, particularly the change in the makeup of the Supreme Court. Describing the impact and potential impact of Southern Baptists, Land stated, "People in Washington, D.C., understand that the difference between the ERLC and other social groups is that we have boots on the ground. We have churches in virtually every community in the U.S., and we have people in those churches who are deeply concerned about these issues and who are already activated on these issues and who are just waiting to be pointed in the right direction." One item of note coming out of the trustee meeting was the fact that President George W. Bush was recognized as the 2006 recipient of the John Leland Religious Liberty Award.[197]

In the remainder of September, Land addressed participants at the "Values Voter Summit" sponsored by the Family Research Council. Land declared, "God is no Democrat or Republican . . . but is pro-life, pro-heterosexual and anti-pornography." Writing to Senator John Warner during this same week, he said, "We are writing to express our support for the inclusion of language protecting the right of military chaplains to pray according to the dictates of their consciences." And in a first-person piece, Land criticized Barry Lynn of the Americans United for Separation of Church and State "for sending out his typical threatening letters to pastors." Land wrote, "In a press release Lynn decries those he says are 'dragging churches into partisan politics;' I am concerned that Lynn's efforts are aimed at dragging Americans of faith off a platform that allows them equal access to the civic marketplace of ideas."[198]

In October, the month before the impending midterm election, Land was a keynote speaker along with James Dobson and Ken Hutcherson at the Stand for the Family Rally held at Two Rivers Baptist Church in Nashville. Tennessee was one of several states holding a referendum on the exclusivity of marriage.[199]

Ten days later, just before the election, Land stated, "Elections have consequences, and people have different visions for where America should go." He elaborated with sober truth, "It goes without saying that there would be vastly different approaches to issues like abortion, parental rights and the Marriage Protection Amendment." Other implications, should Democrats win, were that no more strict constructionist Supreme Court judges would be confirmed and homosexual activists would hope for more advances of their agenda.[200]

On election day, the Democratic Party won the House, 232–202, and the Senate, 51–49. Most values votes won, however, like the Marriage Amendment in Tennessee and six other states. The one glaring moral issue that was lost for conservative Christians happened in Missouri, which approved state support for embryonic stem cell research. Commenting on that loss, Charmaine Yoest, political analyst for the Family Research Council, pointed out that the spending ratio was $30 million to $1 million in support of the bill plus the celebrity factor of

Michael J. Fox, and it only produced a 51–49 percent victory. In her assessment, much deception was also used to confuse issues with inaccurate information.[201]

Yoest, analyzing the overall results of the fall election, also suggested:

> Authenticity is important. That's part of the message we were trying to communicate to the GOP ahead of the election: Values voters brought them into office in 2004 and didn't see the authentic follow up in governing. Our message afterward is that the value voters of 2004 were the integrity voters of 2006. They said, "We voted on this in 2004, but we didn't see a governing coalition on these issues."[202]

The more obvious explanations for the election results were a growing disillusionment with the Iraqi war, discontent over extremely lax borders, and the exposure of hypocrisy in the Mark Foley and Ted Haggard scandals, both of which broke coincidentally just days before the election; and all this was coupled with the "culture of corruption" tag due to the Abramoff scandal. Offsetting the bitterness of the results were the positive reports of pro-life Democrats who were elected like Bob Casey in the Senate and Heath Shuler, Joe Donnelly, and Brad Ellsworth in the House. *Baptist Press* quoted Kristen Day, executive director of Democrats for Life, who said, "Although the Democratic Party is still led by supporters of abortion rights who back the 1973 *Roe v. Wade* decision, and although its platform says Democrats 'stand proudly for a woman's right to choose,' the tide could be turning [for Democrats] to broaden the tent."[203]

With the conclusion of the election cycle, the work of Richard Land and the Commission continued. Gaining another Supreme Court justice or two with a strict constructionist philosophy proved more difficult in the short term. The pro-life agenda faced more obstacles and the homosexual rights crowd found more advocates in Congress. Yet the work went on.

At the conclusion of 2006, Land's executive team consisted of Harold Harper, Kerry Bural, Dwayne Hastings, and Bobby Reed in

Nashville; Barrett Duke in Washington, D.C.; and two consultants, Shannon Royce and Ben Mitchell.[204]

In the past ten years, the ERLC had grown in every aspect of its work. The organization was poised to march into the next decade with confidence and competence. One could say that everything up till now had been preparation. With a solid foundation laid and a committed, talented executive team and staff in place, Land had completed the next crucial step toward fulfilling the ERLC's mission for the glory of God.

Looking to the future, Land was asked what new directions he would incorporate with additional funding. His response was intriguing:

> With a major funding increase, I am convinced that we can change the culture. If I had an extra $5 million per year, for example, we would be on as many radio stations as Dobson; we would hire about four more people in Washington to do public policy, and we would probably hire four regional people, field representatives, to go out and relate directly to the churches and state conventions on a one-to-one basis—go out there and interface with them. We would start doing what Focus does, pay to have pastors come into Washington, recognizing key pastors and getting into personal relationships with them; hire a development man and start a development office so that we could begin to increase the endowment of the agency so that we would have in perpetuity more and more resources to use; start a Fellows program—expand our internship program into a Fellows program where we could pay people a decent stipend to come in for a year, based on competitive admission and begin to build a cadre of younger folks, pastors, and otherwise, who really are committed to our vision of changing America. That's just off the top of my head. I would expand the Research Institute and do our best to relate directly to the grassroots and minister to the grassroots. That would be huge.[205]

And these comments were drawn simply from a spur-of-the-moment response.

As the New Year came, so, too, did the century mark of Southern Baptist engagement in public policy and moral and ethical issues. The Commission, likewise, was celebrating its sixtieth year of service. And in all of this, Southern Baptists have demonstrated from across the years and across the miles that they are a people who intend to stand for what is right because it is a matter of conviction.

Notes

1. Land, Interview, May 7–8, 2007.

2. 1997 *SBC Annual*, 550.

3. Greg Ward, *The Timeline History of the USA* (New York: Barnes and Noble Books, 2003), 351–352.

4. "Religious Freedom Restoration Act" in wikipedia.org.

5. Dwayne Hastings, "Supreme Court strikes down RFRA; peril seen in religious freedom," *Baptist Press*, June 25, 1997.

6. Washington v. Glucksberg in wikipedia.org; Art Toalston, "High Court upholds state bans of physician-assisted suicide," *Baptist Press*, June 26, 1997.

7. Tom Strode, "Clinton issues religion guidelines for workplace with wide support," *Baptist Press*, August 14, 1997.

8. Letter from Land to Congress, August 28, 1997; Tom Strode, "ERLC's priorities are sanctity of life, religious liberty, it tells Congress," *Baptist Press*, August 28, 1997; 1997 SBC Resolution On the Display of the Ten Commandments in Government Buildings; "Congressman Istook introduces religious liberty amendment," *Baptist Press*, May 9, 1997; Tom Strode, "Supporters, foes of RFA wrestle over its impact," *Baptist Press*, July 25, 1997; Tom Strode, "House falls short of two-thirds vote on Religious Freedom Amendment," *Baptist Press*, June 5, 1998; *Light*, May–June 1997, 1, 3–4.

9. Tom Strode, "ERLC's Land: Bill would help U.S. overcome failure on persecution," *Baptist Press*, September 12, 1997; "International Religious Freedom Act of 1998" in wikipedia.org.

10. Dwayne Hastings, "ERLC trustees OK new staff, radio program in first meeting," *Baptist Press*, September 18, 1997. For the record, as a trustee at the Sunday School Board which became LifeWay Christian Resources, I had the privilege of working with my fellow trustees to secure start-up capital from LifeWay in order to launch *For Faith and Family*. Here is another example of LifeWay's expanded influence.

11. Land Interview, May 7–8, 2007.

12. Tom Strode, "Courts 'disordering' liberty Land, others say in statement," *Baptist Press*, September 26, 1997.

13. Dwayne Hastings, "Gore says homosexuality is divine creative act," *Baptist Press*, November 17, 1997.

14. Dwayne Hastings, "Eisner labels Disney critics 'nuts' in national TV interview," *Baptist Press*, November 20, 1997; Tom Strode, "Land: 60 Minutes fails to show offensive products of Disney," *Baptist Press*, November 24, 1997; Tom Strode, "Disney sponsored homosexual benefit before Eisner denied 'any agenda,'" *Baptist Press*, December 9, 1997.

15. Dwayne Hastings, "Eisner won't 'censor' Disney; boycott among key '97 stories," *Baptist Press*, January 8, 1998; Tom Strode, "Pro-life leaders assess progress as Roe's 25th anniversary nears," *Baptist Press*, January 9, 1998.

16. Dwayne Hastings, "Human sexuality timely theme of 1998," *Baptist Press*, January 30, 1998.

17. Dwayne Hastings, "ERLC soon to be within Southern Baptists' reach," *Baptist Press*, February 6, 1998.

18. Tom Strode and Dwayne Hastings, "Church challenged at ERLC seminar to influence sex-dominated society," *Baptist Press*, March 6, 1998.

19. Russell Moore, "Land, other ethicists, evaluate medical dilemmas at conference," *Baptist Press*, March 9, 1998; King Sanders, "Proliferation of pornography poisoning America, Land warns," *Baptist Press*, March 11, 1998; Debbie Moore, "Racial discrimination still a part of some SBC churches, Land says," *Baptist Press*, March 23, 1998; Steve Nelson, "Hunger fund gifts rise as Baptists increase emphasis on world hunger," *Baptist Press*, March 27, 1998.

20. Dwayne Hastings, "Eisner: 'Boycotters' a splinter group with Nazi leanings," *Baptist Press*, April 22, 1998; Dwayne Hastings, "$2 bills, 'buycott' to show homosexual support of Disney," *Baptist Press*, May 13, 1998.

21. Ibid., Hastings, "2 bills . . ."

22. King Sanders, "Land urges moral leadership in comments to congressmen," *Baptist Press*, May 14, 1998.

23. Ibid.

24. 1998 *SBC Annual,* 265–69.

25. 1998 Study Committee appointed by SBC President Tom Elliff: Anthony Jordan (OK)—chairman, William Elliff (AR), Richard Land (TN), Mary Mohler (KY), Dorothy Patterson (TX), Damon Shook (TX), and John Sullivan (FL).

26. 1998 *SBC Annual,* 87–96.

27. King Sanders, "ERLC's Land urges Senate to restore religious liberties," *Baptist Press*, June 26, 1998; See William J. Clinton's "Statement on Signing the Religious Land Use and Institutionalized Persons Act of 2000" in the American Presidency Project at americanpresidency.org.

28. *Cutter v. Wilkinson* in wikipedia.org.

29. Ward, *The Timeline History of the USA,* 352–53.

30. Tom Strode, "Senators again fail to override veto of partial-birth abortion ban," *Baptist Press*, September 18, 1998.

31. Nedra Kanavel, "Christian role underscored in addressing public issues," *Baptist Press*, November 2, 1998.

32. Dwayne Hastings, "Human Sexuality," *Baptist Press*, January 30, 1998.

33. Tom Strode, "China Policy shows Clinton's morality has public consequences, Bauer, Land," *Baptist Press*, May 19, 1998; Dwayne Hastings, "Land: President Clinton should just 'tell the truth,'" *Baptist Press*, August 14, 1998; Dwayne Hastings, "President's 'regret' called short of true confession," *Baptist Press*, August 18, 1998; Tom Strode, "Church's lack of discipline enables Clinton's double life, Mohler says," *Baptist Press*, August 26, 1998; Tom Strode, "Clinton tells religious leaders he has repented, asked forgiveness," *Baptist Press*, September 11, 1998.

34. Tom Strode, "Newsweek article: Baptist moderates laid groundwork for Clinton morality," *Baptist Press*, October 30, 1998.

35. Tom Strode, "House committee approves impeachment; ERLC's Land repeats call for resignation," *Baptist Press*, December 14, 1998; Tom Strode, "Clinton's call for end to 'destruction' hypocritical, ERLC's Land, others," *Baptist Press*, December 21, 1998; Tom Strode, "President 'earned' impeachment, ERLC's Land says of House vote," *Baptist Press*, December 21, 1998.

36. Dwayne Hastings, "'Kingdom of Racial Reconciliation' still awaited in U.S., Land Laments," *Baptist Press*, January 12, 1999.

37. Tom Strode, "NIH to fund stem-cell research, though destroying embryos involved," *Baptist Press*, January 21, 1999.

38. Tom Strode, "Accountability needed on all sides in restoring civility, Land says," *Baptist Press*, January 27, 1999.

39. "Impeachment of Bill Clinton" in wikipedia.org.

40. Tom Strode, "America's culture war isn't lost, Land counters political strategist," *Baptist Press*, February 25, 1999.

41. Ibid.

42. Tom Strode, "SBC's Patterson, Land, others meet, pray with congressional members," *Baptist Press*, February 26, 1999.

43. Dwayne Hastings, "Push for hate crime law threatens religious freedom, Land contends," *Baptist Press*, March 4, 1999; Tom Strode, "Land: President's hate-crimes efforts attack biblical values," *Baptist Press*, April 8, 1999.

44. Art Toalston, "SBC leaders lament 'moral melt down' of families, media's," *Baptist Press*, April 22, 1999; "The Columbine High School Massacre" in wikipedia.org.

45. Tom Strode, "Panel's support for embryo research is 'cannibalism,'" ERLC's Land says," *Baptist Press*, May 25, 1999.

46. 1999 *SBC Annual*, 287–91; Tom Strode, "Southern Baptists will not be silent in leading America to God: Land," *Baptist Press*, June 17, 1999.

47. 1999 *SBC Annual*, 91–101.

48. Art Toalston, "Baptist agency lists '10 Reasons' to oppose hate crimes legislation," *Baptist Press*, June 30, 1999.

49. Tom Strode, "Blocking of Ohio voucher program, 'outrageous,' ERLC's Land says," *Baptist Press*, August 27, 1999.

50. Ibid.

51. Debbie Moore, "Network TV 'worse than ever' in family hour, study reports," *Baptist Press*, September 3, 1999.

52. Dwayne Hastings, "ERLC trustees ask messengers just say no to Disney visit in 2000," *Baptist Press*, September 23, 1999.

53. Land Interview, May 7–8, 2007.

54. Ibid.

55. Steve Achord, "5 of 8 GOP candidates sign pledge for marriage; Gore, Bradley decline," *Baptist Press*, October 21, 1999.

56. Ibid.

57. Tom Strode, "Senate OK's partial-birth abortion ban but again misses veto-proof majority," *Baptist Press*, October 22, 1999.

58. Daniel Walker Guido, "Controversy continues to mount in N. Y. over art exhibit Land calls 'blasphemous,'" *Baptist Press*, November 12, 1999.

59. Tom Strode, "Reports of trade in fetal body parts fuel call for congressional hearings," *Baptist Press*, November 15, 1999.

60. Tom Strode, "SBC bioethicists: NIH guidelines represent 'biotech cannibalism,'" *Baptist Press*, December 3, 1999.

61. Tom Strode, "Land, others ask president to work for peace in Sudan," *Baptist Press*, December 14, 1999.

62. Todd Starnes, "SBC leaders to White House accusations of 'ancient religious hatred,'" *Baptist Press*, December 22, 1999.

63. Letter from Land, et al., to Mrs. Clinton, January 7, 2000; Tom Strode, "Land, others ask White House to reverse itself on sex trafficking," *Baptist Press*, January 10, 2000; Tom Strode, "Trafficking in women, children, staggering problems, panel told," *Baptist Press*, February 24, 2000.

64. Tom Strode, "Vermont panel backs partnerships, not marriage, for homosexuals," *Baptist Press*, February 10, 2000; Karen Willoughby & Todd Starnes, "60% of Calif. voters opt for marriage over same sex unions," *Baptist Press*, March 8, 2000; Tom Strode, "Homosexual 'civil unions' gain OK in Vermont Senate," *Baptist Press*, April 19, 2000.

65. Todd Starnes and Art Toalston, "Broadcasters, SBC's Land defend Dr. Laura against homosexual protest," *Baptist Press*, April 6, 2000; Tom Strode, "Land, other pro-family leaders request meeting with Bush concerning homosexuals," *Baptist Press*, April 26, 2000.

66. Dwayne Hastings, "Carl F. H. Henry offers vision for ERLC Research Institute," *Baptist Press*, February 25, 2000.

67. Tom Strode, "ERLC's Land: McCain's attack on Christian leaders 'despicable,'" *Baptist Press*, March 1, 2000.

68. Tom Strode, "ERLC asks justices for reversals in abortion, homosexuality," *Baptist Press*, March 8, 2000.

69. Tom Strode, "Voucher decision thwarts will of people, ERLC's Land says," *Baptist Press*, March 20, 2000.

70. Todd Starnes, "ERLC head lashes out at 'Gestapo-like' tactics in seizure of Elian Gonzalez," *Baptist Press*, April 25, 2000.

71. Daniel Walker Guido, "Take a stand for faith, Land urges, as Baptists of colonial times did," *Baptist Press*, April 27, 2000.

72. Tom Strode, "ERLC, others urge Congress to oppose PNTR for China," *Baptist Press*, May 5, 2000; "FDA proposal may restrict use of drug, abortion advocates fear," *Baptist Press*, June 8, 2000.

73. See http://baptistpress.com/bpnews.asp?id=6020. Posted June 14, 2000.

74. 2000 BF&M Study Committee appointed by SBC President Paige Patterson: Max Barnett (OK), Steve Gaines (AL), Susie Hawkins (TX), Rudy A. Hernandez (TX), Charles S. Kelley Jr. (LA), Heather King (IN), Richard D. Land (TN), Fred Luter (LA), R. Albert Mohler Jr. (KY), T. C. Pickney (VA), Nelson Price (GA), Adrian Rogers (TN) (appointed chairman), Roger Spradlin (CA), Simon Tosi (AZ), and Jerry Vines (FL).

75. Dwayne Hastings, "Southern Baptists called forth as 'champions for the faith,'" *Baptist Press*, June 20, 2000.

76. 2000 *SBC Annual*, 267–72.

77. Ibid., 76–90.

78. Tom Strode, "SBC ethicists: Society 'ill-equipped' for issues raised by genetic mapping," *Baptist Press*, June 27, 2000.

79. Tom Strode, "Update: High court rules for Boy Scouts, a joint partial-birth abortion ban," *Baptist Press*, June 29, 2000.

80. Letter from Land to Senators, July 14, 2000; Letter from Land to Congressional Representatives, July 17, 2000.

81. Don Hinkle, "Homosexuality instruction in schools at issue in Oregon ballot initiative," *Baptist Press*, July 17, 2000.

82. Dwayne Hastings, "Despite threats, Falwell interview aired on ERLC's 'For Faith & Family,'" *Baptist Press*, July 25, 2000.

83. Tom Strode, "Pro-lifers decry NIH guidelines permitting embryo-cell research," *Baptist Press*, August 24, 2000; "ERLC institute notes relationship between biotech, Christian higher education issues," *Baptist Press*, September 25, 2000.

84. Land Interview, May 7–8, 2007.

85. Art Toalston, "SBC's Land: Analysis of issues is not endorsement for presidential nominee," *Baptist Press*, October 26, 2000.

86. Adam Myrick, "Land warns of 'greatest danger' ahead for religious expression," *Baptist Press*, November 9, 2000.

87. Todd Starnes & Tom Strode, "5–4 Supreme Court drama clears way for Bush presidency, Gore concession," *Baptist Press*, December 13, 2000.

88. Todd Starnes, "Bush nominates evangelical Christian for attorney general," *Baptist Press*, December 22, 2000; Tom Strode, "Ashcroft held to 'double standard' as cabinet nominee, Land says," *Baptist Press*, January 9, 2001; Tom Strode, "Land: Much opposition to Ashcroft amounts to 'religious profiling,'" *Baptist Press*, January 22, 2001; Tom Strode, "ERLC endorses Ashcroft; Land cites abortion, religious liberty as reasons," *Baptist Press*, January 16, 2001; "John Ashcroft" in wikipedia.org.

89. Tom Strode, "Land urges President-elect Bush to tackle pro-life, other issues," *Baptist Press*, January 10, 2001.

90. Tom Strode, "Bush establishes faith-based office; ERLC's Land urges ground rules," *Baptist Press*, January 30, 2001.

91. Tami Reed Ledbetter, "Land tells SBTC crowd ERLC speaks for majority of Southern Baptists," *Baptist Press*, February 9, 2001.

92. Land Interview, May 7–8, 2007.

93. Letter from Land and Mitchell to Bush, March 2, 2001; Tom Strode, "ERLC urges Bush to repeal NIH rules on embryo research," *Baptist Press*, March 6, 2001.

94. Dwayne Hastings, "Land: Cultural breakdown traced to man's failure to heed divine design," *Baptist Press*, March 15, 2001.

95. Richard Land, "First Person: Porn profits reflect its potency versus even Hollywood, rock music," *Baptist Press*, May 4, 2001.

96. Tom Strode, "Bush's judicial nominees the kind needed, Land says," *Baptist Press*, May 16, 2001.

97. 2001 *SBC Annual*, 247–51; Dwayne Hastings, "ERLC dispenses with usual report, recognizes champions for the faith," *Baptist Press*, June 14, 2001.

98. 2001 *SBC Annual*, 72–80.

99. Tom Strode, "White House announces support for comprehensive ban on human cloning," *Baptist Press*, June 21, 2001; Richard Land, "First Person: George W. Bush & the power of a presidential promise," *Baptist Press*, July 26, 2001; Tom Strode, SBC ethicists disappointed in Bush's stem cell decision," *Baptist Press*, August 10, 2001; Richard Land, "Statement: 'Deeply disappointed' yet seeing some 'good news,'" *Baptist Press*, August 10, 2001; Dwayne Hastings, "Land urges family vigilance to 'dark underbelly of the Internet,'" *Baptist Press*, August 13, 2001; Dwayne Hastings, "Lottery & embryo issues fuel on-air stances by SBC's Land," *Baptist Press*, August 28, 2001; "ERLC, others join together to promote pro-life justices," *Baptist Press*, September 5, 2001.

100. Ward, *The Timeline History of the USA*, 357; Todd Starnes, "Terrorists send nation to its knees in New York City, Washington attacks," *Baptist Press*, September 11, 2001.

101. Richard Land, Statement: "Land calls on believers to trust in God," *Baptist Press*, September 11, 2001.

102. Tom Strode & Art Toalston, "Attacks unify Americans in unusual way, Land says," *Baptist Press*, September 12, 2001; According to Land, Our trustee board was in session when this attack took place. We had just commenced our board meeting. When the first plane hit, we were having breakfast; when the second plane hit, we had just gone into session. Fortunately for me, God takes care of those who can't take care of themselves. I told Bobby to go rent every car you can rent. We had 30 some trustees here from thirty some states and all the planes were canceled. We got enough cars to get everybody home, but we did it in tag-team fashion. We had one car that went to Arkansas and on to Oklahoma and on to New Mexico. It took us about a week to get two or three of our trustees who were on the west coast home. We immediately stopped and had prayer. The board was actually in its annual board meeting when the attack took place. Land Interview, May 7–8, 2007.

103. Tom Strode & Dwayne Hastings, "Bush names ERLC president to religious liberty panel," *Baptist Press*, September 17, 2001.

104. Ward, *The Timeline History of the USA*, 357–58.

105. Tom Strode, "America has met criteria for 'just war,' Land says," *Baptist Press*, September 21, 2001.

106. Dwayne Hastings, "Land: Battle plan to compare religious conservatives with Taliban an outrage," *Baptist Press*, January 8, 2002.

107. Dwayne Hastings, "Cloning opponents criticized for 'imposing their moral code,'" *Baptist Press*, January 22, 2002.

108. Dwayne Hastings, "Land: Democrats' block of Bush nominee an outrage," *Baptist Press*, March 21, 2002.

109. "Pro-life ad campaign features former abortion-rights figures," *Baptist Press*, January 15, 2002; Tom Strode, "Health proposal to cover unborn draws fire from abortion advocates," *Baptist Press*, February 1, 2002; Dwayne Hastings, "Land: Critics of prenatal care intent on 'pro-death' agenda," *Baptist Press*, February 5, 2002; Tom Strode, "House passes ban on transport of underage girls for abortion," *Baptist Press*, April 18, 2002.

110. Dwayne Hastings, "Land: Media presents incomplete story about American Taliban," *Baptist Press*, January 30, 2002; Tom Strode, "Land, others rip doctors' group for support of same-sex adoptions," *Baptist Press*, February 6, 2002; Tom Strode, "Children's welfare must prevail over clergy restoration, Land says," *Baptist Press*, April 26, 2002; Tom Strode, "Amendment to protect marriage from courts introduced in House," *Baptist Press*, May 16, 2002.

111. Tom Strode, "ERLC asks Bush to veto campaign reform measure," *Baptist Press*, March 4, 2002.

112. Tom Strode, "Court's decision on child porn 'dark day,' ERLC's Land says," *Baptist Press*, April 17, 2002.

113. Letter from Land et al., to Bush, April 1, 2002; Tom Strode, "ERLC, others displeased at new trafficking report," *Baptist Press*, June 6, 2002.

114. Dwayne Hastings, "Land says Arafat is detriment in search for Mideast peace," *Baptist Press*, April 17, 2002; Tom Strode, "Land, others call on Bush to denounce anti-Semitism," *Baptist Press*, April 26, 2002; Dwayne Hastings, "Land: Citizen's right to bear arms undeniable," *Baptist Press*, May 14, 2002; Land Interview, May 7–8, 2007.

115. "Talk Show featuring Richard Land debuts, to air mid-day Saturdays," *Baptist Press*, June 8, 2002.

116. Richard Land with John Perry, *For Faith and Family* (Nashville: Broadman & Holman Publishers, 2002).

117. 2002 *SBC Annual*, 241–45.

118. Dwayne Hastings, "Land: Cloning debate outcome will direct society's future," *Baptist Press*, June 13, 2002.

119. 2002 *SBC Annual*, 74–81.

120. Art Toalston and Dwayne Hastings, "Land: Military action against Iraq meets ethical standards for war," *Baptist Press*, September 9, 2002.

121. Letter from Land to Bush, October 3, 2002.

122. Tom Strode, "ERLC asks congressional leaders to make cloning ban a priority," *Baptist Press*, January 8, 2003; Richard Land, "First Person: Our Endangered Species," *Baptist Press*, January 22, 2003.

123. Tom Strode, "Court delivers 8-1 win to pro-life, other protesters," *Baptist Press*, February 27, 2003.

124. Dwayne Hastings, "Studies suggest death penalty is deterrent to crime, Land says," *Baptist Press*, January 15, 2003.

125. Tom Strode, "Federal religion guidelines for public schools underscore students' freedoms," *Baptist Press*, February 13, 2003.

126. Letter from Land et al., to Bush, February 27, 2003.

127. Tom Strode, "Land on 'Nightline': 'Truly evil' Hussein justifies force," *Baptist Press*, March 5, 2003; Dwayne Hastings, "Bush right to seek God's guidance in Iraqi crisis, Land says on MSNBC," *Baptist Press*, March 12, 2003; Tom Strode, "Partial-birth abortion ban clears Senate, likely to become law," *Baptist Press*, March 13, 2003; Ward, *The Timeline History of the USA*, 362.

128. "ERLC to focus additional resources on D.C. front toward public policy," *Baptist Press*, April 22, 2003.

129. Minutes of the ERLC Executive Committee Meeting, June 16, 2003; Land Interview, May 7–8, 2007.

130. Ibid., Land Interview.

131. Tom Strode, "Support for Israel 'is biblical' and should never be surrendered, Land says," *Baptist Press*, May 7, 2003; "Land, Rogers, others urge strong stand by White House on 'road map,'" *Baptist Press*, May 22, 2003; Land et al. to Bush, May 19, 2003.

132. Tom Strode, "House passes partial-birth abortion ban with 282-139 vote," *Baptist Press*, June 5, 2003.

133. Michael Foust, "Canadian court approves homosexual 'marriage;' could America be next?" *Baptist Press*, June 12, 2003.

134. 2003 *SBC Annual*, 203–7.

135. Ibid.

136. Dwayne Hastings, "ERLC head: Divorce statistics reflect a culture in trouble," *Baptist Press*, June 19, 2003.

137. 2003 *SBC Annual*, 69–77.

138. Ibid.

139. Dwayne Hastings, "Analysis: SBC sets record straight on convention's abortion stance," *Baptist Press*, June 19, 2003.

140. Lawrence v. Texas in wikipedia.org.

141. "Justice Anthony Scalia's Dissent in Lawrence v. Texas" may be found reprinted at OrthodoxyToday.org.

142. Dwayne Hastings, "Bishop's election embraces deadly theology, Land says," *Baptist Press*, August 6, 2003.

143. Dwayne Hastings, "Runaway judiciary is central issue in controversy surrounding the public display of the Ten Commandments, Land says," *Baptist Press*, August 28, 2003.

144. James A. Smith, "First-Person: Starving a woman to death," *Baptist Press*, October 16, 2003; R. Albert Mohler, "First-Person: Death stalks the innocent," *Baptist Press*, October 20, 2003; Joni B. Hannigan & Michael Foust, "Jeb Bush orders Terri Schiavo's feeding tube re-inserted," *Baptist Press*, October 21, 2003.

145. Tom Strode, "President Bush signs first restriction on abortion since '73 *Roe v. Wade* decision," *Baptist Press*, November 5, 2003.

146. Dwayne Hastings, "World at Risk if U.S. allows freedom to dim, Land tells trustees," *Baptist Press*, September 22, 2003.

147. Tom Strode, "King Sanders, Southern Baptist policy leader, dies," *Baptist Press*, October 31, 2003.

148. "N. J. governor signs bill allowing therapeutic cloning," *Baptist Press*, January 5, 2004; Tom Strode, "Dean says his religious views led to support for same-sex unions," *Baptist Press*, January 8, 2004.

149. Dwayne Hastings, "Equipping for pro-life cause among key ERLC aims, Land says," *Baptist Press*, January 12, 2004.

150. These are *Baptist Press* headlines for January 15; February 6, 23; April 5; May 18; July 12, 30; August 5; September 22, 30; and October 18, 2004.

151. Dwayne Hastings, "ERLC launches voting initiative in view of 'critical' '04 ballot,'" *Baptist Press*, February 17, 2004.

152. Land and Harper Interview, May 7–8, 2007.

153. Ibid.

154. Ibid.; Dwayne Hastings, "Truck rigged for iVoteValues to register & inform voters," *Baptist Press*, June 16, 2004; Tom Strode, "President Bush wins

reelection, exit polls show values voters made the difference," *Baptist Press,* November 3, 2004.

155. Tom Strode, "Bush ready to sign protection for unborn victims of violence," *Baptist Press,* March 26, 2004; Tom Strode, "President signs rights for unborn victims," *Baptist Press,* April 2, 2004.

156. Dwayne Hastings, "SBC's Richard Land in the news from home state to BBC," *Baptist Press,* April 27, 2004; "ERLC biographical sketch of Richard Land;" Dwayne Hastings, "SBC's Land among experts D.C. policy-makers look to," *Baptist Press,* June 9, 2004.

157. Letter from Land et al., to Vaclav Klaus et al., May 18, 2004; Letter from Land to Hastert, June 9, 2004.

158. Jerry Pierce, "Land explains why religious liberty is vital to national interests," *Baptist Press,* June 10, 2004.

159. Richard Land, *Real Homeland Security* (Nashville: Broadman & Holman Publishers, 2004).

160. 2004 *SBC Annual,* 222–26.

161. Dwayne Hastings, "Christians must be informed voters, ERLC's Land says," *Baptist Press,* June 18, 2004.

162. 2004 *SBC Annual,* 81–87.

163. Letter from Land to Frist, June 25, 2004; Letter from Land to Hastert, July 2, 2004; Tom Strode, "Senate hate-crimes vote is 'terrible precedent,' Land says," *Baptist Press,* June 21, 2004; Tom Strode, "Congress challenges Bush stem cell policy," *Baptist Press,* July 16, 2004; Richard Land, "First-Person: Federal Marriage Amendment: Far from dead," *Baptist Press,* August 5, 2004.

164. Erin Curry, "Democratic Party Platform set to push homosexual agenda in America," *Baptist Press,* July 29, 2004.

165. Tom Strode, "Panel: Land, others, discuss church's role in politics," *Baptist Press,* October 5, 2004.

166. Tom Strode, "Thousands rally in nation's capitol for traditional marriage," *Baptist Press,* October 18, 2004.

167. Tom Strode, "ERLC think tank: Embryonic stem cell research is immoral," *Baptist Press,* October 26, 2004.

168. Richard Land, "First-Person: Moral Values," *Baptist Press,* November 5, 2004.

169. Dwayne Hastings, "SBC positions gain national hearing on 'Meet the Press,'" *Baptist Press,* November 30, 2004; Dwayne Hastings, "ERLC's Land: 'Meet the Press' panel reflects debate on whose values should prevail," *Baptist Press,* November 30, 2004.

170. Erich Bridges, "Southern Baptists begin relief efforts in tsunami-battered areas," *Baptist Press,* December 27, 2004; "As death toll rises, Baptist workers ask for prayer, donations," *Baptist Press,* December 30, 2004; R. Albert Mohler, "First-Person: God & the tsunami (Part 1)," *Baptist Press,* January 4,

2005; R. Albert Mohler, "First-Person: God & the tsunami (Part 2)," *Baptist Press*, January 5, 2005.

171. Tom Strode, "ERLC to push protection for unborn, marriage, human rights," *Baptist Press*, January 12, 2005.

172. See the headlines for *Baptist Press* archives, 2005, for each of the dates.

173. Michael Foust, "'Sad day for America': Schiavo dies in Florida hospice, 2 weeks after feeding tube pulled," *Baptist Press*, March 30, 2005.

174. Ibid.

175. 2005 *SBC Annual*, 251–57.

176. Dwayne Hastings, "Land says values voters are new political force in America," *Baptist Press*, June 22, 2005.

177. 2005 *SBC Annual*, 104–12.

178. "Katrina delivers 'catastrophic' damage to coastal region," *Baptist Press*, August 30, 2005.

179. Tom Strode, "Senate confirms John Roberts as chief justice, 78-22; Focus turns to next nominee," *Baptist Press*, September 29, 2005.

180. Tom Strode, "Abortion issue & Schaeffer influence pushed evangelicals to engagement, Land says," *Baptist Press*, December 6, 2005.

181. Letter from Land et al., to Bush, December 20, 2005.

182. Dwayne Hastings, "Foy Valentine, dead at 82, led SBC moral concerns arm 27 years," *Baptist Press*, January 9, 2006.

183. Richard Land, "First-Person: Little cause to celebrate," *Baptist Press*, January 13, 2006.

184. Tom Strode, "Senate confirms Alito, 58-42, provides conservatives hope for high court change," *Baptist Press*, January 31, 2006.

185. Ken Walker, "Prayer in Jesus' name remains an issue in military chaplaincy," *Baptist Press*, February 10, 2006.

186. Tom Strode, "Groups of evangelicals issues global warming stance; several notable names are absent," *Baptist Press*, February 9, 2006; 2006 *SBC Annual*, 115–16.

187. Tom Strode, "Coalition of more than 100 evangelicals presents alternative on global warming," *Baptist Press*, July 31, 2006; Michael Salazar and Calvin Beisner, "First-Person: Getting prepared to deal with global warming," *Baptist Press*, November 21, 2006.

188. Tom Strode, "ERLC to seek gains for life, marriage, human rights," *Baptist Press*, March 14, 2006.

189. "State Department report on Saudi Arabia criticized by bipartisan religious liberty panel," *Baptist Press*, March 16, 2006; Tom Strode, "S. Baptists want immigration enforcement, Land tells Bush," *Baptist Press*, March 24, 2006; Richard Land, "First-Person: Immigration crisis requires biblical response," *Baptist Press*, April 27, 2006; Shannon Baker, "Rally against Darfur genocide prods Sudanese government," *Baptist Press*, May 2, 2006; Tom Strode, "Panel:

Religious freedom threats mount in Afghanistan, Iraq," *Baptist Press*, May 5, 2006.

190. Michael Foust, "Marriage Digest: Al Gore affirms 'gay love,' now 'gay marriage?' Canadian court sides with religious freedom," *Baptist Press*, April 20, 2006.

191. Tom Strode, "Bush urges Congress to put amendment in 'hands' of the people," *Baptist Press*, June 5, 2006.

192. 2006 *SBC Annual*, 291–99.

193. Dwayne Hastings, "ERLC head says faith brings hope to America" *Baptist Press*, June 14, 2006.

194. 2006 *SBC Annual*, 104–21.

195. Tom Strode, "With first veto of presidency, Bush blocks bill that would destroy embryos for stem cells," *Baptist Press*, July 19, 2006.

196. Gregory Tomlin, "Study reveals brain activity of patient in 'vegetative state,'" *Baptist Press*, September 11, 2006; "Princeton prof Peter Singer says killing disabled newborns is acceptable," *Baptist Press*, September 14, 2006.

197. Dwayne Hastings, "Baptists play key role in civic debate, Land tells trustees," *Baptist Press*, September 19, 2006.

198. Daniel Guido, "Land, others, urge Christians to vote their values in election," *Baptist Press*, September 25, 2006; Letter from Land to Warner, September 22, 2006; Richard Land: "First-Person: There he goes again," *Baptist Press*, September 28, 2006.

199. Michael Foust, "Stand for the family rally: Election too important for Christians to sit out, Land, Dobson, other leaders say," *Baptist Press*, October 17, 2006.

200. Tom Strode, "Election '06: Fate of social issues likely hangs in the balance," *Baptist Press*, October 27, 2006.

201. Michael Foust, "7 states pass marriage amendments; partnerships defeated in Colo.," *Baptist Press*, November 8, 2006; Charmaine Yoest in "Religious Voters and the Midterm Elections," event transcript from Pew Forum on Religion & Public Life, November 13, 2006.

202. Ibid.

203. Michael Foust, "Election was 'turning point' for pro-life Democrats, activist says," *Baptist Press*, November 29, 2006.

204. 2006 *SBC Annual*, 497.

205. Land Interview, May 7–8, 2007.

CHAPTER

An Epilogue:
A Matter of Conviction

As stated earlier, "The burden of history falls upon all of us, but Christians bear a particular responsibility to make sense of the past and to evaluate events, issues, and decisions from the framework of Christian moral teaching." In examining the cultural engagement of Southern Baptists in particular, and other convictional Christians in general, we have attempted to work from within a framework and build upon a foundation of our convictions.[1]

The historical framework and foundation has essentially been demonstrated in the overall flow of the book. Beginning with a rationale for engagement and the biblical imperative of functioning as "salt" and "light" within culture, we progressed to the Christian contribution in creating, shaping, and sustaining Western civilization. With particular regard to the United States, Baptists have been engaged officially and unofficially over the duration up to the present time. In the last twenty years or so, Southern Baptists particularly have moved to the forefront in providing moral leadership in the public policy arena.

Accompanying the historical framework and foundation has been the intention of laboring within a theological framework and foundation as well. Scripture instructs believers to function as salt and light in a corrupted and darkened culture (Matt. 5:13–16). Romans 14:23 states, "Whatever is not of faith is sin" (KJV). Its complementary verse is James 4:17, "To him who knows to do good and does it not, to him it is sin" (NKJV). By faith and faithfulness to the task, Christians are obligated to do that which is good in society, doing what they can, while they can, with all they have.[2]

Jesus told His disciples to "render therefore to Caesar the things that are Caesar's and to God the things that are God's" (Matt. 22:21 NKJV). May God give us wisdom to know the difference. Jesus also told His followers, "We must do the works of Him who sent Me while it is day. Night is coming when no one can work" (John 9:4). In other words we all have a brief window of opportunity in which to do God's work and impact this world for eternity.[3]

The third component is the philosophical foundation and framework. This, conveniently, is provided in our nation's Declaration of Independence. Notice that it is not secular but religious in its orientation. Its presuppositions rest in the reality of God, who is identified as Nature's God who has given Natural Law, the Creator of mankind who gives unalienable rights, the Supreme Judge of the World to whom they appealed for the rectitude of their intentions to become a sovereign nation, and the Divine Providence upon whom they firmly relied for support of the just penned Declaration. The framers of our nation had a religious, not secular, orientation that the United States' existence depended upon the sustaining will of God.[4]

The God who allowed this nation to be birthed has revealed certain self-evident truths. The nation was founded by a God who gives truth. It was not founded on secularism or relativism. This God of truth has created all men (mankind) equal. And these equal men are forming a new nation. Moreover, this God of Truth who has created all men equal has Himself endowed all men (mankind) with certain unalienable rights. Unalienable means "incapable of being alienated, surrendered, or transferred." And those rights are life, liberty, and the pursuit of happiness.[5]

This trilogy of rights was adopted from John Locke's ideas on the right to life, liberty, and property from his Second Treatise on Civil Government (see the Fourteenth Amendment). It is arguable that these rights are a descending hierarchy of values with first priority being life, then liberty, then the pursuit of happiness.[6]

To secure these rights, Jefferson, as well as Locke, maintained governments are formed. This, in fact, was done by the United States as they "dissolved" that which connected them to Great Britain and "connected" to each other. This brought the new nation into a "separate and equal station" with other nations, the Declaration maintains. Thus, wrote Jefferson, "the Laws of Nature and Nature's God entitle[d] them."[7]

Here is the philosophical foundation of our body politic. Our nation is (1) God formed, not secular in its presuppositional orientation, (2) founded on self-evident truths, not relativism, (3) conceived on the axiom that all men (mankind) are created equal, and (4) established upon presuppositions that each one is a possessor of unalienable rights, which in a descending order of value are life, liberty, and the pursuit of happiness. As a nation, this is our philosophical foundation.

Southern Baptists, with the Ethics & Religious Liberty Commission leading the way, also have a practical foundation and framework which includes the "what," a clear "vision," and the "how," a clear "mission." The vision of the Commission is, "An American society that affirms and practices Judeo-Christian values rooted in biblical authority." This is what Southern Baptists want to see formed. But the issue is how to move from where we are to where we believe God wants us to be. The Commission expresses its mission by stating that it is attempting "to awaken, inform, energize, equip and mobilize

Christians to be the catalysts for the biblically-based transformation of their families, churches, communities, and the nation."[8]

The Ethics & Religious Liberty Commission, representing Southern Baptists, is working to provide definitions and direction in the culture war of ideas. Its convictions are built on a historical, theological, philosophical, and practical foundation and framework. The field of its work is broad, falling under two main headings: religious liberty concerns and moral issues.

Historically, its first concern has been in the area of religious liberty. For the duration of our nation's existence, Baptists have been active in pleading the case for religious liberty and equality, not just tolerance. It has embraced not a total separationist agenda but an accommodation posture with the mind-set that the original intention of our founding fathers was that religion was to be accommodated. When, in 1954, Senate Majority Leader Lyndon Johnson introduced a rider to an appropriations bill forbidding 501(c)(3), nonprofit, organizations from endorsing political candidates or being involved directly in the political process, this should have been challenged as violating not only the First Amendment's free exercise and nonestablishment clauses but freedom of speech as well. This is an egregious violation that is yet to be corrected. Yet, we find unfolding today what Barry Hankins described as "elites in America . . . pursuing a European model of secularization," explaining, "In church-state matters the federal courts have been moving in a 'French direction—moving toward a government that is antiseptically free of religious symbols rather than simply a government that doesn't favor any particular religious group.'"[9]

The remedy to halt our culture from moving any farther in this direction is multifaceted. First, Christians must reengage the culture. Many losses have been by default. Second, legislators and jurists who understand our heritage and embrace a strict constructionist constitutional philosophy are important. Some reading this may need to run for public office. Third, honest historians must challenge the revisionists who seemingly systematically have attempted to rewrite our nation's heritage to exclude Christian influence.

A second field where we must continue to engage is in the area of equality and racial reconciliation. Although our distant past and conformity to another era's status quo hindered our progress in this area, Southern Baptist leaders have been diligent in their efforts to emphasize the equality of all people regardless of their skin color or national heritage. The 1995 Racial Reconciliation resolution is a major milestone and marker for Southern Baptists. Yet our desire is that this mind-set influences the entire nation. Jesus was serious when He said, "By this all will know that you are My disciples if you have love for one another" (John 13:35 NKJV).

A third field, one which is a great challenge in our day, is in the life issues. Until 1973's *Roe v. Wade* decision, most states in the nation had severe restrictions on abortion, and the assumption was universally embraced that life begins at conception. The central issue in the court case was whether the fetus was a person and thus protected by the Constitution not to mention the foundational assumptions found in the Declaration of Independence.

One wonders what would have happened had Robert Flowers, representing Henry Wade, the Texas district attorney, answered Thurgood Marshall's question differently and intelligently. Marshall asked, "I want you to give me a medical, recognizable medical writing of any kind that says that the time of conception that the fetus is a person." Flowers responded by conceding, "I do not believe that I could give that to you without researching through the briefs that have been filed in this case, Your Honor." Earlier Potter Stewart had asked Sarah Weddington, attorney for Jane Roe (Norma McCorvey), "If it were established that an unborn fetus is a person, within the protection of the Fourteenth Amendment, you would have an impossible case here, would you not?" Weddington responded, "I would have a very difficult case." And earlier Byron White had clarified the issue addressing Weddington, "Well, do I get from this then that your case depends primarily on the proposition that the fetus has no constitutional rights?" She responded that it would, even if conceded, still be weighing one life against another.[10]

As everyone knows, the verdict was in favor of *Roe*, and curiously the majority declared that it was so ruled because of a suddenly discovered right to privacy. White, dissenting, assessed this ruling as an exercise in "raw judicial power," which, in fact, it was.[11]

Eventually, *Roe* opened the door for euthanasia, which was played out graphically in the Terri Schindler Schiavo case previously discussed. And most recently Princeton professor, Peter Singer, has advocated the legitimacy of infanticide. Of course, the whole debate over embryonic stem cell research is rooted in the mind-set that life does not really begin at conception.

Two issues are overwhelmingly problematic. First, the mind-set that anyone has the liberty or the right to decide arbitrarily who will live or die is barbaric, perhaps with apologies to the barbarians. The fact that two preborn children can go to a hospital and one be aborted and the other have a costly life-saving procedure in utero says something foreboding against both our culture and our laws. From this perspective, the practice of partial-birth abortion should be severely criminalized.

Looking deeper, a hideous valuation system is subtly being adopted. It was practiced in Nazi Germany by the highly skilled Nazi doctors at the instruction of political and military leaders. A concept was formulated by two professors, Karl Binding and Alfred Hoche, a jurist and a psychiatrist, respectively, in 1920. The concept was *Lebensunwertes Leben*, "life unworthy of life." The Nazis, according to Robert Jay Lifton, "did not originate this concept, [but] they carried it to its ultimate biological, racial, and 'therapeutic' extreme."[12]

Because some life is not worthy of living, worthy life is free to dispose of it at will. Here is a logical culmination of the survival of the fittest mind-set. And it is antithetical to the Christian faith. Needless to say, Christians have a long way to go in addressing this issue, especially because of the tremendous monetary benefits for those who embrace what has been called the culture of death.[13]

Still another area of critical importance is the area of family. Anyone who is an observer of life in America is aware of the tremendous stress which families are under. Divorce remains at record levels. Rates of cohabitation continue to escalate. Single-parent homes are in many areas the norm. And the homosexual movement is aggressively demanding the right to marry. Making matters worse is the continuing judicial activism that at any moment could legally overturn the exclusivity of marriage as between one man and one woman. In European countries where the "gay marriage" experiment has been tried, heterosexual couples simply cease to marry, deciding instead to cohabit. The outcome is incredible insecurity in the lives of children.[14]

Yet Bible-believing Christians believe that marriage and family are God-ordained institutions. These are well worth fighting for, and again, this will be a long, drawn-out conflict.

Still another area of concern is education in America. Public schools, private schools, and homeschooling are all options. Public schools continue to request more money, demonstrate less than adequate results in way too many instances, and embrace an almost purist secular value system. Part of this is the court's continued rulings separating not just church from state but also Christian values and symbols from the marketplace of ideas. The evolution-intelligent design debate appears to suffer from a stacked deck in favor of Darwin's beliefs; and in the universities, secularism is the dominant philosophy embraced in most locales. The field of education demands our attention.[15]

Concern over our nation's security is another field where our convictions must contribute a voice. Especially since September 11, 2001, concern over security from terrorism is a high priority. Homeland security, the discussion over the nature of Islam and its threats, the security of Israel, rogue states, and nuclear proliferation are all concerns. And they are concerns that should continue to be informed by Christian convictions.[16]

Still another field of concern is in the areas of abuse and addictions. When these are all considered in total—alcohol, drugs, sex, physical violence, gambling, pornography—we find ourselves contending with a culture where abuse and addiction are running at epidemic levels. Certainly Christianity with its convictions can address and minister to people caught in the clutches of these life-devastating problems. Surely God has a better way.

Yet at the same time that Christians must be addressing these and so many more issues in our culture, we find Christianity itself under assault. A virtual anthology of literature has emerged in recent years accusing Christians calling for America to become a "theocracy." Of course, the only way for something like that to happen is for the First Amendment to be removed from the Constitution, and that is virtually an impossibility. Moreover, no one in the conservative Christian community truly thinks in those terms, but it makes a great "straw man." Here is another example of critics forming arguments and accusations and then sadly going unchallenged. Coupled with the accusation that Christians want a theocracy is the ongoing attempt simply to marginalize Christians in the public square. "You have no say so if your beliefs and values are based on the Bible" critics often maintain.[17]

Still another scheme of the critics is the entire cadre of history-revising antics that have attempted to rewrite American history, removing almost all vestiges of Christianity; or if it is mentioned, it is almost exclusively in a negative vein. For example, Howard Zinn's *A People's History of the United States* makes only scant references to Christianity; and where it does, it does so in an almost exclusively negative manner.

Coupled with these distortions are the new breed of militant atheists like Richard Dawkins and his *The God Delusion* and Sam Harris's *Letter to a Christian Nation*. In short, these volumes and their kin seem to have a vendetta against all religions in general and Christianity in particular.

Each of these areas constitutes collectively the field of our endeavor and focal points where the Ethics & Religious Liberty Commission must direct its attention. To stand for righteousness and religious liberty in such turbulent times is a great challenge.

After we have considered the framework and foundation for our convictions, and the field in which these convictions are played out, the question remaining is, how can we further our convictions? Granted, Southern Baptists constitute a great host of "foot soldiers in the field," and granted, we have excellent leadership from our Ethics & Religious Liberty Commission in general and Richard Land specifically, but the issue is, what can the average Southern Baptist Christian do to engage the culture and make a difference? Permit me to conclude with a challenge and a checklist.

One of the most important things that you can do is simply get informed. What issues are important? What legislation is pending? Where are the potential points of ministry within your proximity and circle of influence? Two sources to monitor are *Baptist Press,* which releases articles each weekday. If you examine the Ethics & Religious Liberty Commission's Web page at www.erlc.com, information is readily available.

Next, pray intelligently. Intercede for politicians and those who are engaged in the public life and in the war of ideas. Pray for wisdom, discernment, and courage so that you will know the right and best thing to do. Pray that the Lord will show you His timing. Pray that the Lord would pour out His Spirit once again. Many of history's great revivals came suddenly at a time when the moral landscape looked bleak. Pray Matthew 6:10, "Your kingdom come. Your will be done on earth as it is in heaven."[18]

Grow in your understanding of the Word of God. The more you internalize a Christian worldview, the more effective you will be in the public arena.

Make your voice heard. Call a politician when a bill is pending; write letters to the editor or op-ed pieces. Call in to a talk radio show. Speak up! Make sure your voice is heard.

Next, get involved. No one can do everything, but everyone can do something. Work in a political campaign. Champion an issue you feel strongly about. Volunteer to help a ministry that addresses one of the great moral issues. Look for opportunities where you can make a difference. Some may even need to run for public office.

Give your financial support. In a day when the homosexual rights group, the Human Rights Campaign, is raising over $20 million a year to further its singular agenda of normalizing homosexuality and same-sex "marriage," Christians must put their money where their convictions are.

Support your pastor. Many pastors are afraid to speak out on moral issues because they are attacked for doing so. Stand with him. Let him know that you believe in him and support him and that you are praying for him.

Refuse to be intimidated. One of the enemy's greatest tactics is to attempt to intimidate you into remaining silent. He will make you believe that you are all alone, out of step, or an extremist, and that you are asking for trouble. Do not allow the enemy to intimidate you.

Weigh everything you read or hear in the popular media. More and more it seems to be taken over by a secular, anti-Christian, anti-patriotic agenda. Ask the Lord to give you discernment in what you read and hear.

Refuse to disengage. The enemy will keep telling you, "It's not worth it." We do what we do not for the applause of people but for the approval of God. We are forever tempted to step back, be cautious, or simply disengage. After all, there is always somebody else who can do what you are doing. Or is there?

Look for God's activity. God is always at work somewhere. Where do you sense Him moving and leading? Where do you sense is the place of greatest need? What opportunity matches up with your giftedness, passion, personality, and experience? When you look at our needy world, what do you see? What you see may well determine where God wants you to invest your life working with Him.

Walk by faith. Paul said simply, "Walk by faith, not by sight." We do what is right not because we are successful or we are rewarded but because it is our calling and it is right. Recall William Wilberforce, who labored his entire life to outlaw slavery in the British Empire. The laws finally passed three days before his death. Like Wilberforce, walk by faith. It will be easy to get discouraged if you do not.

Know that winning this war of ideas will require many battles so do not give up! If you lose a battle, do not quit. If you are criticized, do not quit. If you are challenged, do not quit. In fact, winning the battle we are in may well take a lifetime.

Refuse to get bitter. Learn to forgive. Those who oppose us will not fight fair. They will take cheap shots and attempt to wound us in order to stop us. Do not get bitter. Choose to forgive and go on. Life is too short to waste it on being bitter.

Encourage others to get involved. Encourage others to stay involved. Be an encourager. A card, a call, a compliment, a word of thanks can go a long way. Maston, for example, was good at encouraging.

Keep your eyes on the Lord. People might disappoint you. They might let you down. If your eyes are on people, you might get demoralized. Keep your eyes on Jesus! If the entire world opposes you and God is for you, you will be just fine.

Know that ideas have consequences. What you believe, you will live out. So be sure to focus on that which is good, holy, right, pure, wise, and of good report.

Refuse to quit. The enemy would like nothing better than to move you from participant to spectator status. No matter what, refuse to quit. The one who quits will always wonder if he stopped too soon.

Guard your heart and refuse to become cynical. Cynicism is the hallmark of a person who has taken his eyes off the Lord. Cynicism engulfs the person who has ceased to trust God and walk by faith.

And finally, remember this, none of us gets out of this life alive. Are you helping to raise up the next generation of leaders and activists? What will you be remembered for? My prayer is that each of us will be known as men and women who made a difference because what we knew, what we were, and what we did was a matter of conviction.

Notes

1. R. Albert Mohler, "First-Person: Hiroshima and the Burden of History," *Baptist Press*, Augusts 8, 2005.

2. Richard Land, "Citizen Christians Have Rights Too," in Richard Land and Louis Moore, eds., *Citizen Christians* (Nashville: Broadman & Holman Publishers, 1994), 6–10; See Barrett Duke, "Being Salt and Light in a Post-Christian Culture," 127–43 in R. Stanton Norman, ed., *The Mission of Today's Church* (Nashville: B&H Publishing Group, 2007), 127–43.

3. Ibid., Duke, "Being Salt and Light . . ."

4. The Declaration of Independence of the United States of America, 1776.

5. Ibid.

6. Ibid., Charles Hirschfeld, ed., *The Modern World* (New York: Harcourt, Brace and World, 1968), 122–36.

7. Ibid.

8. The "Vision" and "Mission" statements of the Ethics & Religious Liberty Commission of the Southern Baptist Convention.

9. Gregory Tomlin, "What Are You Prepared to Lose?" *Southwestern News* (Spring 2004), 39; Barry Hankins, *Uneasy in Babylon* (Tuscaloosa: University of Alabama Press, 2002), 55–56; See Richard Land, *The Divided States of America* (Nashville: W. Publishing Group, 2007).

10. Peter Irons and Stephanie Guitton, eds., *May It Please the Court: The Most Significant Oral Arguments Made Before the Supreme Court Since 1955* (New York: The New Press, 1993), 343–60.

11. Ibid.

12. Robert Jay Lifton, *The Nazi Doctors: Medical Killing and the Psychology of Genocide* (New York: Basic Books, 1986), 46, 21.

13. Richard Land, *Imagine! A God-Blessed America* (Nashville: Broadman & Holman Publishers, 2005), 25–37.

14. Ibid., 55–93.

15. Jim Nelson Black, *Freefall of the American University* (Nashville: WND Books, 2004).

16. Tony Blankley, *The West's Last Chance* (Washington, D.C.: Regnery, 2005); Richard Land, *Real Homeland Security* (Nashville: Broadman & Holman Publishers, 2004).

17. Gary Hart, *God and Caesar in America* (Golden, Colo.: Fulcum Publishers, 2005); Michelle Goldberg, *Kingdom Coming* (New York: W. W. Norton & Company, 2006); Kevin Phillips, *American Theocracy* (New York: Viking, 2006); James Rudin, *The Baptizing of America* (New York: Thunder's Mouth Press, 2006).

18. Land, *Imagine! A God-Blessed America*, 1–24; Malcolm McDow and Alvin L. Reid, *Firefall* (Nashville: Broadman & Holman Publishers, 1997).

APPENDIX A

Time Line of Southern Baptists Engagement with the Culture

1517	Martin Luther launches the Protestant Reformation
1620	The Pilgrims emigrate to America and sign the Mayflower Compact
1644	Roger Williams pens *The Bloody Tenet of Persecution for Cause of Conscience*
1776	The United States becomes a nation
1788	The Constitution of the United States is ratified
1791	John Leland pens *The Rights of Conscience Inalienable* The Bill of Rights is ratified
1814	The General Missionary Convention of the Baptist Denomination in the United States is formed
1834	The last "state church," Massachusetts, is disengaged
1845	The Southern Baptist Convention (SBC) is formed
1857	The *Dred Scott* decision by the U. S. Supreme Court
1861–1865	The U. S. Civil War
1907	SBC President E. W. Stephens appoints the Committee on Civic Righteousness
1908	SBC Committee on Temperance is formed with A. J. Barton as Chairman
1913	The SBC establishes the Social Service Commission
1914	A. J. Barton elected Chairman of the Social Service Commission. He will serve in this capacity until his death in 1942.
1919	18th Amendment ratified (Prohibition)

1925	Southern Baptists adopt The Baptist Faith and Message and establish the Cooperative Program
1933	Prohibition is repealed
1936	The Committee on Chaplains established during World War I becomes the Committee on Public Relations which will eventually cooperate with the Baptist Joint Committee on Public Affairs (1950)
1942	J. B. Weatherspoon replaces Barton as Chairman of the Social Service Commission
1943	The Social Service Commission receives its first funding from the Southern Baptist Convention
1947	Hugh Brimm elected as the first Secretary-Treasurer (the standard title of an agency head) for the Social Service Commission
1950	The Public Relations Committee of the SBC becomes the Committee on Public Affairs
1951	The Social Service Commission begins to publish *Light*
1953	Acker Miller becomes the new Secretary-Treasurer for the Social Service Commission. The Social Service Commission is renamed the Christian Life Commission (CLC)
1954	The U. S. Supreme Court rules in the *Brown v. Board of Education of Topeka*
1955	Rosa Parks refuses to give up her seat on a city bus in Montgomery, Alabama
1960	Miller retires and Foy Valentine is elected to lead the Christian Life Commission
1963	Martin Luther King Jr. gives his "I Have a Dream" speech in Washington, D. C. The Sixteenth Street Baptist Church in Birmingham is bombed, killing four children President John F. Kennedy is assassinated
1964	The Civil Rights Act of 1964 becomes the law of the land
1968	Martin Luther King Jr. and Robert Kennedy are assassinated

	The SBC adopts the "Statement Concerning the Crisis in Our Nation"
1969	The Christian Life Commission hosts the "Toward Authentic Morality for Modern Man" seminar
1971	The SBC passes the "On Abortion" resolution
1973	The U. S. Supreme Court rules in the *Roe v. Wade* and *Doe v. Bolton* cases legitimizing abortion on demand
1979	The Conservative Resurgence is launched with the election of Adrian Rogers as president of the SBC
1980	The "On Doctrinal Integrity" and "On Abortion" resolutions are adopted by the SBC
	James Dunn becomes Executive Director of the Baptist Joint Committee
1981	People for the American Way is organized
1986	Charles Wade appoints six moderates to the search committee to recommend Valentine's replacement
1987	Larry Baker is elected new head of the Christian Life Commission
	Hal Lane gives a "minority report" for the Christian Life Commission trustees at the SBC
1988	Richard Land elected Executive Director of the Christian Life Commission
1990	The budget allocation to the Baptist Joint Committee is significantly reduced
	The Christian Life Commission receives the program assignment previously held by the Baptist Joint Committee
1991	The Christian Life Commission begins publishing *Salt*
	The SBC completely defunds the Baptist Joint Committee
	The Public Affairs Committee and the Baptist Joint Committee give their final report to the SBC
1994	Leland House, the CLC's Washington, D.C., office opens
1995	The SBC adopts the "Resolution on Racial Reconciliation on the 150th Anniversary of the Southern Baptist Convention" by a nearly unanimous vote

1997	The CLC becomes the Ethics & Religious Liberty Commission on June 19, 1997, as part of the Covenant for a new Century
1998	The *For Faith and Family* radio program is launched
	The erlc.com Web site comes online
	The article on "The Family," drafted by a Convention-elected Committee, which includes Richard Land as a member, is adopted with little dissent as Article XVIII of the Baptist Faith and Message by messengers attending the SBC meeting in Salt Lake City
1999	The ERLC launches its Research Institute
2000	SBC messengers meeting in Orlando overwhelmingly approve revisions to the Baptist Faith and Message, drafted by a committee on which Richard Land serves as part of an executive committee named by chairman Adrian Rogers
2001	Richard Land is appointed by President Bush to the U. S. Commission on International Religious Freedom
2002	*Richard Land Live!* begins airing on weekends
	Richard Land's book, *For Faith and Family*, is released
2003	The *Lawrence v. Texas* case before the Supreme Court rules in the favor of Lawrence
	President Bush signs the "Partial-Birth Abortion Ban Act"
2004	The ERLC sponsors the "iVoteValues" campaign
	Richard Land releases his book *Real Homeland Security*
2005	Land releases *Imagine! A God-Blessed America*
	Richard Land recognized as one of the "25 Most Influential Evangelicals in America" by *Time* magazine
2006	*Light* is renamed *Faith & Family Values*
2007	Richard Land's book, *The Divided States of America*, is released
	The ERLC launches JosiahRoad.com
	Commentary on the Baptist Faith and Message, authored by Richard Land, Chuck Kelley, and R. Albert Mohler, is published by LifeWay Press

APPENDIX B

Recipients of the John Leland Religious Liberty Award from the Ethics & Religious Liberty Commission of the Southern Baptist Convention

1992—JAMES C. DOBSON
1993—ADRIAN P. ROGERS
1994—GLEB YAKUNIN
1995—CHARLES W. LYONS
1996—CARL F. H. HENRY
1997—JOSEPH TSON
1998—JAY ALAN SEKULOW, J.D.
1999—RICHARD D. LAND
2000—CHARLES CANADY
2001—PHIL ROBERTS
2002—NINA SHEA
2003—SAM BROWNBACK
2004—FRANK WOLF
2005—RICK SANTORUM
2006—GEORGE W. BUSH
2007—BOB FU

APPENDIX C

Recipients of the Distinguished Service Award from the Ethics & Religious Liberty Commission of the Southern Baptist Convention

1965—BROOKS HAYS
1966—T. B. MASTON
1967—A. C. MILLER
1971—HENLEE H. BARNETTE
1972—JIMMY R. ALLEN
1973—WALKER L. KNIGHT and ARTHUR B. RUTLEDGE
1974—RANDALL LOLLEY
1975—J. CLARK HENSLEY
1977—WILLIAM M. PINSON JR.
1978—SARAH FRANCES ANDERS
1979—JAMES M. DUNN
1980—GEORGE WILLIS BENNETT
1981—HUGH A. BRIMM and JESSE BURTON
        WEATHERSPOON
1982—PRESIDENT JIMMY CARTER and MRS. ROSALYNN
        CARTER
1983—BILLY GRAHAM
1984—MARK HATFIELD
1985—FOY VALENTINE
1986—OWEN COOPER
1987—CAROLYN WEATHERFORD
1988—SAM CURRIN and DOUGLAS and EVELYN KNAPP
1989—FRED LACKEY and LARRY LEWIS
1990—RICHARD GOODGAME

1991—CHARLES W. COLSON
1992—CARL F. H. HENRY
1993—JAMES T. DRAPER JR.
1994—RICHARD B. NEILL
1995—TONY HALL
1996—JERRY KIRK
1997—VIOLET GALYEAN
1998—DR. A. (ARTHUR) J. BARTON
1999—DR. THOMAS D. ELLIFF
2000—DR. CHARLES L. ROESEL
2001—DR. JOE BOB MIZELL
2002—DR. GARY FROST
2003—DR. RICHARD LAND

Recipients of the Richard D. Land Distinguished Service Award* from the Ethics & Religious Liberty Commission of the Southern Baptist Convention

2003—CLAUDE WITT
2004—REV. DONALD E. WILDMON
2005—DR. PAIGE PATTERSON
2006—TED STONE
2007—DR. BILLY GRAHAM

*In 2003, ERLC trustees voted to honor Richard Land by naming the Distinguished Service Award after him.

APPENDIX D

Installation Address, as 5th President of The Christian Life Commission of the Southern Baptist Convention, delivered March, 27 1989, Kansas City, Missouri.*

"The Salt of the Earth and the Light of the World" by Richard Land

It was the best of times, it was the worst of times,
It was the age of wisdom, it was the age of foolishness,
It was the epoch of belief, it was the epoch of incredulity,
It was the season of Light, it was the season of Darkness,
It was the spring of hope, it was the winter of despair . . .

—CHARLES DICKENS, *A TALE OF TWO CITIES*

Thus Dickens described another revolutionary time when all presuppositions and values were challenged. As twentieth-century men and women, we face a similar epoch. We latter twentieth-century Christians have been called upon to follow the Lord and to be His disciples in a supremely strategic moment in history. It is a moment replete with devastating problems and ripe with promising opportunities.

Numerous people have commented on the increasingly dominant influence of what Carl F. H. Henry in 1946 called "the secular philosophy of humanism or naturalism."[1] One of the most incisive analyses was provided by Alexander Solzhenitsyn, the Soviet exile many consider to be one of the twentieth century's greatest and bravest men. In 1978, Solzhenitsyn warned of the grievous consequences of this fallacious world view:

> "The humanistic way of thinking, which has proclaimed itself our guide, did not admit the existence of intrinsic evil in man, nor did it see any task higher than the attainment of happiness on earth. It started modern western civilization on the dangerous trend of worshipping man and his material needs . . . As if human life did not have any higher meaning."[2]

At the outset of this decade, Carl F. H. Henry described the drastic extent to which twentieth-century philosophies and educational theories have succumbed to a man-centered, rather than God-centered, focus and orientation.[3] Dr. Henry observed that man rather than God "now defines 'truth' and 'goodness'" in most modern universities and that this is the culmination of the present century's having experienced "the greatest overturn of ideas and ideals in the history of human thought."[4]

From this century's mid-point onward, our descent has gained momentum. By the 1960s, we were widely perceived to be a secular culture—aggressively, emphatically secular. Dominant in the opinion-making sectors of our society was the idea that "religion" was to be isolated to the realm of personal piety and the "religious" area of life.

The end result was that for the last half of this century Christianity has increasingly ceased to function in any meaningful way for our culture. By the 1960s, a "Christian mind" did not exist "as a coherent and recognizable influence upon our social, political, and cultural life."[5] A "Christian" piety and practice survived and often even flourished, but it was isolated from the cultural main stream and was driven to the periphery of the culture.

However, things have changed since the 1960s. Rationalistic humanism with its misguided faith in man's capabilities reached its zenith in J. F. K's New Frontier optimism and collapsed with dizzying speed in the jungles of Southeast Asia and on our nation's campuses as the "baby boomers" and "flower power" descended into an abyss of drugs and indiscriminate sexual copulating which was neither "free" nor "love."

Christians today are no longer confronted by a "merely secular" culture, but have now descended "to a pagan society which denies God and has its own idols and own pantheon of new gods," a veritable "neo-pagan age."[6]

The downward spiral of sin outlined by Paul for the Roman Christians has materialized before our very eyes. As "their foolish heart was darkened, professing themselves to be wise, they became fools" and they "changed the truth of God into a lie and worshipped and served the creature more than the Creator."[7] Consequently, "God gave them up unto vile affections" and "gave them over to a reprobate mind"[8]

Christians should draw encouragement, however, from the fact that we face a situation remarkably analogous to the one which confronted our first-century spiritual ancestors. They, too, were immersed in a world dominated by pagan, idolatrous philosophies and lifestyles. Most of them had been an integral part of that world until their conversion. They had to develop a new life, a new mind, a new world view.[9] If they triumphed in their time and place, so can we, with God's power, guidance, and assistance.

How do we begin? I would like to suggest that we start with a renewed understanding that the "kingdom of God embraces every aspect of life: ethical, spiritual, and temporal."[10] We must recover a comprehensive understanding of Christian truth and of its applicability to every area of life. Scripture tells us this will be done through the renewal of our minds (Rom. 12:1–2; Eph. 4:23; Rom. 8:5–10; Col. 3:1–2). What is a Christian mind or outlook?[11] It has been defined as a "Christian outlook that controls our life and our thinking."[12] It is . . . "A mind trained, informed, equipped to handle data of secular controversy within a framework of reference which is constructed of Christian presuppostions, presuppositions," (for example) of the supernatural, of the pervasiveness of evil, of truth, authority and of the value of the human person.[13]

To be truly effective, to change lives, we must first be changed. Conversion to faith in Jesus Christ as personal Lord and Saviour must precede the "renewing of your mind." Conversion does not, however, make that renewal automatic. Otherwise, we would not be commanded and exhorted to "present" ourselves for the Spirit's transformation (Rom. 12:1).

When we have experienced regeneration, and we can begin to allow the Holy Spirit to develop our Christian character, then as citizens of our Saviour's kingdom, we have responsibilities. The scripture passage adopted by the Christian Life Commission for its official seal contains in sublime simplicity the foundation of our Lord's teaching in applied Christianity. In Matthew 5:13–16, Jesus tells His disciples that they are "the salt of the earth" and "the light of the world."

The larger context of the passage tells us that Jesus saw "the multitudes." Jesus saw the people in their lostness, in their degeneration, in their darkness. He, and He alone, sees the complete havoc of sin, because He not only sees what they are, but what God intended for them to be, but for sin. He beholds the world's individual and collective ruin, and He tells His disciples that they are salt and they are light. Since the world is corrupt and degenerating, Christians are to be salt, the agent that preserves from decay and putrefaction. Since the world is in darkness, Christians are to be light, to illuminate the pathway to life. Salt is essentially defensive in nature. It stops the decay. "You do not salt a living thing. You salt a dead one that it may not be a rotting one."[14]

Christians who are fulfilling their role as salt retard evil by their presence. They are people in whose presence it is harder to say or do the wrong thing and easier to say or do the right thing. They act as "a moral disinfectant" in a deteriorating world.[15]

To be salt, Christians must remain pure. If the salt loses its savor, then it is "good for nothing." Light, unlike salt, cannot cease to be light. However, it can be covered and obscured. If these words of Jesus teach us anything, it is that "to be a true Christian in all secrecy, comfortably and enjoyably, is as impossible as firing a cannon in all secrecy."[16]

Jesus leaves no room here either for monastic withdrawal or syncretistic cultural accommodation.

The Christian must be in the world (salt must make contact with what it preserves or purifies and light which is to "shine before men" must be seen by men), but not of the world (James 1:27).

As we face our neo-pagan cultural milieu under the command to be salt and light, we must realize that an ability to do so successfully will first be governed not only by His presence in our lives, but also by the extent we surrender on a daily basis to His lordship.

As Paul challenged the Romans, when we unreservedly "present" ourselves for service, we will discover "that good, acceptable and perfect will of God" for our lives which, as we have seen, includes being salt and light as a priority of the highest order (Rom. 12:1–2).

How does this apply to specific issues? Let us examine a few. Pornography is a plague on our land. It is a multibillion-dollar-a-year industry that shrinks, shrivels, and stunts the souls of all it touches. It shamelessly and cruelly exploits women and children and is grossly dehumanizing. Pornography is one of the great hidden factors in divorce in our nation today, and I don't just mean among non-Christians. Pornography is a major contributing cause to our epidemic of child abuse and rape. As salt, we must assault the decay and seek to be a "moral disinfectant" in stopping further pollution of our young people's minds. For every man driven to hideous crimes by addiction to pornography, there are tens of thousands for whom it has twisted and distorted their capacity to be the loving, caring husbands God intended them to be and designed for their wives to have.

But it is not enough to defend against further decay. It is not enough "to just say no!" We are also commanded to be light. We must take the offensive and aggressively share God's design for the sexual relationship within the boundaries of holy matrimony. The world has taken the sexual union which God intended to bring about, the most intimate, joyous, giving, sharing communion a man and woman can know this side of heaven, and has distorted it to the point that now common slang terms for the sex act are euphemisms for hostility, exploitation, and aggression. We must shed God's light on the sheer beauty and joy of the Genesis accounts of Adam and Eve.

We must shed God's light on marriage as a divinely founded institution and proclaim "marriage is honorable in all, and the bed undefiled" (Heb. 13:4). We must do all within our power to give our young people a positive, pure, holy view of their sexuality and the reasons God graces us with that particular gift. Marriage is under unprecedented assault in our culture, and we must not only seek to preserve as salt, but also to proclaim His truth about the divine estate of holy matrimony.

We must seek to be salt in preserving against the death of drugs and drug dealers. We must also be light. We must address the nihilism, hopelessness, and hedonism of our people which leads them to drugs in a frantic search, if not for happiness, at least for momentary pleasure.

Racism continues to plague our nation and our world. This should dismay us, but it should not surprise us. Racism is an enemy within, as well as without. It is an integral part of our having been born with "a nature and an environment inclined toward sin."[17] Prejudice is at its most basic a sin problem, a spiritual problem, a consequence of the fallen, sinful human heart.

Scripture reveals the ubiquity of sin's curse on the creation, with the consequence that no single person or thing is as God originally intended it to be (Rom. 8:22–23). Isaiah informed us that "all we like sheep have gone astray; we have turned everyone to his own way" (53:6). Jeremiah furthered the diagnosis when he revealed, "The heart is deceitful above all things, and desperately wicked" (17:9). Paul added in inclusive conclusion, "For all have sinned, and come short of the glory of God" (Rom. 3:23).

Racism and all other forms of prejudice and bigotry are at heart a problem of sinful pride and of thinking more highly of ourselves than we ought to think. It is also revolt against God's revelation of the Imago Dei. God has clearly taught us that all persons are created in the image of God (Gen. 1:27) and that while that image has been distorted by the Fall, it has not been obliterated (James 3:9).

The idea that all of us, each individual one of us, is the creation of God, made in His image, and is an invaluable someone for whom Jesus died, destroys the basis for bigotry. We must be salt in opposing racial prejudice as anti-biblical and in addressing it whenever it appears. We must also be light.

We must understand that everyone is victimized by racial prejudice, both the persecutor and the persecuted. We must also hold up the light of hope that is the Gospel. We can be healed and liberated from our past (Col. 2:13–15; Phil. 4:13; 1 John 1:9). Victimizer and victim alike find liberation from their victimization in Jesus Christ!

Abortion is perhaps the supreme contemporary example of our need to be salt and light. Since 1973 abortion, the taking of unborn life in the womb, has assumed staggering proportions in our society. At least 1.5 million babies a year are being killed before they are born because they are considered too expensive, too embarrassing, or too inconvenient. We must proclaim the biblical witness against such carnage (Exod. 21:22; Ps. 139:13–16; Jer. 1:5; Ps. 51:5, etc.). These and other verses indicate that life begins in the womb—unique, planned life.

We must be salt. We must force people to confront the horror of what they are doing.

We must be salt in seeking to preserve life. We must also be light. We have already talked about pagan sexual attitudes which must be addressed and which lead to the supposed need for many abortions. We must also speak to the unborn as God's creation, thus of divine value. We must also preach the forgiveness and healing of God, which is available to all who have been afflicted by abortion, whether the mother who had one, the doctor who performed one, or the parent who counseled one.

We must have, on all these issues and more, what Helmut Thielecke in another context called "simultaniety." In other words, to be faithful to our Lord's mandate, it must never be "either/or," but always "both/ and"—salt and light.

Will we win in our confrontation with the idols of our age and time? Ultimately, yes (John 16:33). In the interim, I knoweth not. Let us heed our Paul's advice and "not be weary in well-doing; for in due season we shall reap, if we faint not" (Gal. 6:9).

If a new pagan age does emerge and flourish, we should draw encouragement from our brave Christian brothers and sisters in China and in the Soviet Union. They have survived a dark night and flourished in the midst of adversity. And as Lord MacCaulay has reminded us:

> *To every man upon this earth*
> *Death cometh soon or late;*
> *And how can man die better*
> *Than facing fearful odds*
> *For the ashes of his fathers,*
> *And the temples of his gods.*[18]

Especially is this so when our ancestors have bequeathed us such a rich heritage, and when the one who is by His grace our God, is also the one true God.

Let us follow our Saviour's example and be about our Father's business. As changed people, let us help other changed people change the world. And when distractions tempt us, remember that though

> *The woods are lovely, dark and deep.*
> *But I have promises to keep,*
> *And miles to go before I sleep.*[19]

*An abridged version of Dr. Richard Land's installation address. Published in the July–September 1989 issue of *Light* magazine.

Notes

1. Carl F. H. Henry, *Remaking the Modern Mind* (Grand Rapids: Wm. B. Eerdmans, 1946), 9.

2. Ronald Berman, ed. *Solzhenitsyn at Harvard* (Washington, D. C.: Ethics and Public Policy Center, 1980), 16–17.

3. *Christianity Today,* May 7, 1981.

4. Ibid.

5. Harry Blamires, *The Christian Mind* (Ann Arbor: Servant Books, 1978), originally published 1963, vii.

6. Denton Lotz, "Christian Higher Education and the Conversion of the West," *The Southern Baptist Educator* (Sept. 1987), 7.

7. Romans 1:21–25.

8. Romans 1:26–28.

9. Oliver Barclay, *The Intellect and Beyond* (Grand Rapids: Zondervan, 1985), 16–17.

10. Charles Colson, *Kingdoms in Conflict* (Grand Rapids: Zondervan, 1987), 86–87.

11. Cf. Blamires, op. cit. and Barclay, op. cit., 13f for an interesting debate on whether the better concept is "mind" or "outlook."

12. Barclay, 15.

13. John R. W. Stott, *Your Mind Matters* (London: Inter-Varsity Press, 1972), 19, quoting Blamires, op. cit., 43.

14. Alexander Maclaren, *Expositions of Holy Scripture* (Grand Rapids: Baker, 1982), vol. vi, 179.

15. R. V. G. Tasker, *The Gospel According to St. Matthew* (London: Tyndale Press, 1961), 63.

16. Søren Kierkegaard, quoted in *Daily Devotion Bible Commentary* (Nashville: Holman, 1974), vol. iii, 24.

17. Baptist Faith and Message, "Man."

18. *Lays of Ancient Rome*, stanza 27.

19. Robert Frost, *Stopping by Woods on a Snowy Evening*.

APPENDIX E

"Is Life a Right?"*
by Richard Land

Is human life sacred? From the very beginning the Bible reveals that it is because human beings are created in God's image (Genesis 1:27).

The Bible portrays God's personal involvement in humankind's creation, and the emphasis throughout is on man's divinely imparted uniqueness as made in God's image. That divine image was distorted but not destroyed by man's fall into sin. God communicated with Adam and Eve both before sin entered the world (Genesis 1:28) and immediately after the Fall (Genesis 3:9), promising His intervention to bring redemption and restoration (Genesis 3:15).

God tells fallen but regenerate human beings, "Be ye not as the horse, or as the mule, which have no understanding" (Psalm 32:9), but instead look to Him to instruct "and teach thee in the way which thou shalt go" (Psalm 32:8).

The central truth that emerges from these Bible verses is that human life is sacred, thus distinct in nature and design from all other life; and the differences are of kind, not degree. We are not merely the most advanced life in the animal kingdom. The Bible tells us that all life deserves respect, but that human life demands reverence.

If human life is sacred, when does it begin? The Bible reveals God's intense interest in each human life from before conception onward. God told Jeremiah, "Before I formed thee in the belly I knew thee; and before thou camest forth out of the womb I sanctified thee" (Jeremiah 1:5). Job said, God "made me in the womb" (Job 31:15).

The psalmist speaks vividly: "For you created my inmost being; you knit me together in my mother's womb. I praise you because I am fearfully and wonderfully made; your words are wonderful . . . your eyes saw my unformed body. All the days ordained for me were written in your book before one of them came to be" (Psalm 139:13–16 NIV).

In Psalm 51:5 David says, "I have been . . . sinful from the time my mother conceived me" (HCSB). God revealed to David that he had a sin nature from the moment of conception onward. Since only human beings with a soul and a spirit possess a sin nature, human life begins at conception.

Is life a right? Since the Bible teaches that life is sacred and that it begins at conception, human life is a right that should be revered and protected from conception onward. God mandates protection for human life: "You shall not murder" (Exodus 20:13; see also Proverbs 6:16–17 NIV).

God is the giver and sustainer of life (Genesis 2:7; Colossians 1:15–20). Our world needs desperately to hear this truth. Human life, from conception to death and at all points in between, is under violent assault. Unborn babies, handicapped infants, the terminally ill, and the aged and infirm are merely the first to be victimized. The Bible tells us that all life deserves respect, but that human life demands reverence.

Many now seek to overturn the Bible's sanctity of life ethic, which sees human beings as possessing a sacred, God-given right to life as an inherent part of human nature. They would replace the Bible's view of humanity with a "quality of life" ethic that makes human beings the arbiters of whether other human beings possess the potential for a sufficient "quality" of life to be allowed continued existence.

Our country since its inception has based its beliefs about human life on a sanctity of life ethic. Our Declaration of Independence declares that "human beings are endowed by their Creator with certain inalienable rights" and "that among these are Life. . . . "

Christians must sound the clarion call against all attitudes and actions that assault the sacredness of human life. We must bear witness by deed as well as by word that human life is sacred. It is a precious, irreplaceable gift from God. We must oppose the barbaric, lethal combination of technical expertise and spiritual ignorance that would deny human life's sacredness and that would abort and experiment on our pre-born, harvest fetal tissue, allow death into the nursery for our mentally and physically handicapped infants and encourage euthanasia in our hospitals and retirement homes.

Let us, as brothers and sisters in Christ, covenant together to pray for the discernment and the diligence to do this and more.

*A very popular tract published by Broadman Press in 1990. Slightly revised and republished in 2003.

APPENDIX F

Nashville Statement of Conscience
September 1994

"The Struggle Against Abortion: Why the Use of Lethal Force in not Morally Justifiable

In July 1994, abortion doctor John Britton and his escort, James Barrett, were shot and killed as they arrived at the Pensacola (Florida) Ladies Center. These murders generated more rhetorical heat than light. The pro-choice and pro-abortion forces claimed such actions were the natural fruit of the conviction that human life begins at conception. The pro-life forces objected strenuously, but did not fully justify their intuitive rejection of these murders.

In September 1994, Richard Land, as head of the Christian Life Commission, convened a meeting of leading Southern Baptist ethicists. Out of that meeting came the Nashville Statement of Conscience, written from a Christian pro-life perspective and designed to clarify the grounds for this rejection of this case of vigilante "justice." It makes the case that the killing of abortion doctors is not a morally justifiable or permissible Christian response to abortion.

"The LORD examines the righteous, but the wicked and those who love violence his soul hates." (Ps. 11:5 NIV)

1. Preamble

1.1 Acts of lethal violence recently have been used in an attempt to stop abortion doctors from performing abortions. Such violence has been perpetrated, in some cases, by those who seek to justify their acts on the basis of Christian moral principles. Dozens of violent incidents of other sorts have also occurred in and near abortion clinics over the past fifteen years.

1.2 The aftermath of these violent acts has made it clear that the views of the perpetrators are not merely idiosyncratic, but instead reflect the perspective of a small number of Americans, some of them Christians, who are strongly opposed to abortion.

1.3 Representatives of a wide range of "pro-choice," "pro-abortion," and "pro-life" positions have offered public statements condemning such use of deadly force and the moral justification of such acts. It has been a rare instance of agreement. We join in condemning these killings.

1.4 However, the divergent reasons that pro-choice and pro-life groups have offered for their moral rejection of such acts as the Pensacola shootings, and of the moral claims that undergird such acts, bear witness to the continuing and seemingly unbridgeable gulf between these polarized parties to the abortion conflict.

1.5 We who offer this statement speak from a Christian pro-life perspective. Even though we share the moral condemnation of the killings that pro-choice groups and leaders have expressed, we have yet to read a statement from such persons that reflects our point of view concerning why such killings are not morally justifiable.

1.6 In particular, some claim that unborn life is not fully human life, and thus that it is wrong to use lethal force in an attempt to prevent abortion. We strongly disagree with the claim that an unborn child is not fully human life, deserving of full protection. We will reject the killing of abortion doctors on other grounds.

1.7 At the same time, we find the response thus far from the pro-life community deserves more elaboration and depth. We are glad to see that all responsible pro-life groups and leaders have condemned such killings, as do we. But mere denunciation, however passionate it may be, is not enough. We believe that the point of view of persons advocating violence against abortion doctors requires serious moral reflection and engagement, more serious than has thus far publicly occurred. A number of profound questions of Christian morality and Christian citizenship are at stake.

1.8 As pro-life Christians, we are concerned about the possibility that some of our fellow pro-life Christian friends and colleagues will drift into an embrace of violence directed against abortion providers. Lack of serious engagement with the views of persons who advocate the use of violence will only increase the risk that this drift will occur. We are equally concerned that such violence will lead pro-life Christians to withdraw from morally legitimate forms of action to prevent abortion.

1.9 This statement, therefore, is intended as a moral analysis and rejection of the killing of abortion doctors, offered from a Christian pro-life perspective. It is at the same time intended as an urgent plea for intensified Christian involvement in all morally permissible forms of anti-abortion activities. We offer this statement in the name of Jesus Christ, our Savior and Lord, to any who will listen, and especially to our fellow laborers in the protection of the unborn.

2. Murder in Christian Perspective

2.1 Murder, the culpable killing of a human being, is an extraordinarily grave offense against civil law as well as against the moral law of God (Exod. 20:13) on which all morally legitimate civil law is ultimately based.

2.2 The Bible teaches that each human life is sacred, for every human being is made in the image of God (Gen. 1:26–27). For this reason, each human life bears divinely granted and immeasurable value. Human beings are not free to take the lives of others, for those lives belong to God, their Creator. This is the meaning of the divine prohibition of murder in the Ten Commandments. "Thou shalt not kill" means that God prohibits the unjustified taking, and mandates the protection, of human life.

2.3 In the Sermon on the Mount (Matt. 5:21f.), Jesus affirmed the prohibition against murder. Indeed, He warned of God's judgment even on intense expressions of anger and contempt for others, while calling His hearers to seek reconciliation with any persons from whom they might be estranged, even their enemies (Matt. 5:43–44). Jesus also proclaimed God's special favor upon those who make peace (Matt. 5:9). While wholeheartedly committed to the spread of the Kingdom of God (Matt. 6:10, 6:33), Jesus personally rejected the use of violence to accomplish even this holy aim.

2.4 The Apostle Paul frequently reaffirmed the centrality of peacemaking and reconciliation, even describing God's saving act in Jesus Christ as an act of divine peacemaking between those who had once been enemies--an act that not only reconciled God to humanity but also reconciled estranged human beings to each other (Eph. 2:11–22).

2.5 Paul also argued that the governing authorities of this world have been established by God. Their mandate in a world deeply marred by sin is to serve God by deterring wrongdoing and bringing punishment on wrongdoers, thus protecting the innocent (Rom. 13:1–7). In this work, Paul writes, the authorities "do not bear the sword in vain" (Rom. 13:4). Most Christians have understood this to be a divine authorization of the use of force by governing authorities, even deadly force at times, when such force is finally required to accomplish government's divinely mandated purposes. Through the centuries, strict criteria have been developed for the just employment of such force.

2.6 In Christian theology a historic split has existed between those who believe that the witness of Scripture prohibits any taking of human life under any circumstance by any person or institution, and those who believe that under the conditions of sin the taking of human life is in a very small number of tragic circumstances morally justifiable and thus morally permissible.

2.7 Those taking the former position could ground a rejection of the killing of abortion doctors in their uniform and absolute rejection of any killing of any human being under any circumstances by any person or institution. This point of view would be coherent and consistent, and no further argument would need to be made.

2.8 While respectful of this position, we believe that the overall witness of Scripture, including Romans 13, leads to the latter conclusion--that there are indeed a small number of tragic and exceptional circumstances in a fallen world in which the taking of human life can be morally justifiable.

2.9 However, from our perspective the Bible establishes a profound presumption in favor of preserving life rather than ending it. God wills that human beings should make peace with each other, should be reconciled, and should treat every life with the respect its divine origin and ownership demands. There is at the very least a *prima facie* moral obligation to refrain from killing. This means that an extraordinarily stringent burden of proof is imposed upon any who would seek to justify the taking of a human life.

2.10 To the extent that United States civil law reflects the divine moral law, it likewise is structured both to deter and to punish severely the unjustifiable taking of a human life. Civil law does generally recognize that under certain unusual circumstances normally involving defense of self or third persons against deadly force, the taking of another human life by a private citizen might be justified. A stringent burden of proof in every case rests on those who would justify any taking of life.

2.11 United States civil law is also structured to recognize the broader mandate of government to use force and the threat of force, judiciously and carefully, to deter and punish evil and to protect the innocent from wrongdoing. The government protects its citizenry from domestic wrongdoers through the law enforcement and criminal justice systems, and from foreign wrongdoers through the armed forces. Private citizens rightly are barred from authorizing themselves to perform these functions.

2.12 Those advocating acts of lethal force against abortion doctors claim that such acts qualify as morally justifiable homicide, despite the current status of civil law in the United States.

2.13 This assertion requires Christian consideration of the moral and legal status of the act of elective abortion, as well as the moral obligations of Christians living in a democratic society that by statute permits elective abortion under most circumstances.

3. The Moral and Legal Status of the Act of Elective Abortion

3.1 Since 1973, the United States Supreme Court has interpreted the United States Constitution in such a way as to create a right of a woman to choose to secure the services of a physician who is paid to "terminate her pregnancy"—that is, deliberately to end the existence of that life which is developing within her body. This state of affairs is justly called "abortion on demand" in that abortion is permitted on the basis of no criteria other than a pregnant woman's demand for an abortion. The abortion workers who have been killed or injured have been relying on this decisional law to justify their conduct legally.

3.2 The moral status of the act of elective abortion is arguably the most bitterly contested moral and, consequently, legal, social, cultural, religious, and political question of our time. This is not the place in which to offer a rehearsal of the arguments that pertain to this question. We will instead simply state our position in the following way.

3.3 As indicated above (2.2), we believe that each human life bears a divinely granted sacredness. We believe that its sacredness begins at conception, when biological life begins. We believe that gestational life—life in the womb from conception to birth—must be understood as human life in its earliest stages rather than as pre-human, non-human, potential, or any other less-than-fully-sacred kind of human life. We know that, if allowed to continue developing without hindrance through a normal pregnancy, a gestating human life becomes a newborn baby. Thus, we are compelled to consider elective abortion the killing of a human being.

3.4 We have already argued that, given the sacredness of human life, the burden of proof is on any who would morally justify its deliberate extinguishing. The terrible flaw at the heart of federal abortion law is that abortions are currently permitted *while requiring a woman to meet only a minimal burden of proof which may be imposed by state laws*. In terms of gestational life, the federal government has wrongfully abdicated its responsibility to protect the innocent and to establish and enforce stringent criteria for the justifiable taking of human life.

3.5 We recognize that for a woman (or, for a couple) an unwanted pregnancy may well be a crisis pregnancy. We acknowledge that women seek abortions for a wide range of reasons. Tragically, these range from the most serious and justifiable (i.e., a threat to the physical life of the mother) to the least serious and justifiable (i.e., gender preference, interruption of vacation plans, and so on). The effect of current abortion law is that any reason for an abortion, or no particular reason, is as good as any other. The great majority of abortions in the

United States are performed for what can best be described as reasons of convenience.

3.6 We recall the biblical principle that it is morally forbidden for a private citizen to end a human life except in the act of self-defense. Only in cases when gestational life poses a serious threat to the physical life of the mother, in our view, does elective abortion clearly meet this self-defense criterion. A significant number of pro-life Christians are willing to grant the possibility that abortion in the cases of rape, incest, and/or radical fetal deformity also ought to be included among those exceptions to the general prohibition of abortion that should be recognized by law. We disagree. But we recognize that rewritten abortion laws framed along those lines would still disallow all but a very small percentage of abortions in this country.

3.7 Instead, our nation continues to operate under a law that requires no significant burden of proof for abortion. This represents a fundamental assault on the sanctity of human life. Human beings are not at liberty to lower the threshold for the taking of human life, but that is precisely what abortion laws have done. Lowering that threshold is one of humanity's greatest temptations, one to which human beings have succumbed all too frequently, especially in our own century of world war and genocide.

3.8 But we need not look elsewhere for examples. Our own violence-wracked nation bears witness each day to the devastating consequences of disrespect for the sacredness of human life. Truly the blood of the murdered cries out from the ground (Gen. 4:10; Lev. 18:28). We believe that abortion on demand is the leading, but not the only, example of a broader national moral and social crisis of disrespect for human life.

3.9 From our perspective, then, the overwhelming majority of abortions represent a morally unjustifiable form of killing. It is a unique form of killing, involving several parties. An abortion is undertaken by a physician who performs abortions, at the request of an unborn child's mother. Often, a woman is pressured by the child's father to have an abortion. Pressure may also come from family members, friends, and others. Her decision is then permitted by the civil law of the United States. Each participant in this act of unjustifiable killing, including the government of the United States (and ultimately "we the people," who are the sovereign of this government and have elected its officials), bears a share of the responsibility.

3.10 For twenty-one years, since the 1973 *Roe v. Wade* and *Doe v. Bolton* Supreme Court decisions, abortion on demand has been the controlling interpretation of the Constitution in the United States. In that time over thirty million abortions have been performed in this country. We believe that this state of affairs can only be called a moral outrage.

3.11 We share the intense frustration of tens of millions of this nation's citizens who grieve each of the lives lost, the futures never realized, the human beings who unjustly have been prevented from ever "seeing the light of day" (Job 3:16). We also grieve for the many mothers and fathers who spend much of their lives profoundly regretting their choice to have an abortion, mourning the children they never had the chance to love and enjoy.

4. Legitimate Forms of Christian Response

4.1 Most Christians who believe, as we do, that the overwhelming majority of abortions are morally unjustifiable acts of killing, rightly feel the need to offer significant moral response. Indeed, millions of American Christians even today are engaged in activities that constitute such a response; most of these activities, in our view, are fully and morally justifiable and quite constructive. They are aimed at saving lives, and are directed at each of the participants in the abortion decision.

4.2 For example, many Christians are involved in supporting absti-
nence- and values-based sex education programs in schools, civic institutions, and churches. The Southern Baptist Convention's "True Love
Waits" program is an effective example. Such programs are rooted
in the biblical moral norm that sexual intimacy is designed by God
to be reserved for marriage (1 Cor. 6:9–20; 7:9; etc.). It is obvious,
but important to point out nonetheless, that the demand for abortion
would decrease radically if God's intentions for sexuality were heeded.
Abortions happen because unwanted pregnancies happen; unwanted
pregnancies happen, most of the time, because of sexual activity outside of marriage. It is important to note again that it takes both a man
and a woman to engage in such sexual activity, and both are responsible for the consequences.

4.3 Christians are also involved in helping pregnant women "choose
life," that they and their children "may live" (Deut. 30:19). Christians
have led the way in establishing crisis pregnancy centers and maternity
homes. In such places pregnant women are cared for and prepared
either to raise their children themselves or to give their children to
others who can do so via adoption. This is a noble form of Christian
ministry to women and their children. We give thanks to God for those
women who avail themselves of these ministries and thus save their
children's lives.

4.4 Pro-life Christians, especially those in the health care professions,
are also on the front lines in the struggle over abortion as an aspect of
medical practice. Such health care professionals bear witness to their
convictions by refusing to "regularize" abortion as an aspect of medical care. They remind fellow health care providers of the "first, do no
harm" provision of the Hippocratic Oath. This kind of witness—a witness of winsome moral suasion and example, rather than invective and
violence—is an important and appropriate part of the struggle against
abortion. It is one of the reasons why very few physicians are willing
to perform elective abortions.

4.5 Abortion on demand became law in our democratic society by the decision of persons who attained their office by legitimate processes, and remains lawful through the same processes. Christians, anguished at this state of affairs, are rightfully involved in the wide-ranging kinds of political engagement afforded us within the democratic process.

4.6 Such involvement includes voting, lobbying, campaigning for pro-life candidates, drafting legislation, writing letters to government officials, getting involved in political party platform drafting, running for office, initiating boycotts, and so on. We believe that there is no doubt whatsover that such activity is our right as citizens and our obligation as Christians.

4.7 Some pro-life Christians are involved in lawful public witness in the vicinity of abortion clinics, such as the handing out of printed materials and the organizing of prayer vigils. We believe that public witness of this type is morally justifiable.

4.8 Some Christians have engaged in various forms of nonviolent, public, civil disobedience in the vicinity of abortion clinics as an aspect of their protest against legal abortion on demand. This kind of activity has been a matter of considerable debate in pro-life circles and concern in the broader society.

4.9 From a biblical perspective, Christians clearly are required to submit to and obey the governing authorities of the lands in which they live. This responsibility flows from the divinely authorized nature of these governing authorities (see 2.5).

4.10 Scripture does recognize, however, that governments sometimes violate their God-given purposes, even to the extent of enacting laws and policies that are in direct and specific conflict with the divine moral law. History bears frequent tragic witness to the same reality. The Bible teaches that Christians are morally permitted, and sometimes even obligated, to violate a civil law that is in direct, specific conflict with the law of God (cf. Exod. 1:16–2:10; Dan. 6; Acts 4:1–31, 5:12–42).

4.11 The burden of proof for justifying civil disobedience rests with those considering it. Besides being intended as a challenge to a morally illegitimate law or policy, such nonviolent civil disobedience should follow the failure of a range of other, less radical forms of action; should have some likelihood of effectiveness; and should have positive consequences that are likely to outweigh negative consequences.

4.12 Christians living in a democratic society who make the grave judgment to engage in public, nonviolent, civil disobedience must willingly submit to the consequences of their actions. Thus, Christians involved in civil disobedience related to abortion should expect to be prosecuted. To break a morally illegitimate law, and to submit willingly to the consequences of doing so, is in fact an attempt to change civil law via moral witness—and thus, to affirm all morally legitimate civil law.

4.13 We believe that laws concerning access to abortion clinics and protests around abortion clinics function as a fence around the immoral law that permits legalized abortion on demand. Because the abortion law is a permission for private citizens to have and to perform abortions, rather than a mandate requiring behavior of one type or another, it is impossible to perform direct civil disobedience in the matter of legalized abortion on demand. This means that nonviolent civil disobedience, if it occurs, can only be directed at subsidiary laws.

4.14 We have outlined several lawful ways in which Christians can offer constructive moral response to the morally illegitimate law permitting abortion on demand. These can by no means be described as having been exhausted. There is much more to be done. This raises the question of whether nonviolent civil disobedience is justified.

4.15 On balance, we believe that acts of *nonviolent* civil disobedience related to abortion, though not morally *obligatory* for Christians, may be seen as morally *permissible*. This is ultimately a matter of individual conscience before God.

4.16 Legalized abortion on demand has become deeply entrenched in our society. What many Christians once hoped would be a temporary aberration has become an institutionalized reality. We must acknowledge that this has occurred because significant portions of our society have wanted it to occur. The tragic and abhorrent legal reality reflects an equally tragic and abhorrent social, cultural, and moral reality.

4.17 Pro-life Christians should work to change these social, cultural, and moral realities in which legalized abortion on demand is rooted. It is a heart-by-heart, home-by-home, city-by-city, state-by-state struggle. We must greatly intensify our efforts in the morally justifiable anti-abortion activities described above. It is our moral obligation.

5. Why Lethal Force is Not Morally Justified

5.1 The killing of abortion doctors by private citizens raises the important question of whether such an action is a morally legitimate Christian response to legalized abortion on demand. We strongly contend that killing abortion doctors is not a moral option for Christians, and respond to the various arguments as follows:

5.2 First, we reject the argument some have made that such killings are valid as an act of defending the innocent from harm. We reply that according to both civil law and divine moral law private citizens are permitted to use lethal force against another human being only if this occurs as an unintended effect of the act of defending oneself or another against an assailant's unjust attack. Private citizens are not allowed to *intend* to kill another human being and are not allowed to engage in *premeditated* acts of deadly force in order to accomplish what they intend. In other words, a private citizen can intend to stop, but not to kill, an assailant regardless of the final result. Attacks on abortion doctors fail this test.

5.3 Furthermore, an act of homicide is unjustifiable if the attacker's victim could have been adequately defended in any way other than causing the attacker's death. We believe that the many pro-life measures outlined in section 4 do offer a range of constructive (even if not fully adequate) forms of defense of the lives of the unborn, and thus, the killing of abortion doctors is unjustifiable.

5.4 We believe, further, that the killing of an abortion doctor in actuality does not constitute a meaningful defense of unborn life. This is the case because an abortion doctor is only one of the participants in the act of elective abortion, and not the most important one. It is the woman seeking an abortion who drives the process. The killing of an abortion doctor does nothing in itself to diminish a woman's demand for an abortion. If abortion is legal, and she perceives no alternatives to abortion, she will find another abortion provider. As long as abortion is legal, if we wish to save the lives of unborn children we must influence the actions of women who are considering abortion. The best and most Christ-like way to do so is lovingly to provide her with viable alternatives to abortion. This does not absolve others, especially the baby's father, who may be exerting enormous pressure on the child's mother.

5.5 Second, we reject the argument that the killing of an abortion doctor is justifiable as a form of capital punishment. We reply that the moral legitimacy of capital punishment in contemporary American society is a point of dispute among pro-life Christians. More germane to the argument is the fact that whatever right there may be to execute a criminal is reserved exclusively to governing authorities, and is never the prerogative of a private citizen. A peaceful and orderly society can have no place for self-appointed executioners.

5.6 Third, we reject the argument that killing an abortion doctor is an act of violent civil disobedience made necessary by the gravity of the moral evil of abortion on demand. It is our conviction that no act of lethal force can be properly ascribed to the rubric of civil disobedience. Moreover, the contradiction between the use of lethal force and civil disobedience is especially glaring in a democracy, in which so many alternative forms of activism for social and legal change are permitted. We contend that such an act is better described as an act of revolution rather than an act of civil disobedience intended to accomplish reform.

5.7 Fourth, we reject the argument that a government that allows legalized abortion on demand has of necessity lost its legitimacy, and that in such a circumstance private citizens are free to resist it "by any means necessary."

5.8 To this we reply that we accept the legitimacy of the government of the United States, despite its failure to protect the lives of the unborn and its sanction of access to abortion on demand. It is the people of the United States who have, in fair and free elections, selected the leaders of our government, and it is these duly elected leaders who have appointed judges to the Supreme Court and other federal courts. The actions and inactions of persons in all three branches of the federal government over more than twenty years are responsible for legalized abortion on demand. In turn, their decisions have reflected the pressures brought to bear on them by citizens of the United States, functioning through the democratic process.

5.9 From this we conclude that it is the people of the United States, acting through legitimate governmental institutions, who are responsible and ultimately accountable for immoral laws permitting and protecting the taking of unborn human lives. We do not believe that laws permitting abortion on demand remove the legitimacy of our government. Rather, the authority of our legitimate government has been perverted to allow and protect abortion on demand.

5.10 To us, legalized abortion on demand is the single gravest failure of American democracy in our generation. But we recognize it as a failure of a legitimate democracy rather than as the imposition or decree of an illegitimate regime. For this reason, we reject what can only be described as *the logic of revolution* that some have articulated. Instead, among our other pro-life efforts, we pledge intensified commitment to change the law through the democratic processes of the United States of America.

5.11 Fifth, we reject the claim that private individuals have a right to circumvent the processes of democratic government by using deadly force where the law sanctions abortion on demand. We realize that what is legal and what is moral are not always identical. Where they diverge, Christians bear a dual responsibility, first to act in accordance with the moral law, and second to respect and obey the legitimate authority of government. So long as a government retains legitimacy, and so long as opportunities for reform remain, individuals and groups must work within the democratic process and must resist the temptation to take the law into their own hands.

5.12 We believe that a government may lose its legitimacy as it sets itself against divine law and loses the popular support of its people. Should such circumstances arise, and should that government preclude all opportunities for reform, then Christians, for sake of conscience, may be forced to consider more drastic measures. We deny that our nation is nearing or has reached such a crisis. Our goal must be reform, not revolution.

5.13 We understand that no government can allow laws against the taking of human life to become a matter of private interpretation without placing its own existence and legitimacy in jeopardy. A private citizen who makes the decision to use lethal force against human life contrary to established law is not merely breaking the law against murder, he or she is also assaulting and undermining the authority of the government itself. Thus, any private decision to break the law against murder—

even where there is an intention to do good—is an act of rebellion that threatens the existing governing authority, contrary to the will of God (Rom. 13:2). It is not simply an act of civil disobedience. It is certainly not an act of legal reform.

5.14 The distinction between nonviolent civil disobedience and the private use of lethal force can be illustrated from American history. Many Christians felt compelled during the 1850s to violate the fugitive slave laws by participating in the Underground Railroad, which illegally assisted slaves in escaping to freedom. That was nonviolent civil disobedience. On the other hand, John Brown and his supporters fomented slave insurrection and rebellion against the state by lethal force. That was the advocacy and exercise of lethal force by private citizens and is beyond the prerogative of individuals, Christian or non-Christian.

5.15 We wish to call attention to the fundamental difference between nonviolent and violent forms of action for social and legal change. We believe that the witness both of Scripture and of history affirms that a social movement's crossing over from nonviolence to violence is a most perilous, and almost always unjustifiable, step. One consequence of such a transition is that resistance to certain *deeds*, such as abortion, is often transformed into attacks on certain *persons*, such as those who perform abortions.

5.16 When the distinction between the wrong and the wrongdoer is obliterated, social change or resistance movements tend to focus on doing away with the wrongdoer rather than taking concrete steps against the wrong. The morally worthy original goal of the movement is replaced by one that is new and unworthy. Any possibility of reconciliation with the wrongdoer, of conversion of that wrongdoer, and of peacemaking, possibilities at the heart of the life and ministry of Jesus, is eviscerated. Instead, efforts focus on how to kill rather than how to make change occur. The people who are the intended recipients of this violence respond in kind. The devastating cycle of violence is intensified.

5.17 Once the bloodshed escalates, social movements embracing violence tend to slide rapidly along the continuum from violent resistance limited to specified targets toward unlimited violence directed at an ever wider range of persons (are judges and politicians going to be the next targeted?). Even at the first stage, innocent bystanders often are injured. One reason God wisely prohibits murder is precisely because of the incendiary effect of bloodshed on the minds and hearts of sinful human beings.

6. Conclusion

6.1 Our conclusion is that the killing of abortion doctors is not a morally justifiable or permissible Christian response to abortion. We utterly reject such conduct as inconsistent with Scripture and call on all Christian people to join us in this stance.

6.2 We believe that Christians are, nevertheless, morally obligated to oppose legalized abortion on demand and to reduce the number of abortions through other, morally legitimate, channels. We must do so more actively and faithfully than ever before.

6.3 Pro-life Christians must act quickly and vigorously to prevent a small but vocal band of militant activists from destroying the credibility, effectiveness, and witness of the mainstream Christian pro-life movement. We pray earnestly that God will bless the efforts of all who employ morally legitimate means in order to save the lives of the most vulnerable among us, the unborn children. We are persuaded that this reflects the mind of Christ.

THE DRAFTING COMMITTEE

Mark T. Coppenger, Ph.D.
Vice President for Convention Affairs
Executive Committee
Southern Baptist Convention
Nashville, Tennessee

David P. Gushee, Ph.D.*
Assistant Professor of Christian Ethics
Southern Baptist Theological Seminary
Louisville, Kentucky

Daniel R. Heimbach, Ph.D.
Associate Professor of Christian Ethics
Southeastern Baptist Theological Seminary
Wake Forest, North Carolina

Richard D. Land, D.Phil.
Executive Director-Treasurer
Christian Life Commission of The Southern Baptist Convention
Nashville, Tennessee

C. Ben Mitchell, Ph.D.
Consultant on Biomedical and Life Issues
The Christian Life Commission
Nashville, Tennessee

R. Albert Mohler Jr., Ph.D.
President
Southern Baptist Theological Seminary
Louisville, Kentucky

*At the Christian Life Commission's request, Dr. Gushee constructed a first draft, which was then revised by the entire draft committee during a Christian Life Commission consultation meeting in Nashville, September 17–18, 1994. Selected Christian Life Commission staff also participated in the consultation.

APPENDIX G

Annual Southern Baptist Convention Sermon*
Southern Baptist Convention, delivered June 18, 1997, Dallas, Texas

"Watchmen on the Wall"
by Richard Land

This is what the LORD says: Stand by the roadways and look. Ask about the ancient paths: Which is the way to what is good? Then take it and find rest for yourselves" (Jer. 6:16 HCSB).

If America dies, she will perish from self-inflicted wounds. It has always been the case and always will be that nations, great nations, die from within, not from without.

That is surely what God's Holy Word is telling us in Jeremiah 1. God sent His prophet Jeremiah, and there can never have been a more direct command to go than the one Jeremiah received from God. Beginning in verse 5, God said, "I chose you before I formed you in the womb; I set you apart before you were born. I appointed you a prophet to the nations" (HCSB). And then Jeremiah said that God put forth His hand and touched his mouth (v. 9). After God put His own words in Jeremiah's mouth, He sent him out to speak them to His people, who were in rebellion and in the grip of pagan idolatry.

In Jeremiah 6:13–17 we hear these words:

"For from the least to the greatest of them, everyone is gaining profit unjustly. From prophet to priest, everyone deals falsely. They have treated My people's brokenness superficially, claiming: Peace, peace, when there is no peace. Were they ashamed when they acted so abhorrently? They weren't at all ashamed. They can no longer feel humiliation. Therefore, they will fall among the fallen. When I punish them, they will collapse, says the LORD. This is what the LORD says: Stand by the roadways and look. Ask about the ancient paths: Which is the way to what is good? Then take it and find rest for yourselves. But they protested: We won't! I appointed watchmen over you and said: Listen for the sound of the ram's horn. But they protested: We won't listen!"

In Jeremiah's day the only real earthly protection that could be afforded to a city was to fortify itself with a wall and place watchmen on it. They would watch through the night and through the day, scanning the horizon. The watchmen were issued trumpets, and at the first sign of trouble, they were to pick up those trumpets and blow a warning blast. The people knew that was their signal to awaken from their slumber or stop their daily activities and defend their homes and families.

In effect, Jeremiah was saying that God's prophets were his watchmen. They had scanned the horizon looking for any threat, but they had turned and seen that the real threat was inside the walls. The watchmen had taken up their trumpets and blown the warning blasts, telling the people to take notice of what was around them, to ask about the old path and look for the good way, then to find rest by walking in it.

Several years ago a reporter asked me, "We've heard a lot from you about what's wrong with America. What would America look like if it was the way you wanted it to be?" And I replied, "Well, a good place to start would be America in 1955, without the racism and the sexual discrimination against women."

America in 1955 was a place where the following things did not happen, as they do now:

Less than half of our children currently grow up in intact families. The divorce rate in America is 45-50 percent for first marriages, 60-67 percent for second marriages, and 70-73 percent for third marriages.[1]

Every year in the last ten years there has been a 400 percent increase in child abuse significant enough to require a doctor's attention.[2]

Every hour our children watch 20 violent acts on television.[3]

Every day in America nearly 2,800 teenage girls get pregnant.[4]

Every day in America 1,106 of those girls snuff out the lives of their unborn children through abortion.[5]

About 8 out of every 100,000 teenagers committed suicide in 2000. For every teen suicide death, experts estimate there are 10 other attempts.[6]

By the time they graduate from high school, 54 percent of our teenagers acknowledge that they have used one or more illegal drugs.[7]

And we are being inundated with a tidal wave of moral relativism that centers on human sexuality.

At 13.3 billion dollars a year, the 2006 revenues of the sex and porn industry in the U.S. are more than the revenues of professional football, basketball, and baseball combined. Worldwide sex industry sales for 2006 are reported to be 97 billion dollars. To put this in perspective, Microsoft, which sells the operating system used on most of the computers in the world (in addition to other software) reported sales of 44.8 billion dollars in 2006.[8]

One out of every 4 girls and 1 out of every 6 boys in the United States will be sexually molested by the time they reach their 16th birthday.[9]

Somewhere in America, a woman is raped every 46 seconds. Every day 4 women are killed by their domestic partner.[10]

Prior to 1960 there were only two significant sexually-transmitted diseases: syphilis and gonorrhea. Both were easily treatable with antibiotics. In the next two decades this began to change. Today there are approximately 25 STDs, and a few can be fatal. Approximately 1 in 5 Americans between the ages of 15 and 55 are currently infected with one or more STDs, and 12 million Americans are newly infected each year. That's nearly 5 percent of the entire American population. Of these new infections, 63 percent are in people under the age of 25.[11]

Yes, things have changed since 1955. That time certainly had its own problems, but this moral filth was not being poured out into our culture.

When I was a Royal Ambassador growing up in a church in Houston, one of the first passages of Scripture I learned was Ephesians 2:8–10 (KJV), "For by grace are ye saved through faith; and that not of yourselves: it is the gift of God: not of works lest any man should boast. For we are his workmanship, created in Christ Jesus unto good works, which God hath before ordained that we should walk in them."

What Ephesians 2:10 tells us is that God has a plan and God has a purpose for every single human life that is conceived. But we are like the prodigal son. We as Americans have aborted nearly 50 million babies since 1973.[12] Have we aborted the next great evangelist? Have we aborted the one that God sent to find a cure for cancer? Have we aborted the next great military mind, the next great president, the next international peacemaker? Each of those American babies was a child—a child with a future and a purpose, sacrificed to the pagan gods of social convention, career advancement, and material well-being.

I can still remember as a young man in Sunday School having a Bible lesson about how the children of God had become so paganized that they went down into the valley of Gehenna and sacrificed their little children to the pagan god Molech. How could I have ever imagined as a young boy that I would live to see the United States of America offering up its unborn children as pagan sacrifices because they are too expensive, too embarrassing, too ill, or too inconvenient! God help us!

We are the prodigal son. We have taken the inheritance of our unborn children and gone to a far city where we have wasted that inheritance in riotous living. And now we are reduced to feeding among the swine for the husks of life. There is only one hope for America, and that is for us to come to our senses as did the prodigal and shake the filth from ourselves and determine to go home to the Father who is scanning the horizon, waiting for His people to come home.

America is not the America of the fifties. The reporter asked me, "Was it really that good in 1955, or do we just know more now?" And I realized that I might as well have been talking about the time of Louis XIV. The reporter was born some 10 years after 1955, while I was nine years old in 1955. Today's young people have never experienced America when it was far more right than it is today. And unless we take the initiative to lead them back to the old ways, to the old paths, then surely we will proceed at an ever-accelerating pace toward destruction. If the present trends continue unabated, think about what America will be like 30 or 40 years from now! I become uncomfortable when I read the Corinthian letters because more and more we find ourselves in the same situation in which the Corinthian Christians found themselves—awash in a tide of moral relativity, a tide of sexual paganism, a sexual abyss.

In 1947, C. S. Lewis described the proper composition of a human being in a little book called *The Abolition of Man*. He said that the head ruled the belly, which was the sensual appetite, through the chest. Lewis defined the chest as consisting of the higher emotions organized by trained habit into stable sentiments—in other words, being taught the Ten Commandments, not the ten suggestions. Lewis went on to say that the higher emotions of the chest were the absolutely essential liaison between the cerebral and the sensual, and without the chest, human beings became worshipers of their own minds, their own appetites. Lewis also said that moral relativism tears out the chest and removes moral character.

"In a sort of ghastly simplicity, our culture removes the organ and demands the function," Lewis wrote. "We make men without chests and expect of them virtue and enterprise. We laugh at honor and are shocked when we find traitors in our midst. We castrate and then bid the geldings to be fruitful." I can think of no better diagnosis for what has happened to a generation and a half of Americans whose fathers and mothers and aunts and uncles and grandfathers and leaders lost their moral compass and lost their moral way and are adrift on a turbulent ocean of relativism.

Yet when we believers try to stand up and speak the truth, we are told, "Oh, you can't do that! That's a violation of separation of church and state!" Nonsense! Foolish and dangerous nonsense!

John F. Kennedy once said the greatest enemy of truth is often not the lie—deliberate, contrived, and dishonest—but the myth—persistent, persuasive, and unrealistic.[13] And it is a persistent, persuasive, and unrealistic myth to say that you can't legislate morality. All law is the legislation of someone's morality.

Romans 13 says that we are to have civil government to punish those who do evil and reward those who do right. You have to legislate morality in order to do that. When we pass laws making murder and theft and rape and racism illegal, we are not so much trying to impose our morality on murderers and thieves and rapists and racists as we are trying to keep them from imposing their immorality on their victims. That is not only our right; it is also our obligation.

When Abraham Lincoln was running for the presidency of the United States in another time of great moral crisis, he got a lot of criticism for making slavery an issue. Here's what he said in 1860, in the midst of the presidential campaign: "You will not let us do a single thing as if it was wrong: there is no place where you will allow it to be even called wrong. We must not call it wrong in the free States, because it is not there, and we must not call it wrong in the slave States, because it is there; we must not call it wrong in politics, because that is bringing morality into politics, and we must not call it wrong in the pulpit, because that is bringing politics into religion . . . " Lincoln concluded by saying, "There is no single place, according to you, where this wrong can properly be called wrong."[14] I'm glad Abraham Lincoln didn't listen to his critics.

We have allowed ourselves to believe this lie that somehow Christians don't have a right and an obligation to be involved in public policy, and we have withdrawn and left the field to those who do not care to hear our faith-based convictions. And we are reaping the consequences. There was a study done several years ago to determine which were the most religious countries in the world. They came to the conclusion that India was the most religious country in the world and Sweden was the least religious country in the world. When Peter Berger, the famous sociologist, was told of this, he commented that if India is the most religious country in the world, and Sweden the least religious, then America is a nation of Indians ruled by Swedes.[15] There's a great deal of tragic truth in that. Do you know whose fault that is? It's our fault! It's our fault for not being willing to get involved and to be part of the process.

Jesus told us we are the salt and the light of the world. Salt is a purifying agent and a preservative, but it must come into contact with that which it would purify and preserve. And it not only purifies and preserves, it also stings and irritates. That's why when Jesus said we were to be salt and light, He preceded it by saying, "Blessed are ye, when men shall revile you, and persecute you, and shall say all manner of evil against you falsely, for my sake" (Matt. 5:11).

I grew up in Southern Baptist churches where it was often said, "Now, we're Southern Baptists. That means we don't get involved in anything controversial. We just preach the Gospel." Folks, that's an oxymoron. And as a graduate of Oxford, I want you to know that an oxymoron is not a moron who went to Oxford. An oxymoron is when you take two seemingly contradictory descriptions and use them to describe the same thing. Take "humble Texan," for example. It is just as much of an oxymoron to say "noncontroversial Christian." If we're being salt and light then we are going to be controversial. Jesus intended for us to be controversial! In the first century Christians were known as the people who turned the world upside down, which means they were turning the world upside right.

There has been a conscious, concerted, and clever attempt by some in our country to marginalize Christians and drive them from involvement in the public policy of this nation. We must not allow them to keep us from our rightful place in the public square.

We must convince Christians to run for elected offices at every level, then encourage them to act on their faith-based convictions while they are in office. We must walk, talk, and vote our values. We must elect those who will appoint judges who understand that the Constitution is what governs us, not judges' opinions about the Constitution.

We must have revival. America is too far gone for anything else to save us. We must have a heaven-sent, Spirit-filled, Christ-centered, Cross-focused, life-changing revival, or we are doomed.

I hope you are familiar with the song "Statue of Liberty." It has special meaning to me. I had been back in America for three days after three years in England. I had moved to Dallas to take a position at Criswell College, and I was taken to Family Night at the Music Hall at Fair Park. They were having their God-and-Country celebration, and it culminated with a rousing rendition of that great song, which says "A rugged cross is my Statue of Liberty."[16] As the screen showed the Statue of Liberty, the song talked about the blessings of being an American. I just broke down and wept.

We live, by the grace of God, in the most blessed country on earth. God has blessed us wonderfully. But He has often blessed us in spite of ourselves. Our salvation will never be in America but in the Cross of Jesus Christ. We must have a revival, and it must be a revival, a revival that blossoms into an awakening and becomes a reformation. It's too late for just a revival. The revival has got to come first, but the revival and the awakening have got to be applied to our government and to our culture. It has to be from the inside out! It has to be a regeneration of our nation through a regeneration of its people that culminates in a reformation that shakes America as Luther and Calvin shook Europe and Whitfield and Wesley shook England and Edwards shook Colonial America for Jesus Christ.

Government can't save us. Government is usually part of the problem, not part of the solution. King Josiah is the perfect example that the government cannot bring revival. King Josiah heard the Word of God, and it broke his heart. He called for reforms. He instituted right and holy worship in the temple. He got rid of pagan excesses. He instituted true religion. And what happened? All of Josiah's reforms died with him because only the king's heart was changed. The people's habits were changed, but their hearts were not. When the king died, the reforms died.

We have a right, we have a responsibility, and we have an obligation to be involved in the civic process. Jesus commanded us to be salt and light. But we must always remember that while the salt of the law can change actions, only the light of the Gospel can change attitudes. The salt of the law can change behaviors, but it is only the light of the Gospel that can change beliefs. The salt of the law can change habits, but it is only the light of the Gospel that can change hearts.

My dear brothers and sisters, when we are in crisis there is always a danger that we will turn to the government and try to make the government our ally. And it is a danger to say, "If we can just get the government to sponsor our religion, we can bring about revival." That always has been and always will be a fatal bargain. When the government sponsors religion, the government thinks it owns religion. When the government puts its arm around you and embraces you, it's like being squeezed by a python. You lose all life and vitality and eventually drop dead.

Government-sponsored religion is government-dictated, government-deluded religion. We don't want the government to sponsor religion! We want the government to quit suppressing our right to be involved. We want the government to guarantee a level playing field and then to get off the field! Does that mean that false religions have the same rights to express their opinions and their beliefs as we do? Sure. Let them come. I never saw Elijah backing away from a confrontation with the prophets of Baal. He just showed them the power of the One True God!

Let us never forget our Baptist heritage. America will never get the proper role of religion in society right without Baptists and our heritage. It's in our genetic code to mistrust government when they come to us and say, "I'm from the government, and I'm here to help you." With government sponsorship, with government favoritism, comes government control. The Baptist Faith and Message says the church should never resort to the state to do its work. It's our job. It's our privilege. It's our work to preach the Gospel of Jesus Christ. But when we preach that Gospel, and God has blessed it and people's hearts and minds have been changed, then they have the right as citizens to come forth in the public arena and say, "This is wrong, and we want it stopped."

For example, abortion is the murder of babies, and we want laws to change it. When we convince a majority of Americans that we are right, that's not called a theocracy, that's called the democratic process.

God knows that I love my country, but Christians, our hope is not in America. America's hope is in Christ. Ask not what your country can do for God. Ask what God can do for your country. And the answer, of course, is everything.

Southern Baptists, let's heed the call to stand in the gap and repair the hedge and claim the promise of God when He said, "If my people, who are called by my name, will humble themselves and pray and seek my face and turn from their wicked ways, then will I hear from heaven and will forgive their sin and will heal their land" (2 Chron. 7:14 NIV). May there be a new birth of freedom, may there be a new birth of morality, may we stand in the ways and see the old paths and heed the watchmen on the wall.

The Bible says, "Where there is no vision, the people perish" (Prov. 29:18). The vision is the Chazon, the entirety of the Word of God, and it is our job to proclaim and preach the Gospel. It is no one else's responsibility. It's the job of those who name the name of Christ. The Cross is our liberty and our salvation.

God bless you, God bless your family, and God bless the United States of America.

---

*The annual convention sermon is delievered by a speaker who is elected to deliver the sermon at the previous year's Convention. Richard Land was elected as the Convention preacher at the 1996 SBC meeting in New Orleans. Statistics have been updated © 2008.

Notes

1. "Divorce Statistics" [online] 2004 [cited 22 April 2007]. Available on the Internet: www.divorcestatistics.org/

2. "National Incidence Study" [online] 2006 [cited 22 April 2007]. Available on the Internet: www.childabuse.com/fs13.htm

3. "Children and Television Violence" [online] 15 April 2007 [cited 22 April 2007]. Available on the Internet: www.abelard.org/tv/tv.htm

4. "Statistics on Teens" [online] 20207 [cited 22 April 2007]. Available on the Internet: www.soundvision.com/Info/teens/stat.asp

5. "Teen Statistics" [online] n.d. [cited 22 April 2007]. Available on the Internet: http://72.14.209.104/search?q=cache:RN54F1bmMxwJ:www.josh.org/notes/file/Internet16-TeenStatistics.pdf+teens+who+get+abortions+stats&hl=en&ct=clnk&cd=1&gl=us&client=safari

6. "Teen Suicide Statistics" [online] 2005 [cited 22 April 2007]. Available on the Internet: www.teendepression.org/articles1.html

7. "Preventing Teen Drug Abuse" [online] 2007 [cited 22 April 2007]. Available on the Internet: www.cqpress.com/product/Researcher-Preventing-Teen-Drug-Use.html

8. "Statistics and Information on Pornography in the US" [online] 2005 [cited 22 April 2007]. Available on the Internet: www.blazinggrace.org/pornstatistics.htm

9. "Keep Your Children Safe" [online] n.d. [cited 22 April 2007]. Available on the Internet: http://sound-learning.com/child_molesters_wabash_indiana.htm

10. "Stop Violence" [online] 2006 [cited 22 April 2007]. Available on the Internet: www.safetyforwomen.com/start.htm

11. "The Epidemic of Sexually Transmitted Diseases" [online] July 2002 [cited 22 April 2007]. Available on the Internet: www.leaderu.com/orgs/probe/docs/epid-std.html

12. "Abortion in the United States: Statistics and Trends," National Right to Life [online] n.d. [cited 2 April 2007]. Available on the Internet: www.nrlc.org/abortion/facts/abortionstats.html

13. "John F. Kennedy" [online] 21 April 2007 [cited 22 April 2007]. Available on the Internet: http://en.wikiquote.org/wiki/John_F._Kennedy

14. "Slavery the Snake of the Union Bed" Speech at New Haven, Conn. March 6, 1860 [online] 2007 [cited 22 April 2007]. Available on the Internet: www.lincolnarchives.us/index.php?sub=/specialfeatures/lincoln_administration&act=lincspeech03061860&left_nav=left_nav_subscription&header=header_1860

15. Philip E. Johnson. "Books in Review: The Culture of Disbelief" [online] December 1993 [cited 22 April 2007]. Available on the Internet: www.leaderu.com/ftissues/ft9312/reviews/johnson.html

16. Neil Enloe. "Statue of Liberty" [online] n.d. [cited 22 April 2007]. Available on the Internet: www.our.homewithgod.com/ewerluvd/liberty.htm

SUBJECT INDEX

SCRIPTURE INDEX

Photo Credits

Pages 1–2
PORTRAITS—(Portraits were photographed by Lucretia Goddard, ERLC staff)
Arthur James Barton—Marie Taylor Barton
Hugh J. Brimm—Jan Rhodes
A. C. Miller—Jan Rhodes
Foy Valentine—Jan Rhodes
N. Larry Baker—June Deaver
Richard Land—John Sanden

Page 3
Early CLC booth at SBC—ERLC Archives
A. C. Miller with chart showing cost of alcohol—ERLC Archives

Page 4
Foy Valentine, A. C. Miller, Hugh J. Brimm—ERLC Archives
Bill Moyers, James Dunn, Phil Strickland—ERLC Archives
Billy Graham/Foy Valentine—Baptist Press

Page 5
President Lyndon B. Johnson—ERLC Archives
President Johnson speaking to seminar group—Charles W. Stoughton
Bayard Rustin—ERLC Archives
Jesse Jackson—CLC, Floyd Craig

Page 6
John Claypool—Dick Barnes
Joseph Fletcher—ERLC Archives
George McGovern—ERLC Archives
Andrew Young—ERLC Archives
Edward Kennedy—ERLC Archives
Rosalyn Carter—ERLC Archives

Page 7
Phyllis Schlafly and Harvey Cox—Mark Sandlin
Martin Marty—ERLC Archives
Ramsey Clark—ERLC Archives
Sarah Weddington—Official Photograph, The White House, Washington
Tipper Gore—ERLC Archives
Marian Wright Edelman—ERLC Archives

Page 8
Dr. C. Everett Koop—ERLC Archives
Jimmy Draper—ERLC Archives
Bill Bennett—ERLC Archives
Paige Patterson—ERLC Archives
Fred Luter—ERLC Archives
Barbara O'Chester—ERLC Archives

Page 9
Charles Colson—ERLC Archives
E. W. McCall—ERLC Archives
Charles Stenholm—ERLC Archives
Jay Sekulow—ERLC Archives
Governor David Beasley—ERLC Archives

Page 10
Richard Land at CLC Trustee meeting—ERLC Archives
Dr. Land's extended family at installation—ERLC Archives

Page 11
Dr. Land at NRLC Rally for Life—NRLC, Dr. Richard Glasow
Dr. Land/Cardinal Mahony/Jim Smith at National Right to Life March—ERLC, Tom Strode

Page 12
Dr. Land before Senate Foreign Relations Committee—ELRC, Tom Strode
Dr. Land/Adrian Rogers/Harold Harper—ERLC Staff

Page 13
ERLC Booth at SBC 2001—ERLC Staff
Dr. Land and Jimmy Draper—*Baptist Press*, Kent Harville
President Bush, Dr. Land, Janet Parschall—The White House

Page 14
Dr. Land at 2004 SBC—*Baptist Press*, Van Payne
Dr. Land with Jack Graham—ERLC Staff
iVoteValues truck—Jill Yochim

Page 15
Immigration Reform meeting President Bush—*Associated Press*, Charles Dharapak
Dr. Land at Save Darfur rally—Shannon Baker
Dr. Land, Morris Chapman, Condoleezza Rice—*Baptist Press*

Page 16
Dr. Land and Sen. Lieberman—ERLC, Tom Strode, 2/8/07
Dr. Land and Sen. Kennedy—ERLC, Tom Strode, 2/27/07
Dr. Land at rally for North Korea—ERLC, Tom Strode, 7/17/07